Debates in Modern Languages Education

Debates in Modern Languages Education offers a comprehensive introduction to and synthesis of the major themes and research evidence in language learning and teaching today, providing an up-to-date, authoritative review of traditional and contemporary issues.

With chapters by leading experts in the field, thematic sections explore:

- the importance of a wide range of different knowledge bases and skills for effective teaching
- how to become an expert practitioner
- approaches to teaching with reference to relevant theories, complex constructs and empirical evidence
- the innovations and ideas that shape and will shape the discipline for the next decade.

Each thought-provoking chapter is supported by reference to further reading and additional material to encourage deeper exploration which will help the reader to fully engage in the debates presented.

Debates in Modern Languages Education is a valuable resource for any student or practising teacher engaged in initial teacher education, continuing professional development and Masters level study.

Patricia Driscoll is Reader in Education at Canterbury Christ Church University, UK.

Ernesto Macaro is Professor of Applied Linguistics at the University of Oxford, UK.

Ann Swarbrick is Languages Education Lead at CfBT Education Trust, UK, and President of the Association for Language Learning.

Debates in Subject Teaching Series
Series edited by: Susan Capel, Jon Davison, James Arthur, John Moss

The **Debates in Subject Teaching Series** is a sequel to the popular **Issues in Subject Teaching Series**, originally published by Routledge between 1999 and 2003. Each title presents high-quality material, specially commissioned to stimulate teachers engaged in initial training, continuing professional development and Masters level study to think more deeply about their practice and link research and evidence to what they have observed in schools. By providing up-to-date, comprehensive coverage the titles in the **Debates in Subject Teaching Series** support teachers in reaching their own informed judgements, enabling them to discuss and argue their point of view with deeper theoretical knowledge and understanding.

Titles in the series:

Debates in History Teaching
Edited by Ian Davies

Debates in English Teaching
Edited by Jon Davison, Caroline Daly and John Moss

Debates in Religious Education
Edited by Philip Barnes

Debates in Citizenship Education
Edited by James Arthur and Hilary Cremin

Debates in Art and Design Education
Edited by Lesley Burgess and Nicholas Addison

Debates in Music Teaching
Edited by Chris Philpott and Gary Spruce

Debates in Physical Education
Edited by Susan Capel and Margaret Whitehead

Debates in Geography Education
Edited by David Lambert and Mark Jones

Debates in Design and Technology Education
Edited by Gwyneth Owen-Jackson

Debates in Mathematics Education
Edited by Dawn Leslie and Heather Mendick

Debates in Modern Languages Education
Edited by Patricia Driscoll, Ernesto Macaro and Ann Swarbrick

Debates in Modern Languages Education

Edited by
Patricia Driscoll, Ernesto Macaro
and Ann Swarbrick

Routledge
Taylor & Francis Group

LONDON AND NEW YORK

First published 2014
by Routledge
2 Park Square, Milton Park, Abingdon, Oxon OX14 4RN

and by Routledge
711 Third Avenue, New York, NY 10017

Routledge is an imprint of the Taylor & Francis Group, an informa business

© 2014 Patricia Driscoll, Ernesto Macaro and Ann Swarbrick

The right of the editors to be identified as the authors of the editorial material, and of the authors for their individual chapters, has been asserted in accordance with sections 77 and 78 of the Copyright, Designs and Patents Act 1988.

British Library Cataloguing in Publication Data
A catalogue record for this book is available from the British Library

Library of Congress Cataloging in Publication Data
A catalog record for this book has been requested

ISBN: 978-0-415-65832-4 (hbk)
ISBN: 978-0-415-65833-1 (pbk)
ISBN: 978-1-315-85655-1 (ebk)

Typeset in Galliard
by Saxon Graphics Ltd, Derby

MIX
Paper from
responsible sources
FSC® C013604
www.fsc.org

Printed and bound by CPI Group (UK) Ltd, Croydon, CR0 4YY

Contents

Illustrations

Figures

Tables

Contributors

Amanda Barton is Honorary Lecturer in Education at the School of Education, University of Manchester, where she teaches on the secondary PGCE in modern languages. Her doctoral research focused on boys' underachievement in languages and formed the basis of her book, *Getting the Buggers into Languages* (Continuum, 2006). Her other research interests include the teaching of languages in primary school and the retention of recently qualified teachers. Having designed and taught a language awareness programme in a primary school she went on to become principal investigator on two research projects evaluating the effectiveness of language awareness programmes in primary schools around the country. She guest-edited two special issues of *Language Learning Journal* on the teaching of languages in primary schools (July 2009, July 2010).

Patricia Driscoll is Reader in Education at Canterbury Christ Church University. She taught in secondary and primary schools before conducting her PhD in 1996. She has experience of teaching both secondary and primary PGCE students and providing professional development for teachers at masters' level. She also supervises and teaches on programmes for doctoral students. Her research focuses mainly on learning and teaching languages in primary schools and teacher education. She has conducted national, regional and local level research studies and has published in professional and academic journals and books. She has also collaborated on two European projects: one project aimed to develop learners' language and cultural awareness through a comparison of attitudes and approaches to healthy eating in seven European countries and the other project aimed to integrate the pedagogies of foreign languages and music education with a view to enhancing language learning for young learners.

John Field is Senior Lecturer in Cognitive Approaches to Language Learning at the CRELLA Research Unit of the University of Bedfordshire. He also teaches at the Faculty of Education, Cambridge University. He is best known as a specialist in second language listening, on which he has published and researched widely and on which he wrote his PhD at Cambridge. Much of his thinking is informed by his background in psycholinguistics, which he taught until recently at the University of Reading. It has equipped him to respond to current interest in the mental processes employed by foreign language learners and test takers. He has also written several books aimed at making psycholinguistics accessible to non-psychologists, particularly teachers, educationalists and linguists. Before becoming an academic, John had extensive experience as an English language materials writer and teacher trainer, working in Belgium, Spain, Jordan, Saudi Arabia, China and Tanzania.

Suzanne Graham is Professor of Language and Education at the Institute of Education, University of Reading. Before moving into teacher education, she taught French and German in schools in England. At Reading she leads the Secondary ITT Programme in Modern Foreign Languages, as well as being the Institute Director of Research. She has published widely in both academic and professional journals. Many of her publications feature on reading lists of second language education courses. Her research focuses on second language learning strategies, particularly in relation to listening, and on second language learning motivation.

Michael Grenfell is (1905) Chair of Education at Trinity College, University of Dublin, Ireland. He has a long association with educational research, as well as involvement in policy forums. He is author of several books including: *Modern Language Across the Curriculum* (RoutledgeFalmer, 2002); *Learning Strategies and Modern Languages* (Routledge, 1999 – with V. Harris); and *Language, Ethnography and Education* (Routledge, 2012). He edited a special series on language learning and teaching – *Modern Languages in Practice* – for Multilingual Matters, which includes some 15 titles. He has published several academic research articles. His own PhD was on the philosophy of language teacher education, and he has also been Chair of the Research Committee of UCET (Universities Council for the Education of Teachers). He collaborated on two major European research projects leading to the publication of the *European Language Teacher* (Peter Lang, 2003) and the drafting of the *European Profile for Language Teacher Education* (2002–2004). He was commissioned to write support articles for the Key Stage 3 Strategy for Modern Foreign Languages in UK secondary schools. He also has a longstanding association with the work of Pierre Bourdieu. He was three times visiting scholar at the *École des hautes études* in Paris. He has authored: *Pierre Bourdieu: Acts of Practical Theory* (Falmer Press, 1998 – with D. James); *Pierre Bourdieu: Language, Education and Culture* (Peter Lang, 2002 – with M. Kelly); *Pierre Bourdieu: Agent Provocateur* (Continuum, 2004); *Bourdieu: Education and Training* (Continuum, 2007); *Arts Rules: Pierre Bourdieu and the Visual Arts* (Berg, 2007 – with C. Hardy); *Pierre Bourdieu: Key Concepts* (Acumen, 2012); and *Bourdieu, Language and Linguistics* (Continuum, 2010).

Vee Harris has recently retired from being Senior Lecturer at Goldsmiths College, University of London. She ran the PGCE modern languages course for over

20 years, published widely and collaborated on several European projects. Her main research interest is the language learner strategies used by students in the 11–15 age group. Working with Michael Grenfell, her most recent study explored the strategies used by non-native students to memorise Chinese characters.

Mairin Hennebry is a Lecturer at the University of Edinburgh. Within this capacity she works with both MFL and EFL teachers from across the world. She trained as an MFL teacher and has taught MFL and EFL in a variety of countries and contexts. Mairin obtained her DPhil from the University of Oxford, investigating the associations between European Citizenship, the teaching of the target culture and learners' attitudes towards and motivations for language learning. Her research spans aspects of applied linguistics and second language acquisition as well as language teacher education, thus yielding publications in the fields of education and language learning.

Philip Hood is Associate Professor in Primary Education at the University of Nottingham and Course Director of the National Primary SCITT Consortium. He has worked in both secondary and primary settings and has been involved in teacher education since 1991. His writing encompasses both language learning and children's early years learning development. In the field of CLIL he has developed masters' level courses, supervised doctoral students, worked as a consultant to the Catalan Ministry of Education and spoken at many conferences. He is co-author of Cambridge University Press's *Content and Language Integrated Learning.*

Katie Horne (formerly Lee), a Germanist, has taught foreign languages for 15 years. Following a short period as a teacher of English as a foreign language, Katie completed her PGCE in 1998. She spent the first five years of her career at Hockerill Anglo-European College in Bishop's Stortford, where Mike Ullmann had founded the pioneering French *Section Bilangue,* based on high frequency 'total immersion' language lessons and an additional curriculum of history and geography taught entirely through the medium of French. Inspired by Mike's teaching and leadership, and working closely with Do Coyle, Katie developed and distilled principles and training for what she terms 'immersion language teaching'. As assistant head and director of specialism at The Willink School she again applied the principles and training, establishing The Willink as a national centre of excellence for language teaching and CLIL and carried out training nationally. Since her move to Whitecross Hereford, she continues to provide advice and training to languages departments and has also facilitated training workshops on teaching oral interaction in the context of the Professional Development Consortium for MFL, working with Ernesto Macaro and Suzanne Graham.

Richard Johnstone is Emeritus Professor of the University of Stirling where he was Director of Scottish CILT and Head of the Institute of Education. He has directed national and international funded research projects on language teaching, learning, teacher education and policy. His research covers modern foreign languages, heritage languages (particularly Scottish Gaelic), community languages (particularly Cantonese and Mandarin) and TESOL within a range of models that include modern languages in primary and secondary education, CLIL, bilingual education and immersion. From 1991 to 2009 he wrote the annual review of international research for the research journal *Language Teaching*. Recently, he has directed research on bilingual education for the British Council and national ministries in Spain, Italy, Portugal and East Asia. In 2004 he was awarded the OBE for services to modern languages.

Jane Jones, Senior Lecturer in Education, is Head of modern foreign languages teacher education at King's College London which includes the PGCE and the MA in MFL as well as doctoral students researching in the field. She is a member of the King's College London Assessment Group. She has been UK co-ordinator of 16 EU-funded projects researching assessment, language teaching and learning, teacher development and leadership, the topic of her PhD. She has published widely on these topics and given many keynote talks across Europe and in the US. Her research focuses on the development of effective formative assessment and the promotion of the pupil voice in all issues relating to their learning.

Jill Llewellyn-Williams leads the Professional Doctorate (EdD) pathway in the School of Education at Cardiff Metropolitan University. After many years teaching in secondary schools, she joined Cardiff School of Education as a teacher educator in 2001. She was chief examiner of GCSE French for the Welsh Joint Education Committee until 2009, completing her EdD later that same year. She is active in the Master's in Education programme, teaching research skills and education policy. In addition, she supervises PhD students in the UK and overseas, mainly in the domain of linguistics and language pedagogy. She is an active researcher, her focus being mainly on subject knowledge development, language memory, attrition and the reactivation of lapsed language skills.

Ernesto Macaro is Professor of Applied Linguistics at the University of Oxford. He was a language teacher in schools in England before becoming a teacher educator. He obtained a PhD from the University of Reading and joined the Department of Education at Oxford in 1999. Since then he has taught on the PGCE teacher education programme and introduced applied linguistics to Oxford for the first time through the MSc in applied linguistics and second language acquisition. He has published five books, some of which have become standard reading on second language education courses, and also published research articles in most of the top second language acquisition journals. His research focuses on second learning strategies and on the interaction between teachers and learners in second language classrooms, particularly the benefits or otherwise of teacher codeswitching.

Rosa M. Manchón is Professor of Applied Linguistics at the University of Murcia, Spain. She was a language teacher in secondary schools in Spain before she joined the English Department at the University of Murcia, where she obtained her PhD. She teaches undergraduate courses in second language acquisition (SLA), as well as postgraduate courses in research methodology, cognitive dimensions of second language learning and use, and language teaching methodology. Her research interests include SLA-oriented L2 writing research and research methods. Recent books are *Writing in Foreign Language Contexts: Learning, Teaching and Research* (Multilingual Matters, 2009), *Learning-to-Write and Writing-to-Learn in an Additional Language* (John Benjamins, 2011), and *L2 Writing Development: Multiple Perspectives* (De Gruyter Mouton, 2012). Her work has also appears in leading journals such as *Journal of Second Language Writing*, *Language Learning* and *The Modern Language Journal*. Together with Christine Tardy she edits the *Journal of Second Language Writing*, and, in her capacity as AILA Publications Coordinator, she is the editor of *AILA Review* and the AILA Applied Linguistics Series (AALS, John Benjamins).

Ron Martinez earned a Master of Science in applied linguistics and second language acquisition from Oxford University and finished his PhD, with a focus on applied corpus linguistics, at the University of Nottingham. He has taught in a wide variety of classroom contexts in the United States, the United Kingdom, Spain and Brazil. He has published widely for both academic and professional audiences. He also regularly serves as a reviewer for academic articles for many prominent journals. He has lectured at a number of universities around the world, including Oxford University and Pontificia Universidade Catolica do Parana (Brazil), where he is also an adjunct professor. His research interests centre on the mental lexicon and vocabulary acquisition in language pedagogy.

Rosamond Mitchell originally trained as a teacher and taught Irish and French in a Dublin secondary school. She later studied applied linguistics in Edinburgh and obtained her PhD in education from the University of Stirling. She has worked at the University of Southampton since 1986, and has conducted research on foreign language education policy and on language teaching and learning over many years in British schools and universities. Her research has focused recently on language learning in the primary school, and on the social networks of British undergraduate students of languages during residence abroad. She is co-author of *Second Language Learning Theories* (third edition, Routledge, 2012), together with Florence Myles and Emma Marsden.

Marie Ryan is currently Deputy Director of the Schools Service for the Catholic Diocese of Arundel and Brighton. From 2003 to 2013 she was Senior Lecturer in Education and subject leader for PGCE Secondary Modern Languages pathways at Canterbury Christ Church University. Marie has conducted research on foreign language teaching and learning over a number of years, with her recent research focusing on language learning and pedagogy in the secondary school and on the development of cross-curricular links. Marie taught modern languages in inner-city comprehensive schools in London and in an international 3–18 school in Brussels before becoming a teacher educator. She is nearing completion of her PhD.

Ann Swarbrick is Languages Education Lead for ITT at CfBT Education Trust and is currently President of the Association for Language Learning. She was languages teaching adviser and Head of initial teacher training at CILT, the National Centre for Languages from 2002–2011. In the 1990s she led the Open University languages PGCE as senior lecturer in education after many years teaching in secondary schools. She was also languages advisory teacher for a local authority supporting the work of secondary languages departments. She has published extensively in the field of languages education including academic works and publications for pupils, and for teachers' continuing professional development.

Robert Vanderplank is Director of Oxford University Language Centre and a Fellow of Kellogg College, Oxford, where he is also Director of the Kellogg College Centre for the Study of Lifelong Language Learning. Prior to moving to Oxford in 1996, he taught in the School of Languages at Heriot-Watt University and before that in the Language Centre at the University of Newcastle upon Tyne. He teaches on the MSc in applied linguistics and second language acquisition in the Department of Education at Oxford, where he is also a member of the Applied Linguistics Research Group. His research interests and publications include lifelong language learning, language maintenance and attrition (www.lara.ox.ac.uk), television and language learning, listening comprehension, learner autonomy and self-assessment. He is also reviews editor of *System*.

Robert Woore is a Lecturer in Applied Linguistics at Oxford University Department of Education (OUDE). He is the lead tutor on the modern languages PGCE course and also teaches on the MSc in applied linguistics and second language acquisition and the masters in learning and teaching. He previously taught French and German at secondary school level. His principal research interest is print-to-sound decoding in a second language, particularly in relation to beginner and near-beginner learners in modern foreign languages classrooms in the UK.

Abbreviations

3Ps	presentation, practice, production
4Cs	content, communication, cognition, culture
AfL	Assessment for Learning
AL	audio-lingual
A-level	advanced level public examination
AS level	public examination falling between GCSE and A-level
CEFR	Common European Framework of Reference for Languages
CILT	Centre for Information on Languages Teaching and Research
CLIL	content and language integrated learning
CLT	communicative language teaching
CPD	continuing professional development
CPR	Cambridge Primary Review
DCSF	Department for Children, Schools and Families
DfE	Department for Education
DfEE	Department for Education and Employment
DfES	Department for Education and Skills
EAL	English as an additional language
E-Bacc	English baccalaureate
ECML	European Centre for Modern Languages
EFL	English as a foreign language
ESL	English as a second language
ESP	English for specific purposes
FL	foreign language(s)
FLES	Foreign Languages in Elementary Schools
GCSE	General Certificate of Secondary Education
GOML	Graded Objectives in Modern Languages
GTC	General Teaching Council for England
HEI	higher education institutions
HMI	Her Majesty's Inspectors of Schools
ICC	intercultural communicative competence
ICT	information and communications technology
ITT	initial teacher training

KAL	knowledge about language
KS	key stage
L1	first language
L2	second language
LAD	language acquisition device
LLS	language learner strategies
MFL	modern foreign language(s)
MLPS	Modern Languages in Primary Schools
NFER	National Foundation for Educational Research
NQT	newly qualified teacher
NUT	National Union of Teachers
PE	physical education
PGCE	Postgraduate Certificate in Education
PSHE	personal, social and health education
RAE	research assessment exercise
RE	religious education
SEN	special educational needs
SLA	second language acquisition
SLC	specialist language colleges
TL	target language
TOEFL	Test of English as a Foreign Language

Introduction to the series

This book, *Debates in Modern Languages Education*, is one of a series of books entitled *Debates in Subject Teaching*. The series has been designed to engage with a wide range of debates related to subject teaching. Unquestionably, debates vary among the subjects, but may include, for example, issues that:

- impact on initial teacher education in the subject;
- are addressed in the classroom through the teaching of the subject;
- are related to the content of the subject and its definition;
- are related to subject pedagogy;
- are connected with the relationship between the subject and broader educational aims and objectives in society, and the philosophy and sociology of education;
- are related to the development of the subject and its future in the twenty-first century.

Consequently, each book presents key debates that subject teachers should understand, reflect on and engage in as part of their professional development. Chapters have been designed to highlight major questions, and to consider the evidence from research and practice in order to find possible answers. Some subject books or chapters offer at least one solution or a view of the ways forward, whereas others provide alternative views and leave readers to identify their own solution or view of the ways forward. The editors expect readers will want to pursue the issues raised, and so chapters include questions for further debate and suggestions for further reading. Debates covered in the series will provide the basis for discussion in university subject seminars or as topics for assignments or classroom research. The books have been written for all those with a professional interest in their subject, and, in particular: student teachers learning to teach the subject in secondary or primary school; newly qualified teachers; teachers undertaking study at Masters level; teachers with a subject coordination or leadership role, and those preparing for such responsibility; as well as mentors, university tutors, CPD organisers and advisers of the afore-mentioned groups.

Books in the series have a cross-phase dimension, because the editors believe that it is important for teachers in the primary, secondary and post-16 phases to look at subject teaching holistically, particularly in order to provide for continuity and progression, but also to increase their understanding of how children and young people learn. The balance of chapters that have a cross-phase relevance varies according to the issues relevant to different subjects. However, no matter where the emphasis is, the authors have drawn out the relevance of their topic to the whole of each book's intended audience.

Because of the range of the series, both in terms of the issues covered and its cross-phase concern, each book is an edited collection. Editors have commissioned new writing from experts on particular issues, who, collectively, represent many different perspectives on subject teaching. Readers should not expect a book in this series to cover the entire range of debates relevant to the subject, or to offer a completely unified view of subject teaching, or that every debate will be dealt with discretely, or that all aspects of a debate will be covered. Part of what each book in this series offers to readers is the opportunity to explore the inter-relationships between positions in debates and, indeed, among the debates themselves, by identifying the overlapping concerns and competing arguments that are woven through the text.

The editors are aware that many initiatives in subject teaching continue to originate from the centre, and that teachers have decreasing control of subject content, pedagogy and assessment strategies. The editors strongly believe that for teaching to remain properly a vocation and a profession, teachers must be invited to be part of a creative and critical dialogue about subject teaching, and should be encouraged to reflect, criticise, problem-solve and innovate. This series is intended to provide teachers with a stimulus for democratic involvement in the development of the discourse of subject teaching.

Susan Capel, Jon Davison, James Arthur and John Moss
December 2010

Introduction

*Patricia Driscoll, Ernesto Macaro and
Ann Swarbrick*

This book offers a comprehensive introduction and synthesis of the major themes and theories in language learning and teaching today. Significant recent changes in policy and practice at school, local authority and teacher education level have created the need for a book that provides an up-to-date authoritative review of traditional and contemporary issues in language teaching.

The book is divided into three main sections. Part I, 'Overview', explores current debates in the subject and how the languages discourse has changed over time. The importance of substantive and syntactic knowledge for effective teaching is discussed and how novice teachers develop their subject and pedagogic knowledge and skill to become expert practitioners. Part II, 'Issues in the classroom', explores current understanding of how learners learn languages and considers approaches to teaching with reference to relevant theories, complex constructs, and empirical research. Part III, 'Educational debates', considers the aims and rationale, values and philosophical principles inherent in languages teaching and learning and examines the innovations and ideas that shape and will shape the discipline for the next decade.

The book begins with three chapters that take a historical perspective and use this to structure their argument. We begin with a look at the broad aim of languages teaching – to develop good linguists and thus to create a nation that is sympathetic to the notion that communicating in languages other than your mother tongue is a good thing. Richard Johnstone charts the efforts made over several decades to help the UK become more multilingual. He charts the successes and blind alleys giving us a historical perspective over 40 years across the four nations of the UK. He proposes that there are four emerging and common challenges across the UK, all of which have emerged strongly, in his view, over the 40-year period:

- How to enable the learning and use of additional languages to flourish when English is increasingly the dominant language not only of the UK but also of globalisation?
- How best to extend the learning of a modern language across the full range of abilities in the early years of secondary education?

- How to achieve good numbers taking languages from the point at which they become optional, usually post-14?
- How best to implement languages at primary school?

He analyses each challenge stating that, in his view, none of the four nations have been successful in meeting any of these challenges in the past 40 years. He warns against taking research findings out of context and outlines a clear role for research and researchers in languages in the future.

We move from this broad policy perspective closer to individual teachers' approaches with John Field who considers the focus in UK classrooms, since the 1970s, on teaching the four skills (speaking, listening, reading and writing) and the distinct set of methods that has arisen since then for teaching each of these separate skills with no particular foundation beyond trial and error. He outlines recent psycholinguistic research about the nature of each skill. In his view, such study allows us to design exercise types that practise specific aspects of the skills in question. He provides a brief overview of the cognitive processes involved in each skill and draws out ways in which the processes can be developed in the languages classroom. For if teachers understand the challenges that each skill presents to languages learners they will be better able to address the needs of developing linguists.

This points to the need for investment in teacher development which is taken up by Ann Swarbrick who develops this theme focusing on the CPD needs of teachers and beginning teachers. She takes four particular issues, and through these draws out why teacher development has not been a success story and what effective teacher development might look like in the future. She points readers to prominent writers and researchers working in this aspect of languages education and asks why, if professional development is worthwhile, more teachers do not engage with it and why, if it is not taken seriously by schools, it is a constant area for policy development.

The second part of this volume turns its spotlight on the location where teaching and learning in modern foreign languages mostly takes place. Of course we recognise that, in a world where technology is advancing rapidly and where access to different world languages is increasingly being facilitated by the internet, students can learn outside the classroom. However, it seemed to us fundamental to engage the readers of this book with the issues related to formal schooling because it is in this context that learners (particularly children and adolescents) will encounter the kind of structured pedagogy that is intended to scaffold their learning in a principled way from beginner to advanced level. Paradoxically, it is in formal teaching and learning contexts that we find a lack of consensus as to how to set about scaffolding that learning – how to set about teaching a foreign language.

It is not surprising then that the chapters in this part each present the challenges faced by the language teacher and the language learner. Indeed Robert Vanderplank in his chapter 'Listening and understanding' begins by asking why listening is such a challenge for language learners. The chapter focuses on one-way listening, that is listening to recorded text which cannot be openly interacted with. However, it is made clear that even this kind of unidirectional listening is far from being a passive process but requires high levels of listener engagement. In contrast the chapter by Katie Horne titled 'Speaking interactively' recognises that speaking is precisely a two-way process requiring a different set of strategies from one-way listening. In both these chapters the authors attempt to overcome the lack of ambition found among some teachers with regard to skill development. Vanderplank argues that training the ear to the sounds of the language are prerequisites to making progress in listening and Horne proposes much greater focus on learners communicating real information and with enhanced spontaneity rather than simply regurgitating phrases handed down to them by the teacher or the textbook.

Robert Woore in his chapter on 'Developing reading and decoding' identifies the challenge of the learner's first language and how to make the presence of that first language an asset rather than a hindrance. This is particularly in the sub-skill of decoding L2 text with beginner learners. But here too the challenge for teachers and learners is to go beyond the over-simplified text where most of the words have been taught or encountered in advance to more complex texts requiring clever guessing strategies and the motivation to overcome the difficulties posed by the L2. Rosa M. Manchón asks the reader in 'Learning and teaching writing' to consider the multiple and complex objectives of writing in a L2 classroom and the challenge of ensuring that whilst learners are being taught to write in a new language they are also being encouraged to learn from their writing. L2 writing therefore becomes not just a controlled form of self-expression but an opportunity to notice the gap between one's current linguistic knowledge and the aspiration to communicate at a higher level.

Ernesto Macaro argues for the learning of grammar (the rule-system of the target language) to be considered as supporting the development of the four skills explored in the preceding chapters rather than as an object of study in its own right. In order for grammar teaching to provide that supporting role teachers have to recognise the limitations inherent in explicit grammar teaching and identify for themselves what their expectations are for their students with regard to observing the development of grammatical accuracy. This supporting role is also promoted by Ron Martinez's chapter on vocabulary acquisition. Just how much vocabulary does one need in order to understand and communicate, what kind of vocabulary would this be, and what level of understanding about a word or a lexical item (e.g. a collocation) should a learner demonstrate in order to operate effectively in a variety of realistic communicative contexts?

Classroom issues such as skills development and linguistic knowledge cannot of course be considered without also considering the contexts in which they exist and are debated. One of those contexts is the culture in which the target language is situated. Mairin Hennebry asks whether cultural awareness should be taught and indeed can it be 'taught'. Here, as with the acquisition of grammar and vocabulary the question is how to consider the object of study. Hennebry analyses the relationship between language and culture and examines how cultural knowledge and skills are integrated into the national curricula in a number of countries. A rich learning environment is at the heart of Jane Jones's chapter on the role of assessment. She considers whether formative feedback (or assessment for learning – AfL) has proven to be beneficial to language learning. She questions whether AfL takes up too much classroom time if it cannot be carried out in the target language for reasons of learner proficiency. Amanda Barton considers a learner's trajectory as they move from one phase of schooling to another. She focuses particularly on issues surrounding student transition from Key Stage 2 to 3 and explores conditions for success so learners' achievements and motivation are sustained. These questions cannot be tackled without referring to the context in which they arise. In England, languages have been continually squeezed out of the curriculum by the demands of other subjects and by unsupportive government policies. Both of these factors present further barriers for successful transition across all Key Stages.

Suzanne Graham focuses centrally on motivation. Her chapter goes beyond the conceptualisations of intrinsic and extrinsic or integrative and instrumental motivation. She explores a more cognitive account and proposes that we can better understand the motivation of learners in a class if we examine their thought processes in relation to the language learning tasks that they are actually required to undertake. She argues that success or failure can play a very powerful part in determining whether one wants to continue with the business of learning. Finally Mike Grenfell and Vee Harris ask why programmes of language learning strategies have not taken hold in the UK and as a consequence why language learners are still highly dependent on the teacher for making progress with their language learning. They relate this to the heady days of the late 1980s and early 1990s in the UK, where the emphasis was to shift from the formal teaching of grammar to more communicative aspirations which did not materialise. To try to unpack this conundrum they argue that the three areas of learning strategies, self-regulation, and autonomy have been wrongly considered as separate domains. All three are predicated on the notion of learning to learn rather than being taught learning and this requires a fundamental shift in how we conceptualise the relationship between the teacher, the learners and the curriculum.

Whilst all of the chapters in the book seek to introduce the reader to the debates and concerns of the languages teacher and teacher educator we have dedicated the final part to one overarching theme which has particular resonance across all education phases. This part focuses on the evolving languages curriculum which will inspire and motivate both learners and teachers through the twenty-first century. Rosamond Mitchell considers the value of languages in education in the era of globalisation. She examines the claims and beliefs about an early start and questions whether age matters. She compares the rationale for teaching languages in primary and secondary school and reviews the cognitive and attitudinal advantages and the potential benefits of language learning to a learner's general education. Marie Ryan continues this theme and explores the transformative qualities of creative teaching and learning in languages. She argues that creativity and knowledge are interdependent and teachers who encourage the creative flow in the learning process stimulate intellectual curiosity and experimentation, which is more motivating than focusing purely on the product of learning.

How to ensure that pupils remain engaged in learning is also developed by Philip Hood in his chapter on 'Content and Language Integrated Learning' (CLIL). He analyses how using the foreign language as the medium for teaching rather than the subject matter of teaching results in more effective learning in both primary and secondary schooling. Furthermore, he suggests viable frameworks for practice and looks at the implications for learner motivation and achievement. Learners' right for an education that meets their needs is tackled by Jill Llewellyn-Williams. She argues that over the last decade, we have seen developments in thinking about differentiation and personalisation that have laid the groundwork for curriculum innovation in terms of new patterns of learning which promote a more inclusive education in schools as leaners and teachers develop greater co-constructive collaborative relationships.

Collaboration is a major theme in Patricia Driscoll's chapter as primary languages become part of the statutory curriculum in England. She examines the changing nature of primary languages as the subject has become more established in schools. She also explores the potential of a community of novice and experienced practitioners and non-specialist and specialist teachers working together across primary and secondary schools. She suggests that through professional collaboration we will be able to sustain and extend existing good practice in primary schools and develop a broader conception of the subject and how it is taught, which will form a solid foundation of learning for the future.

We hope you enjoy reading the book and you find the questions and suggestions for reflective enquiry at the end of each chapter useful to you.

Part I

Overview

Chapter 1

Languages over the past 40 years

Does history repeat itself?

Richard Johnstone

Introduction

Covering all four nations of the UK, the British Academy Report (2013) on the current state of languages in UK society offers a stark message. Among its claims are that 'there is strong evidence that the UK suffers from a growing deficit in languages skills' and that 'the range and nature of languages being taught is insufficient to meet current and future demands'. It argues that 'a weak supply of languages skills is pushing down demand and creating a vicious circle of monolingualism' and it states that 'languages spoken by British schoolchildren, in addition to English, represent a valuable future source of supply' (British Academy, 2013: 4–5).

Given the enormous efforts made over several decades across the UK with the aim of enabling education at primary and secondary school to help the UK become more multilingual, it would be easy to become disheartened. Nonetheless, there have been many successes in languages at school where the aim is not limited to the largely instrumental perspective that properly informs the British Academy Report. The report deserves to be taken seriously, but one remembers another prestigious report (the Nuffield Languages Inquiry, Nuffield Foundation, 2000) that created great interest but was not implemented to the extent that had been hoped. Moreover, although the National Languages Strategy[1] did not apply across the UK as a whole, it was a major initiative, yet where is it now?

When thinking of languages policies in the UK, we recognise that there are four nations, each with its own administration for education at school. Admittedly, there are similarities between England, Wales and Northern Ireland (e.g. the terms 'GCSE' and 'Key Stages') whereas Scotland differs in its curriculum and its national examinations. Moreover, pupils in Scotland go to secondary school one year later than elsewhere in the UK. Scotland, Wales and Northern Ireland are similar, in that education at school in each case has a responsibility for contributing to the maintenance and revitalisation of a heritage Celtic language (Gaelic, Irish and Welsh).

All four nations have significant numbers of students at school with a home 'community language' such as Punjabi, Urdu, Polish, Cantonese. The challenge for our educational systems is to find ways of building on the skills possessed in sometimes partial and halting form by young people at school who belong to communities that speak these languages, so that they benefit from having a home language as well as English and our society benefits both culturally and instrumentally.

FOUR EMERGING CHALLENGES

Despite the variations referred to above, I now turn to four challenges that are common across the UK, all of which have emerged strongly over the last 40 years. These have been and still are:

- enabling the learning and use of additional languages to flourish when English is increasingly the dominant language not only of the UK but also of globalisation
- extending the learning of a Modern Language successfully across the full range of abilities in the early years of secondary education
- achieving good numbers taking languages from the point at which they become optional, usually post-14[2]
- implementing Modern Languages at Primary School (MLPS).

The first of these challenges arises from the nature of UK society. The other three all arise from policy decisions, directions, intentions or aspirations. No nation in the UK has been convincingly successful in meeting any of these challenges. However, I shall reflect on some issues that have arisen over the past 40 years or more and will be happy to share some thoughts at the end.

METHODOLOGIES COMPARED

I was asked that my discussion should start from 40 years ago. This was roughly when I became a member of staff at the University of Stirling. At this time, the fourth challenge (above) was already in difficulty, and the Burstall Report (Burstall *et al.*, 1974) would effectively remove MFL from most state primary schools until a second wave of MLPS would begin in the early 1990s. However, attempts to meet the second challenge (above) were in full swing, and this necessitated a big methodological re-think.

The first research book I purchased in my new post was the *Pennsylvania Project* (Smith and Berger, 1968). Although the project took place in the USA, the issues it confronted applied equally in the UK. It sought to evaluate the relative merits of three approaches to MFL teaching: the traditional method based on grammar-translation (GT); the audio-lingual (AL) method based on teaching functional skills; and a modified version of this. The findings did not show significant differences among the three approaches. Such however was the climate of the times that Rebecca Valette wrote in some frustration: 'succinct press releases have proclaimed the superiority of the traditional method and the disgrace of the language laboratory' (Valette, 1969: 396).

As a pupil at secondary school, beginning in the early 1950s, I experienced the GT approach, and as a young schoolteacher towards the end of the 1960s I tried out AL in class and the language laboratory. I admired the expertise that went into the Pennsylvania research. However, my experience as a student at school and then in schoolteaching had alerted me to possible differences between an approach elaborated by experts and the same approach implemented in class by teachers.

Reflecting for example on the GT approach that I had experienced as a beginner learner of French at age 12 in my first year of secondary education (there being no modern languages in Scottish state primary schools in those days), I enjoyed it. We began by focusing on the phonetic written representation of all of the sounds of French – e.g. the phonetics for the four different nasal sounds in *un bon vin blanc*. This helped greatly with correct pronunciation. Later in our first year we were taught the alphabetical spelling of the words we had learnt phonetically, so we were not knocked off course by the strange-looking way in which these words were spelled alphabetically. Also, we were taught the grammar of written French, and to learn from grammar books and dictionaries. By the end of our second year we had covered all of the tenses of French and were working our way through genuine texts of French literature, such as Jules Verne's *Adventures of Captain Hatteras*:

> C'était un hardi dessein qu'avait eu le capitaine Hatteras de s'élever jusqu'au nord, et de réserver à l'Angleterre, sa patrie, la gloire de découvrir le pôle boréal du monde ... après avoir poussé son brick le Forward au-delà des mers connues, enfin, après avoir accompli la moitié de la tâche, il voyait ses grands projets subitement anéantis!

This ignited my imagination through phrases such as *au-delà des mers connues* (beyond the charted seas). We also learnt Latin. The two languages were taught in the same way: reading, writing, vocabulary and grammar, leading to genuine literature, with no distractions in the form of spoken language. Yes, it was a one-sided approach that suited top-stream pupils and that would not be fit for purpose today. I never met a real French person during my entire time at school, but both French and Latin as a means of creating an imagined reality were superb. Then, as now, the amount of time per week for learning modern languages was very limited, but the approach was ruthlessly efficient in that it almost completely cut out spoken language and emphasised learning on the basis of linguistic principles, taking the willing learner quickly and efficiently to a valued literary pay-off. Some of the problems experienced in modern languages today arise in my view from too much being attempted in too limited a time-frame.

Comprehensivisation

With the advent of comprehensive schooling in the 1960s, the extension of a modern language across the full ability range in the initial years of secondary education got underway. Language laboratories, tape recorders, overhead projectors, film-strips, duplication machines (producing an infinite supply of 'worksheets'), were used in order to make the language accessible to the much wider range of students. A few audio-visual French and German courses came to dominate the scene. These helped but I remember analysing one such course based on a family of white Caucasian ethnicity: a father and a mother (married to each other), two boys (tending to be mischievous), a girl (well-behaved) in a detached house with garage (containing car and bicycles) and garden – not much connection to the lives of many UK pupils learning the language or of young people in the foreign country concerned.

At the time the Scottish Office Education Department was willing to fund research projects on foreign language teaching in schools. I was fortunate to have the opportunity of working with the outstanding Rosamond Mitchell and Brian Parkinson in a study producing a segmental analysis of the discourse of MFL classrooms in the first year of secondary education in 1977/1978 (Mitchell *et al.*, 1981) in which a well-known audio-visual course was used. Classrooms were found to be 'busy, work-oriented places, with a heavy emphasis on oral FL activities' but it was found also that

> these large amounts of oral FL usage were limited in several ways. Most of the observed FL activities involved the intensive, repetitive manipulation of very restricted sets of language elements; extensive exposure to any richer FL diet was rare ... Missing also was any effective individualisation of the language learning process. The pupils in the classes we studied received virtually identical language experiences, which moreover almost always centred on the teacher.
>
> (Mitchell *et al.*, 1981: 66)

Three HMI reports offer a picture of the situation in England. Their 1977 report found that most MFL teachers had difficulty in dealing with low-ability groups. Their 1985 report, however, found sufficient evidence that a foreign language experience for all up to the age of 16 can be feasible and beneficial, but their 1989 report found continuing problems with the teaching of modern languages in inner city or urban schools.

Gradually a more learner-centred approach emerged in the late 1970s and continued through the 1980s. This was the era of 'personalisation' in which pupils were encouraged to learn the MFL so as to be able to talk about their own real selves. This was an excellent idea as an antidote to the audio-visual stereotypes described above, so long as over time it grew in range, complexity and depth in order to keep up with students' emerging interests and cognitive development

– but sadly this did not always happen. This was also a time to work towards 'graded objectives' which were to some extent influenced by functional–notional syllabus design, as enunciated particularly by the Council of Europe, and to engage in a variety of 'communicative' activities. Teachers were encouraged to use diagnostic assessment for providing feedback to learners; and to collaborate across schools, often under the banner of Graded Objectives in Modern Languages, so there was an Oxford group, a Leicester group, a Lothian group etc. Brian Page (2004) rightly argues that GOML was about much more than graded objectives; it was about teachers engaging in reflection, discussion and collaboration across many different aspects of their activity. Collaborative developments such as these made a highly positive contribution to MFL teaching in schools.

Upper secondary school

A major problem has been the diminishing numbers taking a MFL to the highest level in the upper secondary school. Suzanne Graham (2004) indicates that the numbers taking French at A-level in England, Wales and Northern Ireland dropped from 27,245 in 1990 to 15,605 in 2002, while Joanna McPake *et al.* (1999) indicate that in Scotland the numbers taking the Higher examination in French dropped from 11,610 in 1976 to 4,840 in 1997.

Graham's (2004) study looked at students in Year 11, the final year of compulsory education, leading to GCSE; in Year 12 (AS level); and Year 13 (A-level). The Year 11 students were from top-ability sets and expressed positive attitudes towards French, but those predicted to obtain high grades were not convinced they were necessarily doing well at French. Graham considered this might indicate low self-esteem and reported: 'this suggests that students do not feel that success in an external examination is necessarily the same as achieving linguistic proficiency' (Graham, 2004: 186). One of Graham's conclusions was that Learner Strategy Instruction might be a good way of helping learners become aware that their learning might be improved if they learnt to employ strategies appropriately and effectively.

McPake *et al.*'s (1999) study identified a 'climate of negativity' in which a number of negative factors conspired together. These included examiners' comments that the standards of performance at Higher were not necessarily high; the views of some principal teachers that some students taking Higher were not interested in the subject and were not necessarily capable of bridging the big gap from Standard Grade in Fourth Year to Higher in Fifth Year; a more general social view (e.g. among parents and in businesses) that learning languages can be difficult and tedious, allied to the absence of any strong belief in the instrumental value of language learning. As Graham was to find subsequently in England, students judged to be competent by their teachers did not themselves necessarily feel confident about the languages skills they were acquiring. The researchers took the view that this lack of confidence among competent students was the most serious consequence of the climate of negativity. When the students were invited to reflect back on the course they had taken, leading to Standard Grade in Fourth Year, they tended to dislike the 'self-centred curriculum' (too much repetitious 'personalisation'?), the 'excessive emphasis on grammar and vocabulary' and the 'lack of intellectual challenge'. It was interesting that these high-attaining students had found French to be 'difficult' but 'not intellectually challenging'!

MLPS

By the early 1990s there was a 'new show in town' in the form of a second wave of MLPS. It has featured strongly in the policies and the activity of both the European Commission and the Council of Europe.

During the 1990s, Scotland was the UK's front-runner with its national pilot projects followed by the implementation of its generalisation phase. It was considered essential to implement the generalisation speedily, on grounds of equity for all Scottish primary schools. So, a substantial fund was created to allow classroom teachers to obtain a certain number of days release over four terms, in order to receive training in French, German, Spanish or Italian and in MLPS pedagogy. This ensured one trained MLPS teacher in every Scottish primary school – a situation that I applauded.

However, Scotland can no longer claim to be leading the UK. As a result of the National Language Strategy, England has impressively built up its provision. The British Academy Report indicates that, by 2007, 57 per cent of primary schools in England offered MLPS, that by 2010 this figure had risen to 92 per cent, and it stated that languages were on track to become part of the primary school National Curriculum by 2014. An Ofsted report (2011) judged achievement to be good or outstanding in more than half of the primary schools visited. Most progress was in speaking and listening, with not many examples of systematically planned reading. The report stated that pupils' enjoyment was very clear and that teaching was good in two-thirds of the 235 lessons observed. This is not perfect but the show seemed to be heading in a good direction.

Nonetheless, some hard questions must be asked of MLPS. Blondin *et al.* (1998) found that pupils enjoyed learning an additional language at primary school but their spoken language largely consisted of formulaic expressions. This applied across several European countries including those with English as the MLPS language. Pupils did not seem to have internalised a system of rules that would enable them to create their own utterances in spontaneous speech. There could be a number of possible explanations for this, and no doubt improvements could be made through a better-informed pedagogy, but one has to consider whether the MLPS model can reasonably be expected to lead to the sort of creative language use that one would like to see. After all, the MLPS model is based on a drip-feed approach, with relatively small amounts of time each week, and quite often from teachers who lack real confidence and fluency in the MLPS language. As a result, MLPS pupils are highly unlikely to be receiving substantial amounts of MFL input.

Carmen Muñoz (2008), a world expert in this field, has stated that: 'an early starting age produces long-term benefits when associated with greater time and massive exposure, as in immersion programmes, but not when associated with limited time and exposure, as in typical foreign language learning classrooms' (p. 582). When evaluating the National Bilingual Education Project in Spain, I regularly was told that the conventional model of MLPS was not delivering what parents and decision-makers in Spain wanted, hence their interest in exploring stronger models such as Content and Language Integrated Learning (CLIL) and bilingual education.

The Early Language Learning in Europe (ELLiE) project (Enever, 2011), undertaken by experts from several European countries, presents a somewhat more positive picture of MLPS pupils' proficiency than in Blondin *et al.* (1998). For many learners there was a significant increase in vocabulary and complexity during the first years of FL teaching, though formulaic expressions were still the most common type of utterance. ELLiE issues a healthy challenge to the CEFR level descriptors as benchmarks for early primary foreign language learning (FLL), claiming they are not appropriate and suggest a limited appreciation of the real processes of early FLL. It also confirms that early primary FL teachers need a high level of fluency – a view that not everybody involved in MLPS shares, with some claiming it suffices for the teacher to be always just ahead of the class. I also welcomed their perception that some of the characteristics of successful MLPS teachers are generic, not languages-specific, reflecting their role as general primary school teachers. These included capacity to create a positive and safe relationship with the children, being supportive to them, making sure the children have successful experiences, and showing skill in keeping the children focused on task.

Another research report that potentially has something to offer MLPS in the UK is the USA study by Taylor and Lafayette (2010). Their research was focused not on what the pupils could do in the MFL but rather on the impact that their early MFL learning might have on their learning of other subjects such as English, mathematics, science and social studies. Over Grades 1–3 there was a clear advantage for MFL pupils as compared with a carefully matched non-MFL group.

The way forward for MLPS arguably should include: (1) devising a clearer and better-grounded rationale for doing it – there *are* good reasons but these have not been clearly stated or disciplined sufficiently by the best research evidence; (2) making the MLPS model work as well as it possibly can, despite its inherent limitations; and (3) systematically exploring other models where circumstances allow. To put all of our eggs in basket (2) would clearly indicate lack of national ambition, so I favour a variety of provision on the ground with innovations in (3) complementing the main provision in (2), and with a substantial research programme to monitor progress and guide development.

Need for alternative models

Some of the alternative models vary according to the amount of instructional time per week in the target language. I shall mention two.

First there is the (roughly) 25 per cent model, as in Järvinen's (2008) CLIL study of learners at Grades 1–3 in Finland. Students receiving 25 per cent of their curriculum in English were compared with mainstream students receiving MLPS. The CLIL students' English language development was quicker but also different. After a one-word phase in Grades 1 and 2, they were producing 'full-blown' sentences in Grade 3, whereas the mainstream pupils failed to do this even by the end of Grade 5. On three years exposure and instruction at 25 per cent these young learners had developed implicit L2 learning. It was also concluded that teachers needed to focus on accuracy as well as on fluency, to explore deep meaning (e.g. subject-specific concepts and higher-order thinking skills), to challenge pupils' comprehension, and to create opportunities for pupils to produce fairly elaborate spontaneous stretches of expression, not simply one- or two-word utterances.

Second, there is the (roughly) 40–50 per cent model of bilingual education or early partial immersion (EPI). The UK's first experiment in EPI in a foreign language, with local authority and government backing, was in an Aberdeen primary school (Johnstone and McKinstry, 2008). Set in a locality of substantial socio-economic disadvantage, the school provided EPI in French from Primary 1 to the end of Primary 7. The evaluation report stated that the pupils had reached a level of proficiency in French that went far beyond what could be expected of MLPS. They had shown that they could use French in order to access with profit other areas of their curriculum, with no disadvantage to their English, environmental studies or mathematics. Their ability to cope with a fast flow of French input from their native-speaker support teachers was particularly impressive.

However, a hard lesson had to be learnt. Financial difficulties meant that the local authority could not find the funds to continue the project. It no longer exists. The pupils and their parents had been let down. This raises the serious issue of the 'sustainability' of innovative projects. We need innovation, but a 'sustainability plan' needs to be built in from the start.

Complementary schooling

Complementary schooling usually takes place for a few hours at weekends and is run by particular minority linguistic communities to help their children maintain the home language. CILT UK[3] has played a major role in supporting complementary schooling. A study by McPake et al. (2007), reflecting three of the UK's CILTs, indicates the importance of finding ways of providing support for complementary schooling, rather than leaving it to the linguistic communities alone, since teachers in complementary schools often have considerable difficulties in accessing suitable professional development.

Some world-class research has been done on complementary schooling in the UK. Both Creese and Blackledge (2010) and Li Wei (2011) show how dynamic and creative the processes of interaction between complementary teachers and their students can be. Creese and Blackledge discuss the merits of 'translanguaging' as an alternative to the assumption that the community language should necessarily be passed on monolingually. Li Wei similarly discusses Chinese complementary school classroom processes from a multicompetence perspective in which code-switching and mode-switching by both teachers and students can take place. Li Wei claims that the pupils: 'use their language skills to simultaneously further and flout the norms of behavior in the school ... they exploit the full sets of their linguistic resources to showcase their creativity and criticality by challenging the teacher's authority and traditional Chinese ways of teaching and subverting the pedagogic task' (2011: 381).

MFL teaching in mainstream UK schooling can learn from this. There have been times when an almost tyrannical imposition of classroom interaction exclusively in the MFL has taken place. It is important to provide substantial exposure to the MFL, but at the same time pupils' first or national language is a major resource for them as learners. Good teaching finds ways of productively linking the two languages together. The complementary schooling research shows that the instincts and the creativity of pupils can be a resource on which teachers may draw.

X-medium education

One of the greatest success stories in UK languages education over the past 30 years must be X-medium education. The most recent research evidence on Gaelic-medium education by Fiona O'Hanlon (2010) and colleagues confirms a picture which applies to Welsh-medium and Irish-medium also: pupils who have English as the language of their home but who are entered by their parents for this form of education become highly proficient in the immersion language without detriment to their subject attainments. In addition, they gain the cognitive, cultural, linguistic and personal benefits of having become bilingual. Wales has undoubtedly given a lead on this form of education, not only in the UK but also at world level through the expertise of many excellent scholars and innovators, e.g. Colin Baker's seminal *Foundations of Bilingual Education and Bilingualism* (2011). Irish-medium education has also become well-established in Northern Ireland, with 21 stand-alone schools and 12 schools with Irish-medium units attached to English-medium host schools.

The stakes are as high as can be. Without a successful provision of Welsh- and Gaelic-medium education from the early years at school onwards, the future existence of these languages would be at risk, especially Scottish Gaelic with its low speaker-base. As Li Wei (2011) has stated in the context of complementary schooling, bilingualism and multilingualism by their very nature can give rise to tensions, and sometimes to conflict, whether ideological, cultural, personal or other. These tensions have to be confronted in societies, communities and individuals. In Welsh-, Irish- and Gaelic-medium education, I believe that outstanding progress has been made. Those involved are up for the double challenge of providing an excellent education for pupils while at the same time playing their part in the maintenance and revitalisation of three unique indigenous speech communities.

Conclusion

So far as languages education in UK schools is concerned, does history repeat itself? I shall mention two senses in which this may possibly be true to some limited extent, one sense in which the situation has not changed, and one sense in which there is encouraging progress.

The two senses in which history may to some extent be repeating itself are: (1) a clear move at government policy level in England to go back to a more traditional model of modern language teaching; and (2) a clear move in England and maybe also in other parts of the UK to go back towards a situation in which teachers in schools had to do it all by themselves rather than rely overmuch on advice and support from outsiders at local or national level.

I shall briefly explain these two points:

First, I have already discussed the knowledge-based curriculum and grammar-translation-and-literature approach that I experienced as a beginner learner in the early 1950s. Recently the BBC News website of 6 February 2013[4] reported the Secretary for State for Education in the coalition government as saying that 'pupils should be taught a core knowledge of facts and information', and that 'language teaching will have a clear emphasis on the importance of translation, including the study of literature of proven merit'. This echoes my own earlier experience. Although there is some merit in what was said, a much more rounded and better-informed picture of the aims and principles of languages education for today's world is needed.

Second, in my days at school we had teachers but no languages assistants, no local authority advisers, no CILT UK, no researchers. However, from the mid-1960s a significant infrastructure supporting languages at school emerged and made a major contribution in support of teachers. It included local authority (LA) advisers, Association of Language Learning (ALL), CILT and eventually the Scottish, Welsh and Northern Ireland CILTs, plus links with partners on the continent of Europe as facilitated by the European Commission and the Council of Europe, and also with increasing participation from higher education institutions (HEI) staff involved in languages teacher education and research. In my view, the 1980s and 1990s were a brilliant time in which to be a languages professional, as networks at local, national, UK and European levels built up. There was exchange of information and ideas and healthy debate, in which research increasingly played a role.

However, some of this infrastructure has been downsized. LA advisers are less numerous than they were; CILT in London has been moved elsewhere and incorporated into another organisation, losing its invaluable research library (and invaluable library staff); annual funding for the European Centre for Modern Languages (ECML) in Graz has been stopped. We are not back to the days of my schooling but have moved in that direction.

The sense in which I believe the situation has hardly changed at all takes me back to the four challenges that I mentioned earlier in this chapter. They have been with us for decades. Our ways of attempting to meet these challenges have evolved and diversified considerably – but they remain major challenges rather than general success stories.

Let me now identify one area in which history is not repeating itself and in which the future stands a chance of being better than the past. This is represented by a clear growth in the numbers of researchers based in UK universities who do much of their research on languages at school, very often working collaboratively with schoolteachers. Some of the UK university researchers working in this area have achieved real eminence internationally, and thus languages education at school has much to gain. This is a far cry from the teacher trainers of the past, often based in Colleges of Education, for whom collaborative research in schools, with publication in top international journals, was simply not part of their job.

Looking to the future, I believe that university researchers have a major role to play. In fact, I believe that the plethora of advice and information that is now becoming available to teachers from a range of not-very-authoritative sources may be something of a problem. Having studied several UK websites for languages teachers, I become concerned when a report is taken out of context by persons who may be teachers, curriculum developers or policy-makers, its meaning is somewhat distorted and is used for promotional purposes – this is particularly true of some of the claims on behalf of younger learners and also CLIL. University research on schools has much to offer. Rosamond Mitchell (2003) has challenged the notion that progression in the acquisition of an additional language at school is like climbing a ladder. Her view that there are a number of components of proficiency with recurrent trade-offs and backsliding, is superior to the simplistic ladder model. We need to think of ways in which important research insights such as this can inform teachers' thinking and belief systems. As such, I welcome the 8 Principles[5] as elaborated by Ernesto Macaro and Suzanne Graham which seem not only accessible to busy teachers but also arise from research that is of high quality. Finally, I welcome ICT research such as that by Magda Phillips (2010) on video-conferencing between primary school pupils in England and France. Putting people in touch with each other and helping to create new communities of practice, involving two countries, schools, teachers, pupils, and researcher, is a fitting way in which to conclude.

Reflective enquiry

1   Progression in the acquisition of a modern language is often described in terms of climbing a ladder, ever upwards from one step to the next. In this chapter I draw attention to some researchers who challenge this view. So, what are the strengths and weaknesses of the 'ladder' model? Are there better ways of describing 'progression'?

2   Research mentioned in this chapter shows that children learning a modern language at primary school seem to be heavily reliant on 'formulaic expressions' in their spoken output. What is the value of formulaic expressions, and what might teachers do in order to help their students at any stage of their education produce a spoken output that is less formulaic and more creative, flexible and still accurate?

3   Overwhelmingly in UK schools the dominant model in languages education is based on the 'language as a school subject' with limited amounts of time available for it in a crowded curriculum. Two questions arise: (a) What might primary and secondary schools do in order to make this model work as effectively as possible? and (b) What, if any, alternatives to this model exist that would be realistic and sustainable?

Further reading

Enever, J. (ed.) (2011) *ELLiE Early Language Learning in Europe*, London: British Council.

Graham, S.J. (2004) 'Giving up on modern foreign languages? Students' perceptions of learning French', *The Modern Language Journal*, 88(2): 171–191.

Johnstone, R. and McKinstry, R. (2008) *Evaluation of EPPI: Early Primary Partial Immersion in French at Walker Road Primary School, Aberdeen, Final Report*, Stirling: University of Stirling, Scottish CILT, online, available at: www.strath.ac.uk/media/faculties/hass/scilt/research/eppi_book.pdf.

McPake, J., Johnstone, R., Low, L. and Lyall, L. (1999) *Foreign Languages in the Upper Secondary School: A Study of the Causes of Decline*, final report to SOEID, University of Glasgow: The SCRE Centre, online, available at: http://dspace.gla.ac.uk:8080/bitstream/1905/232/1/091.pdf.

Mitchell, R. (2003) 'Rethinking the concept of progression in the National Curriculum for modern foreign languages: a research perspective', *The Language Learning Journal*, 27(1): 15–23.

Ofsted (2011) *Modern Languages Achievement and Challenge 2007–2010*, Manchester: Ofsted, online, available at: www.ofsted.gov.uk/resources/modern-languages-achievement-and-challenge-2007-2010.

Notes

1 The Languages Company was set up in order to support the National Languages Strategy and to implement the Languages Review of 2007. In 2011 the Coalition Government decided not to continue with the Languages Strategy and to cut most central funding for languages. In common with most other bodies, The Languages Company received no further funding from the Government. (www.languagescompany.com/about-us/supporting-the-languages-strategy.html.)

2 The British Academy Report (2013) states that in England in 2004 languages were made optional post-14. In 2011, 43 per cent of the cohort took a MFL GCSE (down from 78 per cent in 2001). In Northern Ireland, in 2007 languages were made optional at secondary post-14, and from 2007–2011 the numbers taking French, German and Spanish dropped 19 per cent. In Wales, a foreign language has never been compulsory post-14 but the HMI (Wales) report (HM Inspectorate for Education and Training in Wales, 2009) indicates that between 1999 and 2007 the numbers taking GCSE in a modern foreign language dropped from 41 per cent to 28 per cent.

3 CILT UK consisted of CILT The National Centre for Languages, based in London, and its counterparts Scottish CILT (University of Stirling), CILT CYMRU (Cardiff) and NICILT (Queens University, Belfast). CILT The National Centre for Languages has since then been incorporated into the CfBT Education Trust, and Scottish CILT is now SCILT (University of Strathclyde).

4 www.bbc.co.uk/news/education-21346812.

5 Downloaded from: http://pdcinmfl.com/category/uncategorized/

Chapter 2

Cognitive processing and foreign language use

John Field

Introduction

Since the 1970s, language teaching pedagogy has embraced the notion that the four language skills (speaking, listening, writing and reading) are not simply ways of putting learnt grammar and vocabulary into practice, but are targets for teaching in their own right. A distinct set of methods has developed in relation to each of the skills, but these approaches have largely evolved by trial and error, and need to be supported by a clearer understanding of the nature of skilled second language (L2) performance.

Recent psycholinguistic research has produced considerable information about the nature of the four skills. Though this information chiefly relates to the way in which first-language users perform, it provides language teachers with a useful set of behavioural targets towards which they can lead L2 learners. By highlighting the various types of process that experienced language users employ, it enables us to design a range of exercise types, either developmental or remedial, which practise specific aspects of the skill in question.[1]

This chapter provides a brief overview of the cognitive processes that underlie the four skills and draws some implications as to the most effective ways in which the processes can be developed in a foreign language learning context. The purpose is to provide intending teachers with a clear set of goals for skills practice and to enable them to understand the challenges that each of the skills presents to language learners in the classroom. It is also to supply some theoretical background for the pedagogical issues raised in Chapters 4 to 7.

THE NOTION OF EXPERTISE

This chapter treats a competent user of a second language as somebody who has acquired a form of 'expertise'. There has been a large body of research into how expert performers behave, originally based upon studies of skills such as driving a car or playing chess. One influential model (Anderson, 1983; see summary in Johnson, 1996: 79–91) suggests that in employing a skill of any kind there is a progression from what is termed 'declarative knowledge' (knowledge *that*) to 'procedural knowledge' (knowledge *how to*). This account, known as 'adaptive control of thought' (ACT), neatly parallels an early distinction made by the methodologist Harold Palmer (1921) between knowing about a language and knowing how to use one; and indeed Anderson, the author of the theory, makes explicit connections with foreign language learning.

Declarative knowledge (think of it as classroom input in the form of grammar rules or of contextualised examples of grammar in use) consists of a series of linked steps which, because they are unfamiliar, demand a great deal of attention from the novice user. Consider the laboured way in which an early-stage learner of French would assemble a conditional sentence such as: *Si j'avais etudié l'espagnol, j'aurais compris* ('If I had studied Spanish, I would have understood'). As a result of extended practice, the initial set of steps goes through two important changes. First, small steps become 'composed' – i.e. combined into larger ones. Instead of constructing the sentence word by word, the user perhaps masters the sequences *si j'avais* and *j'aurais*, each followed by a past participle. What this illustrates for the language teacher is the importance of building up in the learner a repertoire of 'chunks' of language. Most teachers are familiar with lexical chunks such as *in front of, on time, Good to meet you*; but a proficient language user also acquires syntactic chunks such as *I wish I were…* or *I should have done*. These are stored in the mind as complete phonological units which not only makes it easier to produce them fluently, but also means (because they are pre-assembled) that they are grammatically accurate.

Second, the production of sentences becomes more 'automatic', i.e. it demands less and less focused attention and a rapid connection is made between the idea that the speaker wants to express and the means of expressing it (Segalowitz, 2003). An expert speaker or writer is thus one who has immediate access to words in their vocabulary store and who can construct grammatical sequences without having to reflect on them. There is then a similar automatic connection between the words and the physical operations that transmit them (the tongue, jaw, lips etc. in speaking, and the fingers in handwriting or typing). For the listener or reader, automaticity relates to the ability to decode words as they occur: identifying their forms, matching them to known words and accessing the meaning of those words. It also entails building the words into familiar grammatical patterns.

Automaticity is critical to skilled performance. The mental operations associated with producing and understanding language take place in 'working memory' (Gathercole and Baddeley, 1993). One of the functions of this type of memory is to focus extra attention upon anything that proves difficult to handle. However, the drawback is that our resources of attention are quite limited. Novice users of a language – like novice drivers or chess players – have to give a great deal of attention to detail: they have to assemble their own utterances in a very deliberate way and to focus carefully upon an L2 speaker's utterances in order to divide them into words. Because these low-level operations take up so much of their working memory, early-stage learners have little spare capacity to devote to larger-scale considerations. Take novice listeners as an example. Working memory limitations affect them in two distinct ways:

1   They have to concentrate so much on 'decoding' what is being said that they have little attention left to give to higher-level operations like relating the meaning of what they have heard to what went before in the conversation, interpreting the intentions of the speaker or bringing in their own knowledge of the world.
2   When they are listening to a piece of speech, listeners have to carry forward the words they have heard in their minds until such time as they are able to work out the relationships between them (subject, verb, object etc.). If they are giving a lot of attention to recognising an incoming word, they might well forget the words that preceded it.

So how is automaticity achieved? Mainly through extended practice and exposure to the target language. There are certainly messages here for the foreign language teacher. One is that some of the form-based practice drills which we associate with discredited 'behaviourist approaches' to language learning may not have been entirely useless after all. Another is that we should never underestimate the value of giving time and attention in the language classroom to free oral practice, where learners can gain experience in assembling utterances in the target language under pressures of time. A similar comment applies in relation to the receptive skills. It is essential for learners to be exposed to a wide range of listening and reading material so that they can develop an ability to decode rapidly what they hear and see. To make the experience relevant to real-life processing, at least some of this material should be derived from authentic sources, even in the early stages of learning (Field, 2008a: Ch. 14).

THE SKILLS

Cognitive accounts of language skills owe much to an 'information processing' approach (Broadbent, 1958), which tracks the way in which the mind takes a piece of information and progressively reshapes it. In the case of the *productive* skills (speaking and writing), we can identify certain stages that are involved in turning an idea into a string of speech sounds or into marks on a page. Accounts of the *receptive* skills (listening and reading) proceed in the opposite direction, tracing how a group of sounds or written words is turned into an idea.

Though the word 'stages' has been used here, this does not indicate that language users necessarily proceed in a step-by-step fashion. Evidence suggests that our minds operate on several levels at once. While in the middle of producing an utterance, a speaker might be preparing instructions to the tongue, lips etc. for performing the remaining words, monitoring what has been said so far and even thinking of the next utterance. Furthermore, if a message does not fit a language user's goals or is inconsistent with what went before, they can go back at any point to revise it. This kind of behaviour is especially seen in writers, who often backtrack and change part of a text while in the middle of producing it.

Speaking

Speaking can be envisaged as broadly falling into four stages (see Levelt, 1989: Ch. 1; Levelt, 1999: 86–89 for a more complex model):

- *conceptualising:* having an idea to express
- *planning:* preparing an utterance
- *executing:* delivering the utterance
- *monitoring:* checking one's performance.

What has been said generally about automaticity applies especially to speaking. Most forms of speaking take place under pressures of time, so *planning*, especially during a to-and-fro conversation, has to be rapid. A mark of an expert speaker is the ability to make an automatic connection between an idea and the words that express it.

Speakers manage to think ahead while engaged in speaking, but 'planning pauses' (usually at the ends of clauses) are also necessary to enable them to find the necessary language for the next utterance (Hawkins, 1971). These pauses are brief in expert speakers (around 0.2 to 1 second) and listeners generally do not notice them. By contrast, we tend to notice 'hesitation pauses', which often occur *within* clauses and mark where speakers have difficulty retrieving a word, lose track of what they planned to say or change their minds about how to express it (Lennon, 1990).

One way of gauging fluency in L2 speech is in terms of these pauses. Lengthy planning pauses or frequent hesitation pauses suggest that the speaker has not fully mastered the code. They are conventionally attributed to a limited knowledge of grammar and vocabulary. But equally important is how easy it is for the speaker to *access that knowledge* when it is needed. This underlines the importance of free practice in handling the language, as a means of establishing connections between an idea and its expression.

Because of the attention they have to give to assembling an utterance, novice L2 speakers experience limits on how much pre-planned speech they can hold in their minds. This tends to restrict the utterances they produce. Again, freedom to practise using the language is the key: a widely quoted study by Raupach (1980) demonstrated that a stay-abroad period had very positive effects upon the length of utterances produced by German learners of French.

A second means of support for speech planning is to be found in chunking. Indeed, a breakthrough in proficiency often coincides with learners starting to identify chunks in the speech of native speakers and to store them as complete units in their minds (Pawley and Syder, 1983; Wray, 2002). There are three criteria which language teachers and testers take as indicators of speaking competence: *fluency, accuracy* and *complexity*. Chunking supports all three. It supports fluency by enabling several words to be retrieved at a time. It supports accuracy because the chunks that are produced are pre-assembled without requiring the application of a grammar rule. And it supports complexity because stitching together chunks enables speakers to produce more elaborate utterances: a sequence like [*I wish I knew*] + [*what the time is*] can be assembled from only two chunks. The message to teachers is to focus learners' attention on recurrent units of speech that are larger than the word and even to practise them in terms of their rhythm and intonation.

In *executing* an utterance, a novice speaker faces two hurdles: (1) the words to be uttered have to be welded into a group; and (2) uttering them is then achieved by means of signals from the brain that bring about certain positions and movements of the tongue, lips, vocal cords etc. Teachers of pronunciation tend to make much of the second, as do teachers of oral vocabulary. But we should not forget the first. Speakers modify how words are pronounced when embedding them in a larger group. This underlines, once again, the importance of the frequent chunk, which should be a unit for pronunciation practice alongside the word. Pronunciation instructors also need to practise the adjustments that enable words to be run together (Brown, 1990: Ch. 4; Field, 2008a: 140–157): 'ten pounds' is usually pronounced as *tem pounds*, 'next spring' as *neck spring*, 'half-past two' as *huppast two*. These are not examples of slovenly speech. They just exemplify the way in which expert users of a language make it easier for themselves to move from one consonant setting to another.

Finally, how capable are novice speakers of *monitoring*? Behind much oral communication work in the classroom there is an expectation that lower proficiency learners will notice their own inadequacies of expression and learn from them. But if they do not, it may not be a matter of carelessness but one of attention. They concentrate so much mental effort upon assembling an utterance, holding it in the mind and achieving an intelligible pronunciation that they have little attentional capacity to give to checking their performance while they are speaking. There is a simple solution: to encourage learners to record themselves and then listen to their speech once the speaking task is over.

Writing

The path taken by a writer follows that of a speaker in terms of having an idea, converting it to linguistic form, executing the message and checking the end-product. Writing broadly consists of the following stages (adapted from Kellogg, 1994):

- *conceptualisation:* having an idea or set of ideas
- *planning:* organising a set of ideas into a sequence – choosing the next idea – linking it to what went before

- *conversion:* turning the idea into language – storing it in the mind
- *execution:* turning the words into written forms – sending signals to the fingers
- *monitoring:* checking for accuracy and to see if intentions have been realised
- *editing:* revising at word, sentence, paragraph and text level.

A first observation is how much of the skill entails thinking rather than writing. This, of course, reflects the fact that a writer usually has ample time to compose. It gives rise to the expectation that most written texts will be more complex in grammatical structure, more precise in vocabulary and more logically structured than an equivalent piece of speech.

Let us look at each of the stages briefly. *Conceptualisation* poses a headache for the second language teacher. To what extent should we reward a second language writer for originality of ideas; and to what extent should we ensure that a class is provided with ideas from the outset, so that language and expression can be the chief criteria? The solution adopted by many teachers and testers is to provide visual stimuli as a basis for the content of the writing task, or written cues such as a text or email to respond to.

Planning is an extremely important aspect of writing; it is also one that, research suggests, is neglected by learners in the early stages of acquiring a second language (Silva, 1993). There are two likely reasons: the first lies in the time limits associated with writing in class and in tests, which impose pressure on the individual to get started rather than reflecting first on how to structure ideas. The second is that learners at lower levels of proficiency focus heavily upon the effortful process of assembling language forms, preventing them from taking a wider view of the text that they are constructing. One answer is to encourage learners to develop their texts over a period of time: rethinking their plans and submitting drafts to their peers for comments on how coherent and comprehensible their writing is.

An important account of the writing skill (Hayes and Flower, 1980) places particular emphasis on the 'environment' surrounding the task – in effect, the considerations that a writer needs to take into account before beginning to write. They include: the writer's own goals, the identity of the reader (including his/her familiarity with the topic), the topic and whatever has been written so far. In a second language context, the first two of these merit special attention. In order to achieve the writer's goals, a knowledge of 'pragmatics' (the way in which language can be used to persuade, advise, threaten, imply and so on) may be necessary. Similarly, central to an awareness of the reader is the ability to compose at the right level of formality (everything from an email on the one hand to a job application on the other). Attention should be given in any writing class to these language-related issues. However, it is also important to ensure that young L2 writers practise composing the type of text that they are likely to need to produce in their everyday life or in their future use of the L2. All too often in the foreign language classroom or in language testing, writing tasks are restricted to conveying experiences in narrative form to an unspecified reader.

Conversion is used here in preference to the term 'translation' favoured by many L1 writing specialists. This is not just to avoid confusion; it also reflects the fact that, far from being desirable, translation via the first language is the mark of an inexperienced L2 writer. The long-term goal should be for the learner to acquire expertise in moving directly from a concept to a form of words in the L2 that expresses it. One way of building these links is by whole-class activities that employ visual stimuli and invite learners to brainstorm the relevant language to describe them. Another is to make use of 'reading-into-writing' tasks, where a reading text requiring a reply includes language that learners can use themselves in formulating their responses.

The problems posed by *execution* are sometimes treated as involving little more than spelling. But, these days, pupils come to the learning of a second language with advanced keyboard skills in their L1. This means that the physical production of words in the L2 requires more than just a knowledge of how the words are spelt; it also requires that learners suppress highly automatic keystroke sequences that are common in L1 but not in L2. They have to focus additional attention on the keyboard, and the effect may be to limit their ability to retain in their minds the L2 sentence that they are trying to produce. See Bereiter & Scardamalia (1987: 105–111) for a parallel situation with young L1 handwriters focusing on letter formation.

Monitoring and *editing* is well catered for in current 'process writing' methodology (White and Arndt, 1998), where learners plan a short piece of writing in pairs and then submit it to another pair for suggestions, not only on its language, but also on how it might be developed. Nevertheless, teachers should be sensitive to the fact that inexperienced writers are also usually inexperienced readers, whose proofreading skills may be much less reliable than those of a more expert reader. Misspellings in their work may simply be there because they are not good at detecting them rather than because of carelessness.

Reading

The receptive skills proceed in the opposite direction to the productive: starting with language and ending with an idea. Reading does, however, have something in common with writing in that the pace at which readers operate is under their own control. A good reader (Rayner and Pollatsek, 1989: 118) is somebody who manages to adapt their speed of reading to their own goals and to the difficulty of the text. Despite the claims of those who market speed-reading courses, fast reading is not of itself good reading. Tests of reading speed have been proposed for low proficiency L2 readers (e.g. by Nation, 2008); and they do indeed bring benefits in promoting rapid word recognition, but they do not serve to distinguish expert readers from inexpert ones. Another idea that should be treated with some scepticism is the view that readers can only make sense of a text if they understand a high proportion of the words in it (various figures between 95 per cent and 98 per cent are usually quoted – see e.g. Laufer, 1989a). Again, everything depends on the type of text and the reader's goals. In the language classroom, it can be a useful exercise to ask learners to look through an authentic L2 text and to report on its general meaning, without requiring them to report the fine detail. In this way, they acquire 'strategies' for making sense of texts that have only been partially understood – important survival techniques for reading in real-world L2 contexts. Similar techniques equip them to read L2 literature for pleasure without constantly relying on dictionaries to check word meanings.

The five broad components of reading are as follows (Perfetti, 1985, some terms modified):

- *decoding:* identifying words on the page
- *lexical search:* matching words to meanings
- *parsing:* imposing a grammatical pattern on a group of words
- *meaning construction:* enriching the bare meaning of the sentence
- *discourse construction:* linking information to what went before.

The first three are concerned with making sense of the words on the page and will be discussed here. The last two are concerned with building a complete understanding of what has been read, and will be discussed under 'comprehension'.

For some time, a myth grew up in L1 reading circles that *decoding* words was not important; and that general context might enable learners to work out meaning and spare themselves the time and effort of focusing on words (see e.g. Goodman, 1967). The same argument is sometimes heard in relation to L2 reading. Nothing, however, could be further from the truth (Gough and Wren, 1999). It is important for a novice reader, in L1 or L2, to achieve a high degree of automaticity in word recognition. Only when readers are capable of relatively rapid and effortless decoding, can they direct extra attention to thinking about the wider meaning of a passage. Studies of L1 and L2 reading using eye-tracking equipment (Just and Carpenter, 1987), show that weak readers look back frequently to check if words have been accurately recognised. To be sure, stronger readers do regress as well, but they do so less often and in order to check understanding. This suggests the value of very simple word recognition activities in the early stages of studying a language (e.g. using flashcards, setting timed reading tasks or asking readers to run their fingers rapidly down the middle of the page and then report what words they have seen).

A second myth about decoding is that words are recognised by their general shapes. Current evidence (Rastle, 2007) suggests that, to identify a word, readers weigh information at several different levels: letter features (strokes and curves), letters, pairs of letters, letter order and the whole word. There is thus little value in exercises that practise recognising word shapes; it is more useful to draw attention to pairs or sequences of letters which occur frequently in the target language. Taking an example from English, a very productive final sequence is '-ight-', enabling learners who know the word *night* to later identify *fight, right, might* and *tight* by analogy.

Lexical search entails matching a word form to an item in the learner's vocabulary. A learner may well 'know' a word in the sense of recognising it, but that is not the same as being able to retrieve its meaning rapidly. With both L1 and L2 novice readers, a first stage would appear to entail the sequence

$$\text{printed word} \rightarrow \text{word in vocabulary store} \rightarrow \text{meaning}$$

Then exposure to the word over time leads to a more automatic process where readers move straight from printed word to meaning.

Parsing might appear to be a simple matter of applying a grammar rule, but it is not quite so straightforward. Reading takes place linearly, with the reader's eye moving across the page and identifying words one after another. It is only when the reader reaches the end of a clause or sentence that the words can be shaped into a grammatical pattern and then into a basic piece of information, known as a 'proposition'. Meanwhile, the reader has to carry forward in his/her mind all the words that have been read so far. Curiously, these words appear to be stored in phonological form and not as images of what has been seen on the page. The explanation often given for this 'voice in the head' is that it enables the reader to separate words read previously from the ones currently being decoded. But it raises interesting questions about L2 readers (Walter, 2008): is parsing fundamentally different in somebody whose knowledge of L2 phonology may be quite limited?

The operation of carrying forward words in the mind makes considerable demands on working memory. As already noted, working memory is limited in how much it can hold at any one time; and novice or poor readers have to give a great deal of that capacity to decoding words on the page. The result is that they sometimes fail to retain what has just been read, and have to go back and re-read it. Once again, this illustrates the importance of automatic decoding: the more efficiently words can be recognised; the more able the reader is to store a sentence in order to parse it.

Listening

Listening involves a similar set of processes to reading (Field, 2013):

- *decoding:* matching acoustic sensations reaching the ear to the sounds and syllables of the language
- *lexical search:* dividing connected speech into words and matching them to words in vocabulary
- *parsing:* imposing a grammatical pattern on a group of words
- *meaning construction:* enriching the bare meaning of the sentence
- *discourse construction:* linking information to what went before.

But the skill is much more complex to understand and to teach – partly because of time pressures (the speaker sets the pace) and partly because the input that the listener receives is much less standardised. Also important is the fact that speakers produce their utterances in a form that is transitory. Like readers, listeners have to retain in their minds the words they have heard until they are able to form them into a grammatical pattern – but the difference is that they cannot look back to check understanding.

There is evidence (Marslen-Wilson, 1973) that listeners decode speech about a quarter of a second (roughly the length of a syllable) behind a speaker. But there is also evidence (Pollack and Pickett, 1964) that it is very difficult to accurately recognise syllables or even words if they are excised from a recording of natural speech. A task known as 'gating' in which an utterance is presented in ever-increasing segments has demonstrated (Grosjean, 1985) that L1 listeners often have to go back – sometimes by as much as three words – to revise their impressions of what they heard. So we have to envisage listening as a *tentative* process in which hypotheses about what is being said keep having to be revised. L1 listeners accept this ambivalence without even noticing it, except when there is an occasional 'slip of the ear'. But L2 listeners find it difficult to deal with the uncertainty, and tend to blame their own unfamiliarity with the language. Learners often cling to their first impression of what a speaker said in the face of contrary evidence (Field, 2008b).

Let us consider the first three ('perceptual') stages of listening. *Decoding* is not as straightforward as in reading. Readers can rely on a standardised spelling system or set of symbols. It may have quirks and exceptions; but the fact is that each word has its own agreed written form. Speech is very different. The sounds ('phonemes') of any language vary considerably according to the sounds that come before and after them, and it has proved difficult to find acoustic features that serve to identify any given phoneme and distinguish it from all others (Nygaard and Pisoni, 1995). Some speech scientists (e.g. Dupoux, 1993) have suggested that the syllable is a more reliable unit for the listener than the phoneme, as it is more constant. It can be argued that too much pronunciation instruction focuses on the phoneme and that more time should be allowed for the recognition of syllables and of (see above) frequently occurring chunks of language.

In addition, speech varies according to who is speaking: speakers differ greatly in the pitch of their voices and in how precisely, how rhythmically and how fast they speak. We tend to take it for granted that L2 learners will be able to adjust to an unfamiliar voice very quickly, because that is what occurs in their first language. But it is necessary to allow them time in order to come to terms with voice quality and speaking style. Here is one reason why listening classes conventionally allow learners a preliminary hearing of a recording before they listen to it in depth and answer questions on it.

Speakers also vary in their accent. In some languages such as English, the differences are largely carried by vowels. This is problematic because vowels last longer than consonants and therefore provide more reliable clues to word identity. In these cases, learners should only be exposed to regional accents very gradually.

In languages such as Spanish, where varietal differences are mainly carried by consonants, learners can be expected to adjust to new accents more readily.

Identifying whole words in *lexical search* is also a complex operation. It is incorrect to suggest, as some commentators do, that listening is a step-by-step process where listeners build phonemes into syllables, syllables into words and words into clauses. Instead, at any given moment, a listener is likely to be weighing clues at several levels (phoneme, syllable, word and adjacent words) in order to determine the closest match between a piece of the input and an item in his/her vocabulary (McQueen, 2007). In this process, resemblance to a complete word tends to outweigh phoneme information. Imagine you hear an English speaker utter the word 'veshtable'. You may not even notice the incorrect phoneme 'sh' because of the closeness of match to a word you know well. This is sometimes referred to as a 'top-down' process in that a larger unit of knowledge (a word) is being used to determine a smaller one (a phoneme). L2 listeners seem to transfer this effect when listening to a foreign language they do not know well – no doubt because they have greater faith in their lexical knowledge than in their ability to confidently identify the sounds of L1.

However, even words are not completely reliable forms in speech. They undergo considerable variation according to how important they are in an utterance and according to how precisely a speaker is articulating. Consider the enormous difference between the 'citation form' of the English word 'where' and the way the word is often said in connected speech, where it may be reduced to little more than [w] (as in 'W'you going?'). Given how greatly words vary, it is understandable that what learners extract from a piece of L2 speech is often incomplete – even where they know all the vocabulary. Early-stage L2 listeners characteristically identify 'islands of reliability', a few words or clusters of words in which they have confidence. They decode far less than is generally supposed by teachers and there is not necessarily a close connection between speaking and listening proficiency, as is sometimes assumed. The result is that learners are heavily dependent upon 'listening strategies' (Macaro *et al.*, 2007) to fill gaps in their understanding.

Another major source of difficulty is that there are no consistent gaps between words in connected speech as there are in writing. This means that it is the listener who has to work out where one word ends and the next begins. You can imagine the potential traps if you consider the English word *university*, which contains *you, knee, verse, it* and *tea*. There are also problems with sequences like 'the way to cut it'/'the waiter cut it', which can be 'segmented' in two different ways. Researchers (e.g. Cutler, 1994) have suggested that listeners use the rhythmic characteristics of a language in order to identify word boundaries. This is straightforward in the case of 'fixed-stress' languages such as Czech, Finnish or Polish, where stress nearly always falls on the same syllable of a word (first, last or penultimate).[2] Though English does not have fixed stress, L1 listeners appear to operate on the premise that each stressed syllable marks the beginning of a new word, a technique that pays dividends because 90 per cent of the content words (nouns, verbs, adjectives) in everyday English speech do indeed consist of or start with such a syllable (cf. *BIcycle* and *CYcle*).

Early-stage L2 listeners tend to rely on their native technique when trying to locate word boundaries (Cutler *et al.*, 1992). For English speakers, this can cause problems in French, where stress is generally on the last, not the first, syllable of a word stem (*monTAGNE, gatEAU, terminUS, finIR*). To complicate things further, it largely disappears in connected speech, leaving only weak cues to word boundaries – which may explain why L1 French listeners appear to segment speech syllable by syllable (Cutler *et al.*, 1986). A different situation arises in Spanish, where stress is variable and stressed syllables are not as distinctive as English ones (compare the duration of the stressed first syllable in the English word *NAtional* with that of the Spanish word *NAcional*).

The solution here is to provide listeners with extensive practice in segmenting connected speech into words – by listening to the same short utterance several times and attempting to transcribe it little by little or to report how many words it contains. Learners' attention should be drawn to any relationship between a language's rhythm and the location of word boundaries, and to common prefixes and suffixes which serve as clues to word onsets and endings.

As noted earlier, *parsing* in listening is demanding because learners need to hold what they have heard in their minds until such time as they are able to trace a grammatical pattern in it. Their ability to achieve this may be diminished at lower proficiency levels by the attention they have to give to identifying words in incoming speech.

It would seem that listeners build up certain expectations as an utterance proceeds: for example, hearing the verb 'give' alerts them to expect mention of a gift and a recipient ('I gave a present to Marie'). But some sentences give rise to 'garden path' situations where expectations are thwarted. If somebody hears *The lawyer questioned...* they might reasonably expect a direct object (the witness); but this hypothesis would have to be radically revised if the sentence went on *...by the judge admitted lying*. As briefly mentioned above, L2 listeners have difficulty in making this type of U-turn and tend to cling to a first interpretation.

Comprehension

Once parsing has taken place, the reader or listener is no longer dealing with a piece of language but with a piece of information. The processes applied are similar across the two skills, though a listener has a more demanding task because of the lack of evidence to refer back to.

First, the reader/listener adds to the bare meaning what has been extracted from the utterance. If somebody says 'Be careful!' we can understand the sense of the words used, but we need to place them in a 'context' – ice on a pavement, a reckless cyclist, a warning about mentioning a sensitive topic. Help comes from world knowledge, knowledge of the speaker, knowledge of the current situation and recall of what has been mentioned so far. For an extended account of the relationship between external information and perceptual input in listening, see Chapter 4.

The reader/listener may also have to make 'inferences' to fully understand a piece of language. Writers and speakers frequently say less than they mean, assuming that connections will be made. In order to make sense of two sentences like: *The road was blocked. A tree had come down in a storm*, you need to infer that it is the tree that is blocking the road and that storms often involve high winds that bring down trees. On top of that, comprehenders may have to use their understanding of pragmatics in order to recognise the intentions of a writer or speaker.

These processes are often given low priority in L2 comprehension. Learners may have to focus so much effort on decoding that they have little attention left for wider meanings and for interpretation. In addition, their understanding of the finer shades of meaning may be restricted by their cultural assumptions or by limited familiarity with L2 pragmatics and markers of politeness.

Once an enriched meaning has been developed from the input, it has to be connected to what one has read or heard so far – a process of 'discourse construction'. As each new piece of information comes in, a reader or listener has to:

- *choose:* decide if it is important or not – and thus whether to retain it in detail or in a generalised form;
- *combine:* link it to the previous point;
- *compare:* check for consistency between new information and what has previously been read or heard; and
- *construct:* build an overall argument, with major and minor topics.

(Field, 2008a: Chapter 13)

Again, L2 comprehenders may not achieve some or any of these processes because their attention is so focused on the task of identifying words and parsing them. They often fail to identify what is or is not important or to recognise links between points in an argument. They also tend not to monitor their own performance. If they form an assumption about what they have read or heard, they do not register how confident they are in this guess and check it against what comes next. A misunderstanding early in a text may thus lead to further misconceptions piling up as the text proceeds.

Commentators sometimes refer to 'reading comprehension' and 'listening comprehension' as if these two skills demand little more than extracting meaning. The irony is that it is precisely the level of deeper meaning that current materials often fail to target. Open-ended comprehension questions all too often focus on discrete pieces of factual information and do not require learners to trace connections between points, use inference or identify the main point of a text. With more closed types of question, a great deal depends on the format. Multiple-choice items are not without their problems[3] but they can be used flexibly to target logical links, inference or main point – even if in practice this rarely happens. By contrast, lessons that feature gap-filling tasks are not at all flexible and reinforce the learner's tendency to focus attention at word and phrase level.

Conclusion

This chapter has described the four language skills in terms of the behaviour that underlies them. The logic has been that cognitive insights of this kind provide a set of performance goals that can and should guide the pedagogical choices made when teaching the skills in a MFL context.

A better understanding of the processes that make up speaking, writing, reading and listening assists teachers in two broad ways. First, it serves to define a set of behavioural objectives. It highlights aspects of expertise such as automaticity that deserve attention; and it enables us to design tasks that focus on and develop the various strands that compose the skills. Second, it enables teachers to align their teaching with the real-world needs of their learners.

Reflective enquiry

The context of a second language classroom is a highly artificial one that cannot ever fully replicate the type of communicative event that occurs in a natural encounter with a user of the L2. Nevertheless, teachers can still ask themselves the following questions:

1   How closely do the processes elicited from learners by the tasks employed in my lessons correspond to those they might use in real-life events?
2   Do learners rely heavily on loopholes in tasks and materials that enable them to sidestep normal language behaviour just to get the right answer?

A better understanding of language processes also enables teachers to take a more critical overall look at skills programmes:

3   How comprehensive are the various types of processing that my tasks and activities demand? Do I rely too heavily on certain levels of processing and side-line others?

Further reading

The following titles provide reader-friendly overviews of central areas of psycholinguistics.

Aitchison, J. (2012) *Words in the Mind*, Oxford: Blackwell, 4th edition.
——(2008) *The Articulate Mammal*, Abingdon: Routledge, 5th edition.

Field, J. (2004) *Psycholinguistics: The key concepts*, Abingdon: Routledge.

——(2003) *Psycholinguistics: A resource book for students*, Abingdon: Routledge.

Whitney, P. (1998) *The Psychology of Language*, Boston, MA: Houghton Mifflin.

Notes

1   For further examples of how psycholinguistics can inform our understanding of language learning, see the 2008 Special Issue of *TESOL Quarterly*, 42(3) (ed. Field, 2008c).

2   The reference here is to lexical stress, which serves to distinguish a word like *INsight* from *inCITE*. It is not the same as focal (or tonic) stress, which marks out the most important word or words in an utterance: *I bought the flowers on SATurday.*

3   Written multiple-choice questions do, of course, need to be short and simply worded in listening, to ensure that the exercise does not end up targeting the learners' reading rather than listening ability.

Chapter 3

Evidence-informed practice as an effective approach to teacher development

Ann Swarbrick

Introduction

Though professional development has been available to teachers in the past few decades, it rarely gets a good press, if any kind of press at all. But an informed and up-to-date profession is a strong profession, a confident profession. This is why pre-service courses put such great store in developing teachers who question what they see in school rather than remain acquiescent. This chapter is designed to give some historical perspective on professional development – what have been the issues and what might be its future. It gives some idea of prominent writers and researchers working in this aspect of languages education. It asks why, if professional development is worthwhile, more teachers do not engage with it and why, if it is not taken seriously by schools, it is a constant area for policy development. The chapter is designed to direct you towards accessible and inspiring readings. Teacher development has a wide literature which is not subject based, but I have combined this with languages-specific references to give you both a focused and a broader view on this topic.

As graduates take up their posts in schools across the country it is not unusual to hear them complain as newly qualified teachers (NQT) that much of what they learnt about in the training year, for example innovative effective practice, is neither respected nor looked for in school. Some meet with intransigence and tired practice which gradually saps them of any energy they once had for thinking about what their languages learners need and want from them. From talking to alumni from my own pre-service course it is the collegiality and debate that they miss, the time to reflect and the time to develop new ideas with colleagues to improve and energise their teaching. There is in-service training happening in their schools but this is usually of a whole-school nature and directly linked to the school development plan. Agendas of departmental meetings are corralled to be in line with what the senior management team require (which is often in line with what the Ofsted inspection process requires) and this is rarely in line with departmental needs; or it is filled by the requirements of the examinations and assessment process. The notion of professional development being relevant to the needs of subject teachers is not a priority in many secondary schools. It is an aspect of teaching which has the potential to transform and affirm a teacher's practice and, as we discuss below, raise standards of both teaching and learning. But the crucial factor in developing effective professional development is the extent to which the teacher is in control – doing rather than being done-unto.

This chapter focuses on the area of teacher development that has variously been referred to as practitioner research or action research, teacher-as-researcher or enquiry-based research. The word 'research' is problematic in the context of teacher development because, though now most *pre-service* courses in England have an element of research study in them – most courses have master's level credits attached to them – the classroom is so all-consuming a context in which to work that it is rare to find an experienced teacher with the time or inclination to engage in 'research' off their own bat. And when teachers do engage in 'research' this is not widely respected within the academic community because it is considered either too subjective or not rigorous enough. Validity is the issue. But validity for whom? This kind of research is valid for the people doing the research whatever the view of professional education researchers. I will consider this issue in a little more depth in the chapter by using examples from two recent classroom enquiry-based initiatives in which the teachers involved engaged in small-scale, systematic enquiry into their classrooms. It has become clear to me from being involved in such work that languages teachers are eager to question their practice if they are convinced that it will affect their pupils' learning for the better.

CHANGING PERSPECTIVES IN LANGUAGES TEACHER DEVELOPMENT

Some of the recent literature in languages education focuses on how research methods are integrated into pre-service courses and how this does or does not have an impact on teachers' (and student teachers') views of themselves as reflective practitioners (for example Gray, 2013; Hulse and Hulme, 2012; Lawes, 2010). In addition, there are examples of researchers working alongside experienced languages teachers which have given rise to a body of work which, in various ways, demonstrate the constraints on teachers but also the impact of such work on them as they take hold of the research agenda (Macaro and Mutton, 2002; Lamb and Simpson, 2003; Macaro, 2003; Borg, 2010).

Teacher education in England, initial (ITE) and continuing professional development (CPD) is currently in a period of intense change. The reform creates the mechanism by which newly designated Teaching Schools will play a central role in the provision of localised professional development: 'Their remit includes both the development of existing teachers through peer-to-peer training, coaching and mentoring and also supporting the training of new teachers. All teaching schools will undertake these core roles, along with school-to-school support' (DfE, 2011b: 12).

The speed of change is rapid with both schools and higher education institutions (HEI) needing to react to policy reform faster than they can create systems and processes to support it. This theme of research in professional development is likely, therefore, to become increasingly debated as the agenda for school-led research embeds into the system. But the idea of the school as the place and context for training, classroom research, teacher development and reflection has a long history. It in itself is not new but it is enjoying a new emphasis in policy development. What constitutes teacher education and how it should happen and where, is part of this agenda for change.

SOME BACKGROUND TO CURRENT DEVELOPMENTS

Borg (2010) provides a wide-reaching review of the origins of the idea of classroom-based enquiry. He considers the 1970s as a significant decade for the UK, with the ascendancy of the work of Stenhouse (1975) who believed that teachers should enquire into their own practice, becoming researchers themselves. Postholm more recently echoed his view,

> It is not sufficient to just study teachers' work, as teachers also need to study their own work ... teachers are the best researchers of their own classrooms because they are the ones who really know the history and background of their pupils and the classroom activities taking place there.
>
> (Postholm, 2009: 551)

It was Stenhouse who coined the phrase 'teacher as researcher'. Here, research is seen as an ideal way in which teachers can develop their understanding of their own practice. This movement was not without its detractors both in the academic and teaching world – Stenhouse was seen as muddying the academic waters by promoting a lack of rigour in educational research and he was seen by some traditionalist teachers as infringing the teacher's right to professional autonomy and meddling in pedagogy (Elliott, 1990: 9).

There was a substantial amount of support for school-led research in the 1990s, for example the Teacher Training Agency for England was influential in promoting teaching as a research and evidence-informed profession throughout the decade. It provided research grants of £3,000 for teachers to carry out small-scale classroom enquiries. It launched the School Based Research Consortia initiative which formed four partnerships between schools, Local Authorities and HEIs which, over a period of three years, explored ways in which teachers could improve teaching and learning through engaging in enquiry. In 1999 the DfEE launched a larger-scale programme of funding for teachers – the Best Practice Research Scholarship scheme. The General Teaching Council for England (GTCE) and the National Union of Teachers (NUT) also developed a research- and evidence-based CPD strategy developed in partnership with academic education researchers (Cordingley, 2004).

Borg sees the 1980s through to the 1990s as a time when practitioner research started to be a focus in languages teaching in the UK. In the 1990s, the research agenda was developing in university departments of education due mainly to the Research Assessment Exercise (RAE) through which funding for universities was decided. If Schools of Education were to retain status and funding within their institutions then they would have to increase their research output. This saw the blossoming of research publications focusing on the (foreign) languages classroom in the UK (for example, Coyle, 2007a; Grenfell, 2002; Macaro and Mutton, 2002; Graham, 2003). Many of these researchers worked closely with classroom teachers of languages often through initial teacher education courses. Macaro in particular focused on bringing clarity to classroom enquiry for teachers, outlining why it was valuable to teachers and pupils alike and demystifying the research process considerably by working in schools alongside teachers. His current work with Graham developing a national, school-based modern foreign languages (MFL) CPD network is the latest iteration of this work in which researchers work closely with teachers in their individual classrooms over time and engage the teachers in theorising the findings. Their blog is available at http://pdcinmfl. wordpress.com (accessed 20 March 2013).

The discussions around teachers enquiring into their own classrooms have remained decidedly similar since the 1980s. This is surprising given central government intervention into teachers' professional development in this country over the last two decades. Brighouse and Moon (2012), for example, estimate that the Department for Education brings professional development centre stage about every two years, the latest intervention being in 2010 with a paper entitled *The Case for Change*. I will take four issues which, for me, are at the centre of any debate about new approaches to teacher development to structure the rest of this chapter.

1   Forms of teacher development most likely to encourage teachers to change their practice.
2   The bad reputation of educational research in schools.
3   The optimum time to engage in research.
4   Is classroom-based enquiry undertaken by the teacher 'research'?

Forms of teacher development most likely to encourage teachers to change their practice

External intervention

As young teachers in the early 1980s my colleagues and I participated in CPD sessions in which the agenda was set by the 'provider' (often the local education authority), always off-site, external to the school and through which we developed ideas to try out in our classrooms. These were one-off events designed to develop methodology. This was a time when, as teachers, we had autonomy over what we taught; a time of creativity. We saw ourselves as curriculum *makers* rather than curriculum assessors – able to decide what we thought was best for our pupils rather than jumping to the tune of a national curriculum with a national assessment system and national accountability measures through which schools would be judged. The problem was that very little *deep* learning went on in these one-off sessions. They were often intellectually superficial and they were not cumulative. There was a common feature in most of these sessions; we were virtually never asked to reflect on our own classrooms, our own pupils. They were set up as inputs, not part of a process that would lead to lasting change. There was no thought as to outcomes and what should happen as a result of engaging in the training. In that sense they were not the kind of professional development as experienced by other professions – they did not matter; they did not fundamentally change our practice; they did not give us points towards promotion, and how could they for there was and is no performance-related system of professional development for teachers in England? In Dadds' view this approach was doomed to failure as a model for professional development because teachers do not attend such training events as 'empty vessels'; they go to CPD courses,

> Brim full of thoughts and feelings; with implicit and explicit beliefs about education and their work with children. They come with differences, disagreements, preconceptions, uncertainties, missions. These are useful resources which can be drawn upon and studied in CPD processes.
>
> (Dadds, 1997: 32)

As she says, during this time, teachers 'learnt to seek the expert outside but deny that there might be a potential expert within'. And this continued well into this century. Centralised programmes of professional development to support the introduction of government initiatives in England (for example the Keystage 3 Strategy and the introduction of the Keystage 3 Framework for Languages), relied on the 'expert outside' rather than nurturing the 'expert within'. Indeed, those engaged in delivering this training were given a script and a set of resources and were asked not to stray from them. And so little local adaptation was possible, there was little real reflection on the starting point of teachers coming to training events. The emphasis was on effecting change which was imposed from without. But, in the early 2000s this type of activity was often the only CPD on offer and was supported by a huge local authority workforce of consultants. We have seen in this subsequent decade that such initiatives have a sustainability problem because of their inability to respond to local need and local contexts but they also rarely survive a change of government. For example, though millions of pounds were spent on a huge bank of resources developed to support the implementation of the Keystage 3 Strategy in England, when the government changed from Labour to a Conservative/Liberal Democrat Coalition in 2010 all of these resources were immediately archived or removed from public use even though they were found useful by schools and in teacher training programmes. No long-term evaluation has been made of the effects of these initiatives and indeed the Keystage 3 Framework for Languages, the use of which was variable across the country during its lifetime, disappeared from schemes of work very quickly post-2010. This implies that it had not become embedded in the practice of teachers probably because it was imposed upon them rather than arising from a need that they themselves had recognised. Worse was the cultural change that happened in schools. Teachers became deskilled and began to question their ability to make decisions for themselves; creativity seeped from the classroom and staffroom as Ofsted descended and demanded more and more adherence to nationally imposed norms on teaching and learning – the objectives written on the board, the three-part lesson, the starter (arrival activity), the plenary (end of lesson summary).

Dadds' 'expert outside' was not an effective form of CPD if CPD is about teachers developing their practice. She was highly critical of this approach, associating it with the 'delivery concept of education reform, in which the teacher is positioned as the uncritical implementer of outside policies' which she sees as 'inappropriate for developing a well-educated teaching force'. Dadds considers that, unless the agenda for development is set by the individual teacher involved, it will not be effective, it will not be sustained. Stoll *et al.* (2006) added to this debate with their research which showed in the mid-2000s that most teachers felt that CPD in England had been driven by school development needs and that national priorities had taken precedence over individual CPD needs.

And so what of Dadds' 'expert within'? Could approaches to teacher development which arose from their own statement of need help to engage teachers in developing their practice where one-off events could not?

Internal, school-based professional development

In England, teachers are required to participate in five in-service training days per year. Useful time for teachers to engage in professional development, you would have thought. However, Brighouse and Moon consider research evidence in this field which demonstrates that these training days are 'rarely well organised, are seen of as little use by participating teachers, and represent a wasted resource … the use of consultants is common, although there is often little evaluation of these inputs, and sourcing expertise relies heavily on word of mouth' (Brighouse and Moon, 2012: 3); unless of course *teachers* set the agenda. Effective CPD, as argued by Jackson and Street (2005) is directly linked to school priorities and the most fertile ground is where head teachers have created conditions that allow teachers to work collaboratively in school. Where this happens what are called variously 'professional learning communities' and 'professional learning networks' are established – groups of teachers sharing and critically interrogating their practice 'in an ongoing, reflective, collaborative, inclusive, learning oriented, growth promoting way' (Stoll *et al.*, 2006: 223).

Externally supported school-based professional development: an example

There are arguments that suggest that schools cannot and should not 'go it alone' but should use outside agencies such as universities to support teachers' development. This is important to consider in an education system which is on the brink of giving schools complete control over the teacher development agenda. Stoll *et al.* quote Fullan (1993) whose conviction was that 'seeking outside help was a sign of a school's vitality; that organisations that act self-sufficient "are going nowhere"'. Schools in Stoll *et al.*'s view need external intervention 'to promote, sustain and extend Professional Learning Communities'. An approach to sustained professional development, with external support, has been developed by my own organisation, CfBT Education Trust. We have developed a model for classroom-based enquiry, based on that of the National Foundation for Educational Research (NFER), which supports teachers in undertaking enquiry in their own classrooms and schools. In the past year we have focused on work with languages departments involved in two particular projects – the Graduate Teacher Programme (pre-service) and the Languages Support Programme (CPD) which was developed with thirty-four new Teaching School Alliances which have established languages as a priority area of development. We have found through evaluations and research summaries that teachers working within these programmes are eager to engage in enquiry into their classrooms and departments so long as it has a direct impact on the learning outcomes of their pupils. The model adopts a three-phase approach which includes an initial workshop run by a professional researcher considering the theory and the practice of 'research' engagement, question design, qualitative and quantitative research methodologies; data analysis; and research ethics and scope. In Phase Two teachers form teams (which may be within one languages department or across a network of schools) and conduct their project in their own schools. The researcher plays a supporting role, commenting on final questions, project design and methodology, advising teams on data analysis and interpretation and helping teams to make sense of their findings (including challenging teachers to consider the evidence as objectively as possible). The researcher undertakes school visits to support research development and writing up. In Phase Three, teachers write a research report and submit it to the researcher who encourages them to identify opportunities for dissemination. Importantly, all of the research reports are published both in book and online form. Themes chosen by the teachers in both primary and secondary schools involved have so far included the development of spontaneous talk in the target language; gender difference in extended writing; a study of what motivates boys in learning Spanish; an exploration of pupils' views about different approaches to listening activities in languages lessons; an exploration of the use of 'Group Talk' and its effect on writing as well as speaking; and an evaluation of 'content and languages integrated learning' on pupils' attitudes and skills development.

Though teachers involved have reported positively about the impact this work has had on them and on their pupils, there are obstacles to this way of working. The main constraint quoted by most teachers involved is time to devote to it when their main responsibility is to their pupils. And as we see throughout the literature time is crucial for any deep learning to take place. However, despite this we have found that tight deadlines have helped teachers focus their classroom investigations and, crucially, that the opportunity to have the resultant work published has given urgency and status to the work in the eyes of school senior management teams. We have also seen a raising of status for this work in the eyes of headteachers who were required to write a reflection on the impact of the programme.

> There is now a learning culture shared by the project schools, which has led to a change in ethos – more of a risk-taking culture where teachers can work together to deliver training and support.
>
> (Headteacher in Bishop's Stortford)

> The most important success of the programme has been the difference it has made to the learners in all the schools involved in terms of engagement, challenge and enhanced motivation for languages.
>
> (Headteacher in Altrincham)

> The greatest achievement of the programme is the impact on pupil confidence through the Action Research findings regarding the centrality of talk. This in turn has had an impact on progress in the four skill areas.
>
> (Headteacher in Sheffield)

We are yet to understand the impetus such work has had in the medium to long term on our teacher colleagues but Stoll and colleagues' research on Professional Learning Communities suggests that, in schools where there are positive professional communities, students achieve at higher levels. Indeed there is ample evidence (Stoll *et al.*, 2006; Galanouli, 2010; Dadds, 1997; Timperley, 2008; Furlong *et al.*, 2003; Boyle *et al.*, 2005; Levin and Rock, 2003) to suggest that the closer to the classroom the CPD is, the more focused it is on the needs and interests of the individual teacher, the more effective it is.

This then suggests that sustained, school-based CPD with the agenda set by the teacher or the school is more effective than one-off external input and that centrally imposed training cannot work unless it has 'buy-in' by those it is designed to support.

THE BAD REPUTATION OF EDUCATIONAL RESEARCH IN SCHOOL

When the word 'research' or 'researcher' is uttered in staffrooms or teacher gatherings, reactions can be gauged on people's faces. There are those who glaze over, those with scepticism written all over their faces, those who immediately perk up with interest. The spectrum is wide. What is it about the word which never fails to get a reaction? Conversations with some NQTs would have you believe that educational research does not reflect the reality of the classrooms beginner teachers inhabit. Is it the external expert, invited in, inadequately briefed about the context of the school? Is it the research reports that seem to show research proving intuitive truths which are considered not worth researching in the first place? (For example, the research reported in *The Guardian* in July 2007 which studies the time-use of 1,500 teenagers for a year and concluded that girls who play computer games do less homework.) Whatever the reason for the divide it is still the case in the minds of many teachers that research in schools and about schools has a bad name and is somehow not for them; that what matters and what works is intuition. Educational research seems not to be regarded as the place to go for answers to questions about learners and about classrooms. Classrooms seem somehow too context bound ('Yes, but you haven't been to my school').

Just as strident is the tension within the *research* community which has teacher-as-researcher at one end and a real scepticism about the seriousness of research undertaken by teachers at the other. The tension lies in the subjectivity factor, that a teacher focusing on his/her own practice will not be rigorous enough.

In his consideration of the issue of the inaccessibility of some classroom research and his study of teachers' attitudes to research in second language acquisition Macaro (2003) talks about the teachers he has worked with being eager to inform their practice and indeed change their practice but cited 'not knowing where to look', 'too technical' and 'findings too detailed' as reasons that put teachers off reading research papers. In the same article he regrets that this should be the case as he sees research-informed practice as being a powerful way of keeping power within the hands of the teachers,

> Research-informed practice stops government agencies imposing practice-related policies on L2 classrooms, policies which have little or no basis in the research evidence and which are usually generated by an elite group's desire to impose uniformity on a complex system for the purposes of professional control.
>
> (Macaro, 2003: 4)

Much more needs to be done along these lines if 'research' is to gain a foothold in the professional development of teachers.

THE OPTIMUM TIME TO ENGAGE IN RESEARCH – THE VALUE OF CLASSROOM-BASED ENQUIRY IN EARLY PROFESSIONAL DEVELOPMENT

Since the early years of this century teacher education in England at postgraduate level has been reformed, mainly to ensure parity of academic standards. From 2003 all postgraduate courses, including initial teacher education courses, were required to comply with master's level benchmarks. Programmes changed to bring assessment criteria in line with this. This has meant that there has been a research element in all programmes leading to postgraduate teaching qualifications since early 2000. This begs a number of questions, for example: in a one-year training programme in which two-thirds of time has to be spent in school, is there enough time to conduct academic research; is there any true value in this research? Is it a realistic proposition or does it impose pressures on trainees which adversely affect their progress in developing their teaching skills? Are conventional master's criteria appropriate and achievable within a one-year professional course? Colleagues of Lawes (2010: 163) saw such research practice as 'a desirable, but unrealistic goal within the initial period'.

These questions are important to this debate about teacher development because of the influence that initial training has on people in the first few years of teaching. If teachers have their awareness raised about research in their training year, and have a positive experience in undertaking it, they will be more inclined to be drawn towards it once they have begun teaching. Indeed Lawes (op. cit.) argues the case for master's-level study early on in a teacher's career because it can have an impact on how teachers define themselves,

> Teachers who start their careers with a strong sense of professional identity, founded on a critical intellectual engagement with teaching and learning, and education in general, will not only wish to improve their practical teaching skills collaboratively with their colleagues, but – more importantly – will also want to continue to develop their theoretical and professional knowledge ... ultimately this will do more to enhance their capabilities as classroom practitioners.
>
> (Lawes, 2010: 155)

However, there is the issue of readiness to engage with research. For many trainees the main preoccupation of the training year is the development of practical teaching skills – often their fears and preoccupations revolve around control and behaviour management. Their knowledge base about the context which they are being asked to research is underdeveloped and superficial. The time factor is a problem. Indeed in Hulse's research on one cohort of trainees undertaking postgraduate teacher training (PGCE) (Hulse and Hulme, 2012) 41 per cent of her group reported that, though positive about the outcomes of their research, they felt under pressure to gain a master's qualification and considered that it would be better to wait until they were more experienced before they undertook classroom research. Interestingly, a number of these students who already had master's level degrees in their subject discipline 'seemed to have difficulty accepting action research as a valid method of enquiry' (Hulse and Hulme, 2012: 320).

It may be that the training year is valuable for raising awareness but that more experienced teachers have the background to get more out of it. However, as discussed above, time to undertake research is the issue here too. Without time to devote to research and reflection, classroom-based enquiry will remain a poor relation to research. Which leads us to what research actually is in the school/teacher perspective.

IS CLASSROOM-BASED ENQUIRY UNDERTAKEN BY THE TEACHER 'RESEARCH'?

In 2010 the NFER conducted an annual survey of teachers on behalf of the General Teaching Council for England (Poet et al., 2010), exploring teachers' experiences of the different forms of support they receive to help them maintain and develop their teaching practice. In the survey, 33 per cent of teachers said they had undertaken research to improve their teaching in the previous twelve months. In this context, one question that arises from this debate about classroom-based enquiry is what kind of research and was the research actually research?

From my own experience of working with teachers in setting up such small-scale research projects, the themes of this research always arise from the imperatives of their own classrooms. These projects are not unlike those in the Teacher Research Grant Pilot Scheme set up by the Teacher Training Agency in England in 1996. In his evaluation of this scheme Peter Foster (1999: 383) asked the question 'Were all the projects research?' For Foster the primary aim of research is the production of knowledge which is 'pursued by the employment of systematic and rigorous methods of data collection and analysis'. Commenting on the Research Grant projects he went on,

> The central goal of a significant minority of the projects appeared to be prac-
> tical: concerned with the improvement of teaching, learning or educational
> achievement, rather than the production of knowledge.

Under this definition, the classroom-based enquiry my colleagues in school have undertaken would not be classed as research, rather investigation. This is important in the context also of the PGCE discussion of Gray (2013) and Hulse and Hulme (2012) cited above where similar small scale research projects are set as academic assignments. Claims cannot and should not be made from small-scale classroom-based enquiry but this does not mean that work undertaken in school by practising teachers cannot be useful to other practitioners. The issue is the generalisability of such work and the extent to which research in one classroom can be said to be true of many or all classrooms. Because of the limited time teachers have and the limited scale of some of their classroom-based enquiries it would be difficult for them to add entirely new learning to the debate. However, this kind of work can contribute to understanding of what works and it can deepen and refine professional knowledge. In this sense it does have an important place in the teacher development debate. Olson (1990: 17), cited in Borg (2010) usefully defines the benefits of such teacher-led enquiry as:

- reducing the gap between research findings and classroom practice
- creating a problem-solving mindset that helps teachers when they consider classroom dilemmas
- improving teachers' instructional decision-making processes
- increasing the professional status of teachers
- helping teachers to influence their own profession at classroom … and national levels
- offering the overriding and ultimate advantage of providing the potential for improving the educational process.

The NFER survey (2010) quoted above reported that teachers felt 'repro-fessionalised' by contact with research and research processes. The experience of the teachers I have worked with certainly reflects these findings.

Research and teaching are significantly different roles which depend on different types of knowledge and skill. Whilst it is useful to see and understand the difference it is not useful that two such distinct communities should be in an oppositional debate about relevance and status. The move in England to place the onus of teacher development on schools themselves points, in my view, to a need for a new paradigm that questions the old tension, the old 'oppositional dilemma' (Hulse and Hulme, 2012: 314) which places research and teaching at different ends of a spectrum.

Conclusion

There is an increasing literature about how education needs to become more evidence-based. Given the speed of change, this is becoming an imperative if education is not to become the yoyo of the government of the day which has been the pattern of the last two decades in England. If schools are to take the reins of teacher development, then they need to address the needs of teachers and the needs of the profession in terms of research and development; there needs to be increased engagement in what effective development is and the conditions required to nurture it.

We have seen in this chapter that there is plenty of evidence to suggest that the most effective agenda for change is that which individuals and schools define for themselves. If this is the case then intuitive responses to problems need to take a back seat and schools need to fully appreciate the value of research, accepting that it takes time and expertise. Educational researchers will be needed in this new evolving world and universities need to wise up to this. For example, let us imagine a longer pre-service training option, first introduced to me by James Burch at Cumbria University, which divides training between, first, developing basic teaching skills and then, in a second year, master's-level study based in the host school. This would require HEIs to work more closely with schools and could give rise to university education researchers being located, at least some of the time, in school. There is a good opportunity here for the research community, through initial teacher training departments, to support this initiative in schools and to help train a new generation of classroom-based researchers. This could be a very powerful mix.

Reflective enquiry

1   Your school may have been involved in the kind of research described in this chapter for many years. If it has, explore teachers' attitudes to this approach and how pupils benefited. If not, it is useful to explore the same area i.e. teachers' attitude to teacher research and how pupils can benefit from teacher research. As part of your exploration, consider the obstacles and the possible gains for the school and for the individual teachers.
2   Find out what the relationship is between the school and local HEI.
3   A useful source of research reports written by languages teachers is available on the CfBT website (www.cfbt.com, accessed 27 August 2013). These might give you some ideas for your own research project. Consider a research question which would support your work in school.
4   You will find a useful collection of instruments, materials and stimuli used to elicit data for research into second and foreign languages at www.iris-database.org (accessed 25 March 2013).

Further reading

Bartlett, S. and Burton, D. (2006) 'Practitioner research or descriptions of classroom practice? A discussion of teachers investigating their classrooms', *Educational Action Research*, 14(3): 395–405.

Borg, S. (2003) 'Teacher cognition in language teaching: a review of research on what language teachers think, know, believe and do', *Language Teaching*, 36(2): 81–109.

Reis-Jorge, J. (2007) 'Teacher conceptions of teacher-research and self-perceptions as enquiring practitioners: a longitudinal case study', *Teaching and Teacher Education*, 23(4): 402– 417.

Volk, K.S. (2010) 'Action research as a sustainable endeavour for teachers: does initial training lead to further action?' *Action Research*, 8(3): 315–333.

Part II

Issues in the classroom

Chapter 4

Listening and understanding

Robert Vanderplank

Introduction: outlining the key issues

Why is listening in a second language such a challenge for learners? There are some obvious answers: the speech comes too quickly, you can't recognise the words you have spent so long learning, you have no time to think about what you are listening to, the word boundaries all run together, it sounds odd, and so on. In this chapter, I focus on what is called 'one-way' listening, that is listening to TV and radio, talks, plays, rather than 'two-way' listening or taking part in conversations, interviews, etc. The latter form of listening is largely dealt with in chapters in this book that deal with interaction, communication strategies and communicative activities.

John Field, in his book on teaching listening in a foreign language, takes as his starting position that 'the listening lesson has been little discussed, researched or challenged; and there is a tendency for teachers to work through well-worn routines without entire conviction' (2008a: 1). Given the easy availability of foreign language speech in the form of internet broadcasts, DVDs and CDs, this seems paradoxical, yet is certainly the situation in many parts of the world, not least in the United Kingdom.

How does this paradox arise and what issues does it help to throw light on? Is it produced by a methodology which places emphasis on communicating the message, whether in two-way interaction or in one-way listening? Is it a consequence of teacher training which has tended to relegate phonology to the sidelines in favour of tasks and topics which are supposed to foster second language acquisition along the lines of first language acquisition? What role does listening play in learning a foreign language anyway? How do we think learners learn to develop their listening ability in the foreign language? Does the way we listen in our mother tongue have any relevance to the way we listen (or learn to listen) in a foreign language?

When we listen as native speakers of a language, we have at our disposal a wide range of knowledge and skills, both linguistic and non-linguistic. We are able to decide how to deploy our resources according to the demands of the listening or our interest in it. For example, in listening to a news programme, we may draw on our prior knowledge of the news item in order to understand what is being reported; we don't start listening from scratch in a passive way but actively engage our own thoughts and language. We may characterise this invoking of existing knowledge in order to understand what is being said as 'top-down' processing. It goes without saying that this is a rapid, efficient and usually accurate process. With new and unfamiliar news items, we may need to give far more attention to what is actually being said. Indeed, there will often be unfamiliar topics or accents when even a native speaker is reduced to following the words of the language spoken. This is often referred to as 'bottom-up' processing. All native speakers (including children from the age of about 10–11) can follow or 'shadow' spoken language accurately in their heads, sub-vocally or out loud at very high speeds. It is one measure of being a native speaker (or near-native speaker) of a language. In research I carried out some years ago (Vanderplank, 1988a), I made the distinction between native and non-native speakers 'following' and 'understanding' according to the difficulty of what was being heard and compared the extent to which native and non-native listeners could vary their following and understanding. Not surprisingly, native speakers were far more flexible in switching between 'following' and 'understanding' according to the demands of the content of the listening, the speed of delivery, speaker's accents, etc.

In terms of the current issues in listening in a foreign language, we can see from the simple example above that native-speaker listening ability is made up of active 'top-down' and 'bottom-up' attributes: prior knowledge of topics, wide vocabulary knowledge, familiarity with how words are produced and perceived in running speech, variations in pronunciation etc., together with feedback loops to monitor how well we think we are understanding the message and adjust our listening accordingly.

A key issue then is the extent to which we should be explicitly training our learners in developing the attributes of native-speaker listeners rather than leaving them to develop their knowledge and skills through regular exposure to listening texts. Another issue is whether we should give priority to strategies such as predicting what is likely to be heard, marshalling prior knowledge or trying to identify key content words as a means of maximising limited learner resources and building confidence, while the learner slowly increases linguistic knowledge and skill. Or, alternatively, given limited class time, should more time be given to basic training in the perception and pronunciation of the running speech of the target language. What would such focus mean for the teacher's own knowledge and skills?

In this chapter I hope to provide a clear conceptualisation of why listening has continued to be a problematic area in foreign language learning in spite of the ample evidence for good practice which has been accumulated over the years together with an outline of what research is telling us the way forward should look like in terms of classroom practices.

ANALYSIS OF THE MAIN THEMES AND DEBATES

Ever since David Mendelsohn and others opened the debate on listening strategies (e.g. Mendelsohn, 1994), there have been intense and sometimes acrimonious exchanges on the value of training learners in listening strategies. It is important to understand the context in which interest in the role of listening strategies arose. In many contexts and settings the communicative approach has been well nigh all-conquering in name if not in practice, along with the predominance of the role of 'input' and 'interaction' in the foreign language as the key theoretical underpinnings for second or foreign language acquisition. In the UK, this has meant an emphasis on what might be termed the 'comprehension approach' in listening, whereby learners are played spoken texts and attempt to grasp the essential gist of what they have heard together with 'key word' detail.

It is within this context and model of language learning that the role of listening strategies has gained ground as a means of guiding learners to facilitate their understanding. However, they have been viewed by some in the field (e.g. Poulisse, 1990; Kellerman, 1991; Skehan, 1998) as merely compensating for lack of linguistic knowledge rather than helping learners to confirm accurate understanding of both language and content. A key question in this debate is whether our model of foreign language learning, loosely based on early child first language acquisition, has become a hindrance to developing the skills, knowledge and confidence required for reliable foreign language listening.

Another theme, which has emerged more recently, is the question of how to order listening tasks and activities. Should teachers prioritise the activation of existing knowledge, both linguistic (e.g. predicting vocabulary) and non-linguistic (e.g. knowledge about topics) or should there be more emphasis on breaking down a listening text, focusing on the difficult linguistic aspects of the foreign speech stream itself? This may seem a marginal debate as experienced teachers will vary the ordering of activities according to the nature and difficulty of the listening text. However, as will be seen, the choice to prioritise one activity over another may suggest an altogether different conceptualisation of how knowledge and skills for listening in a foreign language are developed.

CRITIQUE OF THE LATEST RESEARCH EVIDENCE

Strategy use, strategy training and listening comprehension

Research into the listening strategies used by learners has been an important strand of the second language acquisition (SLA) research agenda. A critical review of the research evidence for both strategy use by learner-listeners and training in listening strategies by Macaro, Graham and Vanderplank (Macaro *et al.*, 2007) found that it was difficult to distinguish successful strategy use from linguistic proficiency (for example, grammatical and lexical knowledge), which was more often than not inadequately controlled for in the studies reviewed. In an article reviewing both theory and methods used to gather data, Santos, Graham and Vanderplank (Santos *et al.*, 2008) illustrated the difficulty of comparing studies in learner strategies which follow different methodologies, or, if they appear to follow the same methodology, such as 'think-aloud', have significant differences in how data are gathered, or which assess linguistic proficiency in different ways.

For example, a key figure in listening strategy research, Larry Vandergrift (1997, 1998, 2003) looked at the strategies used by high school learners whom he termed 'more successful' and 'less successful' or 'more skilled' and 'less skilled' listeners in French as a second language in Canada using 'think-aloud' protocols in which learners listened to a text and, while listening, paused to record their understanding and how they arrived at this understanding. In general, the higher the level of proficiency, the more 'successful' his subjects appeared to be in terms of strategy use and the more varied the strategies used. The studies had several weaknesses: lower-level learners recognised very little of the language listened to and had to rely on familiar words and cognates, while with higher-level listeners, it was difficult to separate out strategy-related success from just being able to recognise more words on which to base an inference. In other words, while 'successful' or 'skilled' listeners may have used different strategies from 'less skilled' or 'less successful' ones, success may be equally well explained by greater linguistic knowledge.

A rare study which controlled for lexical and vocabulary knowledge (Chien and Wei, 1998) did find some evidence that strategies made a difference to listening comprehension success with learners at the same level of grammar and vocabulary, though the strategies identified were 'listening out for single words', translating into the L1 and 'relying on vocabulary lists', while Peters (1999), investigating the development of strategies used by younger learners of French in Canada found that during the period of a school year, lower-level learners were able to abandon early guessing strategies as their linguistic proficiency improved.

In a series of articles, Graham, Santos and Vanderplank (Graham *et al.*, 2008, 2010, 2011) reported on the difficulties which English secondary school students (Year 12) learning French as a foreign language at intermediate level (CEFR A2/B1) were experiencing when listening to the types of listening texts used in their normal classes through think-aloud procedures linked to multiple-choice questions. In two studies (Graham *et al.*, 2008, 2011), they report on whether strategy use changed at two time points, six months apart, with different levels of French proficiency. On the whole, there were clear differences between levels at both times in terms of their preferred strategies and there was little change in strategy use from the first time point to the second across the proficiency groups. Those at lower levels who improved appeared to take a more questioning approach to selective attention after six months. The ineffective use by the weaker learner of 'good' strategies such as comprehension monitoring underlines the challenge to the notion that learners with lower proficiency can be helped by teaching them the strategies that tend to produce results for 'good' or 'skilled' listeners. No link was found between teachers' approach to listening and students' strategy use, mainly because teachers regarded listening as a practice exercise rather than as a skill to be taught.

In another study (Graham et al., 2010), they found that most of their 23 listeners engaged in a form of prediction about the vocabulary that they expected to hear based on the multiple-choice questions rather than thinking about the topic and what they knew about it. Rarely did they anticipate that what they heard on the recording might not correspond exactly to what was in the questions.

In their review of studies in which there was an element of strategy instruction for listening comprehension, Macaro et al. (2007) reported that most studies showed at least partial improvement in learners' listening but given the variety of studies, with learners at differing levels of proficiency and instruction occurring over different periods of time, it was difficult to identify what the key elements of successful listening strategy instruction might be. The most effective ones (Thompson and Rubin, 1996; Kohler, 2002) were more focused on the development of metacognitive strategies such as strategy evaluation and comprehension monitoring.

Graham and Macaro (2008) describe a key study involving training in listening strategies for French learners in UK secondary schools (aged about 16–17 and at B1/lower intermediate level). The three groups were tested before the intervention, immediately after and after a six-month delay. Results at Time 2 showed that the group that had received most training and feedback in strategy use had scored significantly higher than either the group which had received a lower level of strategy support or the comparison group which had continued with their usual listening lessons. In the longer term, after six months, scaffolding made a significant difference. The authors suggest that the positive results for the two scaffolded groups were obtained by high levels of focus on specific clusters of strategies such as prediction, directed attention and phonemic segmentation, combined with metacognitive strategies of monitoring and evaluation.

While this well-conducted study confirms the value of an active teacher-led approach, it is strikingly different from previous strategy instruction research in including what are certainly bottom-up language skills in its battery of scaffolding. These skills included perception of words and phrases in French to address the phoneme–grapheme problem in French together with training in segmentation strategies based on intonation patterns in French. As they say, 'strategy deployment might be impossible without that knowledge' (Graham and Macaro, 2008: 762). It might have been helpful if the authors had made more of this aspect of the training provided in their discussion of the findings.

Metacognitive strategies and the metacognitive approach to teaching listening

Research studies by Goh and Taib (2006), Vandergrift and Tafaghodtari (2010), Cross (2010), Bozorgian (2012) and Birjandi and Rahimi (2012) have all focused on investigating the potential benefits of a metacognitively based sequence of instruction in listening comprehension, centred on raising learners' awareness of strategies such as predicting, monitoring, problem identification and evaluating what they have listened to. In general, the studies found that lower-proficiency learners made more progress in strategy use than higher-level learners. As Macaro *et al.* (2007) noted, simple strategy instruction which raises awareness or 'opens learners' eyes' may be all that is needed to improve performance.

The metacognitive approach appears to follow the questionable principle that this is what successful listeners do; therefore, if we take this approach and raise our listeners' awareness of these strategies, together with focused practice, we will improve their listening skills and ability. The issue of the link between language proficiency and strategy use is not really tackled head-on, nor is the issue of what native and near-native listeners do in more or less difficult listening situations. Vandergrift and Tafaghodtari also concede that adding a 'bottom-up' component to the final phase of their listening sequence would have been a valuable contribution, while Cross comments that although the metacognitive approach may be useful pedagogically for weaker and less strategy-aware learners, it may not benefit all learners in a class and would probably work best when implemented with other forms of instruction.

Affective factors and listening

An important strand of research has looked at the role of so-called affective factors such as motivation, anxiety, and self-efficacy (see Chapter 13, this volume) on the behaviour of foreign language listeners as they listen, how aware listeners are of these factors in their behaviour, and how these factors are linked to foreign listening ability.

Vandergrift (2005) investigated the relationship between motivation, metacognition and proficiency with 57 immigrant adolescents learning French in Canada, using a listening comprehension test and his Metacognitive Awareness Listening Questionnaire (MALQ), designed to assess awareness of processes, strategies and motivation. The findings were decidedly mixed; the relationship between higher intrinsic and extrinsic motivation and the use of listening strategies was quite limited.

Graham (2006a) and Graham and Macaro (2008) have explored the issue of the role of self-efficacy in listening comprehension in 16–18-year-old UK secondary school learners. Graham found that most learners saw listening as their weakest skill and mentioned problems of perception, particularly regarding the speed of delivery of texts, difficulties caused by missing or mis-hearing supposedly vital words, and problems in identifying words because of the speakers' accent. The interviews reported gave a strong sense of passivity and helplessness – learners felt that they were just no good at listening in French and the tasks were too difficult.

Graham and Macaro (2008) included a measure of self-efficacy in their study of Year 12 learners reported above and found that self-efficacy in listening improved significantly compared to the control group. The importance of developing learners' confidence in listening in a foreign language should not be underestimated. Native speakers assume that they will be at least able to follow the language of what they hear even if they do not fully understand the meaning of a new or complex topic. In this respect, the findings of this study add significant weight to the importance of building up the learners' knowledge and skills with the objective of following listening texts at an appropriate level confidently.

The role of prior knowledge

Several studies have considered to what extent learners may be helped or hindered in their listening in a foreign language by deploying their prior knowledge of a topic as a compensatory strategy. For example, Young (1996, 1997) explored the way in which a group of Hong Kong students used a cluster of strategies, including the use of prior knowledge, to understand familiar and unfamiliar listening passages. She found that her subjects were able to use an 'elaboration' strategy to help them link up their personal knowledge with the content of the listening text, though some did over-extend their use of prior knowledge. With unfamiliar passages, those who listened accurately tended to make use of their better linguistic knowledge combined with metacognitive strategies.

A key piece of research that illustrates how successful listening in a foreign language involves the flexible use of both prior knowledge and linguistic knowledge is the comparison by Tsui and Fullilove (1998) of Hong Kong English listening examination scores over seven years. They found that, in some questions, the deployment of prior knowledge would not lead to the correct answer, requiring instead close listening to the text. They conclude that there is a need to balance the 'top-down' strategy of deploying prior knowledge with 'bottom-up' processing. Contextual support may be useful to compensate for limited linguistic decoding skills but guessing based on prior knowledge may lead to errors.

Perception and production

John Field is prominent among those who have recently reported empirical studies on specific linguistic features causing problems in listening comprehension. Field's research has proved to be a valuable counterbalance to strategies-based research and takes us back to a time in language teaching when basic teaching skills included knowledge of the phonology of both one's L1 and the L2 to be taught, together with the pedagogical skills to train learners in essential perception and production skills.

In one study, Field (2004) tested 48 EFL learners in a UK language school with low-frequency words that they were unlikely to know but which resembled high frequency words which they were likely to know, such as 'They're lazy in that office, they like to shirk'. Field found that in over 33 per cent of responses his subjects substituted a known word for an unknown word even though it was semantically inappropriate and was contrary to the evidence that the listener was hearing. He proposes that his listeners were using a lexical strategy, simply choosing a word they knew which roughly matched the sound that they were hearing. Is this top-down or bottom-up processing? Field suggests that it is neither, since listeners are disregarding any contextual information and they are altering their perceptual information to something they know.

The link between accurate perception and production of sounds in English has focused in particular on lexical stress. Field (2005), building on earlier work by Cutler and Carter (1987), Vanderplank (1988a), Munro and Derwing (1995), Derwing and Munro (1997) as well as Dalton and Seidlhofer (1994), asked groups of native and non-native speakers to listen to and transcribe 60 disyllabic words in standard, stress-shifted and stress + vowel quality shifted patterns, for example 'foLLOW' instead of 'follow' in the stress-shifted pattern. Field found variable losses in intelligibility by both groups which depended on the direction in which the stress was shifted and whether the vowel had been changed in quality. Wrongly perceived sounds and stresses may shape the learner's expectations of what is to follow, despite the information provided for the listener beforehand.

Romanini (2008) also highlights the complex relationship between perception of sounds and their production in a foreign language in her study of whether high intermediate ESL learners would benefit most from training in either production or perception of suprasegmental stress in English in terms of language gains in the target structures – in this case, accurate perception and production of stressed syllables in two- and three-syllable words. From the (albeit limited) evidence in this study, it appears that training in perception alone does not assist learners greatly while training in production alone helps both perception and production. Romanini attributes the success of the production-trained group to two main factors: first, the fact that although they were ostensibly trained in production, they had to hear and pay attention to their own performances, thereby making use of the 'phonological loop' (Baddeley et al., 1998) to store unfamiliar sound patterns in short-term memory. Second, the exaggerated articulatory training helped learners to pay attention to crucial factors in their articulatory settings, increasing self-awareness of what they were perceiving in their own production.

Reading comprehension and listening comprehension

Reading in a foreign language as a skill to be practiced and developed in tandem with listening has also been neglected. In particular, and of relevance to listening, relatively little research of relevance to the UK context has been conducted until recently (Woore, 2010; Macaro and Erler, 2011) into the role of L2 phonological decoding (i.e. the value of teaching learners grapheme–phoneme correspondences (GPC) and reading aloud). It has been known for a long time that sounding out mental representation of words helps to trigger meanings in long-term memory (see Woore, Chapter 6, this volume).

A much-quoted study by Mecartty (2000) looked at the relative importance of lexical and grammatical knowledge in reading and listening comprehension in Spanish. In the listening part of the study, 77 students at roughly 'late-beginners' level took tests of lexical (LK) and grammatical knowledge (GK). As one might expect, both LK and GK played a significant role in comprehension. However, LK appeared to play a more important role, though the relative contributions of these factors varied widely. The language learner who has strong lexical knowledge is also a good reader and is most likely a good listener. However, on the basis of the findings, the same strength of assertion could not be made for GK. In other words, lexical knowledge was found to be more important than GK, especially for reading. As Mecartty concedes, using a one-time measure of listening comprehension to investigate such a complex and dynamic construct certainly compromises the generalisability of the findings.

Field's (2008d) study of native and non-native listeners' focus on function and content words helps illuminate Mecartty's findings. Field tested 46 EFL learners at two levels of proficiency using a paused transcription technique (in which learners listen to a recording, which is paused from time to time, at which point listeners write down the last few words heard). He found that learners across a wide range of languages tended to focus on content words such as 'television', 'money', 'home'. Function words, such as 'up' and 'on' which, though high frequency, had much lower perceptual salience, tended to be missed. Field suggests that learners direct their limited attention capacity towards getting meaning and how, even at relatively high levels of proficiency, function words may remain quite unclear. In his view, learners require listening practice which may focus on function words, particularly those in clusters such as 'from time to time' or 'I'm looking for the photos' compared to 'I'm looking at the photos'.

Subtitles and captions

Being able to listen to the radio or watch films and TV programmes in a foreign language is one of the milestones for a language learner. Unfortunately, until learners are at quite a high level of proficiency, both radio and TV are very difficult to access and the 'how to use TV and video in the language classroom' books and articles have usually played down the verbal side of TV and focused on the visual. However, there is a substantial body of research evidence stretching back over three decades that indicates that TV and films subtitled in the same language for the deaf and hearing-impaired (usually known as 'captions') can not only transform programmes in a foreign language into accessible (and enjoyable) material for learners but they can also be of great value in language learning, both inside and outside the classroom. Vanderplank (2010) provides a state-of-the-art summary of research using video for language learning, with and without these

same language subtitles. With respect to listening, watching captioned video is useful for training in listening skills and aural word recognition (Vanderplank, 1988b, 1990, 1999; Markham, 1989, 1999, 2001) and exposure to captions appears to improve listening-based recognition of words that are also present later without captions and also implicit learning of words (Markham, 1999; Bird and Williams, 2002).

Winke *et al.* (2010) provide a more recent example of well-conducted research comparing viewing with and without subtitles in several different languages. In it, 150 university students learning Arabic, Chinese, Russian or Spanish watched three- to five-minute-long clips from a documentary with and without captions in random order. Spanish learners had two additional groups: one watched the videos twice with no captioning, and another watched them twice with captioning. The students took tests of reading and listening, with and without captions together with stimulated recall tests and interviews. In the Spanish groups, those who watched with captions both times scored significantly higher in the tests than the no-captions group. For all language groups, those who watched with captions first did better on the tests than those who watched first without and then with captions.

A major question posed by sceptics about the value of captions is whether their presence merely enhances access to programmes and films which would otherwise be inaccessible to learner-viewers or whether the enhanced comprehensible input enables learners to 'tune in' to the foreign language faster and better than they would otherwise. Vanderplank's (1990) study over several months indicates that there are benefits for those who actively pay attention to the language of the programme rather than 'sitting back'. More recently, a high quality study by Mitterer and McQueen (2009) has helped to reinforce the view that captions help learners to 're-tune' their perception, in this case, adapting to an unfamiliar foreign accent. After only the short 25-minute exposure Dutch participants who watched with English captions had adapted their ears to regional accents and even new words were spoken better with captions. However, it was also found that translation subtitles in Dutch *hindered* adaptation. The authors suggest that when we are exposed to print, phonological knowledge is automatically retrieved.

THE RELEVANCE OF THE RESEARCH TO THE UK CONTEXT

While it is certainly true that a great deal of research into listening comprehension in a foreign language has been carried out in second language contexts where there is easy access to the language being learnt (e.g. English in the UK, Hong Kong, Singapore and the United States; French in Canada), as we have seen from the research reported above, there has also been a substantial amount of relevant foreign language research recently within the United Kingdom.

Below are some of the key points we may take from the research reported:

1   The value of providing guidance in using certain strategies to activate existing knowledge and to process what is heard actively.
2   The value of a systematic approach to using listening texts in order to activate existing knowledge and skills and focus on new features of the spoken language, whether sounds, vocabulary or grammar.
3   The importance of paying attention to specific language difficulties in the connected speech of the target language.
4   The importance of building up learners' confidence.

RECENT INNOVATIONS AND FUTURE TRENDS

Social networking, online communities, streaming video

The nature of language learning worldwide has been changing as the internet makes ever greater inroads into our daily lives. What we are seeing now is the dynamic creation of personal agendas for developing foreign language skills in which learners stream foreign language programmes, learn foreign language songs and chat about their life and shared viewing experiences on social networking sites in the foreign language. A good example of this phenomenon is reported by Sockett and Toffoli (2012) in which five non-specialist English learners at the University of Strasbourg kept two-month long diaries of their use of the internet in their spare time to watch, read and listen to English, and also communicate in English, notably in online communities through social networking websites.

Captioned films and TV programmes in many languages

Although the work of Vanderplank (e.g. 1990, 1999) and Winke *et al.* (2010) among others makes it clear that extensive scaffolding is required for learners to benefit from the enhanced access to TV and films provided by captions, the future does look very encouraging for the use of captioned programmes in modern foreign languages classrooms and home viewing. Thanks to supportive EU-wide legislation, many countries now provide programmes with captions and DVDs sold in those countries usually contain optional captions.

Conclusion

From the evidence of the research reported, we appear to be moving to a position which will be familiar to anyone who began their teaching career in the 1970s in which there should be greater emphasis on teaching the basic phonological skills needed to decode messages and produce accurate sounds in the foreign languages combined with raising awareness of strategies (especially metacognitive ones) which may prove useful to learners at all levels of foreign language proficiency. Through this change of approach, we may also address the issue of developing learners' confidence in being able to understand the spoken foreign language. In addition, the easy availability of social media and foreign language programmes, especially those supported by same language subtitles, offers real opportunities for motivating students to engage with authentic foreign language exposure and exchange in informal, out-of-school settings.

Reflective enquiry

1   Think about your own listening in English and in a foreign language (or more than one). Try listening to both familiar and unfamiliar topics. How do you go about listening when the content is unfamiliar? Are you able to 'shadow' the speech in English? Are you able to do this in the foreign language(s) equally well? If not, what difficulties do you encounter?

2   There is clearly still conflict between those who advocate a focus on skills-based training in listening and those who advocate a more strategies-based approach, with a strong focus on brain-storming, prediction and monitoring of listening. On balance, where does the weight of evidence lie?

3   What is your own model of how learners develop and improve their listening comprehension ability? Is it at odds with the research evidence?

4   From the research evidence presented, what do you think would be an effective cycle of presentation and practice for a listening text? How would you go about testing your view?

5   Several flaws were identified in research on using the 'pedagogical cycle' of the metacognitive approach. How would you design a study which would rectify these flaws?

6   In the light of the evidence from research, can an input-based or comprehension approach provide the necessary conditions for listening development to take place in foreign language contexts?

7   How much language-specific work should there be? Should training in word segmentation and specific problems of listening to running speech in the target language occupy the majority of the time with lower-level learners? How would you design a small research project to test this?

8   Production or perception training: which should come first?

9   Does training in accurate pronunciation to produce intelligible speech have a role of developing listening comprehension? What is the evidence for this?

10   Does your school have a language laboratory? How could it be used best for training in listening comprehension?

11   There is clear evidence for the value of captioned videos in developing a range of skills in the target language. How would you go about exploiting a captioned video in the listening class for different levels?

12 How does your own approach to teaching listening differ from the implications for teaching of the research reported? For example, are you sufficiently trained in or knowledgeable about the phonology of the target language to be able to train learners in accurate perception and production?

Further reading

Larry Vandergrift and Christine C.M. Goh (2012) *Teaching and Learning Second Language Listening*, New York/Abingdon: Routledge. While its academic style is quite heavy going and the writers write with a mission, this book is full of good ideas for listening activities and sequences which would work well.

John Field (2008) *Listening in the Language Classroom*, Cambridge: Cambridge University Press. A very thorough critique of the comprehension approach followed by excellent examples of basic perception and production problems for learners of English and how to remedy these. Field's work can easily be applied to other languages.

Robert Vanderplank (2010) 'Déjà vu? A decade of research on language laboratories, television and video in language learning', *Language Teaching*, 43(1): 1–37. Critical review of research from 1999 with a lot to say about the teaching and learning listening in a foreign language.

Tony Lynch (2009) *Teaching Second Language Listening*, Oxford: Oxford University Press. A very readable and personal account of teaching listening, mainly, but not exclusively in English for Academic Purposes. Full of insights and ideas.

Ernesto Macaro, Suzanne Graham and Robert Vanderplank (2007) 'A review of listening strategies: focus on sources of knowledge and on success' in Andrew Cohen and Ernesto Macaro (eds) *Language Learner Strategies*, Oxford: Oxford University Press, pp. 165–185. Quite heavyweight but a thorough, critical review of the research literature on listening strategies.

Chapter 5

Speaking interactively

Katie Horne

Introduction

The aim of this chapter is to outline principles and provide practical guidance for developing spoken interaction in the MFL classroom. This will entail an exploration of what authentic oral communication consists of, how its characteristics can be transferred to the MFL classroom, and what the roles of the MFL teacher and learner are in developing speaking.

WHAT ARE WE AIMING FOR?

I was recently involved in interviewing candidates for a language teaching post. I observed all candidates teaching competently across a range of learning activities designed to practise speaking and listening. I struggled to identify what it was that I had been looking for in the lessons but had not seen. I then realised that although the class had demonstrated progress in speaking, they had not once engaged in authentic *communication,* and not one of the activities was designed to facilitate this.

Before looking in more detail at the characteristics of an authentic communication process, let us remind ourselves of what linguistic product we are aiming for. We would expect speakers with fully developed linguistic skill, to be able to speak fluently (albeit with hesitations), using an appropriate range of vocabulary and linguistic structures, accurately applied, and for the words to be pronounced so as to be readily comprehensible to a native speaker. Fluency is often defined as the length of a run of speech between two pauses (Towell *et al.*, 1996). These are also the measures by which we judge a non-native speaker and they have formed the basis of assessment frameworks for GCSE and A-level.

Yet, as many teachers and learners testify, it is entirely possible for a student to produce such foreign language utterances entirely from memory. Although I do not think anyone would argue that this is the way to train a true linguist, exam boards even advise that this can be an effective way to get high marks. So what is the difference between this kind of memorised utterance and one produced authentically? The difference is in the communicative intention.

What is authentic communication? First, it is usually a *two-way* process. Either the person speaking expects a response, verbal or non-verbal, or they are responding to the other person. Second, and because of this, it involves an interactional *relationship*. At the very least, it is assumed that the other person wants to listen to what is said. Third, it contains *personal emotion or thought*. Whatever it is that I am saying is what *I* decided, needed or wanted to say. It is intrinsically motivated. Because of this, authentic communication usually follows an unpredictable pathway. I do not usually know what you are going to say before you say it. Fourth, and following on from this, authentic spoken communication fulfils some *function*, from simple information transfer through practical request to expression of thoughts or feelings. These characteristics of authentic communication are true regardless of the linguistic developmental stage of the speaker.

There is nothing more important, when considering how best to develop speaking skills in our learners, than to keep a picture of this kind of communication process in the forefront of our minds. Because of the intrinsically motivated nature of authentic communication, applying the same model to learning a foreign language, leads to accelerated progress and more independent learners.

HOW WILL WE GET THERE?

Having described the characteristics of authentic foreign language communication, let us now look at how it can be achieved in the MFL classroom. What implications does this have for the teacher? The following five principles provide a rationale for the practical advice that follows.

1   The functions fulfilled by authentic interactions will be limited to those applicable within a classroom situation. Typically, in MFL lessons I have observed, these relate to the acquisition and use of classroom equipment or the carrying out of classroom routines and administration. However, it is possible to *substitute and re-create the functionality of language* in a much broader way in the MFL classroom.

2   The teacher and learner will be communicating to a certain extent in accordance with a 'teacher-role' or 'learner-role' template. Typically, the teacher leads learning through instruction, modelling, correction etc. This is likely to be steered by a learning programme based on building vocabulary fields and linguistic structures. Typical learner utterances are characterised by copying and/or adapting the utterances of others. However, it is possible to *broaden the personal aspect of communication* much more than is typically practised.

3   Trainees are often taught a classic 'Three Ps' lesson structure of 'presentation', 'practice' and 'performance'. Since, 'performance' risks being interpreted as something script-based done in public, I prefer therefore to

use the term 'communication' for this third phase. Because our MFL learners in the UK tend to start off as absolute beginners, with no experience of the foreign language in question, either taught or absorbed from the world around them, much time will be spent introducing and assimilating new language before they can progress to the third phase. It is therefore important to *incorporate as many aspects of authentic communication as possible into the presentation stage* of language learning.

4   It is helpful to differentiate between 'guided practice' and 'free practice' (Harmer, 1991). Approaches to practising language operate on a continuum between simple repetition and independent practice (e.g. role-play). *It is important that the 'guided practice' phase (i.e. where the expected response is prompted in some way and predictable language is used by teacher and learner) does not become an end in itself.* Memorised language or guided interactions cannot be a substitute for the authentic communication defined above, though it can be used as a means to that end.

5   A crucial ingredient is that which takes the communicative intention described above, and combines it with linguistic knowledge (achieved in the 'presentation' and 'practice' phases) to give it form. It is the 'know how' rather than the 'know what' – the ability to *apply* linguistic knowledge to a communicative situation: this is termed *strategic competence* (Canale and Swain, 1980). The speaker needs to choose from a potential range of vocabulary and structures which are the most appropriate and, conversely, needs to be able to cope if certain words or structures cannot be found. Strategic competence is necessary at all developmental levels of spoken interaction. In the MFL classroom, it is the difference between the learner who can *use* their linguistic knowledge in authentic oral communication, and the learner who knows information about the language but struggles to use it in an unpredictable situation. This learner may excel in highly teacher-supported writing and may be able to memorise chunks of language to recite, even managing to simulate spontaneity, but they have got stuck at the practice phase and have not achieved authentic communication. In order to avoid this, *MFL learners need to be trained in strategic competence.*

At this point the reader may be surprised at the lack of mention in these principles of 'the target language'. It has purposely not been included. 'Use of the target language' is a phrase that has pervaded policymaking and teacher training for many years. Guidance has varied but has failed to provide a real rationale for, or even a clear understanding of the recommended approach. Significantly, research has also shown that teacher 'use of the target language' does not necessarily lead to learners using it (Macaro, 2001a). I hope that both my definition of authentic communication as the aim of MFL learning, and the planning principles we have drawn from this, can provide us in the following sections with some sort of rationale for teacher and learner use of the foreign language in the classroom, shifting the emphasis from quantity to quality, and matching the means to the end.

DAY ONE IN THE MFL CLASSROOM

So, with our authentically communicative end in mind, how *do* we move our learners forward from their absolute beginner starting point? Many school children in non-anglophone countries will already be able to sing the lyrics of a favourite English or American song or quote from English language films they have watched. They will also know many English words from social media and the internet. Without this experience, *our* learners lack the basic concept of the foreign language as a means of authentic communication and it is here that we therefore need to start, by facilitating this experience in the classroom.

In addition to this, we need to give them from the start a consciousness and understanding of themselves as language learners. By this I mean that they are able to reflect on their efficacy as learners, by naming strategies that enabled them to communicate, and by giving them ways in which to recognise and measure their own progress.

I know of no better way to achieve these two things than by 'immersing' learners in the foreign language from Day One, starting with the natural communicative potential of the classroom context, and *explaining the rationale* to the learners. We then build in *learner-strategy reflection* points, including helping learners to deal with their *feelings* about the experience constructively from the start. This 'immersion' imitates or re-creates a mother-tongue learning experience, something all foreign language learners can identify with, and from which they have an immediate precedent for success. Upon this we superimpose the reflective layer (initially carried out in English), which provides emotional support and guides learners to learn from their successes. In a mother-tongue learning situation, if children were only exposed to two or three hours a week of communication, they would progress extremely slowly. The reflective layer *accelerates* this process in foreign language learning, exploiting the relative intellectual and emotional maturity of the learner.

So how should this 'immersion' experience of the foreign language take place? There is no set way, as long as it is carefully planned to achieve minimum stress for learners and a maximum feeling of success in understanding and communicating. Getting to know the class and introducing some classroom routines provide a naturally authentic communicative context. The act of asking and giving names, in a new class, fulfils all the criteria for this: it is two-way, relationship-based, personal and functional. However, if your class already know each other and know you the teacher, you could choose another context to start with, such as simple opinions on a relevant object/person of interest. Making learners laugh by deliberately forgetting names or coming out with some outrageous opinion provides additional authenticity and at the same time lowers stress levels. It is best if you can include at least two different kinds of activities within this initial immersion experience so that learners experience the joined-up nature of authentically communicative acts. Perhaps one could be conversational and one practical. In a typical start-of-year class, there is usually some administration to get through, such as kit checks or the handing out and labelling of books. Although some response may be non-verbal, these act as a practical function and can therefore provide an opportunity for authentic comprehension and communication.

Simulating authenticity

Let us deal with the issue of learner comprehension in an 'immersion' situation, since confidence in understanding words in context is the first step towards actively using them. It is essential that the learner can trust the teacher from the start to speak in a way that makes it possible for them to understand the meaning of what is being said. If they do not, they will lose interest or become negative. Authentic communication does not have to be complex and *'meaning' can operate on two levels* in an immersion classroom. These levels can be likened to the 'head' and the 'stomach'. At the 'stomach' level, certain words or phrases will be understood from their context and will not necessarily be 'decoded' or translated into English by the learner (at 'head' level). It is essential that the teacher considers and actively exploits this level of meaning when deciding what to say and how to say it, starting with very simple and unambiguous units of meaning. Meaning is made up of many elements, such as intonation, accompanying gestures, others' responses, accepted roles, previous experience, logical progression and so on. To give an example, if the teacher picks up a pile of books, hands a few out, and then offers the pile to a learner, saying, 'Can you help?' in the foreign language, it is pretty clear from the context what is meant.

The teacher must learn to trust the learner as well! I have witnessed teachers who, being nervous about learner comprehension, have overcooked their own communication so that it is no longer authentic but forced. This undermines the 'stomach' level of meaning, subtly changing natural body language and intonation. In the example above, an authentic thing for the teacher to do would be to say 'Thank you', as they hand the pile over, then turn away to get on with something else. This reinforces and completes the meaning for the learner.

If possible, choose words with similar or near-sounding equivalents in English to start with. This can help build confidence and trust, although learners will soon have to move beyond familiar sounds, as too much reliance on cognates can be problematic. Sometimes cognates are not obvious to a learner's ear and, assuming the spelling is also similar, writing the foreign word on the board while you say it is a good way of drawing attention to the equivalence, and at the same time lays the foundation for phonetic understanding.

Be absolutely clear in your head what words or phrases you are expecting learners to respond with and check that you have *scaffolded* the lesson to provide and practise these – an illustration is given below. Do not hesitate to *give* them words they need if you sense them wanting to respond but hesitating due to lack of vocabulary (but see below about recording words). Do not worry about approximate pronunciation, unless others start copying it or it leads to hesitation or reluctance to communicate. In such cases you can *repeat* a phrase with the whole class. Remember the aims of this initial immersion experience (p. 69) and resist the temptation to turn this into a 'guided practice' phase, where the teacher would correct all deviations from the standard language immediately.

A good way of avoiding this is to insert *follow-up* comments or questions. If you find that a more open follow-up question slips out naturally, although you know the learner does not yet have the language to answer it, give them two or three easily comprehensible and repeatable options (e.g. 'It is good/bad', 'I don't know') to choose from, in order both to sustain the communicative experience and to reassure the learner from the start that unpredictable questions are surmountable.

A further way of sustaining the experience is to *exploit naturally occurring events* for their communicative potential. These could be a late arrival to a classroom, or another interruption or distraction. Wasps, exploding pens, accusations of cheating and chairs collapsing are all part of the natural narrative of the classroom.

To put this 'classroom language' in the context of an example, a typical getting-to-know-the-class, immersed conversation might include a 'core' question such as, 'What is your name?', and 'My name is...', but also, 'Who is that?', 'I've forgotten', 'Have you forgotten?', 'Sorry', 'Is that...?', 'That is...', 'You are...', 'Are you...', 'Yes' and 'No'. A proportion of this language will be actively used by the learners and the rest will be passively understood but not yet uttered. Learners will of course differ in the speed with which they actively produce language they hear repeatedly. The teacher may aim for a minimum that they would like all learners to have used by the end of the lesson, and would therefore give these phrases the most airing. Appendix 5.1 is another example of how such a section of lesson might sound; showing how language meanings can be introduced and scaffolded, with new language elicited in as authentically communicative a way as possible.

Let us analyse the language in the example above. The 'core' question and answer is probably the minimum that the teacher would be aiming for all learners to actively use by the end of the lesson. Then there are the simple closed follow-up questions ('Have you...?', 'Is that...?', 'Are you...?'). There is also a peppering of generic interactional language ('Yes', 'No', 'Sorry', 'I've forgotten'). These elements encompass all the characteristics of authentic communication (two-way, relationship, personal, functional). However, note also the repeated variations on the commonly used verbs 'to be' and 'to have' in different phrases. What we are seeing here is that the teacher has an important role to play not only in sustaining and simulating authenticity, but also paradoxically, in choosing and steering the language content.

Choosing words with the most common denomination, as illustrated in the example above, means that learners can quickly communicate more by recycling them in other contexts. Combinations of such words can be re-used as starters for many sentences (I refer to these as 'hubs'). An example that I use in German is to teach personal introductions using, 'I am' (*ich bin*) rather than 'I am called' (*ich heisse*). This hub can then be easily re-used to talk about personal characteristics and with other adjectives. At the same time, it provides a springboard to introducing the other forms of the verb 'to be', as in the examples above. The other auxiliary verb 'to have', and all the modal verbs, are particularly useful hubs for recycling in different contexts and at the same time provide a sound base for manipulating language for different time frames ('I have a book', 'Do you have a book?', 'I have forgotten my book', 'You should have a book').

Another important way of 'creating' authenticity, given that you are teaching a class not a single individual, is to *create a three, or multi-way communicative situation* by getting other learners to comment on what has been said. This can be as simple as agreement/disagreement. Getting learners to engage verbally with each other reinforces the personal aspect of communication. At the same time, if wisely exploited through whole-class reflection, this invaluable habit can effectively multiply the individual's learning experience by thirty, and should be fostered from Day One.

Learner strategies: emotional and reflective competence

The initial 'immersion' experience may have lasted anything from fifteen to thirty minutes, depending on the activities used and how the class responded. It is better to cut the experience short, on a high, before any frustrations overcome feelings of success. At the same time, the learner-strategy reflection will work optimally if the learner has experienced a significant level of challenge. Having created for our absolute beginners an experience which gives them the concept of the foreign language as a means of authentic communication, how do we now move them on to a position of consciousness and understanding of themselves as language learners?

At this stage, we shed our co-communicator role, don our teacher–expert hat and speak in English. We need to help the learners go through the following processes, based on their immersion experience. This kind of strategic discussion is to 'the lesson' what stage directions or prompts are to a play script. They exist to enable the play to be performed well, but they are not part of it. Thus, the authenticity of the language of 'the lesson' is not undermined.

1   *Own the initial achievement*
     The learners are helped to recognise what they have achieved. Raising this to consciousness provides the cornerstone of their identity as active and reflective learners ('Wow! How was that? You have managed to function completely in a foreign language for however-many minutes! How did that happen?! You didn't know the language!'). Knowing they 'can do it' provides an *intrinsic motivation* to gain further feelings of success.

2   *Understand reflection-mode*

Learners are led by the teacher in thinking about how they coped with being immersed in the foreign language. They will typically mention the importance of looking at body language and actions accompanying the words as well as the recognition of similar-sounding words in English. Through this exercise they start to become familiar with the idea of reflecting on and analysing their performance, initially at least in English, as distinct from functioning in the foreign language in the lesson. A 'bird's eye view of the lesson' or the stage directions analogy above are good ways of explaining this concept and provide a clear rationale for the use of English.

3   *Plant emotional competence*

Being immersed in a foreign language can give rise to intense emotional responses. It is important that learners know that there is no right or wrong way to react. Their feelings are typical and have no bearing on their ability to progress. Naming their individual responses and hearing those of others can reassure them and help them feel more in control next time. A simple way of helping them do this is list a few typical responses in the context of a 'Hands up if you...' survey. For example, '...understood absolutely every word you heard!', '...were hoping I wouldn't talk to you', '...felt a bit silly saying the words', '...watched what other people did when you didn't understand...' (a good starter-strategy), '...found it harder/easier than you'd expected', '...feel proud of what you've just achieved'.

4   *Accept and define the challenge – what success will look like*

If you intend to continue to use the 'immersion' approach that we have started to explore after Day One, this is the time to tell the learners in simple terms what to expect ('I'm going to speak German to you and I will expect you to speak German to me'). One way of helping learners visualise and measure their progress is to give them a date by which they can aim to function for the whole of the lesson in the foreign language. Given three foreign language sessions a week, it is possible to build sufficient learner strategies to achieve this in less than a term, though you should explain that there is a difference between this initial target of 'being able to function' and the overall aim of being able to speak fluently. Communicating with minimal language can feel very 'high risk' for someone who is used to using full sentences and nuances of meaning and grammar. It is therefore helpful to remind learners of their own mother-tongue learning progress and I often use the term 'baby-German' to describe what they might sound like or aim for to start with.

5   *Understand the rationale*

Explaining why you have chosen this approach to teaching them, and how this will benefit their progress, will provide learners with an extrinsic motivation for accepting further challenges.

Particularly with younger learners (Year 7 and below) and those experiencing MFL learning for the first time, I favour the order above (i.e. immersion in the foreign language followed by reflection in English) since it allows for inductive rather than deductive learning. Because learners have to think of strategies they have already used, these are not only associated with success but also tend to be more easily memorable. In addition, in the secondary school context, the initial authentic communicative situation is not compromised by learners' experience of the teacher speaking English (unless they are also a Year 7 tutor). With older learners, those who have previous and different experience of learning a foreign language, or where the class has significant previous experience of the teacher relating to them in English, I would pre-explain the immersion experience by giving a rationale in English first, and anticipating together which strategies could be used.

SUSTAINING AUTHENTIC COMMUNICATION

Reminders of what success will look like, as well as reflection on the rationale for the chosen methods, should be a common feature of language learning. Learners should also be prompted to consciously track their own development in emotional competence. Seeing how their ability to cope has improved since their initial feelings on Day One is an enormous confidence boost and yet another way in which learners can gauge their own progress. Crucial to developing emotional competence is the ability of learners to compare their own experiences with those of others – ideally not just class peers but also learners of their own language and a school exchange is a perfect context for this.

Learners say that they remember words better when they have to use them for real purposes. By sustaining and building on an authentic communicative experience we can help them do this. The foreign language can be used for all functions of a lesson: not only 'core' language, but also for instructions, practical organisation, explaining, clarification, negotiating activities and homework etc.

I have found that a system of *immediate* points or stickers is the best initial encouragement of authentic communication by learners, providing positive reinforcement of good habits. I have two principles, which I explain to the learners when awarding points: points for speaking are reserved for spontaneous or creative language rather than in guided practice situations, and the threshold for receiving a sticker is raised at an individual learner level, as their communication strategies develop, so that they are always rewarded for improving strategies rather than for the actual linguistic outcome. The effect of the rewards is multiplied if the teacher highlights the new learner strategies being used.

Despite their progress in using the foreign language for spontaneous communication, learners will inevitably still feel more comfortable in English and this will be their natural instinct. It is a common reflex action for them to call out an English translation either out of pride at having decoded what has been said, or to seek reassurance that they have indeed understood. I tell learners that I prefer them to *show* me that they've understood, rather than translate aloud. The same goes for reflex questions in English: these can interrupt the flow of functionality in the foreign language. It is usually possible to respond, without appearing to do so (thus discouraging further questions), by inserting an answer to their question into the lesson 'coincidentally' or by giving non-verbal reassurance, such as a nod or smile. As time progresses, and as an aid to eliminating unwanted English or calling out, the points system can be duplicated at team level and include minus points – although I always make sure that individuals keep a personal credit for their efforts, even if team points are removed.

The approach outlined so far will necessitate a different approach to many established schemes of work. 'Topics' or typical GCSE vocabulary fields, although providing a backbone to the development of language and to planning, will play second fiddle, certainly in the initial stages, to the more everyday and skill-based needs of the classroom that arise, and will probably have to progress more slowly. Conversely, fast progress will be made in language for questions, opinions, time references, past participles and a wide range of verbs. I find that this time invested is more than repaid in the independent and accelerated quality of subsequent learning.

BUILDING VOCABULARY AND STRUCTURES

The most useful kind of words and phrases to give learners at the start are those which will help them increase their understanding and productivity in the language. Teaching them these systematically right at the start is also a major psychological reassurance for facing the challenge ahead. To use an analogy, they are like the float that a child uses when thrown (immersed!) in the deep end for the first time. More sophisticated strokes will come later. The 'floats' can be categorised into those which the learners need to understand (e.g. 'Write…', 'Say…', 'Read…', 'Listen…', 'Look…', 'Put your pen down…', 'Find…') and those which they need to use (e.g. 'I don't understand…', 'How do you say/ spell…?', 'Can you/I…?', 'Which page…?'). It helps enormously not only to teach these explicitly but to also have these available visually for easy reference by the teacher and, increasingly, for learners, as they take their first tentative float-less strokes towards functioning in the foreign language.

A learner strategy that will be needed from the start is that of using vocabulary lists. This can happen naturally, as learners copy and develop the teacher's use of 'floats'. A very effective vocabulary list is one which is self-created during authentic communication. This may include words that learners have asked for, or words that the teacher needed to write up for clarification. New words should be written on the board with their English translation (although it is best not to verbalise this), so that learners can copy them down at an appropriate time, or re-use them during conversation. Self-created vocabulary lists are another important way in which learners can visualise and measure their progress. They are also an important aid to the personal aspect of authentic communication, as they contain words reflecting the learner's own interests and experiences. Vocabulary lists operate at the 'head' level, where meaning is very much decoded, although the words themselves are often provided in a spontaneous 'stomach' context, where the learner starts a sentence that they cannot finish.

Another way of generating effective and personalised vocabulary lists is for the teacher to provide a generic list of phrases and words, by listening to authentic English communication between learners during tasks. In effect, these take the initial 'floats' idea a step further into *peer communication*. Having noted the English words that learners tended to use in order to achieve a specific task, this new language is then presented or elicited, in context, with examples (e.g. 'You/I say...', 'Good idea', 'Your turn'). Finally, learners repeat the same task, using the new language to achieve it.

Some learners, once instructed to keep a vocabulary list, will take naturally to the habit, while others will need more encouragement, for example, by allocating time for a minimum number of words from the board to be noted each lesson, or by setting individualised learning tasks. These words form a stock for the teacher to recycle in follow-up questions and comments, or in selecting and eliciting words for other situations. The same words (particularly questions, connectives, opinions and time references) are often requested or needed repeatedly. This is a golden opportunity to engage others in the class, who have remembered or noted them, to supply words or peer prompt.

LEARNER STRATEGIES: VERBAL COMPETENCE

Work carried out by the Professional Development Consortium in Modern Foreign Languages (2013) has shown that understanding of the following strategies can improve learner confidence, motivation and fluency.

Paraphrasing and *describing*: The teacher can model 'off-stage' a thought process. For example, 'What words in that sentence do you already know how to say?', 'What word do you know that means something similar?', 'Which are the most important words for getting across your message?'

Avoidance: Not everything that the learner wants to say needs to be said. Certain things may need to be saved and said in English outside the lesson, since in an authentic foreign language situation it is not always possible to communicate everything one wants to.

Guessing/coining: Once learners start to 'get a feel' for the language they may be confident enough for this. For example, they may conjugate a verb according to a familiar pattern or take an English word but pronounce or intonate it appropriately to the foreign language. Alternatively, a learner may replace with a foreign language morpheme a part of a word which they have experienced as equivalent to that morpheme in a similar word.

These attempts may produce accurate or inaccurate results. Either way, the strategy should be recognised and praised. In such instances of authentic, spontaneous communication, it is important to respond initially to the sentiment or meaning of the utterance, rather than its form (i.e. with a follow-up comment or, if the learner has asked for something, a practical response), *before* highlighting any error.

Coping with a lack of words: One implication of learners using vocabulary lists to help them communicate is the time it takes mid-sentence to find a particular word. This is an authentic characteristic of foreign language learner communication and should be accepted and encouraged. With such use over time, words will pass from learners' 'head' to their 'stomach' vocabulary, so don't worry that they will become 'dependent' on them – that will only happen if you fail to provide them with opportunities to use the words in a communicative context.

LEARNER STRATEGIES: PARA-VERBAL COMPETENCE

These strategies operate alongside the verbal ones and support them by providing extra meaning when words are scarce or lacking. We saw in the section on simulating authenticity how the teacher can exploit this meaning to aid learner comprehension. However, the teacher can take this one step further and actually model it as a communication tool – it is no bad thing for learners to see their teacher struggling to convey meaning.

Facial expressions and *gestures:* These will arise naturally if the teacher is aiming to keep their vocabulary at an appropriate level for learners yet at the same time respond to unpredictable learner needs. It is an authentic – and often amusing – aspect of foreign language communication if used sparingly.

Intonation: This happens naturally if learners are allowed to communicate authentically. They will tend to use English intonation (as opposed to pronunciation) initially, particularly when communicating from the 'head' (i.e. thinking of the English meaning as they go along). This does not matter because it helps them be understood – both by teachers and peers. (In any case, English and foreign intonation will often be indistinguishable from each other.) I do not think this is a bad thing and have, in fact, consciously exploited the strategy myself to aid learner comprehension.

'Fillers': A native speaker of any language has a stock of sounds to fill the gaps and buy thinking time. In English we say 'um', 'er' and 'sort of'. The equivalent foreign language phrases can be explicitly taught or modelled and much fun had practising them and getting them to move from 'head' to 'stomach'.

Conclusion

If our goal for MFL learners is to be able to communicate authentically, using a range of language fluently and accurately, it makes sense to take the elements of authentic communication as guiding principles for language teaching. On this basis, I have argued that a very generous helping of carefully planned foreign language teacher-input and carefully elicited learner-output, combined with explicit training in strategic competencies will best lead us to our goal.

Reflective enquiry

1   Self-audit: what *features of authentic communication* can you identify in foreign language interactions involving the learner in your own classroom (teacher–learner or learner–learner)? Get someone to observe you, using this checklist to tick or record verbatim every time they notice one of the characteristics. Alternatively, record a lesson, using a digi-recorder and do the same exercise yourself:

   a   two-way (involves response)
   b   interactional relationship (hearer wants to listen)
   c   personal emotion or thought and therefore follows unpredictable pathway (speaker wants to speak and is engaged with content)
   d   fulfils a function (practical request through to expression of thought of feeling)

2   Are you *presenting new language* as authentic language by maximising real meaning, either through context (cf Simulating Authenticity p70ff) or response (see points a–d above)?
3   What strategies are you using to *sustain* authentic communication as the term progresses? (cf p74ff)
4   What emotional and reflective strategies have you taught your learners to aid their progress? (cf p72ff; p76ff)

Further reading

Harmer, J. (1991) *The Practice of English Language Teaching*, London: Longman.
Shrum, J. (1984) 'Wait time and student performance level in second language classrooms', *Journal of Classroom Interaction*, 20(1): 29–35.
Swain, M. (1995) 'Three functions of output in second language learning' in G. Cook and B. Seidlhofer (eds), *Principle and Practice in Applied Linguistics: Studies in honour of H.G. Widdowson*, Oxford: Oxford University Press, pp. 125–144.

Appendix 5.1: German taster lesson devised for Year 6

Objectives:
Perform simple communicative tasks using single words, phrases and short sentences
Listen for specific words or phrases
Recognise some familiar words in written form
Experiment with the writing of simple words.

Outcomes:
•   understand and respond to simple sentences (Listening + Reading level 2)

- respond with short phrases from memory (Speaking level 2)
- copy words accurately (Writing level 1).

Preliminaries:
Class teacher introduces me beforehand, saying that we're going to have a 15–20 minute session where they ONLY hear and speak German. *When they understand something, they should SHOW that they understand it (by smiling, nodding, responding) rather than calling out the English translation.* Just relax, the teacher will help them to understand and respond.

Teacher	*Pupils*
Greet class and individuals:	
Hallo! Hi! Guten Tag! Grüß dich!	**Hallo! Hi! Guten Tag! Grüß dich!**
Introduce self:	
Ich bin Frau Lee *(write up)*	
Das ist mein Name	
Meine Schule ist The Willink	
Deine Schule ist BSM	
Kommst du zur Willink im September?	
Wer kommt zur Willink im September?	
Ja? Nein?	*Hands up*
Gut! Super! Fantastisch! Schade!	**Ja**
	Nein
Introducing other people:	
(recap) **Ich bin Frau Lee**	
Und das ist Frau Moreton	
Und das ist Frau ...	
Wer ist das? *(Susan Boyle, Simon Cowell picture)*	**Das ist ...**
Wer ist das? *(indicate individuals in class)*	**Das ist ...**
(Greet individual identified) **Hi ...!**	**Hallo/Hi/Guten Tag!/Grüß dich!**
Class names memorising game:	
Okay, ich memorisiere ...	**Nein! Ja!**
das ist ... und das ist ... ja?	**Das ist ...**
Nein?	
Wer ist das? *(indicate individual)*	

Und du? ... Tom? Michael?	Ja/nein – Joe
(Model) Ich bin ...	... Ich bin Joe
(Hold up Susan Boyle/Simon Cowell, mimic them and elicit repetition)	
Ich bin Susan Boyle	Ich bin Susan Boyle
Ich bin Simon Cowell	Ich bin Simon Cowell
(Resume asking individuals)	
Und du? Wer bist du?	Ich bin ...
Hold up Susan Boyle picture and speech bubble. Model	
Ich bin musikalisch	
Hold up Simon Cowell picture and speech bubble ... Model	
Ich bin kritisch	
Stick up all celebrity pictures. Hold up and model adjectival phrases in speech bubbles. Elicit name of celebrity:	
Wer ist ... musikalisch/kritisch/ intelligent/sportlich/kreativ/ amüsant? *(stick up bubbles)*	*Names of celebrities*
Elicit whole-class repetition of bubbles:	
Ich bin ...	Ich bin muskalisch/kritisch/ Intelligent/sportlich/kreativ/ amüsant
Say what I am like:	
Ich bin ... und ... aber nicht ...	
Ask class what they are like:	
Bist du ... kreativ? Sportlich?	Ja/nein!
Ja? Nein? Bist du nicht sportlich?	Ich bin muskalisch/kritisch/ Intelligent/sportlich/kreativ/
Throw the frog with question and answer. Model	amüsant (Nicht ...).
Ich bin kreativ – und du?	Ich bin sportlich – und du?
Hand out poster template. Explain in English. Class teacher to post class set to Willink. Displayed at induction day. Can do celebrity if prefer.	

Chapter 6

Developing reading and decoding in the modern foreign languages classroom

Robert Woore

Introduction

How can we help learners become more proficient and confident readers in their second language? This chapter attempts to provide some answers to this question by drawing on research into first language (L1) and second language (L2) reading. Underpinning this approach is the view that research evidence has an important role to play in informing teachers' professional decisions about their practice – albeit considered critically in light of their knowledge of their own particular classrooms and students.

One problem in linking research and practice, as Grabe and Stoller (2011) point out, is the wide variety of settings in which L2 reading research has been conducted: for example, with learners of different ages and proficiency levels, having different first and second languages and set in different national contexts. It is not always easy to see how a given study's findings relate to modern foreign language (MFL) classrooms in the UK, which may be seen as a distinctive context in certain respects: for example, many MFL students face 'highly challenging systemic pressures' (Pachler, 2002: 6), such as limited curriculum time and sometimes low motivation levels. MFL learners are also younger and less proficient in the L2 than the participants in many research studies. Therefore, whilst this chapter considers evidence from a range of settings, it prioritises, where possible, research conducted in UK MFL classrooms.

The chapter has three parts. Part I explores the nature of reading and the processes involved in fluent L1 reading. This is intended to provide a reference point for considering L2 reading and its development. Part II explores some key challenges facing beginner L2 readers and considers the aims of L2 reading instruction, viewed from the particular perspective of UK MFL classrooms. Part III critically discusses some suggestions for reading instruction derived from research evidence.

UNDERSTANDING READING

Deceptive simplicity

The term 'reading' is so commonplace that we may easily overlook the many layers of complexity involved. First, reading is commonly classified as a 'receptive' language skill, perhaps suggesting a simple flow of information from text to reader. However, as Kingston (1961: 105, cited in Carver, 1977: 11) argued, reading comprehension 'can best be understood as a product of communication that results from interaction between the reader and writer'. Many current definitions of reading comprehension reflect this view, portraying the reader as actively involved in 'the construction of meaning from a printed or written message' (Day and Bamford, 1998: 12), rather than simply 'extracting' or 'receiving' information from the text. This implies a need for teachers to be aware of the knowledge and resources which learners bring to the task of L2 reading comprehension.

Second, the term 'reading' may include various kinds of activity. For example, Carver (1977) distinguishes five reading 'gears' (or speeds): thus, we may scan a dictionary page for a particular word (fastest gear); skim a newspaper article to see what it contains of interest; read a novel for pleasure (middle gear); work carefully through a scholarly article to learn about a new concept; or read a quotation repeatedly in order to memorise it for an exam (slowest gear). For Carver, only the middle gear is 'normal' reading. The other gears may involve rather different processing mechanisms; in fact, they may 'only marginally involve the comprehension of meaning' (Sadoski and Paivio, 2007: 341). This should be borne in mind when designing reading activities in the MFL classroom: the tasks we set may lead students to process the text in particular ways. For example, they may be able to 'find the French for X' simply by scanning for certain words, rather than engaging with the text as a whole.

Finally, the rapid, effortless nature of fluent reading belies the enormous complexity of the processing involved. Indeed, according to Snowling and Hulme (2005: 207), 'to fully understand reading comprehension would be to understand most of the fundamental problems in cognition'. Being aware of this complexity makes clear the scale of the challenge facing beginner L2 readers.

How we read

Based on an extensive review of L1 reading research, Grabe and Stoller (2011) outline a model of reading which consists, metaphorically speaking, of 'lower-level' and 'higher-level' processes (There is no implication that higher-level processes are 'better' or more important than lower-level ones; both are essential for effective comprehension). Lower-level processes consist of: (1) word recognition (accessing the meanings of words from their written forms); (2) syntactic parsing (extracting grammatical information from the written forms);

and (3) semantic proposition formation (combining word meanings and grammatical information to give basic clause-level units of meaning). The higher-level processes are: (4) constructing a 'text model', a representation of the meaning of the text as a whole resulting from the accumulation of clause-level units of meaning; and (5) constructing a 'situation model', the reader's interpretation of the text model in light of her or his own goals, feelings and expectations. Readers' background knowledge plays an important role in constructing the text model and situation model, helping them to interpret and contextualise new information from the text. Finally, reading is overseen by 'executive control processes', which monitor comprehension and direct the reader's attention as necessary to address any problems that may arise.

All these processes take place in working memory, sometimes described as a kind of 'mental workbench' (Walter, 2008) in which information is temporarily stored, manipulated and integrated with other information. However, the workbench has limited capacity, storing information only for a very short time (one or two seconds) unless it is reactivated in some way. Fast and efficient processing is therefore essential for fluent comprehension. This in turn relies on the automatic operation of various reading processes, such as word recognition and syntactic parsing (LaBerge and Samuels, 1974; Perfetti, 1985). Automatic processing can be contrasted with 'controlled processing' (Schneider and Shiffrin, 1977), the former being quick, effortless and subconscious, the latter slow and attention-demanding. Since automatic processes place low demands on attention and working memory, they leave more of these limited resources available for the higher-level processes of text comprehension. However, as Grabe and Stoller (2011) note, the development of automaticity requires countless hours of practice in reading – something that may be difficult for MFL learners to achieve.

According to various 'compensatory' models of reading, controlled processing may be deployed when deficiencies occur in automatic reading processes (e.g. Stanovich, 1980; Walczyk, 2000). For example, readers may use contextual clues to 'figure out' the meanings of words that they cannot identify visually. However, as the preceding discussion of automaticity makes clear, using this alternative route to identify words has drawbacks: it is slow and uses up attentional resources, which are then unavailable for the higher-level processes of meaning construction and interpretation. In other words, fluent reading is disrupted. Such compensatory models are helpful in conceptualising L2 reading at low proficiency levels, where readers may know few words in a text and lack automaticity in recognising them.

THE CONTEXT OF L2 READING INSTRUCTION

Before considering the teaching of L2 reading, we need to be clear about both our starting point – the nature of MFL learners and the challenges they face – and our desired goals, that is, the purposes of reading instruction in the MFL classroom. These issues are discussed in the following two sections.

The beginning MFL reader

There are some important differences between learning to read in an L2 compared to an L1. In many ways, the L2 learner's task is harder. First, whilst there is a clear imperative for students in the UK to become literate in English, MFL learners may not perceive a clear instrumental purpose for learning to read, say, French or German. Second, L1 readers benefit from many hours of focused literacy instruction and subsequently encounter written English throughout their school curriculum. This provides the repeated practice necessary to automatise lower-level processes. By contrast, MFL learners often have limited curriculum time available for L2 reading (and indeed for all L2 learning). Third, beginner L1 readers at primary school already have considerable knowledge of the spoken language, whereas many MFL students begin reading in the L2 at the very outset of learning the language itself. One consequence of this is that sounding words out to discover their meaning – the basis of phonics instruction – will often be ineffective for beginning L2 readers, since they may not know the words orally in the first place.

Conversely, most beginner MFL learners are cognitively more developed than beginner L1 readers and are already literate in English, giving them a head start in various aspects of learning to read the L2. For example, they may be skilled users of a range of reading strategies and have better world knowledge to support their comprehension, including knowledge of some conventions of written texts (e.g. text types; the use of headings and paragraphs). They will also understand some underlying principles of written language, so fundamental that it would be easy to overlook them: for example, they know that written words represent spoken language – something they had to learn from scratch as beginner L1 readers. Since English is an alphabetic language, they are also aware that the written symbols (graphemes) which make up written words map onto individual sounds (phonemes) of the language; this understanding can then be transferred to other alphabetic languages, such as German, Russian or Arabic. Going one step further, the most frequently taught languages in UK schools – French, Spanish and German (Tinsley and Han, 2011) – all use the same Roman alphabet as English, albeit supplemented by diacritics such as accents and umlauts. Learners therefore do not need to learn to recognise these written symbols afresh: they already recognise them automatically. However, as will be argued below, this automaticity in processing L2 written symbols is also problematic in some respects.

There will of course be individual differences between learners in all the areas mentioned above. For example, students may vary considerably in their English reading proficiency, so that their knowledge of various aspects of the written language cannot be taken for granted. In turn, this is likely to affect their feelings towards L2 reading: they may approach the task as an enjoyable challenge, buoyed by previous success in L1 reading; or they may dread it based on a long history of struggling with written texts. Second, increasing numbers of students speak first languages other than English (NALDIC, 2011a, 2011b); some may also be literate, or partially so, in languages which use different writing systems, such as Arabic or Chinese. These students may experience some additional advantages or obstacles compared to those who know only English. Finally, students are increasingly reaching secondary school having learnt an L2 at primary school (though not necessarily the same L2 as the one they learn in the first year of secondary). Further, their primary MFL teaching may have emphasised literacy to different degrees. All this strongly underlines the importance of knowing and responding to learners as individuals.

Purposes of L2 reading instruction

This chapter starts from the assumption that the goal of MFL teaching is to develop students' communicative competence in the L2. Following Canale and Swain's (1980) seminal model, this includes – alongside grammatical and sociolinguistic competence – the notion of *strategic competence*, consisting of 'the compensatory communication strategies to be used when there is a breakdown in one of the other competencies' (p. 27). This occurs, for example, when learners lack the grammatical or lexical knowledge to communicate effectively. Interpreted in relation to L2 reading, learners therefore need to develop strategies for comprehending written texts that contain unfamiliar language, of the kind they may encounter when travelling abroad. Further, the comprehension strategies developed in relation to a given language should be transferable to other languages that they may encounter in the future. In other words, we want students to become strategic L2 readers, not just readers of a specific L2.

Another aim of reading instruction in MFL classrooms, it may be argued, is to help students use literacy effectively as a tool for L2 learning – one of the great advantages available to older language learners, who 'approach the enterprise with a very different set of potential strategies from those available to pre-linguistic infants' (Wells, 1999: 248). The same point is made by Cook (2001), who recalls students in an audio-lingual classroom 'surreptitiously writing down the dialogues they heard under their desks' (para. 3c). In MFL classrooms, of course, learners are often encouraged (or indeed required) to note down new vocabulary and structures to aid subsequent memorisation; however, for this to work efficiently, learners must be proficient in encoding and decoding the L2. That is, they must be able to use L2 symbol–sound mappings to spell the words they hear and to pronounce what they have written down. Clearly, developing these basic literacy processes also provides an essential foundation for those students who may continue learning the language to A-level or beyond, which will inevitably involve considerable amounts of reading and writing in the L2.

Finally, any programme of reading instruction must contribute to the wider aim of developing students' motivation for L2 learning, already identified as a key challenge for MFL teachers. Commentators on L1 reading consistently underline the importance of providing engaging texts which learners read for genuine understanding (e.g. Stanovich, 1986; Cunningham and Stanovich, 1998; Dombey, 2010). Yet it appears that MFL reading activities rarely live up to this description. In history lessons, Year 7 students may be reading about the French Revolution or 'the making of the United Kingdom'; by contrast, as Andon and Wingate (2012) memorably point out, a glance at many KS3[1] textbooks reveals a predominance of texts composed of very simple language, covering topics as trivial as the contents of a pencil case. What could be less likely to convince students of the benefits of learning to read in another language?

TEACHING L2 READING

The following sections explore three approaches to L2 reading instruction which, it is argued, are supported by evidence from research. However, given the range of settings in which this research was conducted, the points raised in the previous section need to be borne in mind when assessing the applicability of the findings to MFL classrooms.

Develop language knowledge

Various studies of L2 reading have found support for the so-called 'threshold hypothesis' (e.g. Carrell, 1991; Lee and Schallert, 1997; Yamashita, 2002). This holds that a certain level (or threshold) of L2 proficiency must be reached before general reading skills – already developed by literate learners through reading in their L1 – can be transferred to the comprehension of L2 texts. More recently, Walter (2007) has argued that, rather than talking about the *transfer* of reading abilities from L1 to L2, it would be more appropriate to think in terms of L2 readers *accessing* their existing comprehension processes, once a certain level of L2 proficiency has been reached.

The linguistic threshold has mainly been interpreted in terms of lexical (vocabulary) knowledge. Clearly, this lexical threshold is not absolute: rather, it must be interpreted in relation to the particular text being read. Easier texts, containing fewer words or higher frequency words, will require lower levels of overall vocabulary knowledge. Some studies have tried to identify the level of lexical coverage (that is, the percentage of words in a text that are known by the reader) which is necessary for the adequate understanding of that text (Laufer, 1989a; Hu and Nation, 2000; Laufer and Ravenhorst-Kalovski, 2010). This of course depends on the definition of 'adequate' understanding, but all of these studies have suggested lexical thresholds of 95 per cent or more. By contrast, Schmitt *et al.*'s (2011) findings suggest a relatively linear relationship between lexical coverage and degree of comprehension: in other words, the more words their participants knew in a given text, the more of it they understood; no evidence emerged of any particular lexical threshold beyond which comprehension suddenly improved. However, all participants in this study had lexical coverage levels of 90 per cent or more – still a high figure when viewed from the perspective of KS3 MFL classrooms.

The studies outlined above suggest some important pedagogical implications. If, given sufficient lexical coverage of a text, L2 learners can access general reading abilities developed in their L1, then 'it is worth doing everything possible to increase learners' vocabulary knowledge' (Schmitt *et al.*, 2011: 39). Further, there is no need to develop their general reading abilities, since they possess these already. Swan (2008: 267) makes this case forcefully: whilst acknowledging that certain forms of strategy training can be valuable, he argues that 'much of the work that is done in classrooms in order to "teach" reading skills or strategies is more or less a waste of time'; instead, the aim should be 'to give students the language they need in order to read texts, not to teach them to manage as well as they can without that language'. Extensive reading has itself been suggested as an efficient way for learners to increase their vocabulary knowledge (Day and Bamford, 1998); however, there is evidence that this is less effective for beginner learners, precisely because they lack the linguistic proficiency needed to read anything but the most basic texts comfortably (Pichette, 2005; Pulido and Hambrick, 2008).

Besides the importance of vocabulary knowledge, the model of reading outlined earlier also suggests that rapid, efficient lower-level processes are necessary for effective reading comprehension. In a review of research into reading fluency, Grabe (2010) therefore concludes that, in addition to teaching vocabulary, L2 reading instruction should focus on developing automatic word recognition. Since automaticity develops through very large amounts of practice, it has been argued that L2 learners need to spend plenty of time reading easy texts containing high percentages of familiar words (Grabe and Stoller, 2011; Schmitt *et al.*, 2011).

Overall, then, there is clear evidence that the development of learners' vocabulary knowledge and automatic word recognition are important priorities for L2 reading instruction. However, an approach based solely on these principles may present some difficulties in the UK MFL context. First, if learners need to know around 95 per cent of the words in a text in order to read it comfortably, then the diet of reading offered to many MFL students in order to develop their fluency and automaticity would be severely limited. As we have seen, this may negatively affect their engagement and motivation; given the limited curriculum time available, it could be a very long time before students amass enough vocabulary to read 'comfortably' anything of genuine interest to them. Second, if a goal of MFL teaching is to equip students with the communicative competence to understand texts above their current proficiency levels, then they need practice and support in doing so. This theme is explored in the following section.

Develop strategic reading

This section focuses on helping learners acquire the tools for comprehending texts above their current linguistic level, thus opening the door to more cognitively engaging L2 material which can be read for authentic purposes. Crucially, learners need to see such texts as a challenge to overcome rather than as something daunting and demotivating. The discussion here draws on the large body of research into learner strategies, which – unlike some other fields of research in Second Language Acquisition – includes a number of recent studies conducted in UK MFL classrooms. Researchers have not always agreed on how to define strategies, but for the purposes of this chapter, they are viewed as 'actions selected deliberately to achieve particular goals', such as resolving comprehension problems (Paris *et al.*, 1991: 611).

How do effective L2 readers make sense of challenging texts? One approach to this question has involved classifying the strategies deployed by more and less effective readers, using labels such as 'top-down', 'bottom-up' and 'metacognitive' strategies. These terms are sometimes used in different ways in the Second Language Acquisition literature; however, reflecting the usage in the studies reported here, bottom-up strategies are interpreted as those focusing on the words on the page (e.g. sounding out words to discover their meaning; looking for cognates), whilst top-down strategies draw upon the knowledge that the reader brings to the text (e.g. making inferences using background knowledge). Metacognitive strategies are those involved in 'planning, evaluating or monitoring one's … strategy use' (Macaro and Erler, 2008: 95).

An example of this approach is provided by Chamot and El-Dinary's (1999) investigation of the strategies used by young L2 learners (Grades 3–4 in the US) in French, Spanish and Japanese immersion classrooms. Participants were divided into two groups according to whether their teachers judged them as having high or low L2 proficiency. They were then asked to 'think aloud' whilst reading a challenging L2 text. Two statistically significant differences were found between the two groups (that is, differences that were highly unlikely to occur by chance): low-proficiency students relied much more extensively on the bottom-up strategy of 'phonetic decoding' (sounding out words), whilst higher-proficiency students made greater use of top-down strategies such as inferencing and making predictions. The authors also found differences in the *way* that strategies were used: higher-proficiency learners appeared to be 'more flexible with their repertoire of strategies and more effective at monitoring and adapting their strategies', whereas lower-proficiency learners were more likely to get 'bogged down by details' and to 'cling to ineffective strategies either through unawareness of their ineffectiveness or inability to adapt strategies to the task demands' (Chamot and El-Dinary, 1999: 328). What is unclear, however, is whether such differences in participants' strategy use actually led to differences in their reading comprehension outcomes, or conversely whether differences in participants' L2 proficiency caused their differing patterns of strategy use. For example, the higher-proficiency learners may have mentioned decoding less often simply because they already accomplished this lower-level process automatically and subconsciously, in turn leaving more resources available for inferencing and metacognition.

Various other studies have reached similar conclusions: namely, successful L2 readers are 'strategic readers' (Grabe, 2004: 53) who actively monitor their ongoing understanding of a text and effectively orchestrate their use of a range of comprehension strategies. For example, in one strand of Macaro's (2000) investigation of adolescent L2 learners (aged 14–15) in English and Italian secondary schools, 16 participants were asked to think aloud whilst translating L2 text slightly above their current linguistic level. More successful learners were found to tackle the text holistically as a problem-solving exercise and were prepared to doubt their initial interpretations. By contrast, less successful readers tended to rely too heavily on identifying cognates – a strategy which, though clearly useful in some cases, may misfire if learners are not sufficiently suspicious of 'false friends'. They also made wild guesses not corroborated by other evidence in the text, sticking to these initial guesses even in the face of countervailing evidence.

Having identified some aspects of the behaviour of effective strategic readers, the crucial question is whether we can help other students to adopt similar practices and thus improve their L2 reading comprehension. Grabe (2004: 53) argues that, whilst there is considerable evidence to suggest that L1 reading comprehension is positively affected by 'instruction that emphasises the coordinated use of multiple strategies whilst students actively seek to comprehend texts', such evidence is much more limited in relation to L2 reading. However, since the publication of Grabe's (2004) review, studies based in UK MFL classrooms have begun to find positive effects of strategy instruction on both listening and reading comprehension.

As an example, Macaro and Erler (2008) evaluated a programme of reading strategy instruction with a sample of 116 learners from six secondary schools. Half the participants formed an 'intervention group' who received 'scaffolded' practice in a series of comprehension strategies: for example, they indicated on a checklist (in L1) which strategies they had employed whilst reading challenging texts and received personalised feedback (again in L1) on their strategy use. The feedback therefore focused on the *process* of reading (how they went about it and how to do so more effectively) rather than on the *product* (how many marks they got and what 'level' they achieved). The instruction took up about ten minutes of normal lesson time per week. Compared to the 'comparison group', who did not receive the strategy instruction, the intervention group performed significantly better on a reading comprehension test at the end of the study, based on a text about the Iraq War which was considerably above participants' current linguistic level. Further, 97 per cent of the intervention group were prepared to have a go at understanding this very difficult text, compared to only 77 per cent of the comparison group. Responses to a questionnaire at each time point also showed that, at the end of the study, two strategies were used significantly more often by the intervention group than the comparison group: 'scan for words that look familiar and try to guess the meaning of the text from them'; 'look up many words in the dictionary or glossary'. Conversely, two other strategies were reported significantly more often by the comparison group: 'wait for the teacher to go through the text'; 'wait and see if the teacher says what it means'. In other words, it appeared that the participants who received the strategy instruction became more likely to engage actively with the text, whereas the comparison group actually became less likely to do so over time – perhaps retreating from what they saw as an insurmountable obstacle. Thus, although further research is needed to corroborate these findings, Macaro and Erler's (2008) study suggests that well-designed strategy instruction can help beginner and near-beginner MFL learners become more effective and more confident readers of challenging L2 texts.

Develop phonological decoding

Various studies over the last twenty-five years have investigated L2 learners' print-to-sound decoding, that is, their ability to 'extract phonological information from printed words' (Hamada and Koda, 2010: 513). Although decoding has generally been viewed as a component of reading comprehension, it can also be argued to underpin various other aspects of L2 learning. This section reviews evidence suggesting that the development of L2 decoding should be an explicit focus of reading instruction in MFL classrooms, at least when teaching an alphabetic L2 such as French, Spanish or German.

Why is decoding important? First, sounding out words to discover their meaning – which plays a crucial role in early L1 reading (Share, 1995) – has been reported by MFL students as an important strategy for dealing with unfamiliar words when reading French (Erler and Macaro, 2011). However, as argued above, the effectiveness of such sounding out may often be limited for beginner L2 learners, since they do not know many words orally. Data gathered as part of Woore's (2011) study of beginner-learners' decoding in L2 French illustrates this point: in a vocabulary test, one Year 7 student guessed that *morceau* meant 'more so', *colline* meant 'clean' and *la langue* meant 'along'. It appears that this learner could decode the French words with some accuracy, but did not know the meanings of the resulting phonological forms, associating them instead with similar-sounding English words.

The inverse of this argument, however, is that accurate L2 decoders can generate for themselves the pronunciations of new words which they first encounter in written texts, rather than depending on the teacher or other spoken source to provide the pronunciation. Decoding proficiency therefore enhances learner autonomy, providing a self-teaching mechanism for L2 vocabulary acquisition. These arguments also apply to the intentional memorisation of vocabulary which students have already encountered, such as when learning for homework a list of words which the teacher has presented orally in class. Away from the classroom, poor decoders lack the means to recover the words' pronunciations, should they forget how the teacher said them. The use of literacy as a tool for L2 learning is thus undermined. Indeed, in Erler's (2003) investigation of Year 7 MFL students' experiences of reading French, some participants actually complained that what they were reading 'look[ed] like a different word than what you've been repeating [in class]' or sounded different 'in their head' than the pronunciations produced by their teacher. These comments also suggest that the initial oral 'drilling' of words may not be sufficient to prevent students mispronouncing them in their subsequent reading.

Finally, there is evidence of a link between decoding proficiency and wider motivation for L2 learning. Erler (2003: 308) concluded that learners of French who lack basic L2 literacy skills, such as the ability to pronounce written words accurately, 'are bound to take offence and become disaffected learners'. It may be that, despite their progress through the levels of Attainment Target 3 (QCA, 2007a), they nonetheless perceive themselves to be stuck at the absolute beginner stage in relation to written texts: for many of them, the last time they were so inaccurate and hesitant in reading aloud was in KS1, when they were first learning to read English. Erler and Macaro (2011) investigated this issue further with a large, nationally representative sample of 1,735 learners of French in English KS3 classrooms, finding that better and more confident decoders were significantly more likely to express a wish to continue learning French post-14.

Despite the apparent importance of decoding, several studies based in English MFL classrooms have found that – in the absence of explicit decoding instruction – KS3 learners have very poor decoding proficiency and make little progress in this area (Erler, 2003; Woore, 2009; Erler and Macaro, 2011). Participants in these studies have also been found to compensate for their lack of L2 decoding proficiency by using L1 (English) symbol–sound mappings (Erler, 2003; Woore, 2011) – which doubtless comes as no surprise to many MFL teachers accustomed to anglicised renditions of French words. This problem has been interpreted as the result of automatic (and therefore rapid and involuntary) L1 decoding processes being triggered by L2 input (Koda, 2007), which will be helpful where the two systems overlap but unhelpful where they differ. For example, in French, many consonantal graphemes are pronounced similarly to their English counterparts (and are therefore likely to be decoded correctly), whereas vowels are often pronounced differently. Other languages will show different patterns of facilitation and interference. Words that have similar or identical spellings in the L1 and L2 may be particularly likely to trigger automatic L1 connections. Thus, whilst French–English cognates such as *national* and *télévision* may be helpful for accessing meaning, they are likely to be particularly disruptive in terms of decoding. As Woore (2010) argues, a first step in developing L2 decoding proficiency may therefore involve learners consciously 'overriding' the automatic activation of L1 symbol–sound correspondences, where these differ from those of the L2. In turn, this will allow new, L2-based mappings to become established and, eventually, automatised through practice.

Is it possible to help students become better L2 decoders? Various national documents issued over the past ten years – such as the KS3 Framework (DfES, 2003; DCSF, 2009) and the National Curriculum (QCA, 2007a) – have assumed that it is, although little research has convincingly demonstrated the effectiveness of L2 decoding instruction or its impact on wider L2 learning. Two recent studies (Woore, 2007, 2011) have examined this issue in MFL classrooms. The former study was a small-scale action research project, in which Year 7 students received explicit instruction in German grapheme–phoneme correspondences (GPC), delivered during short starter activities over 18 lessons. Students also memorised short German poems designed to exemplify these GPC and practised using an 'analogy strategy', using words in the poems to help them pronounce unfamiliar L2 words with similar spellings. Students who had received the instruction showed a small but statistically significant advantage over a comparison group in terms of the progress made in decoding German. Woore (2011) subsequently conducted a larger-scale evaluation of a programme of explicit decoding instruction with 186 Year 7 learners of French, drawn from ten classes in four schools. Five classes received explicit French phonics instruction during starter activities over a period of six months, focusing on problematic French GPC and giving students practice in pronouncing unfamiliar words containing these graphemes. The other five classes received no explicit decoding instruction. The intervention group again made significantly more progress than the comparison group in French decoding, although the amount of progress they made was rather small. Work therefore remains to be done to identify the most effective approaches to L2 decoding instruction. In line with previous studies, however, the comparison group in Woore (2011) made virtually no progress at all in French decoding. Given the likely importance of decoding proficiency for wider L2 learning, this suggests that its development is not something that MFL teachers can afford to leave to chance.

Conclusion

The evidence reviewed in this chapter suggests a number of implications for reading instruction in MFL classrooms. First, Part I highlighted the complexity underlying the apparently simple term 'reading'. Fluent L1 reading may appear effortless, but it involves the rapid and coordinated operation of both automatic processes and conscious strategies on many levels. Reading in an L2 multiplies this complexity further; indeed, at lower proficiency levels or where challenging texts are tackled, it may in some ways resemble a conscious problem-solving activity rather than what we usually think of as reading. As MFL teachers, we should bear this complexity in mind and ensure that students are adequately supported in developing the competencies and strategies needed to approach written texts as confidently as possible. There are reasons to be wary of simply asking students to 'read this text' or to 'do the reading activity on page X for homework'.

Second, MFL classrooms are in some respects a distinctive setting for L2 learning. In particular, students' motivation for L2 reading (and for L2 learning more generally) represents a key challenge for teachers. This chapter therefore endorses calls made over the past 20 years (e.g. McGowan and Turner, 1994; Ofsted, 2011) for students to encounter – at least some of the time – texts that cover cognitively engaging topics, coupled with more authentic, open-ended comprehension tasks. The facility with which L2 texts can be accessed online also opens up possibilities for more tailored L2 reading programmes, in which students might identify and read texts of particular interest to them. To borrow words used by Dombey (2010: 13) in relation to L1 reading, if we want students to engage with written texts, 'we have to give them a diet that is attractive, nutritious and satisfying'.

Third, there is considerable evidence to suggest that improving learners' L2 vocabulary knowledge and automatic word recognition is central to improving their reading proficiency. However, it is assumed that an important additional aim of MFL teaching is to develop students' communicative competence, including the ability to tackle written texts which go beyond the language they have already been taught. To achieve this, students need practice in reading challenging texts (thus opening the door to more engaging reading materials, as advocated above). Further, studies have begun to show that targeted strategy instruction can help L2 learners become more effective strategic readers, and that this can in turn improve both their reading comprehension and their confidence when approaching difficult texts. Strategy instruction is therefore argued to be a worthwhile use of at least some of the limited classroom time available. This approach implies a shift in pedagogical focus from the product to the process of reading.

Fourth, we should not neglect the role of phonology when teaching reading. Proficiency in print-to-sound decoding has been argued to underpin various aspects of L2 learning, promoting both learner autonomy and wider motivation for learning the language. By contrast, for those not proficient in decoding, a central tool available to the literate L2 learner is impaired. Several studies have shown that, without explicit instruction, many MFL students in KS3 make little or no progress in decoding French; conversely, there is some evidence to suggest that explicit decoding instruction can help MFL learners become more proficient decoders, although this may not be a quick or straightforward endeavour (at least in French). The most effective instructional methods in this area remain to be established. However, as a first step, it is likely to be helpful for teachers to highlight explicitly the differences between L1 and L2 GPC, and to provide practice in reading texts aloud that contain unfamiliar as well as familiar words (as will inevitably occur when more challenging texts are used). Particular attention should be paid to words that are orthographically close to familiar L1 words, such as cognates. It should also be borne in mind that learners' progress in decoding will depend on the particular L2 involved and its relationship to the L1 writing system.

Finally, this chapter has underlined the importance of individual differences between learners. Year 7 students arrive in the MFL classroom not only with different interests and levels of motivation, but also with different levels of proficiency and confidence in English reading, different L1 backgrounds (perhaps including knowledge of the written language) and different levels of L2 proficiency as a result of MFL learning at primary school. All this highlights the complexity of L2 reading instruction. It implies an approach that validates learners' existing linguistic knowledge (of whichever languages and to whichever levels), and that anticipates that individual learners may encounter different challenges and advantages when learning to read a given L2. Encouraging students to work collaboratively on the comprehension and phonological decoding of challenging, engaging L2 texts, with appropriate scaffolding and evaluative feedback, may be one way of taking a few steps towards this ambitious aim.

Reflective enquiry

1   What is the 'diet' of L2 reading offered to the students in your classrooms? To what extent is this diet 'attractive, nutritious and satisfying'?
    One approach to this issue might be to consult the students themselves about their interests. This could then inform the choice of reading materials used in class. You could also help students to identify for themselves L2 texts which are both of interest to them and of a suitable difficulty level.

2   To what extent do the reading tasks in your classroom help students 'grow' as L2 readers (i.e. focus on the process) as opposed to simply assessing the outcomes (focus on the product)?
    If your students are used to brief reading tasks (for example, where they answer comprehension questions on a short, simple text) on which they obtain a mark or 'level', try adopting a deliberately different approach. Use a more challenging text and open-ended comprehension task, perhaps one which they complete collaboratively. Afterwards, discuss with the class any difficulties they encountered and the strategies they used to overcome these, but do not give a final mark or level. This is to send a message to learners that the focus is on helping them to *develop* their L2 reading, not simply on assessing it.

3   What strategies do your students currently use to help them comprehend written L2 texts above their current productive level? How effective is this strategic behaviour?
    Ask your students to 'think aloud' in pairs or to use a strategy checklist whilst tackling a challenging written text, to help them become aware of the strategies they use; follow this up with a whole-class feedback session, exploring and discussing what they have found out. Then repeat the whole process after having provided some strategy instruction, to see whether their strategic reading has developed.

4   To what extent are your students able to pronounce accurately the words they encounter in written texts (both familiar and unfamiliar words)? To what extent can they do so fluently?

Ask learners to read a text aloud to each other in pairs. Circulate around the class, listening to their pronunciations and making a note of any particular words or graphemes they struggle with. Given appropriate support, they could also peer assess each other's pronunciations. Repeat this exercise periodically to gauge their progress in their L2 decoding.

Further reading

Erler, L. and Macaro, E. (2011) 'Decoding ability in French as a foreign language and language learning motivation', *The Modern Language Journal*, 95(4): 496–518.

Grabe, W. and Stoller, F.L. (2011) *Teaching and Researching Reading*, second edition, Longman: Harlow.

Macaro, E. and Erler, L. (2008) 'Raising the achievement of young-beginner readers of French through strategy instruction', *Applied Linguistics*, 29(1): 90–119.

Note

1   Key Stage 3, secondary school phase between ages 11 and 13.

Chapter 7

Learning and teaching writing in the foreign languages classroom

Fostering writing-to-learn approaches

Rosa M. Manchón

Introduction: writing and foreign language education

Foreign languages (FL) programmes almost without exception incorporate learning objectives related to the development of writing competencies as well as curricular guidelines concerning the typology of texts students are expected to be able to write during a given instructional period, and the way in which the learning and teaching of such texts should be sequenced and implemented.[1] In addition to the learning of writing itself, it is not unusual for FL education to consider writing also as a means to learn, teach or test the students' knowledge of the FL culture. Finally, and this is particularly relevant for the issues to be discussed in the rest of the chapter, writing can be, and often is, viewed and taught as a means to learn the second language (L2), a pedagogical approach based on the recognition of the key role that literacy experiences may play in instructed second language acquisition (SLA), a role that in the case of writing may well go beyond its use as 'a convenient form of language practice' (Ortega, 2012: 409). This use of writing as a language learning tool will be more evident as we progress through the chapter.

It follows from the above that there may exist two (complementary rather than mutually exclusive) overarching purposes for the teaching of L2 writing in instructed SLA: 'learning to write' and 'writing to learn'. As I have detailed elsewhere (Manchón, 2013: 2), *learning-to-write* (LW) settings are those in which 'writing is learned and taught as an end in itself and the ultimate aim of the teaching program is to facilitate the development of (multi)literacy for educational or job-related purposes, as well as for full participation in society'. In contrast, *writing-to-learn* conditions encompass both *writing-to-learn-content* (WLC) and *writing-to-learn-language* (WLL). WLC refers to the use of writing for the learning of disciplinary subject-matter in the content areas, as would be the case, for instance, of writing in French in a geography class in a Content and Language Integrated Learning (CLIL) programme (see Chapter 16, this volume). In contrast, WLL refers to the learning and teaching of L2 writing in the FL classroom as a tool for language learning, i.e. as a means to help students in the two main tasks involved in L2 learning: acquiring (explicit/implicit) knowledge about the L2, on the one hand, and developing the ability to put acquired knowledge to use, on the other.

This chapter will focus on the WLL dimension of L2 writing. Before we do so, a general observation might be appropriate: teaching writing is a socially situated phenomenon, which means that one-size-fits-all pedagogical prescriptions are simply inappropriate (see Chapter 15, this volume). Instead, locally relevant pedagogies need to be sought in recognition of the fact that each educational setting represents a unique interaction of educational, contextual, material and personal variables that do not transfer across contexts, programmes and learners. The recognition of this socially situated nature of learning and teaching FL writing has important implications with respect to the various purposes of writing referred to above, of which I shall mention two. One is that principled decisions need to be taken regarding which purpose(s) or specific combination of purposes for the learning and teaching of L2 writing from those mentioned above are prioritised in each educational setting and why. Following from here, the idiosyncrasy of the foreign language classroom, in opposition to the second language (L2) classroom, must be brought to the fore (see Manchón, 2009; Reichelt et al., 2012). The implication would be that, as argued by several scholars (cf. Leki, 2001; Lee, forthcoming; Manchón, 2009, 2013; Ortega, 2009), the way to proceed is to 'think local' and not to adopt (just perhaps 'adapt', when relevant) writing pedagogies developed for L2 (often university) instructional contexts. This socially situated approach to pedagogical decision-making might not be an easy task as it will entail several educational, material and ideational challenges, critically scrutinised by Leki (2001).

What follows is a discussion on the WLL dimension of L2 writing. This choice of focus is based on two main considerations. One is the conviction of the relevance of exploring the WLL dimension of L2 writing in discussions of FL education given that primary and secondary school FL classrooms are writing-to-learn-language contexts par excellence, which should not be interpreted to mean that LW approaches have no place in the FL classroom. A second reason for a focus on WLL is the almost total neglect of crucial aspects of the WLL dimension of L2 writing in teacher education programmes and language teaching methodology books.

My aim in the chapter is to summarise the theoretical predictions for and some of the empirical evidence on the language learning potential of L2 writing, and to offer some pedagogical reflections from the analysis of the available theory and research. The chapter closes with some questions for further analysis.

WRITING TO LEARN THE LANGUAGE: THEORETICAL PREDICTIONS AND EMPIRICAL EVIDENCE

It has been repeatedly argued (cf. Belcher, 2012; Bitchener, 2012; Harklau, 2002; O'Brien, 2004; Reichelt *et al.*, 2012; Williams, 2012; Wolff, 2000) that writing has an important role to play as a learning tool in instructed SLA. Wolff (2000: 111) goes as far as suggesting that 'writing is probably the most efficient L2 learning tool we have, more efficient than reading or the communicative skills'. Yet, the study of the potential of writing for language learning is a newcomer to the fields of SLA and L2 writing, two areas of research that have up until recently developed independently of each other. Thus, SLA scholars have traditionally been uninterested in written language learning (see Ortega [2012] for possible reasons) with the result that the role that writing may play in language development has seldom featured in SLA research agendas. Similarly, L2 writing specialists have been primarily concerned with the LW and, to a lesser extent, the WLC dimensions of L2 writing (see Hirvela [2011] and Hyland [2011] for overviews of these two strands), with the corresponding neglect of the WLL perspective (reviewed by Manchón, 2011b). However, a vibrant SLA-oriented L2 writing research agenda is rapidly developing and the rich outcome emerging from it is making its way into main publications venues in both fields. Collectively, this body of publications has contributed to theorising the language learning potential of L2 writing and to setting up a challenging future research agenda, in addition to providing a wealth of empirical evidence on the manner in which writing itself and the processing of feedback can contribute to L2 development.

In what follows I shall briefly synthesise the theoretical tenets in support of the language learning potential of L2 writing as well as key findings from the available empirical evidence. I will be drawing on several sources (cf. Bitchener, 2012; Bitchener and Ferris, 2012; Manchón, 2011a, 2011b, 2013; Manchón and Roca de Larios, 2007; Ortega, 2011, 2012; Polio and Williams, 2009; Sheen and Lyster, 2010; Williams, 2012; Williams and Polio, forthcoming) and the reader is referred to these publications for a full elaboration of the issues briefly discussed here.

Theoretical underpinnings

As shown in Figure 7.1, several SLA theories provide the theoretical under-pinnings for the purported language learning potential of L2 writing, including those of a cognitive nature (mainly Skill Learning Theory, the Focus on Form research, the Noticing Hypothesis and the Output Hypothesis), as well as sociocultural approaches to language learning and use. Under the umbrella of these theoretical perspectives, the discussion of the language potential of writing revolves around two main questions: what is unique about writing that can lead

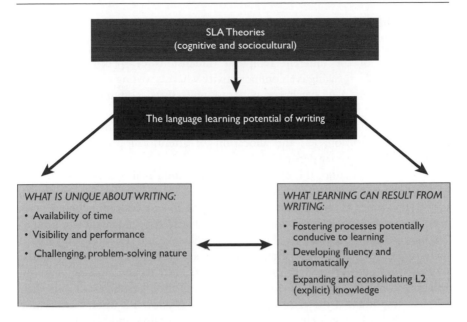

Figure 7.1 Theoretical underpinnings of the language learning potential of writing.

to advancing language competences, on the one hand, and what kind of learning can be expected to derive from written output practice, on the other. As we will see, both dimensions are closely interrelated.

What is unique about writing that can potentially lead to advancing language competences?

It has been suggested that written output practice can potentially lead to language learning as a result of: (1) the availability of time; (2) the visibility and permanence of both the written text and the feedback on it; and (3) the challenging, problem-solving nature of the writing activity. The pace and permanence of writing make it possible for L2 writers to be more in control of their attentional resources, more prone to prioritise linguistic concerns (in contrast to oral production) and, accordingly, more likely to focus on language during both their composing activity and their processing of the feedback received. Similarly, the problem-solving activity engaged in during writing requires decision-making (at various levels) and deep linguistic processing with potential beneficial effects on learning. These issues are further elaborated upon in the sections that follow.

The availability of time

The rationale for the purported learning potential of writing partly rests on the consideration of the different temporal dimensions of speech and writing (Williams, 2012): speaking is an online activity whereas writing takes place offline (with the exception of synchronous computer assisted communication). This means that most forms of writing do not suffer from the time constraints imposed by the production of speech in real time. Three main learning advantages related to (1) task execution; (2) the allocation of attentional processes; and (3) motivational factors may derive.

As for task execution, the offline nature of writing makes it possible for L2 writers to engage in dual task performance (i.e. being able to focus on two things at the same time) as well as to devote more time to task conceptualisation, task planning and task completion, three processes closely associated with attention to language-related concerns. In this respect Williams and Polio (forthcoming) claim that the availability of writing makes it possible for writers to 'reflect on the linguistic demands of the task, plan on how to meet those demands, draw on different knowledge stores in doing so, and use these resources to edit their output'. Importantly, the extra time available may allow L2 writers to become aware of their language deficits i.e. what they do not know and need to know in order to convey the message they want or have been asked to convey. This process, known as 'noticing the hole', may translate itself into actions aimed at solving the communication problems experienced, including both the use of outside sources (dictionaries, the teacher, peers, etc.) and one's own knowledge of the L2 (Ortega, 2012; Williams, 2012). It has been posited that this greater and deeper focus and reflection on language facilitated by the availability of time can help in the consolidation of the L2 user's knowledge sources. Therefore, it would be pedagogically sound to take measures to optimise these potential learning opportunities.

The temporal characteristics of writing also allow for ample opportunities to engage in the process of 'cognitive comparison', an attentional process implemented while processing feedback in order to notice what is new in the input obtained, and to compare what is noticed with one's own representation of the L2 (i.e. what is new in the feedback or what is different from what one already knows). However, as Polio (2012a, 2012b) notes, the delayed temporal nature of written corrective feedback (WCF) may represent a drawback as compared to the immediate provision of oral corrective feedback (OCF), the immediacy of the latter making it in principle more effective. Nevertheless, this potential disadvantage would be compensated by its visibility and permanence: because of the slower pace of writing, writers can go over and over again the feedback received if needed, which is not always possible when processing OCF (see Bitchener, 2012; Polio, 2012b). In short, the temporal dimension of writing offers potentially more favourable conditions for uptake of the feedback received provided by the learner's own agency and active involvement in the processing of feedback. This agency can be greatly facilitated by the teacher's scaffolding and guidance, a point I shall return to in a later section.

Finally, the slower pace of writing can have positive motivational effects: students can work at their own pace and this can avoid the kind of frustration that may derive from oral production in which the flow of time is often other-imposed and where, as a consequence, there might not be time to solve the problems experienced while conveying meaning. But, as Ilona Leki (2001: 206) aptly put it, 'pen and paper (or keyboard) are patient, and flexible. They adapt to any level of English proficiency and bear any alterations or adjustments the writer might care to make'. And she added the important pedagogical challenge that this represents for teachers, who need 'to find ways to promote these students' linguistic and intellectual development by helping them to create L2 texts that come to reflect their maturity and expertise, since writing, even L2 writing, gives the leisure to reform the text to do so' (ibid.). This potential learning outcome of an increase in motivation might partially, although crucially, depend on time-on-task considerations when designing tasks for learners.

Permanence and visibility

Both the written text itself and the feedback on it are permanent and visible. The permanent character of feedback can increase its effectiveness as compared to oral feedback because, as argued by Bitchener (2012), written feedback is always explicit (even if provided as indirect feedback. See Ellis [2010] for a full elaboration of feedback types), and hence more likely to be noticed. It is also permanent, which increases the opportunities to engage in reflection and analysis in the L2 learner's own time.

Written texts are also permanent, and hence potentially useful for testing one's knowledge of the L2 given that L2 users can engage in the process of cognitive comparison mentioned earlier. Nevertheless, the permanence and visibility of the written text can also have negative effects for the writer. Leki (2001: 205) suggests that the permanence of texts leaves L2 writers 'vulnerable to criticism of the writer's ideas, style, and ability to manipulate language correctly and effectively', which can be particularly frustrating for

> writers educated and experienced enough to have established a writerly identity or voice in L1, the loss of one accomplished textual voice under a blanket of awkward, incorrect, or insufficiently expressive or imaginative use of L2 may be especially discomfiting
>
> (2001: 205)

It is equally possible, however, to predict that this potential negative effect of the permanent nature of texts can in fact be an incentive for L2 users to set up higher and more complex goals for themselves, in the sense of pursuing the achievement of more complex aims at different levels (ideational, linguistic, textual, paying attention to audience concerns, etc.) while planning, generating and revising their texts (see Williams, 2012). In other words, the permanence of writing may prompt L2 writers to produce what in the SLA literature has been referred to as 'pushed output', i.e. output that is not only accurate, but also precise, coherent, cohesive and appropriate. In her original formulation of the Output Hypothesis, Swain (1985, 1995) claimed that the production of pushed output could be conducive to learning because learners would pay attention to language (hence increasing the chances of noticing gaps in one's own linguistic resources), test their hypothesis about the L2 (both while writing and while processing feedback) and increase their metalinguistic awareness of the L2 as a consequence of the reflection and analysis of language (including the writer's own linguistic resources) that take place while generating and revising one's own output.

Problem-solving activity

The consideration of writing as a tool for language learning also derives from the demanding, problem-solving nature of the act of composing, as propounded in cognitive accounts of writing. The demands of writing are a consequence of having to distribute one's (limited) attentional resources concurrently among several goals (ideational, linguistic, stylistic, textual, etc.). Therefore, and this would be a first dimension of the problem-solving nature of writing, strategic decisions need to be taken regarding which attentional resources to devote to which of the various demands that may be concurrently competing for attention. As can be anticipated, the constraints are even greater when writing under timed conditions, hence the relevance of time-on-task considerations. The problem-solving nature of writing also results from the fact that the goals that may be pursued might not be reached instantly and automatically, but rather through a search for potential solutions. For instance, in a quest for precision and appropriateness in lexical choices, lack of access to the relevant vocabulary may be solved by consulting external sources, searching for a solution via a reformulation of the intended meaning in the L1 which is then translated to the L2, or looking for a synonym in the L2, among other options. In short, L2 writers (as L1 writers) need to look for and implement appropriate problem-solving strategies, which also require time.

It has been argued (cf. Manchón and Roca de Larios, 2007) that this strategic behaviour in the control and execution of composing activities will entail deeper processing on the part of the L2 writing with potential language learning. For instance, in a study of university level L2 students, Manchón and Roca de Larios (2011) have shown that the setting up of higher-order goals at ideational or textual levels (partly prompted by the L2 writing instructional intervention) prompted the students to engage in the kind of linguistic processing that potentially lead to language learning.

Needless to say, teachers have an important role to play in fostering the L2 writer's problem-solving activity through the writing tasks they ask their students to perform and the way in which they guide them during task implementation, as we will see later.

What learning can result from written output practice?

As the previous discussion makes clear, writing should not be considered a mere form of language practice. Instead, the role of writing in language learning is much more encompassing and hence considerably more relevant than what may be inferred from well-established accounts of what L2 learning entails, how it develops and how it should be fostered in the classroom. Basically, writing offers conditions that either indirectly or directly may be conducive to learning (Figure 7.2. See Williams, 2012 for further elaboration).

The indirect learning outcomes result from the engagement in the set of crucial learning processes that writing facilitates because of its pace, permanence and problem-solving nature, as discussed above. In a previous review (Manchón, 2011b) I concluded that empirical research has shown that these processes include noticing and attentional focus-on-form processes, the formulation and testing of hypotheses about the L2, production and self-assessment of one's own linguistic options and metalinguistic reflection. All these processes can indirectly lead to advancing language competences.

Writing can also have a more direct contribution to learning by helping learners develop fluency and automaticity. This is because writing offers ideal conditions for practice, communicative practice, which is essential for making progress in language learning. DeKeyser (2007a) explains that practice helps to improve performance in terms of speed (less time is needed to say or write more in less time), accuracy (writing becomes more accurate with practice) and amount of attention required to execute any given task (with the result that dual task

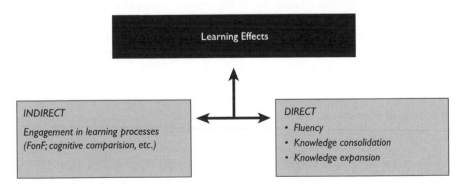

FonF = focus on form.

Figure 7.2 Indirect and direct potential learning effects of L2 writing.

performance may be eventually possible in the case of complex tasks such as writing a demanding text).

As seen in Figure 7.2, writing itself (provided it entails problem-solving) and the processing of feedback (provided the learner's engagement with it) can play a role in developing explicit knowledge about the L2. Whether this explicit knowledge eventually becomes the kind of implicit knowledge needed for fluent and efficient communication is still an open question that future research will have to elucidate.

Research evidence on the language learning potential of writing

Several recent publications provide comprehensive overviews of the main empirical findings available on the language learning potential of writing itself (Manchón, 2011a, 2011b; Williams, 2012) and of feedback (Bitchener, 2012). What follows is a brief summary of some of the findings reported in these state-of-the-art accounts.

- Concerning the potential learning outcomes of the act of producing written texts, research has provided abundant empirical evidence for the purported linguistic processing mentioned in the previous section: L2 writers have been found to devote many of their attentional resources (both in individual and in collaborative writing) to thinking about language and to solving linguistic problems. Rather crucial from a pedagogical perspective are the empirical findings in support of the theoretical prediction that individual and task-related variables mediate potential learning outcomes, particularly: time-on-task conditions; the challenging nature of the writing task; and the learner's engagement in explicit, deep linguistic processing of the feedback received. Recent research also shows that the learner's own perception of the language learning potential of writing can become both a goal and a motivating factor: learners may want to write in order to learn the L2 (and hence engage in language learning actions while writing), while the sense of achievement (i.e. of progress in language) fostered by writing may motivate learners to keep on writing (Manchón and Roca de Larios, 2011).
- As for the language learning potential of feedback, the picture that emerges is that, as theoretically predicted, feedback can contribute to learning by helping learners to expand their explicit knowledge and to increase the accuracy of their use of the L2. It has also been found that the combination and interaction of several sets of factors appear to mediate these potential learning effects (Bitchener, 2012). These include feedback factors (which type of feedback is provided and how); task factors (types of writing tasks); linguistic factors (which linguistic elements were targeted in the feedback provided); and individual factors, including cognitive factors (analytic ability), linguistics factors (L2 proficiency), and affective factors (beliefs,

goals and attitudes). Very importantly, a crucial element is, as suggested above, the learner's own engagement with and reflection on the feedback received.

PEDAGOGICAL REFLECTIONS: FOSTERING WLL APPROACHES IN THE FL CLASSROOM

The theory and research presented above leads to some pedagogical reflections related to: (1) the written tasks included in a FL/L2 writing programme; (2) task implementation procedures; and (3) the pedagogical intervention regarding the provision and processing of feedback.

Regarding *tasks* to include in FL/L2 programmes, the above discussion makes clear that those tasks that engage learners in problem-solving and represent a real challenge for them in ideational and/or linguistic terms have more chances of contributing to learning, in terms of consolidation or extension of knowledge, hence the relevance of taking principled decisions regarding criteria for task selection. In addition, the pedagogical intervention also entails finding ways to engage students in the writing tasks set, such engagement being related to the three well known components of motivation applied in this case to writing: having reasons to engage in the writing task, deciding to engage in the kind of problem-solving behaviour required to pursue the goals set (rather than reducing such goals and engaging in problem-avoiding behaviour), and maintaining the effort required during the entire duration of the task at hand. Although obvious, the potential motivating role of computer-mediated writing in the primary and secondary school FL classroom must be mentioned. Finally, an important issue in pedagogical decision-making, this time derived from the task-based literature (see Bygate, 1996, 2001; Larsen-Freeman, 2009), is whether it is more pedagogically sound to opt for task repetition or for task variation in terms of the language learning potential each option may foster. In the case of writing, the potential learning outcomes that may derive from task repetition may be different from those in oral tasks (see Bygate, 1996, 2001; Larsen-Freeman, 2009): task repetition may compensate for the time constraints that characterise oral interactions, whereas in the case of writing, given the availability of time, task repetition may facilitate the gradual complexification of goals being pursued. In some way, this learning potential was at the basis of the kind of 'internal task repetition' fostered by the process approach to the teaching of writing and its conceptualisation of writing as rewriting and the several drafts technique.

Concerning *task implementation*, the crucial role to be attributed to time-on-task considerations is to be emphasised once again: L2 writers should not be expected to approach their L2 writing as a problem-solving activity if ample time-on-task is not available (see Manchón and Roca de Larios, 2007). In addition, L2 writers need guidance throughout the whole process: guidance in task conceptualisation and task execution, as well as guidance in their processing of feedback.

In terms of the *provision and processing of feedback*, three further observations are pertinent. First, the distinction between 'feedback for accuracy' and 'feedback for acquisition' (Manchón, 2011a) becomes relevant. It is mainly the latter that relates to WLL pedagogies as this type of feedback would be aimed at promoting language learning. Accordingly, the processing of feedback for acquisition would entail the learner's engagement in explicit learning processes and self-reflection through various iterations of writing, noticing and reflection, and rewriting (see Manchón, 2011a, 2011b). Second, motivational issues should be mentioned: teachers need to find ways of responding to student writing in meaningful ways to initiate and maintain their motivation and to encourage them to solve problems of a different degree of sophistication from those the students posed themselves in the first place. This problem-solving activity, as noted in an earlier section, can be potentially conducive to language learning. Finally, the socially situated nature of learning and teaching L2 writing mentioned above also applies to the provision of feedback: as aptly expressed by Lourdes Ortega (2012: 411): 'Teachers are main actors in the provision of error correction, in writing as orally, and they make their choices in the social context of the classroom rather than in a social vacuum' (see also Lee, 2009).

Conclusion

In short, the available theory and research makes it clear that if WLL approaches are to be fostered in the FL classroom, sound and well-principled decisions must be taken regarding the tasks we ask our students to engage in, the task conditions we set (time considerations being particularly relevant), the scaffolding provided during task execution, the feedback we offer, and the guidance offered to students for their processing of the feedback they are given.

Reflective enquiry

1   What have you learned in this chapter with respect to the relevance of time considerations in terms of both the writing activity itself and the processing of feedback?

2   What arguments would you use to explain why one-shot writing activities (i.e. those following a sequence of prompt–writing–feedback) are in principle less conducive to language learning than activities that entail a sequence of processes?

3   After reading this chapter, which previous ideas of yours about L2 writing learning and teaching have been challenged and which ones have been reinforced?

4   What have you learned in this chapter about the socially situated nature of L2 writing learning and teaching and what implications can you draw for the context where you teach?

Further reading

Hyland, K. (2002) *Teaching and Researching Writing*, London: Pearson.

Leki, I. (2001) 'Material, educational and ideological challenges of teaching EFL writing at the turn of the century', *International Journal of English Studies*, 1: 197–209.

Polio, C. and Williams, J. (2009) 'Teaching and testing writing' in M.H. Long and C.J. Doughty (eds) *The Handbook of Language Teaching*, Oxford: Blackwell, pp. 486–517.

Williams, J. (2005) *Teaching Writing in Second and Foreign Language Classrooms*, Boston, MA: McGraw-Hill.

Note

1   See for example in England the National Curriculum Attainment Target in Writing: www.education.gov.uk/schools/teachingandlearning/curriculum/secondary/b00199616/mfl/attainment/writing.

Chapter 8

Grammar

The never-ending debate

Ernesto Macaro

Introduction

The question of whether to 'teach the grammar' of the target language (henceforth the second language, or L2) has been debated internationally for as long as I can remember. It has been debated in school staffrooms, university cafeterias, and in journals about language learning. It has been commented on by politicians and written about in newspapers both of the enlightened and less enlightened variety. In this chapter I do not intend to provide a historical account of the great grammar debate. Instead I want to explore some myths about the relationship between teaching grammar and language learning success, try to delve deeply in what we actually mean by teaching grammar, provide some research evidence on the subject and, finally, come up with some general guidelines that teachers may want to follow.

OUTLINING THE KEY ISSUES: WHAT IS GRAMMAR?

I often start teaching a session on the topic of grammar by simply asking participants (student-teachers or teachers) what they think grammar actually is. Not surprisingly, I get a whole host of different ideas. Some people say 'it's a framework of rules that give you accuracy'. Others say 'it's like the building blocks of the language'. And still others say 'it's the words you need to describe a language, like noun and verb'. Some wax quite lyrical and talk about 'the glue that holds a language together' or 'the weave of the cloth'. What I find particularly interesting are two things. First, it is this recourse to metaphor in order to describe what grammar is, almost as if it is a concept that cannot be defined in any other way. Second, the definitions of grammar rarely refer to actual human beings using it to communicate, but rather to some kind of external entity that has created a thing called 'the grammar' in order to help all of us speak the language properly.

Of course, we can say that grammar is a way of describing and categorising language. That is what grammar books do. Some grammar books' mission is indeed simply to try to describe a language as carefully and as fool-proofly as possible. Now there's a thought: my computer has just told me that there is something wrong with me typing the word 'proofly' by underlining it in red suggesting the word does not exist in the dictionary. It has not underlined it in green to suggest that there is a grammar mistake somewhere in it or around it. However, I know that the noun 'proof' exists (see! no problem according to Mr Gates!) and I know that the morpheme or suffix 'ly' exists because I can put it on the end of another noun, 'man'. So why can't I put it on the end of 'proof'. Is it a lexical mistake? Or is it a grammatical (by which I mean morphological) mistake? Never mind, let's move on but I don't think a grammar book would tell me why 'fool-proofly' is unacceptable.

Not all grammar books are of the type that try to describe a language as carefully and as accurately as possible. Pedagogical grammars try to be helpful to the L2 learner by making the explanation of rules as simple, coherent and non-technical as possible and try to give examples of the grammar in normal usage. They also tend to be selective in the grammatical elements that they describe perhaps believing that these are the important ones that an L2 learner should know at various stages in their learning trajectory.

We should note that both these types of grammar books are written by people, as it were, 'contemplating a language' that already exists. Nobody has invented the grammar of 'natural' languages – grammar has evolved over many centuries, usually many centuries ago.

Another way that we can talk about grammar is 'a series of patterns inside an L2 learner's head'. In the L2 acquisition literature this is often referred to as a learner's 'interlanguage'. The idea here is that the patterns may or may not be the same patterns as those that a native speaker of the language would have in his/ her head but they are patterns nonetheless. The patterns may be wrong (not target-language-like) because of 'transfer' from the learner's first language (L1) or they may be wrong because of over-generalising from the L2 (I know that 'manly' exists, so I reckon that 'proofly' must exist). The fact that a learner has arrived at these wrong patterns by making these two types of computations in his/her head is not something we should laugh at or deride. They show the brain working, not carelessness. They show an attempt at hypothesising about the target language, not stupidity.

Another way that some people talk about grammar, in relation to L2 learning, is related to a learner's ability to talk about and explain rules, whether by using the right terminology (the metalanguage) or his/her own language. However, as we shall see, there is not necessarily a correspondence between being able to talk about rules and being able to use them correctly when speaking or writing.

ANALYSIS OF THE MAIN THEMES AND DEBATES

The debate in language teaching circles appears to have been not about whether grammar should be learnt but whether it should be taught. This statement may seem to you to be unnecessarily problematic.

So let's begin to unpack the statement by asking what would be our expectations of learners in terms of their grammatical knowledge in the first three years of learning a language. The five expectations described below are not, of course, mutually exclusive but, I want to argue, to expect all of them creates tensions.

1   Learners should be able to communicate meaning.
    In other words, taking into account the number of years they have studied the L2, a teacher might expect a learner to be able to say, in non-scripted conversation, something that the teacher can understand without difficulty. The implication is that the patterns of the language are sufficiently correct for the meaning to be understood (e.g. *hier, *je mange* au restaurant chinois avec ma famille*). I doubt that many teachers would disagree with this expectation after putting considerable effort into their teaching.

2   Learners should show evidence of growing awareness of patterns.
    Whilst a teacher might accept that a perfect sentence is not easily achieved in non-scripted speech, they could reasonably expect that, over time, the pattern might become more target-like, even if only gradually. We will return to this progression below when looking at research into the perfect tense in French.

3   Learners should be able to use some of the rules of the language correctly in focused grammar tasks.
    For example, this could be a task where they have to provide the correct inflection for a verb when given in the infinitive or put a series of words in the correct syntactical order. Put differently, a teacher might expect that, having explicitly taught a particular rule, learners should now be able to provide evidence that they have remembered how that rule works by doing these kinds of tasks.

4   Learners should be able to explain a rule in their own words.
    Having taught the rule a teacher might expect that the learners should be able at least to give their own rendition of how the rule works back to the teacher at some later point in time. This might provide evidence that they have remembered how the rule works and can call it up at any time.

5   Learners should be able to use at least some metalanguage with respect to the rules that they have been taught and can remember.
    Whilst very few teachers might expect (school-aged) learners to use such terms as 'determiners', 'di-transitive verbs' and 'pseudo-clefts', they might expect learners to be able to use the terms 'noun', 'verb' and 'adjective'. The problem regarding this expectation is, where do you stop? Would you expect learners to be able to use 'adverb'? Is an adverb something that modifies a verb? If so, how easy is it to understand that 'tomorrow' is an adverb? And what about 'tomorrow's performance will take place…'?

Most student-teacher groups I have taught have no problem with expectations 1 and 2. There is near-unanimous agreement on them. Of course they want learners to be able to communicate and to show signs of progress with their speaking and their writing with regard to grammatical correctness. The unanimity breaks down on expectations 3, 4 and 5. Opponents say things like 'doing grammar tasks is not what you do in real life'. Supporters say things like 'but it's one good way of finding out if they have learnt what I've taught them'. Some opponents then say 'but I find that even if they can do the grammar task doesn't mean they get it right in a role-play activity'. It is always a really interesting debate!

HOW AND WHEN CAN GRAMMAR BE TAUGHT?

Hopefully we are in agreement that we would want to see evidence in our learners of a *development* in their *use* of the language (in terms of syntax and morphology) over time through their spoken and written productions. So the question then is how do we best achieve that development? There are basically three ways to develop the patterns in the heads of our learners.

Developing grammar through 'natural' interaction

This is probably the most contentious of the methods. It is an approach often associated with Stephen Krashen (Krashen, 1985; Krashen and Terrell, 1988) who has been unjustly pilloried, in my view, for trying to make language teaching more interesting. What Krashen was basically saying in the late 1970s and 1980s is that if you expose learners to a lot of input from the teacher, and provided that input is at the right level for their current linguistic knowledge (their knowledge of vocabulary and grammar) they will understand it. He called this 'comprehensible input' and he argued that they could (or at least should be able to) understand it because they can use the context to fill in the unknown bits in the teacher's input. The problem with Krashen is that he tried to go a big step further. He tried to set up a theory (aka 'the Comprehensible Input Hypothesis') that if a learner was able to understand the teacher's simplified input, s/he would also be able to 'acquire' *subconsciously* the patterns of the language contained in that input and that subconscious acquisition was different (and better) than 'conscious learning' of rules. His argument was that they might learn subconsciously in the same way that a toddler might 'acquire' their L1 from the input around them. As you might imagine, this pretty soon caused an uproar among certain linguists (e.g. Gregg, 1984) who set about destroying Krashen's hypothesis by demonstrating that it had little empirical basis and by pointing out that constructs such as 'comprehensible input' and 'acquisition' were irresponsibly vague.

Some researchers tried to save the situation through a kind of compromise. They suggested that acquisition could take place through oral interaction between teacher and learners and among learners (for an overview see Gass, 1997). In other words they were saying that one-way 'input' was not enough; learners had to be involved in negotiating their understanding of the input by asking questions, asking the speaker to modify further what they were saying and by providing confirmation that they had understood. There may be some implicit or explicit feedback on mistakes or even grammar-focused short episodes on occasion, but these should not undermine the general communicative (meaning-focused) orientation of the lesson. Even this approach (aka 'the Interaction Hypothesis') however, has failed to convince a number of people that grammar can improve through this (still fairly natural) interaction. To sum up then, this more 'natural approach' to teaching grammar has fallen out of favour and it is rare to see it happening in L2 classrooms, of the beginner or intermediate type. You may perhaps see it briefly at the beginning of a lesson when a teacher tries to have 'a real conversation' before launching into the main lesson objectives, but even then I doubt that the teacher's intention is to be 'teaching grammar' through natural conversation.

Developing grammar through 'implicit form-focused' exposure and practice

In this approach a teacher selects an element of morphology and/or syntax and in some way makes that element both *salient* and *frequent* during the course of a lesson or series of lessons. If you look at most textbooks contents pages you will see that chapters/units are divided into 'topics' such as 'meeting people for the first time' but also you will be told what the morphology or syntax that the chapter/unit is focusing on.

A teacher following this approach will expose learners to texts that have a particular pattern in them. Of course a lot depends on what the teacher asks the learners to do with these texts, the task associated with them. An associated task that has a very narrow, grammatically driven focus such as 'underline all the negative phrases in the text' or even 'what were all the things that Claudette said she *didn't* want to do?' will be very different from a task that requires a more 'global' understanding of the text (see Chapter 4 by Vanderplank, in this volume).

A teacher following this implicit but form-focused approach might also make their own talk rich with a particular grammatical element and when asking questions of learners might expect that their response would contain that element in them. If a learner then made a mistake in their response that was associated with the grammatical element in question then the teacher would have to make a decision (either on the spot or pre-planned) as to whether to draw the learner's/ learners' attention to the mistake or let it go.

Learners will be less likely to make mistakes if the circumstances are not conducive to them doing so. For example, if they have been told to copy down a response with the target grammatical element in it they are unlikely to make a grammatical mistake when asked to respond to a teacher's questions if they simply read it out. Similarly if the response is very 'standard' and repetitive they will not have to think very hard in order to provide it; the cognitive challenge will be quite low. So some people would advocate that in this 'more implicit' approach, learners should be encouraged to say things which they are not sure are correct. This is related to what Swain (1995) calls 'pushed output'. By taking a risk with the language the learner achieves a number of things. First of all they notice the relationship between what they want to say (the function of the message) and how to say it (the form of the message) and perhaps also notice that there is a gap in their linguistic knowledge allowing them to formulate the message. Second, by having the potential to make the mistake they will create an opportunity for feedback as discussed above. This may give rise to two things. The learner may attempt to reformulate their incorrect utterance and both the initial formulation and the reformulation will provide the teacher with evidence of the effectiveness of their implicit approach. Last, and very importantly, encouraging learners to say things they are not sure are correct creates the sort of classroom environment where learners feel safe to say things in front of their peers without fear of ridicule. Making mistakes becomes part of the learning experience.

A more implicit approach to grammar learning requires two more dimensions. First, it has to show that learners can transfer an element learnt in one context to another context or situation. As a consequence, implicit learning of a grammatical element is not a one-off thing that a teacher can tick off on their scheme of work. It requires constant recycling and reapplying. Second, the progression is not merely from incorrect to correct and from use in one situation to multiple situations. If has also to show a progression from supported or scaffolded interaction (where the teacher or other students have helped a learner with a particular production) to spontaneous productions, ones that perhaps do not occur in the middle of the interaction in which that particular grammatical element is being rehearsed. These spontaneous productions would reassure the teacher that the grammatical element has truly been learnt.

Another way of assessing whether a grammatical element has been learnt is to ask students to carry out a piece of writing on a particular topic where there is an obligatory requirement to use the element. Again, a typical example would be to tell a story from a series of pictures in the past tense or describe an incident that happened recently. If this task were done without the use of supporting grammatical materials then correct productions would make the teacher feel reasonably confident that the implicit approach had been successful.

So far so good. But what do we know of how the grammatical element has been structured in the learner's head? Is it the case that s/he can therefore only have a kind of implicit knowledge of the element in question? In other words when they think about what they have said or written they might say 'it feels right'. Is there a simple relationship between the teaching approach and the way that the knowledge is stored in the brain? To believe that would be to deny the fact that humans are 'free agents' in terms of their cognitive processes. Learners are capable of trying to build up explicit knowledge from implicit information (for a more in-depth discussion of implicit and explicit knowledge see Ellis 2005; Ellis 2004). They may try to formulate rules from the input, the interactions and the productions that they have been involved in. As we mentioned earlier those rules may not always be correct but it is part of human nature to try to see a pattern in reoccurring language data and try to come up with some sort of rule because it is more economical to have a rule than not to have one.

So the question then is, should the teacher try to encourage that process of rule building? For example, after exposure to the pattern and after interaction and productions using that pattern, should the teacher simply leave it at that or should they say: 'can anyone tell me what the rule is'? (The inductive approach). The answer to this is tricky. It might seem obvious to say 'yes, ask the learners to try to generate their own rules'. However, there are a number of problems associated with this. The first is that not all the learners in the class will be at the same stage of having fixed the pattern in their heads through the implicit process and therefore providing them with a peer's explanation of a rule (regardless of how clever that explanations is) will actually revert the learning process for some students to an explicit learning process. The second difficulty is that not all patterns in language are easy to explain. One of the most difficult patterns in languages such as French and Italian is 'aspect'; when to use the perfective and when to use the imperfective. So we might start by making a distinction between hard rules and easier rules. We will return to this question later.

Developing grammar through the 'explicit teaching' of grammar rules

As in implicit approaches there are many variations on how to teach grammar explicitly. However, one fundamental component is that at some point there is considerable focus on 'language as object'. Instead of focusing on the target element by *using* the language, teachers and learners start talking *about* the language. One possible sequence might be:

1   Start the lesson with an explanation of a grammar rule. Perhaps get the students to write down the rule or draw their attention to where an additional explanation is to be found in the textbook. If the pattern differs from the L1 pattern draw the learners' attention to this difference.
2   Provide lots of example L2 sentences that contain the pattern to which the rule refers. Perhaps ask the learners to translate them into their L1.
3   Listen to a recording in which the pattern occurs frequently and look out for the pattern in some way.
4   Provide learners with sentences where they have to fill in the correct pattern in a sentence or a paragraph. Then go through the answers with them referring to the rule explanation.
5   Ask learners to translate a short L1 text into L2. This forces them to use the target pattern rather than avoiding it.
6   Ask learners to do some free writing which requires them to use the pattern. Correct any mistakes in the text they produce by referring to the rule.

Now I have been deliberately 'extreme' in presenting this explicit learning sequence. One could of course mix some implicit approaches with the explicit ones, but I hope it serves the purpose of demonstrating the fundamental differences. One of the hypotheses behind this approach is that learners can convert their explicit knowledge of the target grammatical element into proceduralised knowledge (for an overview, see DeKeyser, 2007b). This means that gradually, with practice, it becomes automatic and the speaker or writer no longer has to think about the rules or the pattern – it just comes out.

DEALING WITH LEARNER ERROR

One final section before we move on to some research evidence. We need to try to understand what we mean by a mistake and *why* one of our students is making a mistake.

One way to categorise non target-like productions is to divide them up into errors, mistakes and slips. These are just convenient labels of course. We could label 'an error' an incorrect production which is likely to have been caused because the learner has never been exposed (or rarely exposed) to the correct target feature. We can label 'a mistake' an incorrect production which the learners have been exposed to and may even have used in the past. As we have discussed earlier in the section on 'interlanguage' this is not the result of carelessness. When you think about it, it is actually quite difficult to think of a mental process where carelessness is the prime cause. I suppose it *could* be 'I can't be bothered to put the correct ending on this verb so I'll just stick on the first ending that comes to mind'. However, why would that 'first ending' come to mind any more than the 'correct ending'? It is highly likely that the first ending that comes to mind is the one that they think is correct. We could label 'a slip', when the speaker (it is harder to detect in written form) produces an incorrect utterance and then almost immediately self-corrects. Clearly they know the correct form but at some point during the production some other form has competed with it.

There is one other form of 'mistake' (as now defined) which we need to think about. This is when a learner at one time point starts off by producing the correct form and later starts to produce incorrect forms! Why are they going backwards? An explanation that has been provided for this is that of 'U-shaped curves of learning' (Bardovi-Harlig, 2002; Myles *et al.*, 1999). In this explanation a learner may start off with perfect formulations. This is usually because they have committed to memory a set phrase that they have been taught.[1] Gradually they begin to break down that set phrase, to unpack it. The reason for doing this is that the set phrase is too restrictive to express what the speaker wants to say or write. It is at this point that errors might start to occur. But to consider it to be 'going backwards' would be unhelpful. So teachers will need to accept that learners' productions may get worse before they can get better.

A SELECTION OF RESEARCH EVIDENCE

Now we come to the difficult part. What does the research evidence tell us is the best way for learners to make progress with producing correct patterns of the language? It is difficult because it is almost impossible to find convincing studies which have juxtaposed the three approaches to teaching described above and done so, over time, under controlled conditions, and in *real* classrooms!

So what we have is a hotchpotch of studies, some of which have tried to isolate a particular grammatical element, expose participants to two approaches (usually in laboratory conditions) and then measured (usually immediately only, rather than immediately *and some time later*) which approach was more effective.

Norris and Ortega (2000) carried out a meta-analysis[2] of 45 studies (published 1980–1998) covering a range of L2s and reported that some kind of focus-on-form was more beneficial than focus-on-meaning only, although there appeared to be no apparent distinction between implicit and explicit focus-on-form.

However, the authors very honestly concede that these results might be hiding a number of problems and are very careful about making huge claims about language teaching. They admit that most of the studies they reviewed tested the resulting learning via grammar exercises – thus biasing the more explicit approach. Most of the studies were not done in real classrooms. The authors were only able to look at studies which had been published, thus eliminating from their review studies which were possibly not published because no significant differences had been found.

I would add more limitations to this meta-analysis. The vast majority of studies were about adults. We are not told what grammar elements were being studied so we cannot make a judgement about relevance and breadth of grammatical learning. We should also look carefully at the title of this meta-analysis 'effectiveness of L2 instruction' which suggests all sorts of possible desirable outcomes: being able to talk fluently, read comfortably, listen without getting frustrated, produce good quality writing, maybe even becoming highly motivated. However, what the title actually refers to is 'if you teach certain grammatical patterns in a certain way do learners learn these patterns?' – and by which generally is meant, can they do a grammar exercise?

Another meta-analysis was carried out by Spada and Tomita (2010) reporting on 34 studies between 1990 and 2004. They report better results for explicit instruction over implicit for both complex and less complex rules. In this analysis the authors try to take into account some of the problems associated with the Norris and Ortega analysis. Nevertheless here too we find problems. Classroom studies were mainly from a very short time period (2005–2006). Omitting studies from the 1980s biases researchers who might be deliberately attempting to counter the communicative drive of that decade. In most studies the delayed interval (the period between the instruction and the final testing) was very short. From a UK perspective two further limitations: only studies of English as an L2 were considered, and once again the vast majority involved adult learners.

What both these meta-analyses do not tackle is the question of 'at what cost?' What cost to other aspects of language proficiency does a particular teaching approach concerned with grammar development have? In order to answer that question we need much broader and more longitudinal studies.

A different way of asking this 'at what cost' question is to look at the general picture in a number of countries. For example, we might look at how English is taught in Japan in general and see what the general outcomes are. This is of course not scientific but I am told by many Japanese colleagues and Japanese students that learners there are taught very consistently by an explicit grammar approach and there is evidence that Japanese learners of English rank 155th out of 155 countries in TOEFL speaking scores (Hobbs *et al.*, 2010). Now that might just be a coincidence or it may be telling us a greater truth than a meta-analysis.

Let us look at my own selection of studies. Incidentally, I am not claiming any lack of bias here!

A study that is often cited with reference to explicit or implicit grammar teaching is one by Green and Hecht (1992). Although it is now quite old, I think it nevertheless sets the scene for the kinds of investigations that other researchers have carried out or could carry out in the future. It is also one of the few studies dealing with learners below adulthood, which makes it relevant to this volume. The researchers asked a large sample of secondary school students in Germany (studying English as an L2) to correct 12 incorrect sentences and to provide explanations of the rule in question. The sample was divided into 'academic students' and 'less academic students' by virtue of the fact that in Germany students go to different types of schools. The researchers checked that all the rules in question had been taught fairly explicitly to all the students in their previous years of learning. They found that the majority of the students could not explain a rule they had been taught. Although they could not explain that rule, a majority were able to correct most of the sentences. So Green and Hecht concluded that there is not an automatic link between knowledge of a rule and being able to spot correct and incorrect patterns.

Similar research seems to be telling us the same story (see for example, Bialystok, 1979; Frantzen, 1995). There is a gap between learning some aspect of grammar explicitly and being able to use it in a productive task involving speaking or writing. Students may be able to fill in a gap or put the correct ending on a verb but when it comes to producing it spontaneously (or even with some deliberation) they repeatedly make mistakes. Macaro and Graham (2008) gave students in England (16–17-year-olds) on an advanced French course a short story to write based on pictures which obliged them to use the *passé composé*. Despite having been extensively taught this tense at some point during their previous five years of learning, most students struggled to produce correct past tense sentences.

A different result was obtained by Erlam (2003) when considering the teaching of direct object pronouns in French to 14-year-olds in New Zealand. She designed a study whereby one class got explicit teaching and another got implicit teaching of the pattern (she calls it deductive and inductive). She provided them with a series of tests including productive language and found that immediately after the treatment the explicit group outperformed the implicit group. However, at delayed test the explicit group dropped their scores more than the implicit group. Thus it is possible that explicit teaching is more effective in the short term but whether it is more effective in the long term is still open to debate. One problem with this study is that quite a few of the tests used were very explicit-grammar-based thus favouring the explicit approach. We should also note that the direct object pronoun pattern in French is a relatively easy one to explain and it has few exceptions.

The relevance of the research to the UK context

I would like, first, to dispose of two myths regarding the MFL situation in the UK. The first myth is that MFL classrooms are communicative classrooms – by which I mean that most of the lesson is taken up with communicating meaning. In my experience this is simply not the case. A lot of lesson time currently is expended on teaching vocabulary explicitly along with a number of set phrases and asking students to reproduce them, and there is in fact very little focus on developing real communication skills.

The second myth is that students do not know the grammar because they have not been taught it *properly*. Students in many classrooms are indeed taught the rules of the language, required to do practice exercises, and asked to write the rules in the back of their books. This has not led to them being able to use those patterns in real language situations.

Both these myths need to be constantly exploded if we are to make headway with promoting foreign languages among our young and adolescent learners.

In the UK the average amount of lesson time, between the ages of 11 and 16, dedicated to language learning is two hours per week. The immediate reaction to this paucity of exposure to the language might be 'in that case we have to take short-cuts and teach the grammar explicitly'. I certainly believe that the research evidence (what convincing evidence there is) suggests that a diet of 'free conversation', two hours a week, will not easily develop the rule system. On the other hand I am reasonably convinced by the evidence, and my own experience, that simply teaching a grammar rule does not necessarily lead to correct 'free use' of that pattern in conversation or in unsupported writing.

So what is the answer? A number of researchers and commentators have proposed that there is a difference between hard and easy rules, or between rules that have lots of exceptions and those that have very few.

One conclusion for the UK context therefore might be 'don't be afraid to teach easy rules explicitly but be very wary of teaching complex rules explicitly'. I mentioned earlier the study of the *passé composé* (PC) and how surprisingly badly students did in a free writing test. Suzanne Graham and I then tracked over time how students improved with this complicated tense. To convince you that it is a complicated tense try to work out[3] how many mental computations an English learner of French has to go through to arrive at the equivalent (written) verb phrase in French: 'Laura and Louise hurried to the station'. What we found in our study was that the crucial first step towards acquiring (and by that I mean producing without help, dictionary or grammar book) the PC was the insertion of the auxiliary. Once that mental leap (so different from the English) was made, the rest of the rules seemed to come more swiftly. This, and some of the other research cited, would suggest to me that teaching the PC's rules all at once and explicitly is not the most effective way of ensuring progress with the tense.

In the end it all comes down to what you want your learners to achieve and the amount of time that you have to do it in. If you want your learners to make progress with skills but only have a few hours a week in which to develop those skills you simply will not have the time to go into a number of grammatical elements in depth. The returns on your investment (and that of the learners) are just not large enough. However, don't forget that learning doesn't all have to take place in the classroom. One approach might be to say, in the few hours that I have, I am going to focus predominantly on skills with some brief focus on form supporting the development of those skills. This does not mean that outside the classroom learners cannot engage with more formal aspects of language.

Conclusion

A teacher's problem is not what is a good activity and what is a bad activity for the learners to engage in, but prioritising in order to get most out of the time available. Language teachers often have to try to kill two birds with one stone: do a reading comprehension activity and learn some vocabulary as a by-product; do a role-play activity and hope that not only fluency and spontaneity will develop but also some accuracy.

So research evidence is important when considering how to teach, but it has to be analysed, problematised and challenged before being accepted.

Reflective enquiry

1   Write out a list of lots of grammatical elements of the L2 you are teaching or going to teach (e.g. future tense; possessive adjectives). Give the list to as many teachers and trainee teachers that you can and ask them to divide the list into easy and hard rules/patterns.
2   Video-record yourself explaining a rule explicitly and providing examples. Then ask individual students to look at the video and tell you what was going through their heads when you were explaining it.
3   Teach a complex pattern/rule implicitly to one class and explicitly to another (the two classes will need to be very carefully matched for achievement level). Devise a spoken and/or written task which reliably measures whether they have internalised the pattern. Carry out the assessment immediately after the teaching sequence and then some three weeks later.

Further reading

Erlam, R. (2003) 'The effects of deductive and inductive instruction on the acquisition of Direct Object Pronouns in French as a second language', *The Modern Language Journal*, 87(2): 242–260.

Macaro, E. and Graham, S. (2008) 'The development of the passé composé in lower intermediate learners of French', *Language Learning Journal*, 36(1): 5–19.

Myles, F., Mitchell, R. and Hooper, J. (1999) 'Interrogative chunks in French L2: a basis for creative construction?', *Studies in Second Language Acquisition*, 21(1): 49–80.

Notes

1   These are sometimes called formulaic phrases but this can be confusing. The set phrases that students are taught in class are selected for pedagogical purposes (*J'aime* for expressing the function of liking in the first person). Formulaic language ('upside down') exists already in the language community in question and has been arrived at for very different purposes.

2   A meta-analysis is where a reviewer pools all the statistical results of various studies into a single statistical analysis based on effect sizes, that is, how big is the effect of different treatments (in this case, ways of teaching grammar).

3   Or if you don't speak French try to ask someone who does.

Chapter 9

Vocabulary and formulaic language

Where to begin?

Ron Martinez

Introduction

Vocabulary knowledge has been consistently shown to correlate strongly with all language abilities (Alderson, 2005; Schmitt, 2010). In other words, and quite obviously, one needs to know words in the target language in order to listen, read, speak and write – and the more the better. However, students learning a foreign language are not necessarily interested in possessing the same vocabulary size in the L2 as they have in the L1. Instead, what is mostly aspired to is a certain pedagogically meaningful size 'threshold' that affords a given student the ability to perform adequately (or better) as per his or her learning needs. However, just how much is enough? There are hundreds of thousands of words in most languages – where would one begin?

In addressing concerns about his ability to communicate effectively with his players, it was reported in *The Times* (UK)[1] that the manager of England's national football team, Italian Fabio Capello, claimed he only needed to know '100 words of English' to do his job. Unreasonable though that figure may sound to some, he perhaps was not as far off base as the press made his estimate appear. First of all, research would support his assertion that the question of 'how many words do I need to know?' is not answerable by an absolute number but through the follow-up question of 'what do you need to do?' – which is perhaps a particularly relevant question when it comes to applied linguistics and second language education. After all, L2 learners often only need to use the target language in a much narrower range of situations and contexts than native speakers, particularly if they are not living in the country in which the target language is spoken (Kirkpatrick, 2007; Pennycook, 2001; Seidlhofer, 2005). Furthermore, although surely 100 words would not suffice to do much in any language, there has been mounting evidence over the years that while there are hundreds of thousands of words in a language like English, even native speakers only really use and come into contact with a fraction of those words on a day to day basis (Nation, 2001; O'Keeffe *et al.*, 2007). A large part of what the present chapter aims to address is the nature of that 'fraction' that is supposedly used more than the rest, and how it may affect the four language skills (reading, writing, listening and speaking), and therefore how language teaching and the taught syllabus may be affected. By the end of the chapter, it will be shown that there are important elements of vocabulary that are insufficiently accounted for in current language textbooks and national curricula. Outlined first are some of the main concepts central to any discussion of vocabulary, followed by a critical analysis of those concepts as they relate to language pedagogy.

THE 'LEXICAL SPACE': BREADTH, DEPTH AND FLUENCY OF VOCABULARY KNOWLEDGE

According to Zechmeister *et al.* (1995), the average educated adult native speaker of English possesses a receptive knowledge of around 20,000 word families.[2] To arrive at their estimate, the researchers tested students and older adults (n = 112) on 200 'functionally important' words (i.e. entries generally considered 'vocabulary words' [p. 202]) randomly selected from a dictionary. Participants were asked to rate each word from one to five, with a value of five indicating that the participant knew the word well enough to give its definition (p. 204). To verify reported word knowledge, the researchers then administered a multiple-choice test, and found that around 80 per cent of older adults could demonstrate some knowledge of over 20,000 word families.

It is clear, however, that participants merely showed, on a relatively superficial level, the extent of their word knowledge (i.e. how many words), otherwise known as 'breadth' (Figure 9.1).

Although participants in the Zechmeister *et al.* study did demonstrate they knew what the words meant that they had claimed to know, what they in fact demonstrated was knowledge of *a* meaning of each word on some receptive level.[3] For example, the word *chivalry* appeared with the following alternatives on the multiple-choice test (p. 205):

> *a. warfare   b. herb   c. bravery   d. lewdness   e. courtesy*

However, nothing in that test item assesses whether or not participants knew that it is usually men that show chivalry towards women (by cultural convention), and that it can also denote the set of qualities 'expected of a knight'.[4] Nor does the above test item check if participants know the pronunciation of the word. We

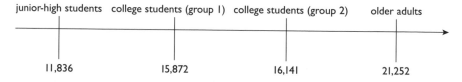

Figure 9.1 Breadth of word knowledge in the Zechmeister *et al.* (1995) study.

cannot know if the participant could use it appropriately in a sentence, or even spell it correctly. And we cannot extrapolate other important knowledge, such as if the candidate knows that *chivalry* is an uncountable noun (i.e. its grammar), or that it can become an adjective by dropping the *-y* ending and adding *-ous* (i.e. its morphology). In other words, the Zechmeister *et al.* (1995) research does tell us something about how many words the participants tested knew (breadth), but provides little insight into the completeness of that knowledge, or *depth* (Figure 9.2).

Beyond the breadth of how many words one knows, and in addition to the depth of one's knowledge of those words, another important dimension of the mental lexicon is how readily one is able to recall and use a word, and the relative ease with which it is used. This notion, which typically involves the speed and accuracy with which a given word can be used by an individual, is known variously as 'automaticity' (e.g. Segalowitz, 2003) and 'fluency' (e.g. Meara, 2002). Altogether, *breadth*, *depth* and *fluency* form a kind of three-dimensional 'lexical space' (Daller *et al.*, 2007), as illustrated in Figure 9.3.

The concept of a lexical space is central to nearly any discussion of vocabulary and the way it is taught, learned and tested. For example, students and teachers should be made aware of the dimensions in Figure 9.3 because, generally speaking, the ability to recognise a word and its meaning is an element of word knowledge that can occur relatively quickly, as when children 'fast map' the meaning of new words they encounter (Heibeck and Markman, 1987), however, that is not

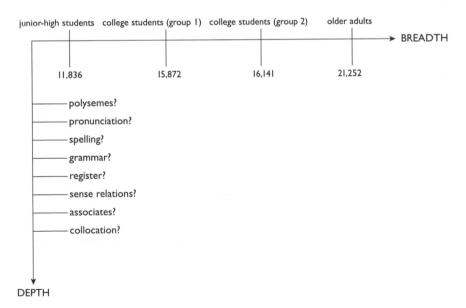

Figure 9.2 Breadth of vocabulary knowledge in Zechmeister *et al.* (1995) study and unknown knowledge depth.

Figure 9.3 The lexical space: dimensions of word knowledge and ability (Daller *et al.*, 2007: 8).

usually the case in the other dimensions of the lexical space (Nation, 2001). The acquisition of vocabulary depth and fluency tends to occur incrementally (Schmitt, 2010: 19), through, for example, multiple exposures to the same word in different contexts (Elley, 1989; Waring and Takaki, 2003; Webb, 2007). Although this incremental process seems to occur largely naturally and subconsciously in the L1 (Hoey, 2005; Nagy *et al.*, 1985), what research suggests is that the same holds for L2 vocabulary acquisition, but to a lesser degree (Laufer, 1998).[5] What seems to be of greater benefit to L2 learners is some kind of form focused instruction to complement the incidental acquisition that may take place outside (or even inside) the classroom (Paribakht and Wesche, 1997; Sonbul and Schmitt, 2010). In both the L1 and L2 learning contexts, however, the benefit of incidental learning or direct teaching of vocabulary will be affected by frequency of exposure, an issue which will be returned to later in this chapter. The take-home message for now, in terms of classroom implications, is that while activity such as extensive reading should definitely be encouraged, one should not rely on the relative vagaries of independent reading alone as a dependable source of steady vocabulary input and growth for most language students to fill that lexical space.

THE CONSTRUCT OF 'WORD'

What counts as a word will obviously influence estimates of vocabulary knowledge and size. For example, estimates of vocabulary size do not generally count how many individual word forms one knows. Take, for example, the very word *word* – which itself can have different meanings. It is reasonable to assume that when an adult native speaker of English knows the word *word*, she or he also knows its plural – *words*. Words and their grammatical inflections (e.g. *do, does, did, doing, didn't*) are called lemmas (Nation, 2001: 7), and a lemma and all its inflections are generally considered to be stored together in the mental lexicon (Aitchison, 1987). Perhaps more controversial, in terms of mental representation, are morphological derivations from a lemma, such as *word → wordless*. Such shifts in form also generally change – to varying degrees – what the word means (Moon, 1987: 89).

Bauer and Nation (1993) claimed that some lemmas have forms created by derivational morphology (i.e. prefixes and suffixes) that should really be grouped together. For example, according to the authors, since words such as *wordy* and *wordless* derive from a known word, those three words – *word, wordy* and *wordless* – are actually part of 'word family':

> From the point of view of reading, a word family consists of a base word and all its derived and inflected forms that can be understood by a learner without having to learn each form separately. [...] The important principle behind the idea of a word family is that once the base word or even a derived word is known, the recognition of other members of the family requires little or no extra effort.
>
> (Bauer and Nation, 1993: 253)

On the basis of the above assertion, Bauer and Nation (ibid.) devised a seven-level model of affixation to systematise what words should be included in a word family, using the following criteria (Nation, 2001: 267):

- frequency (how commonly used the affix is);
- regularity (how much the word changes as a result of the affixation);
- productivity (how usable the affix is on other words); and
- predictability (how transparent/narrow in meaning the affix is).

In Bauer and Nation's model, the lower the level, the more reasonable it is to include a given word in a word family. Therefore, since -*y* and -*less* belong to the 'easiest' stage in the Bauer and Nation classification, it would be safe to assume that *wordy* and *wordless* should be considered part of a one word family, as their recognition requires, reiterating Bauer and Nation's claim, 'little or no extra effort' from a person already familiar with the lemma *word*. At the same time, the concept of a word family adds strength to the rationale for the formal instruction of affixation in a foreign language. For example, if a learner is aware that the suffix -*ría* in Spanish is indicative of a type of shop (*zapato* = shoe, *zapatería* = shoe store; *mueble* = furniture, *mueblería* = furniture store, etc.), then even if a base word ending in -*ría* is unfamiliar to an L2 reader/listener, knowledge of that suffix alone can increase the chances of the learner successfully inferring the meaning of the word.

What is important to bear in mind for the present is that the validity of the word family only holds as long as the inflected or derived forms do not represent too far a departure from the meaning of the base word. So, for example, although the word *cavalo* ('horse') is contained in the word *cavalheiro* ('gentleman'), it is difficult to argue that the suffix *-eiro* would facilitate an accurate guess for a learner of Portuguese who only knows the word *cavalo*.

FREQUENCY

The word 'frequency' as it pertains to vocabulary can actually mean different things – all of which have bearing on the present discussion. 'Frequency' from the perspective of the language learner, for example, can refer to frequency of exposure, i.e. how often that learner reads or hears a word (whether consciously or otherwise). It is a variable that is controlled for in vocabulary-related studies to try to better understand, for example, how many exposures a learner needs on average in order for a word to begin to enter the mental lexicon (e.g. Pellicer-Sanchez and Schmitt, 2010; Rott, 1999). As alluded to in the previous section, frequency of exposure has also been shown to have influence on depth of vocabulary knowledge, at least among native speakers (Lessard-Clouston, 2006).

On the other hand, a lexicographer compiling a learner dictionary might understand 'frequency' to refer to how common, relatively speaking, a given word is – usually (in recent years) according to corpus[6] data. Such information is seen as important in learner dictionaries, and indeed an indication of frequency is often attached to the most common words in those works of reference. Frequency is also one of the ways some lists of the most common words are ranked, such as those in the *Word Frequencies in Written and Spoken English* (Leech *et al.*, 2001) and the *Frequency Dictionary of Contemporary English* (Davies and Gardner, 2010), in which the latter authors state plainly that 'corpus-derived frequencies are still the best current estimate of a word's importance that a learner will come across' (Davies and Gardner, 2010: viii).

Such a data-driven perspective on this type of frequency stands in contrast to what actually happens in language coursebooks, which usually involves the authors merely including vocabulary which 'seems' frequent and useful according to their own instinct, shown to be an unreliable source of frequency information (Alderson, 2007). Moreover, it has also recently been argued that most coursebooks are organised around 'topics' (e.g. food, family, entertainment, clothing, etc.), which are relied upon for the bulk of lexical input. Moreover these topics do not vary greatly (and in fact are often repeated with slight variations from level to level), such that there is very little 'lexical stretching' in coursebook design (Reda, 2003). As a consequence learners receive very little exposure and/or explicit attention to 'mid-frequency vocabulary' (Schmitt and Schmitt, 2012), shown to be vital for reaching a proficiency level at which successful lexical inferencing of unknown vocabulary can occur (Schmitt *et al.*, 2011). Häcker (2008), for example, examined German as a foreign language textbooks published from the 1990s to 2006, and found fault with a method that organises vocabulary around topics:

> [T]he vocabulary of German FL textbooks does not lead to the acquisition of a core vocabulary. The current method of introducing vocabulary in lexical sets is not the most effective way of introducing new words; it suits the teaching method, but does not facilitate the learning process.
>
> (p. 225)

In terms of the present discussion regarding issues of frequency, what is particularly relevant is the natural tendency for shorter, common words to account for the bulk of most texts, with highest-frequency words (e.g. the top 2,000) comprising nearly 80 per cent of the running words (Nation, 2001: 11; O'Keeffe *et al.*, 2007: 32). It is on the basis of this tendency in the frequency distribution of the lexicon that the assumption is made that the most common words are also those most likely to be acquired first and possibly learned naturalistically, through exposure by extensive reading, for example, and listening to people speak the target language (e.g. Krashen, 1989). This supposition, however, is further predicated on the concept of frequency of exposure. Most relevant studies seem to indicate a necessity of six to ten exposures to a new lexical item (in different contexts, in spaced intervals) for acquisition to occur (see Zahar *et al.*, 2001 for a review). Cobb (2007), however, has shown that it takes a very generous diet of naturally occurring input to have a chance at more than six exposures of a given lexical item, in particular at frequencies lower than the 3,000 word-family threshold – arguably the range that might begin to separate lower and intermediate/higher levels of proficiency. In fact, Hill and Laufer (2003) have calculated that a learner would need to read over 8 million words of text in order to go from knowledge of 2,000 words, for example, to 4,000 words. In most cases, one cannot assume a steady listening/reading regimen of thousands of words a week for most students, hence the dilemma of how to foment learning conditions conducive to continuous vocabulary growth that does not depend solely on the vagaries of extensive reading, for example.

VOCABULARY THRESHOLDS

As mentioned in the introduction, while it is clear that the '100 words' Fabio Capello suggested as sufficient to carry out his coaching duties is probably too conservative a figure, it is equally clear that the 20,000 word families some studies have shown native speakers to know is also probably more than most learners need. Therefore, when discussing second language vocabulary learning, the question of *How many words are really necessary in order to…?* arises (e.g. enough to be able to cope in the target country, or to go on to academic study in the target language), otherwise known as 'functional thresholds'. After all, to be able to put a concrete number on the amount of words one needs to know to function in the target language is to be able to set teaching goals, divide proficiency levels and see a proverbial light at the end of the L2 learning tunnel (Schmitt, 2010). However, the answer to that question has also proved somewhat complex, requiring identifying not so much how many words one needs to know in absolute terms, but rather how many words a learner needs to know in order to understand a text in spite of unknown vocabulary.

Basing their assertions mostly on the assumption that 'pleasurable' reading occurs only when a reader knows almost all words in a text, Hirsh and Nation (1992) stipulated the ideal percentage of words known in an unsimplified text at around 98 per cent. To further test this hypothesis, Hu and Nation (2000) gave 66 adult learners studying in New Zealand a relatively short (673 words) fiction text to calculate the relationship between the density of unknown words and reading comprehension. The researchers replaced varying amounts of low frequency words in the text with nonsense words in order to establish a minimum level of reading comprehension. For example, in the 95 per cent coverage version, 5 per cent of the running words were replaced with nonsense words (32 words), and in the 90 per cent coverage version, 10 per cent of the original words were replaced (about 67 words), and so on (p. 410). Following comprehension measures which included multiple-choice tests and cued written recall, the authors concluded that when participants read the version in which 20 per cent of the text consisted of nonsense words, no instance of 'adequate comprehension' occurred (p. 415). ('Adequate comprehension', according to Hu and Nation's criteria, meant accurately answering at least 12 out of 14 questions correctly on the multiple-choice measure and 70 out of 124 on the written recall questions – arbitrary numbers by the authors' own admission.) When 5 per cent of the running words were nonsense words, less than half of all participants achieved adequate comprehension. Since it was only at 100 per cent text coverage (i.e. all words understood) that the vast majority of participants showed minimally acceptable reading comprehension, the authors postulate that 'around 98 per cent coverage' (p. 419) is what is probably needed for learners to gain adequate comprehension. Nation (2006) estimates that knowledge of at least 8,000 to 9,000 words is needed to reach that coverage. However, again, what has been so far underexplored is what the exact nature of that 'knowledge' and those 'words' is.

A MORE CRITICAL LOOK

As mentioned in the previous section, current research suggests that 8,000–9,000 words can provide around 98 per cent coverage of most texts (Nation, 2006). However, Nation's recommendations are for a '8,000–9,000 word-family vocabulary' (p. 79), which does not necessarily mean knowing 8,000 *words*. In the lists Nation and other researchers have used to calculate word knowledge, a word can include a base form and over 80 derivational affixes (Nation, 2006: 66), resulting in 'some large word families, especially among the high-frequency words' (ibid.). A word like *nation*,[7] for example, may include a word family of over 20 separate words, which means that 8,000 words in the lists Nation and others refer to may actually translate to well over 30,000 separate words (Schmitt, 2008: 332). Although some research suggests that native speakers often group morphologically related words together in the mental lexicon (Bertram *et al.*, 2000; Nagy *et al.*, 1989), the same may not apply to non-native learners.

Schmitt and Meara (1997) have demonstrated that language students do not often readily know the derived forms of words or their associates in the same way an L1 user typically does. The researchers gave a word association and affixation test to three groups of Japanese learners of English, and received some surprising results. Although the learners performed adequately on the inflection suffixes (59 per cent correct), they only managed to get 15 per cent of derivation suffixes right (p. 26). In a separate study, Hay (2001) has shown that when a derived form is more frequent than its base form (e.g. *difference = differ + ence*), the affixation becomes less transparent, and the semantic meaning more distant. In other words, it is possible that many of the derived words currently included in word families should really be listed as separate words for pedagogical purposes. However, current word lists have another potential limitation beyond what constitutes a word family: word frequency lists only list individual words. For example, one could argue that a word like *llevar* ('take') is one of the most common and basic words in Spanish, and therefore it is a word that should be taught and learned early on, but more recent research is showing that many of the commonest words in a language are actually merely tips of phraseological icebergs (Figure 9.4).

Sinclair (1991) posited the notion that most texts are not, in fact, composed entirely of individual words, but also of formulaic sequences that should not be broken down into separate parts. He called this theory the 'idiom principle': 'The principle of idiom is that a language user has available to him or her a large number of semi-preconstructed phrases that constitute single choices, even though they might appear to be analyzable into segments' (p. 110).

However, such 'semi-preconstructed phrases' have generally not been included in wordlists or the research into vocabulary thresholds.

FREQUENCY REVISITED

There is a fairly pervasive claim in the existing literature on vocabulary learning that it is pedagogically worthwhile to focus on the 2,000 to 3,000 most common words of a language (e.g. Coady, 1997; Laufer, 1991; Nation, 2004; Nation and Waring, 1997; Stæhr, 2008), the implication generally being that encouraging

Figure 9.4 An underlying complexity of phraseology.

students to learn these words will somehow facilitate accessing meaning in texts. Although knowledge of 2,000 words will only provide around 80 per cent text coverage (Nation, 2001: 11; O'Keeffe *et al.*, 2007: 32), the purported advantage is that there is a greater pedagogical 'payoff' in learning those very frequent words:

> There is an obvious payoff for learners of English in concentrating initially on the 2000 most frequent words, since they have been repeatedly shown to account for at least 80% of the running words in any written or spoken text.
>
> (Read, 2004: 148)

Indeed, Read is correct: that figure does generally reflect the research. However, corpus-based research also tells us that those most common words that 'do most of the work' (O'Keeffe *et al.*, 2007: 32) also tend to have 'less of a clear and independent meaning' (Sinclair, 1991: 114). Hence, the suggestion that there is a pedagogical benefit in focusing on the commonest words in a language in order to allow for maximal comprehension of a text, for example, may in fact be somewhat misleading. Those frequency figures, and the lexical complexity that may underlie them, should be given more careful consideration. According to Sinclair, not only are the most frequent words more prone to polysemy (i.e. multiple meanings for the same word form), but they also are prone to lose even their 'basic meaning' because they tend to feature in formulaic sequences:

For example, we think of verbs like *see*, *give*, *keep*, as having each a basic meaning: we would probably expect those meanings to be commonest. However, the database tells us that *see* is commonest in uses like *I see, you see, give* in uses like *give a talk* and *keep* in uses like *keep warm*.

(Sinclair, 1987: vii)

A good example of very frequent individual words combining to form independent, complex meanings is the phrasal verb in English. Consider the verb *pick*, which occurs 14,274 times in the British National Corpus (BNC), but 9,997 of those occurrences are as a phrasal verb, or precisely 70 per cent of all instances (Gardner and Davies, 2007: 348). Add to that number a whole host of other idiomatic expressions in which *pick* occurs, such as *take your pick, pick a lock* and *pick and choose*, and it is likely that *pick* recombines with other very common words to form separate multiword units of meaning over 80 per cent of the time. The verb *pick* is clearly the tip of its own phraseological iceberg, but it is obviously not alone in exhibiting this behaviour, and is improbable that such a phenomenon does not somehow affect reading comprehension.

Martinez and Murphy (2011) developed a two-part test of reading comprehension, with the texts in each part having perfect lexical symmetry (i.e. constructed using the exact same words), sampled from the 2,000 most frequent words in the BNC – the same word threshold mentioned in the previous section as widely perceived as useful for language learners to focus on. The main difference between the two parts of the test was that, although both parts were written using the exact same high-frequency words, the arrangement of those words in one part was such that they often formed formulaic expressions of varying degrees of compositionality. The learners were required to answer true/false questions about each text, as well as assess how well they believed they had understood the text on a self-reported rating scale. The results show that the participants not only vastly underperformed on the measure of reading comprehension when the text contained formulaic sequences, they also tended to significantly overestimate how well they comprehended the reading passage as a function of the very common words contained in the multiword expressions which they often did not recognise. Instead, they tended to focus on the individual words – words they thought they should know because of how 'common' they are. What the Martinez and Murphy study would seem to provide evidence for is an apparently unattended need for students – and teachers – to move beyond the prevailing concept of 'vocabulary learning = learning lots of words'.

Conclusion

We therefore return to our original question. It has so far been argued in the present chapter that a view of vocabulary as constituting the incremental learning of words is probably not pedagogically useful. While it is true that, vaguely speaking, functional thresholds of vocabulary do exist, thus replacing any need to strive to possess the same vocabulary size in the L2 as the L1, it would not be productive to simply try to memorise the 3,000 most common words in the target language, for example. As shown in this chapter, the more common those words are, the more likely they are to be steeped in complexity, such as polysemy and collocational behaviour. On the other hand, it has also been shown that one cannot usually depend on incidental learning of lexical items alone to realise sizeable vocabulary gains in the L2 (Cobb, 2007). Since lexical inferencing (i.e. the guessing of unknown words) has, at best, been shown to only be effective when no more than 1 out of 20 words is unknown in any stretch of text (Liu and Nation, 1985), the success rate of effective acquisition of new lexis by incidental means only appears reliably high once a sizeable lexicon in the L2 (i.e. at least 5,000 words) has already been attained.

The most practical solution for language educators is to view vocabulary acquisition in the same fashion as language acquisition in general: sensitive to early input and interaction. Since incidental learning of vocabulary really seems to mostly benefit those who have already reached higher levels of proficiency, language educators should focus on a programme that provides generous guidance and explicit focus at the early stages of learning in hope of providing the necessary bootstrapping for later, more autonomous, vocabulary learning. This early input should encourage an awareness-raising of how common words students might think they know are actually words that resemble other words, or mean something different from the canonical meaning they are familiar with (Laufer, 1989b; Nassaji, 2003). Both students and teachers tend to focus on the learning of 'new words', but as has been discussed in the present chapter, there are many words that are actually components of multiword expressions (Martinez and Schmitt, 2012), and these expressions will often go unnoticed by students when encountering those items due to a mistaken belief that since they already 'know' the individual words that they should also comprehend the text as a whole. The explicit attention, therefore, in any early L2 language programme should not be on the constant addition of new words alone, but also on the constant revisiting of words students already 'know'. The language teacher should take it upon her/himself, especially at the early stages of learning, to focus on building vocabulary depth. How can this be achieved? As shown in Waring and Takaki (2003), although incidental exposure has not been shown to be a particularly efficient way to learn new words, extensive reading does seem to strengthen and enrich partially known vocabulary (or, put another way, words students think they already know but actually do not). What therefore seems like a valid approach to vocabulary instruction is to encourage naturalistic exposure to the L2, but not to expect it to help make sizeable gains in vocabulary breadth, but rather as a builder of vocabulary depth. The teacher's job, again, particularly in the early stages, should be on developing those tools amongst students that will build awareness of the components of vocabulary depth, such as knowing a word's phonology, synonymy and phraseology. This can be achieved through the guided use of dictionaries in the classroom, for example, and even internet search engines that will show the various contexts in which a word can appear (and which in turn can affect the meaning of the item in question). Since it is the teacher – it is assumed – who already possesses knowledge of the extent of the depth of any given lexical item, it should be the teacher who offers early and consistent intervention at every given opportunity to raise awareness of the lexical complexity of words, particularly the most common ones.

Although it is probably true that Fabio Capello really does need more than 100 words to carry out his coaching duties, in the end, if the depth of knowledge of those 100 words is extensive enough, he may not be that far off after all.

Reflective enquiry

1   Has this chapter challenged your beliefs about teaching vocabulary? Discuss with a more experienced colleague the implications for teaching, monitoring and giving feedback to students about their use of vocabulary.
2   Video record two consecutive lessons with one class of students. Watch and listen to the recording. Is there a difference in the vocabulary you use when teaching and your students use in the lesson? Compare this vocabulary with that in the textbook (if applicable). Are there certain times in the lesson when you use more vocabulary? What does this tell you about your approach to teaching vocabulary? What are your strengths? What further opportunities could you create for teaching vocabulary?
3   Discuss the results of the audio recording with your students. What are their views about how and when they learn vocabulary best? Do all students learn vocabulary in the same way? What vocabulary do they feel would be useful and why?

Further reading

Martinez, R. and Schmitt, N. (2012) 'A phrasal expressions list', *Applied Linguistics*, 33(3): 299–320.

Martinez, R. and Murphy, V. (2011) 'Effect of frequency and idiomaticity on second language reading comprehension', *TESOL Quarterly*, 45(2): 267–290.

Schmitt, N. and Schmitt D. (2012) 'A reassessment of frequency and vocabulary size in L2 vocabulary teaching', *Language Teaching*, doi: 10.1017/S0261444812000018.

Notes

1   29 March 2011.
2   A word family consists of a headword, its inflections and other derived forms that still retain most of the original semantic meaning of the headword.
3   Rating knowledge of a word as a five in the Zechmeister *et al.* (1995) study meant the participant claimed to be able to actually write a definition for the

word, which would indicate a level of productive knowledge. However, this assertion was never followed up with actual testing of that ability.

4   As defined in the Macmillan English Dictionary (Rundell and Fox, 2007: 250).

5   There can be many reasons for this difference (e.g. age, working memory limitations), but one that is widely accepted is the fact that one is exposed to the L1 usually on a daily basis when growing up, and therefore hears and reads many of the same words again and again. Since language is considered to be an interconnected network (Hudson, 2007; Meara, 2009), the connections are often made stronger and at a faster rate in the L1 because the activation of one word also strengthens the network to which it is connected in the mental lexicon.

6   A corpus in the present chapter will be taken to mean a collection of texts that are analysable by computer.

7   **nation**: *national, nationally, nationwide, nations, nationalism, nationalisms, internationalism, internationalisms, internationalisation, nationalist, nationalistic, nationalistically, internationalist, internationalists, nationalise, nationalised, nationalising, nationalisation, nationalisations, nationhood* (Nation, 2006: 67).

Chapter 10

Cultural awareness

Should it be taught? Can it be taught?

Mairin Hennebry

Introduction

This chapter examines the relationship between language and culture, before considering the meaning of cultural awareness in the context of language teaching, and the ways in which it is represented in policy and practice as exemplified in national curricula for language teaching. An exploration of the teacher's voice in research studies completes this exposition.

It has been argued that culture is the marginalised sister of language. Byram *et al.* (1994) suggest that theoretical approaches to language teaching show appreciation of the target culture only as a means to support the development of linguistic proficiency. Perhaps compounding this problem is the representation of two distinct approaches to the teaching of culture through language. The first approach, high culture, refers to the teaching of the art, literature, history, etc. of the target culture. This approach is perhaps viewed as more traditional and has received little attention in the literature. The second approach refers to a development of Intercultural Communicative Competence (ICC). Within this approach, considerably more popular in the literature, culture is reconceptualised as a dynamic construct evolving around a shared way of life. The focus here is on attitudes and behaviours, the understanding of which relies on skills development rather than knowledge acquisition. Pedagogically ICC offers some advantages since it does not require a specific knowledge base from either student or teacher. Perhaps in part due to this, but also because of an emphasis on community cohesion, ICC has been more popular in policy documentation both at national and European level.

However, an essential element of ICC is the need for critical evaluation of one's own and other cultures. In turn, critical thinking requires domain knowledge about which to think critically. Arguably this is the contribution that high culture can make, whereby learners build a knowledge base about the target culture, which they learn to evaluate through the application of the principles of ICC. Such a dual approach might go some way to bridging the current dichotomy between high culture and ICC.

The teaching of culture through language in mainstream classrooms has yet to be fully and systematically integrated. Consideration of this matter, however, is essential in light of the contribution that cultural understanding and intercultural communication can make to social cohesion and in turn to democratic citizenship at national, European and global levels.

CULTURE AND LANGUAGE

The relationship between language and culture can be conceptualised from a communicative and a social perspective. Language is the primary tool for preserving and transmitting culture, 'linking individuals into communities of shared identity' (Phillipson, 1992: 79). Within communities, language defines boundaries that unify speakers as members of a single speech community. Language acts as a tool for social identification providing linguistic markers used to implement social stratification (Saville-Troike, 2003). It is instrumental in socialisation processes, offering the means through which we manage political, economic and social structures, outwardly express emotion and verbalise our thoughts. Crystal (1997) adds that social development and the perpetuation of culture relies on the preservation of history and a knowledge base for future generations through the medium of language.

Two educational implications stand out: language teaching has a unique role to play in the development of cultural and intercultural understanding; and, intentionally or otherwise, the foreign language teacher introduces the learner not simply to a new language but to another sociopolitical and cultural system. The extent to which language teachers consider it their task to fulfil the role of what Sercu (2006) terms the 'foreign language and intercultural competence teacher' will decisively impact on learners' engagement with the new culture.

The nineteenth and twentieth centuries saw rapid innovation in second language teaching, no doubt due to the rate of industrialisation and later globalisation, creating increased demand for communication across linguistic communities, moving gradually away from the traditional grammar-translation methods that did not address the purposes for which language learners were now required to communicate. This development in teaching approaches was accompanied by increased recognition of the need for cultural understanding, informing culturally appropriate language use, thus fostering effective cross-cultural communication.

The need for cross-cultural understanding is not new. As long as there have been civilised societies there has been a need to select appropriate ambassadors of one linguistic or cultural group to another and this has always been at the heart of successful diplomatic relationships (Byram, 1997). What is new is the increased accessibility to interactions between linguistic and cultural communities to those outside the diplomatic or professional fields. This expansion has caused national and supranational bodies to outline a need for education that equips language learners for effective communication based on cross-cultural understanding (e.g.

the Nuffield Language Inquiry, 2000; the House of Lords European Union Committee, 2005; Commission of the European Communities, 2008).

This chapter is concerned with the broader sense of language learning as going beyond linguistic proficiency and permitting learners access to the culture for the development of positive communication between cultural communities. The teaching of culture through language has fallen into two general approaches; that of teaching 'high' culture and that of seeking to develop ICC. Kramsch (1995: 84) offers a helpful way of understanding these two main conceptualisations of culture as relating to language. The first focuses on the way social groups represent themselves and others through what she terms their 'material productions'; 'works of art, literature, social institutions, or artefacts of everyday life, and the mechanisms for their reproduction and preservation through history'. The second refers to 'the attitudes and beliefs, ways of thinking, behaving and remembering shared by members of that community' (Nostrand, 1989: 51 cited in Kramsch, 1995). The first has given rise to an approach to the study of culture relying on a tradition of texts, of understanding the present and imagining the future in light of the past, arguably akin to a 'high' culture approach. The second leads to observation and the gathering of data, to understanding the present by viewing current events in light of their social diversity and their relation to other contemporary events, more closely related to an ICC approach.

CULTURE IN THEORY

'High' culture, sometimes referred to as 'Culture with a capital C', reflects traditional understanding, implying the teaching of literature, the arts, music and so on, of the target country. This approach to cultural awareness traces back to the very beginnings of language learning. Until early in the eighteenth century, foreign language learning in the European context was largely confined to the learning of Latin, primarily seen as a means of developing intellectual capabilities; it was taught through a focus on grammar and rhetoric. The eighteenth century saw the introduction of modern foreign language (MFL) teaching taught very much through the same approaches previously applied to the teaching of Latin. Heavy emphasis was placed on an understanding of Culture. The research literature has given little attention to this conceptualisation of cultural awareness.

Intercultural and cultural understanding can be viewed as precursors to ICC, a concept largely attributed to Michael Byram, bearing associations to the developing field of critical pedagogy in language teaching. Essentially the model of ICC offers a systematic way of understanding the concept as well as developing pedagogies that address it. ICC is the area on which the literature has primarily focused.

The model of ICC is based on a reconceptualisation of culture, from an emphasis on history, literature, philosophy and the arts to a definition of culture as a dynamic, shared way of life, inextricably linked to people as agents of social change, conceivably aligning itself with the second approach identified by Kramsch. Byram *et al.* (2002: 5, original emphasis) propose that the intercultural dimension of language teaching should aim to develop

> *intercultural speakers* or *mediators* who are able to engage with complexity and multiple identities and to avoid the stereotyping which accompanies perceiving someone through a single identity. It is based on perceiving the interlocutor as an individual whose qualities are to be discovered, rather than as a representative of an externally ascribed identity.

'High' culture is seen as presenting that 'externally ascribed identity'. Instead the focus shifts to learners developing an understanding of multiple identities to be discovered through interaction.

In seeking to operationalise ICC, Byram suggests a model based on five *Savoirs* represented in Figure 10.1.

In his volume *Teaching and Assessing Intercultural Communicative Competence* (1997), Byram offers a detailed explanation of the five *Savoirs*. Notably, Culture is not included in the model; rather, the emphasis is on interaction skills and what might be termed socialisation.

This idea of ICC leaves its mark on national curricula for modern language teaching. Perhaps a key strength is that it makes considerable strides in clarifying the teaching of cultural awareness. Byram's model offers a foothold for teachers to design pedagogies equipping language learners for engaging in meaningful

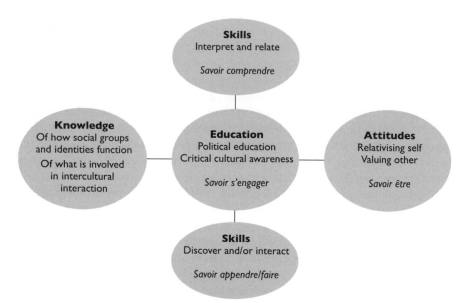

Figure 10.1 Byram's model of Intercultural Communicative Competence.

and productive dialogue furthering intercultural understanding. The European Commission has implicitly adopted this understanding of the aims of language teaching, seen to underpin active citizenship and to promote cohesion in a multicultural and plurilingual society.

At the core of the five *Savoirs* lies an ability to relate and consider other perspectives. Willingham (2007: 8) proposes that critical thinking entails 'seeing both sides of an issue, being open to new evidence that disconfirms your ideas'. Thus the overlap between critical thinking and Byram's model of ICC is clear. The link is strengthened through Willingham's suggestion that the critical thinker should also be self-directed, should identify situations that call for critical thinking and engage in such thinking independently. Thus, in developing ICC, teachers would seek to equip learners with the tools they will need to self-direct in this aspect. The field of cognitive science indicates that critical engagement cannot be separated from domain knowledge since, in order to think critically, the thinker needs not only the meta-cognitive strategies that allow them to know when and how to think critically, but crucially the thinker needs also the domain knowledge about which to think critically. As such, only the combination of the two could lead to a complete cognitive model of critical thinking. Despite this, more 'Western' educational approaches seem to favour style and form of argumentation rather than content, reinforcing an incomplete cognitive model of critical thinking (Biggs, 2003; Egege and Kutieleh, 2003). In order for learners to critically evaluate their own culture and that of others, they arguably need knowledge of both cultures and of how the values and beliefs that they are called on to evaluate have been shaped. In principle then, perhaps a development of an ICC approach integrating Culture or 'high' culture might be more fruitful than one or other approach alone. In other words, if culture is indeed dynamic and evolving, in order to truly understand a culture we need to understand the social, political and economic processes that have brought it to the point it is at today. Conversely, a culture arguably expresses itself through its art, media, music, literature, creations, inventions and so on, such that being unaware of these expressions would imply an incomplete understanding of the cultural community. In turn, such awareness would provide the content base from which to develop critical evaluation of cultural practices.

To understand the current emphasis on ICC, it is helpful to consider two key pragmatic concerns: the question of what to teach, since the Culture associated with any country is vast, therefore, trying to determine what should be taught and what not is ostensibly a difficult task. The challenge is compounded in the case of the English language where the question of which culture needs also to be considered. The same argument might be extended to any language representing more than one cultural community (e.g. French, Spanish, German, Mandarin etc.). Thus, in a helpful practical guide for teachers on developing the intercultural dimension in language teaching, Byram *et al.* (2002) propose that ICC can never be completely acquired. They argue that because of the challenges outlined above, it is not possible to anticipate all the knowledge learners might need in interacting with people of other specific cultures. Indeed they see attempts at such preparation as a shortcoming of subjects such as *Civilisation* in the French curriculum and *Landeskunde* in the German school system. It is this rationale that seems in part to underpin the conceptualisation of knowledge in an ICC model as '[Knowledge (Savoirs)] of social groups and their products and practices in one's own and in one's interlocutor's country, and of the general processes of societal and individual interaction' (p. 8).

On the one hand this approach may provide comfort for teachers who have not had exposure to the target culture or who lack confidence in their own cultural awareness. On the other hand, while in theory the model does encourage taking learners beyond linguistic competence, the outworking of ICC could very quickly be reduced into no more than current forms of communicative language teaching that do little to develop cultural awareness.

The case of the European dimension is different in that it is a concept that was developed in response to a growing need to engage European citizens. Introduced in 1993, this new dimension was intended to filter through all aspects of school education. It was considered that the role of language teaching in this regard was to develop in learners an understanding of other cultures that would encourage them to foster positive interactions with those of other European countries, thus contributing to a cohesive European community; 'Languages are also the key to knowing other people. Proficiency in languages helps to build up the feeling of being European with all its cultural wealth and diversity and of understanding between the citizens of Europe' (European Commission, 1995: 47).

Much of the literature argues that through developing an understanding and appreciation of other ways of life, the intercultural aspect of language teaching makes an essential contribution to education for democratic citizenship, both at national and European level (e.g. Byram, 1992; Breidbach, 2002). Citizenship and language learning share the goals of addressing learners' identities and promoting and developing skills for communication and participation, making them ideal companions (Osler and Starkey, 2005). However, addressing learners' identities is also very much a cultural matter. Our identity is tightly wrapped up in our culture and our understanding of others' identities. Indeed, the European Commission continues to support the view of language teaching as making a unique contribution to the development of European citizenship (Commission of the European Communities, 2008).

In summary, the literature focuses primarily on the development of cultural awareness through the skills-based approach of ICC. The role of Culture is seen as problematic in its breadth while ICC emphasises the individual nature of culture and the skills of understanding, evaluating and relativising. Drawing on cognitive science might suggest that this approach, while no doubt a positive development from the exclusive teaching of Culture, may be incomplete in its neglect of the crucial role of knowledge as a foundation to all forms of critical engagement and evaluation. Sercu (2006) suggests that it is now a commonplace assertion that foreign language teachers should teach not only communicative competence but also ICC and indeed this seems to be true of the literature. The next section considers the issue of cultural awareness in practice.

CULTURE IN THE NATIONAL CURRICULUM

The integration of culture manifests itself in different forms through the national curricula of the various European countries. Examples have been selected from Europe in order to allow the reader to contextualise the previous discussion of recommendations for the role of language teaching in the development of European citizenship. Consideration is given to examples of secondary curricula during the common years of compulsory language learning.

Table 10.1 shows the general aims and objectives in four of the five examples as tending towards a conceptualisation of culture as ICC. We see, for instance, reference to comparison of similarities and differences between cultures; developing an appreciation of one's own culture and that of the target language, critical evaluation through being able to see another's perspective. In some cases there is a 'teaching Culture' approach. In the case of France, for instance, there is specific reference to history and geography. Finland includes basic knowledge of one's own culture and the culture of the target country as 'core content'. It is one of the few countries to go one step further, including cultural skills as a descriptor of 'good performance at the end of the sixth grade'. The importance attributed to acquiring cultural skills is less evident in other curricula. In the case of Ireland and England, the phrasing suggests a more optional approach, such that England's national curriculum suggests that developing an appreciation of the richness and diversity of *other cultures COULD include different aspects of other cultures* and enabling students to *recognise that there are different ways of seeing the world* does not equate to students knowing what those other ways may be. Meanwhile the Irish curriculum does not go beyond the general aims and objectives in its inclusion. On the other hand, by referring to possibilities for pupils to directly access the culture and to participate in social and cultural activities which may involve some use of the target language, it encourages experiential forms of learning highlighted by Byram and colleagues as being particularly effective for the development of ICC. The table shows general support for the idea that language and culture go hand in hand. It needs, however, to be contextualised through the voices of learners and teachers, in order to reflect on the extent to which this positioning of culture compares in practice.

Table 10.1 The inclusion of culture in selected national curricula for foreign language teaching in Europe.

	France	Ireland	Spain	England	Finland
General aims and objectives	Students should be aware of similarities and differences that exist between their own culture and that of the target country and should learn to be open to changing their perspective of each.	To give pupils an awareness of another culture, and thus a more objective perspective of their own culture; To give pupils the possibility of access to sources of information, culture enrichment and entertainment through the target language; To encourage and equip pupils to consider participating in social and cultural activities which may involve some use of the target language.	(The general aims here refer to the Common European Framework for Language learning but make no reference to culture).	The study of languages should include: Learning about different countries and cultures; Comparing pupils' own experiences and perspectives with those of people in countries and communities where the target language is spoken.	The tasks of the instruction are to accustom the pupils to using their language skills and educate them in understanding and valuing how people live in other cultures too… As an academic subject, a foreign language is a cultural and skill subject. In grades 3–6: The pupil is to realise that languages and cultures are different, but not different in value.

Specific references to culture	Sociocultural contents	Key concepts	Objectives
There are no more specific references to culture in the curriculum at the Junior cycle. At the time of writing, MFL at the Senior cycle is under review. [During the sixth and fifth years] students learn to tell and describe through the medium of a variety of authentic materials (songs, advertisements, film extracts, stories, poetry, sayings, etc.). [Students] learn about the main historical events and geographical landmarks.	Pupils should acquire an awareness of the society and culture of the communities in which the target language is spoken… The following topics will be considered in the language learning process: Daily life (festivals, timetables, etc.). Living conditions (home, work, etc.). Personal relations (social structures and relationships between the members of the linguistic community). Values, beliefs and behaviours (institutions, art, humour, etc.). Body language (gestures, visual contact, etc.). Social conventions (behavioural conventions and taboos). Ritual habits (celebrations, ceremonies, etc.).	**Intercultural understanding:** (1) Appreciating the richness and diversity of other cultures. (2) Recognising that there are different ways of seeing the world, and developing an international outlook. **Explanatory note:** **Intercultural understanding:** [It] provides unique opportunities for pupils to explore national identities and become aware of both similarities and contrasts between the cultures of different countries, including their own. **Other cultures:** This could include different aspects of other cultures, such as everyday life, social customs, school life, festivals and events of national importance. **Different ways of seeing the world:** These include religious beliefs, social customs, traditions, values, attitudes towards other countries and reactions to world events.	**Cultural skills:** The pupil will get to know the culture of the target culture and will gain a preliminary introduction to the similarities and differences between that culture and Finnish culture. Learn to communicate with representatives of the target language culture in everyday situations, in a manner natural to that culture. **Core contents:** Situations and subject areas from the perspectives of the language regions of the pupil's language and the language being studied. Basic knowledge of one's own culture and the culture of the target language, possibly including the target language culture in Finland, depending on the language. **Description of good performance at the end of the sixth grade:** **Cultural skills:** The pupils will know the main contents of, and key similarities and differences between the culture of their own language and the target language. Be able to interact with speakers of the target language in simple everyday situations.

Sources: Ministère Education Nationale (2012); Irish National Council for Curriculum and Assessment (2012); Ministerio de Educación y Ciencia (2007); Department for Education (2011); Finnish National Board of Education (2004).

CULTURE IN PRACTICE

Given the European context, a number of studies on cultural awareness published during the 1980s–1990s might be attributed to historical events, including the expansion of the European Union and increased globalisation. The particular focus at the time of the 'communicative language teaching' approach, calling for a view of language teaching for real communication, might also have borne an influence on the research field. A resurgence of interest now is possibly in part attributable to an increased need to re-engage young people in social and political processes that cross cultural and linguistic borders. Other contributing factors may be the increasing realisation that communicative language teaching, despite its emphasis on language for real communication, has not engendered language learners who are able to engage in positive and effective cross-cultural dialogue, to the extent that was envisaged, while the dwindling numbers of school exchanges and language assistants in some countries may raise concerns as to a reduction in possible direct sources of cultural knowledge.

The number of empirical studies in the field is limited. A considerable proportion of the available studies seem to favour a theoretical or discursive approach. Where empirical studies have been conducted they are largely of a descriptive nature. Studies that examine the issues in a school rather than higher education settings are unusual. Those that do exist focus often on contexts outside Europe. The European dimension discussed earlier remains a largely under-researched area, particularly for the relationship between European citizenship and language teaching. Thus, much of the discussion of cultural awareness in language teaching lacks as yet an evidence base.

A number of key empirical studies in the school setting stand out in this sparsely populated field. As a means of focusing the discussion, the following review concentrates on studies that explicitly examine the role of language teaching and its associations with cultural awareness.

In the early 1990s Europe was experiencing a time of considerable geopolitical change. In the context of and seemingly motivated by these developments and the opportunities and challenges that they would present, a number of studies took up the task of investigating the perceptions of teachers as to the teaching of a cultural, even at times a European dimension, in language lessons. One such study was conducted by Byram and Risager (1999), investigating the relationship between language teaching and the cultural dimension within Denmark and England, where questionnaires and interviews with modern language teachers took place. Both countries were considered Eurosceptic at the time. The study suggested that despite the apparent national Euroscepticism, teachers in both countries were positively disposed to the introduction of a European cultural dimension to the curriculum, being concerned about the lack of European identity they perceived among their learners. However, the study raised practical challenges, emphasising the need for school management structures that were equally well disposed and that would offer the necessary support. A notable 69 per cent of the teachers in England indicated that they felt ill-equipped for the task of teaching a cultural dimension in language lessons since their initial teacher training had not offered preparation for the task.

In fact, a number of studies reveal a similar dichotomy between a positive attitude among teachers and the apparent obstacles that lie in the way of a cultural approach to language teaching. Adopting an approach akin to ICC, Starkey (2007) proposes that an additional challenge facing modern language teachers is the persistent tendency for available teaching materials to present the target culture as exotic in an attempt to make it exciting and appealing to learners. The author proposes that such materials reinforce stereotypes and encourage a world view that places the 'unproblematic we in opposition to the exotic other' (p. 58).

Starkey's paper presents data gathered between 1999 and 2002 through teacher interviews with modern language teachers working in the UK. Once again evidence suggested that teachers were eager to teach intercultural competence with particular emphasis on their students disassociating being monolingual from being mono-cultural, endorsing the ICC principle of understanding multiple identities. The study reports the difficulties the participants had, when faced with xenophobia among their students and the compounding issues such as inappropriate syllabuses and textbooks, which continued to address topics such as daily life and routines, stressing differences.

In 2005, Sercu and colleagues published a study focusing on foreign language teachers and the teaching of intercultural competence. The study was conducted in seven countries (Belgium, Sweden, Mexico, Spain, Greece, Poland and Bulgaria) and consisted of questionnaire data provided by MFL teachers in the seven countries. Teachers in the study were asked a series of questions which, in part, sought to examine their views on the teaching of intercultural competence, and whether they felt this would have a positive effect on their pupils, whether they believed such teaching should be confined to MFL or should be cross-curricular and whether they thought that the linguistic competence of the students mattered in this regard. The majority of teachers in Sercu's study were willing to teach intercultural competence but were not convinced of the effect this would have on their pupils. They also felt that such teaching would be dependent on the linguistic competence of their students and showed a tendency to prioritise linguistic competence over ICC, thus offering support to Byram's critique.

A recent study bringing several of these themes together, focused on the impact of formal modern language instruction for adolescent Europeans on developing active European citizenship. As part of the study, data was gathered from 19 language teachers in secondary schools in England, Ireland, France and Spain, to examine their perspectives on teaching the European dimension. The data were gathered through semi-structured interviews with the teachers in their native language. Table 10.2 offers a summary of the teacher sample.

Table 10.2 Summary of teaching experience distributed across schools and countries.

Country	Inner city	Years of teaching experience	Rural	Years of teaching experience
England	Nottingham	Teacher 1: 30 Teacher 2: 15	Oxfordshire	Teacher 1: 20 Teacher 2: 10 Teacher 3: 13
France	Paris banlieue	Teacher 1: 36 Teacher 2: 33	Boulogne-sur-Mer	Teacher 1: 3 Teacher 2: 32
Spain	Madrid	Teacher 1: 31 Teacher 2: 2 Teacher 3: 30	Peñaranda de Bracamonte	Teacher 1: 15 Teacher 2: 28
Ireland	Cork	Teacher 1: 12 Teacher 2: 18 Teacher 3: 20	Ballincollig	Teacher 1: 10 Teacher 2: 19

Teachers in the sample commonly cited their passion for the country and the culture as their motivation for entering the profession. This in itself may help explain the overall positive tendency displayed in the research field, towards the inclusion of a cultural dimension. Of the 19 teachers not one suggested they had become language teachers to teach linguistic proficiency. This endorsement of a cultural dimension to language teaching was evident when teachers were asked to describe how they perceived their role as language teachers:

> You're trying to inspire them to have some kind of love for it, to say … it can get you out of your little box and make you see that there's something bigger out there and your job is to make that happen. (England)

> The ultimate goal would be to encourage the pupil to get to know people in the target culture; encourage them to reach out to other cultures. (France)

The teachers displayed a range of perspectives on the role of culture. On the one hand there was a perception of cultural awareness as a means of enhancing language learning motivation, arguably a view of culture as a means to an end rather than an end in itself: 'If we did more culture with them I think that would have a big impact on their desire to learn' (England).

Similarly some teachers viewed culture as positive but perhaps optional:

> They *hopefully also* experience some of the literature of the country which will open up their perspective on the culture … and then it will bring them to the whole political-social strata that will really open up their knowledge of the country, how it works and even the social fabric of the country. (Ireland, emphasis my own.)

On the other hand, a number of teachers considered an awareness of culture as an essential aspect of the language learning process: 'The most important thing is that opening of the mind and when you learn a language it opens you up to knowing other cultures' (Spain). 'Culture has to be part of the language that you teach ... you're making a huge mistake by alienating it and children are fascinated' (Ireland). 'Teaching languages is mostly a cultural question ... through the means of the language one should try to get people to understand each other better and to live constructively alongside one another' (France).

Also evident is variation in the extent to which culture in any form is seen as integral to the language teaching process. At this point numerous challenges arose from teachers in the four countries, the interviews with the teachers in England strongly indicating that the problems they faced were severely compounded by a prescriptiveness of the national curriculum and national examinations, not including a cultural aspect. While this prescriptiveness was not unique to the English context it was, for instance in the Irish case, combined with inclusion of a cultural dimension: 'They [the curriculum] try to insert cultural aspects but in any case the language teacher is very free. You can do a lot to deliver the target culture and more and more this is becoming a priority' (France). 'We are given the syllabus with various topics to cover and there is an emphasis on the cultural element; this must be covered' (Ireland).

These comments contrasted starkly with those of teachers in England: 'Because of the demands of the course we don't have the time to think or to look at it as much as perhaps we'd like to' (England); and

> Creativity is what's missing and with that could come more of a cultural understanding but if you stop what you're doing so that you can do a little project on whatever it is, then when you next come to try and do it there's even less time for it and the trend is towards compressing the languages curriculum. (England)

The curriculum was also described by teachers in England as 'horribly tight', 'to do with jumping through hoops', 'very grammar based'. One teacher commented:

> I think in some ways what we've got is the result of people, course-book writers and exam boards and things struggling over the years to get a balance. I think when you get in close, yes sometimes it's not appropriate or it's badly presented in the books. (England)

> The teacher, who's a very busy person, will tend to rely on the materials that are easily to hand, so I think having that content in a course-book would be very useful. (England)

In addition to the issues surrounding curriculum and materials, the interviews in England highlighted issues of learners' linguistic proficiency as an obstacle:

It's a vicious circle that before you can look at cultural stuff and particular authentic materials on a particular topic and say this comes from, you know, this is what actual German pupils would use in school, they need to reach a certain level of German and so you're actually trying to build up their language but they're doing that out of context so contextualising is a tricky part of it. (England)

The study provided rich data, discussed in other publications (Hennebry, 2011a, 2011b, 2012). The findings clearly indicated support from teachers who might be represented on a continuum from those who see such a teaching Culture approach as primarily supporting linguistic proficiency to the majority of teachers who view it as an inextricable component of language teaching.

Interestingly, teachers did feel sufficiently equipped to teach a cultural dimension. When referring specifically to a European dimension as a means of contributing to active citizenship, they were more hesitant since that would entail developing political understanding for which they felt considerably less equipped.

Conclusion

Through examination of the literature on the issue of culture and language teaching, a number of themes emerge. There is agreement among theorists, researchers and practitioners that the teaching of language goes hand in hand with the development of cultural awareness. The second theme that emerges is the existence of varying approaches to the teaching of culture. This in turn inevitably implies varying understandings of the outcome measures that might be applied to assess cultural awareness. Examination of some of the available curricula for language teaching hints at a lack of a systematic approach to the teaching of culture, with only the Finnish curriculum referring to the evaluation of cultural awareness as an indicator of successful learning. Nevertheless, the relative flexibility of some curricula does allow teachers the space and freedom to develop this aspect of language teaching, England being the notable exception. Indeed, in England, language teachers highlight a number of obstacles to cultural awareness. These include, the limited time allowed for language teaching in the school curriculum, the current emphasis on linguistic proficiency placed by the curriculum as well as in national examinations, to the extent and manner in which culture is presented in available textbooks and other materials. Teacher education may need to also equip language teachers with the skills and strategies for the development of cultural awareness among their learners, within these constraints. Underpinning any pedagogical strategy there needs to be a rigorous evidence base that provides an understanding of effective means of developing cultural awareness moving beyond a descriptive approach to the analysis of outcomes of interventionist models.

The need for cultural awareness appears on track to continue gathering momentum and import. Therefore, current approaches to language learning need urgently to adapt and keep pace with the demands of the times such that they reflect the arguably greater need for an intercultural rather than an exclusively linguistic competence.

Reflective enquiry

1   In your view, what are the extents and purposes of the concept of cultural awareness within the scope of modern foreign language teaching?
2   What do we mean by the expression 'second language acquisition'? To what extent can a second language be said to be acquired where there is an absence of cultural awareness?
3   Is it possible to fully achieve Intercultural Communicative Competence with the exclusion of the historical and philosophical perspectives from the target community?

    a   If it is possible what might this look like? And what outcome measures might practitioners look for?
    b   If it is not how might we integrate these elements into a modern foreign language curriculum?

Further reading

Byram, M. (1997) *Teaching and Assessing Intercultural Communicative Competence*, Clevedon: Multilingual Matters (focus on Chapter 2: 'A model for Intercultural Communicative Competence' and Chapter 3: 'Objectives for teaching, learning and assessment').

Celce-Murcia, M. (2007) 'Rethinking the role of communicative competence in language teaching', Chapter 3 in E. Soler and M. Safont Jorda (eds) *Intercultural Language Use and Language Learning*, Springer.

Chapter 11

Developments in formative assessment

A retrograde step for teaching and learning?

Jane Jones

Introduction

Formative assessment and the practical implementation of this by teachers in classrooms, widely referred to as Assessment for Learning (AfL), has taken a central place in the educational assessment arena in recent years. AfL has been given prominence by government education policy as part of its standards and school improvement agenda (DCSF, 2008). The OECD Report (2005: 1) on an intercontinental investigation into formative assessment defines it thus: 'the frequent assessments of student progress to identify learning needs and shape teaching'. Early work into formative assessment by Black *et al.* (2002) suggested five main types of activity as potentially effective: sharing success criteria with learners; classroom questioning; comment-only marking; peer and self-assessment; and formative use of summative tests. The OECD report (2005: 44) identified similar key elements from their case studies and related research that provide useful pegs for this exploration of the problematical issues and potential of formative assessment in languages:

1   Establishment of a classroom culture that encourages interaction and assessment tools.
2   Establishment of learning goals, and tracking of individual student progress towards these goals.
3   Use of varied instruction methods to meet diverse student needs.
4   Use of varied approaches to assessing student understanding.
5   Feedback on student performance and adaptation of instruction to meet identified needs.
6   Active involvement of students in the learning process.

These resonate strongly with the discourse of effective teaching and learning (Harris, 1998) and in spite of certain difficulties, formative assessment in the practicable guise of AfL techniques is, in fact, much in evidence in many language classrooms. What is less clear is what the impact of those techniques has been on improving language learning and teaching (Willis, 2011). Assessment as a topic is always subject to considerable contestation and debate on the topic can be quite emotive. In recent times, after initial enthusiasm for AfL, a sense of frustration has become visible and in some areas there has been a backlash against aspects of it in some language classrooms. In results-driven school cultures, for example, it is claimed by some teachers (based on an element of misconception) that there is not enough time for AfL-type activities. There is also some research (Goodman, 2011) to indicate that some pupils resist the move to be given fewer grades and more formative comment, after a school career dominated by grades, and the same goes for their parents as Perrenoud (1993: 107) has found – '*Touche pas à mon évaluation!*' Other teachers comment on the insidious creeping back of English into the languages classroom. Black *et al.* (2003: 72) found that schools had difficulty in embedding formative assessment into languages in their research, and suggested that

> part of the difficulty is that in UK classrooms, there is an orthodoxy that the vast majority of communication between the teachers and the students should take place in the target language ... based on a mistaken application of the idea of 'immersion' in the target language.

They argue that: 'if the rigid adherence to the monopoly of the target language is abandoned, then even modern foreign languages create many opportunities for good formative assessment' (ibid.: 73). However, an AfL approach certainly needs to and can work in tandem with optimal target language use.

In this chapter, I will suggest that AfL needs to be better understood in terms of a firmer grasp of formative assessment and managed by teachers in the languages community of practice in a way that supports recent classroom developments and beliefs about languages teaching and learning. Although formative assessment is based on certain fundamental principles of learning, there is a degree of subject-sensitivity as has been discussed before (Hodgen and Marshall, 2005; Jones and Wiliam, 2008). Whilst formative assessment may seem less easy to integrate into languages than into other more discursive subjects such as English and history, and the core subjects of science and maths where learning is often centred on problem-solving, it is possible for languages to exploit formative assessment to create a productive language-learning environment and to significantly increase the use of pupil target language (TL) in a collaborative learning context.

Before considering the challenges AfL has posed for languages and suggesting ways in which teachers can make formative assessment work for languages, I begin by identifying the basic principles of learning on which formative assessment is built and at the heart of which self-regulatory skills are crucial.

THEORISING ASSESSMENT FOR LEARNING

Principles of learning

Common-sense knowledge indicates that formative assessment supports learning in general. Jones and Wiliam (2008: 5) designate four principles that facilitate learning in a languages classroom where formative assessment is put into practice, followed by some concrete examples:

The *first principle* involves meeting the pupils at their level of knowledge: that requires revisiting prior learning. This involves identifying and building on the learners' previous knowledge, and revising it in order to provide a context for new learning. Critically, secondary teachers need to ascertain the pupils' languages coverage and also ways of learning in the primary school and build on these, and the same again at other transitional learning points.

The *second principle* is that the learners must be active in the learning process, the learning done by them and not for them. In such a case, teachers need to desist from just telling pupils e.g. giving them vocabulary items, and rather to employ strategies that involve the learners discovering such things for themselves. This might typically involve the learners having a moment to think about a grammatical rule for example, or to research items for themselves, consulting the teacher as a last resort.

The *third principle* requires the learners to know what they are working towards, where they are currently in relation to the objectives and criteria of work expected, and to have strategies or be able to discover ways to achieve those objectives. Formative assessment has become arguably at its most visible in language classrooms in the ubiquitous identification of learning objectives at the beginning of lessons, typically flashed up on a whiteboard which often pupils laboriously copy down. There is a danger of this becoming an unthinking chore rather than an orientation to support the learning. Nonetheless, sharing, even negotiating the learning objectives with the learners, and revisiting them, is important.

The *fourth principle* posits that learners need to talk about their work, drawing on discussion, feedback and questions arising from peer- and self-assessment as well as feedback from the teacher. This requires much more pupil talk and less teacher talk; teachers need to be less linguistically controlling and encourage the pupils to 'have a go'.

Such principles resonate with the core tenets proposed by the Assessment Reform Group (ARG, 2002: 2), aimed at ensuring that assessment policy and practice reflect relevant research, and that endorsed the concept of AfL as a tool for raising standards and achievement in schools, defining it as 'the process of seeking and interpreting evidence for use by learners and their teachers to decide where the learners are in their learning, where they need to go and how best to get there' (ibid.). James (2006) shows how formative assessment is not associated only with one theory of learning but manifests itself in behaviourist, cognitive, constructivist and socio-cultural, situated and activity theories of learning; she suggests 'possibilities for eclecticism or synthesis' (p. 58) in a more inclusive theory of learning.

A model of formative assessment

Black and Wiliam (2009) on the basis of the aforementioned principles, have theorised a model of formative assessment that relates to classroom realities as set out in Figure 11.1.

The interlinking grid in the figure draws on the trilogy of key processes in learning and teaching first identified by Ramaprasad (1983). These intersect with the five key strategies (a)–(e) as in the model. The processes have become ubiquitous in assessment discourse yet they are fundamental to focusing learning in any scheme of work and lesson frame. *Where the learner is going* requires clearly thought out learning objectives, or intentions, so that the learning is oriented and can be evaluated in terms of those objectives. The memorable findings of the small-scale but powerful research by Lee *et al.* (1998) in Barking and Dagenham that showed some 95 per cent of Year 9 pupils (thus aged 14) had no idea what they were supposed to be doing in their languages lessons and remained 'in a fog' throughout. The omnipresent learning objectives have probably dispelled the fog to some extent but, as previously mentioned, this important orienting can so easily become a mindless lesson starter, the objectives never being revisited again

	Where the learning is going	**Where the learner is now**	**How to get there**
Teacher	(a) Clarifying learning intensions and criteria for success	(b) Engineering effective classroom discussions and other tasks that aid understanding	(c) Providing feedback that moves learners forward
Peer	Understanding and sharing learners' criteria for success		
		(d) Activating students as instructional resources	
Learner	Understanding learning intentions and criteria for success	(e) Activating students as owners of their own learning	

Figure 11.1 Aspects of formative assessment (modified from Black and Wiliam, 2009: 5).

in what could be a helpful check on progress. The learners need to know not just where they are heading but how they will know when they get to that point: what will be the criteria for the successful completion of task? Progress cannot be assumed but needs to be carefully monitored.

As in Figure 11.1, the starting point for deciding the objectives needs to be based on an evaluation of *where the learners are*. This requires the teacher to have evidence of learning through a careful selection of activities that will enable the learners to show what they can do and where they are unsure as well as a learning roadmap for *how to get to the learning objectives*. The notion of lesson plan can be an obstacle if this is not seen as a flexible frame to allow the teacher to act on contingencies and to be responsive to learners' needs as they emerge. Learning cannot be pre-planned nor can the teacher be sure that what she teaches is what the learners will learn (Heafford, 1990). Perrenoud (1998) emphasises the unpredictable nature of classroom learning since, he asserts, we cannot ever really know what the learner uptake will be from the teacher input. This lack of predictability Perrenoud likens to a 'bottle at sea' image of pupil learning, because we cannot be sure that the 'messages' from our teaching in the 'bottles' will find a receiver in the ocean of learners around us. Student teachers often make the mistake of evaluating their own performance, the contents of the bottles, rather than looking for evidence of learning and trying to relate it to their teaching and to the feedback given to and received from the learners. Feedback is a cornerstone of formative assessment.

Feedback

A large British meta-study (Coffield *et al.*, 2004a) showed that feedback and formative assessment proved to be very learning-supportive. The meta-study by Hattie and Timperley (2007), attaching 'effect sizes' to numerous factors relevant to learning in schools, has attracted considerable attention and caused much debate in educational circles. It has also given strong support for many of the practices and principles central to AfL, giving credence to the small-scale action research projects in schools and in networks of schools where AfL has been introduced and developed. Perrenoud (1998) states that feedback, or rather the impact of feedback, is not as simple as is sometimes thought. He is of the view that teachers have a considerable challenge in needing to shift from a traditional view of feedback that is minimal (*'Très bien!'*) or judgemental (*'Non, ce n'est pas tout à fait correcte'*), to one that can take learners forward with responses that act as 'cognitive stepping stones' (*'Oui, on pourrait bien dire ça, quelqu'un peut ajouter d'autres détails?'*). Feedback intertwines with feedforward to 'stir' the learner to the next step. Teachers are urged to create and seize on contingent opportunities for interaction (Van Lier, 1996) and for the explicit development of meta-cognition (talking about learning). In such a case, the pupils are a source of self-regulation, and formative assessment for the teacher is an aspect of the management of learning.

SELF-REGULATION

Self-regulated learners

Much has been written about the role of motivation in successful language learning (Dörnyei, 2001, 2008; Williams and Burden, 1997; Williams *et al.*, 2002). There are studies into the psychology of learning that have focused on the association between motivation and learning outcomes (Boekaerts, 2002; Dweck, 2000; Pintrich, 2000). Boekaerts (1995) postulated from her research that motivation – an essential element of successful learning, and conceptualised in her research as a specific self-regulatory skill – was necessary for learners to experience success in educational outcomes. She suggested that motivational beliefs, which serve as a frame of reference for pupils' feelings and actions in a given subject or task, are a result of learning experiences. Students who have positive beliefs about their capacity to learn have higher achievements. Well-motivated learners were found to be capable of using their self-regulatory skills, i.e. their capacity to control and manage their own learning effectively for higher achievement. Boekaerts distinguishes between meta-cognitive skills (learning goals oriented that refer to the learners' capacity to generate cognitive strategies in a context-specific way), meta-motivational and self-management skills (not necessarily learning goal restricted), to explain the types of self-regulatory skills which are 'concerned with the control of behaviour in general, including motivation control, action control, emotion and social control' (1995: 10).

Since there seems to be a direct link between motivation to learn and proficiency in self-regulatory skills, it would seem plausible to suggest that pupils who are encouraged by their teachers through skilful questioning, helpful feedback, well-planned learning activities involving peer-work and assessment, self-assessment and other activities conducive to developing self-reliance, all recognisable features of AfL approach, can become independent and well-motivated learners capable of high achievement. In this can be seen resonance with what is described by e.g. Rubin (1975) and Griffiths (2008) as the 'good language learner'; good language learners can be defined as self-regulatory and making use of strategies (O'Malley and Chamot, 1990; Oxford, 1990), meta-cognition and autonomy to frame their learning.

Implications for teachers

The implications for the teacher are many. Perrenoud (1998) affirms that well-regulated classroom environments that focus on the learning outcomes before any learning occurs and adjusting teaching to pupils' responses, support the regulation of learning. Therefore, appropriate teacher intervention is crucial to enable students to develop their self-regulatory and motivational skills, allowing them to be less teacher-dependent. Boekaerts (1995: 17) concluded that 'teachers should make these self-regulatory skills explicit educational targets', an exhortation that resonates with the Learning to Learn agenda (James *et al.*, 2006) and Claxton's notion of 'learning as learnable' (2004). Rogers (1991: 276) asserts that: 'The only kind of learning which significantly affects behavior is self-discovered, self-appropriated learning' which emphasises the importance of the pupils' involvement in their own learning.

Baumert's research (1993) identified the important role of school processes as a whole school culture in influencing self-regulation where learners assumed a sense of responsibility for learning. Gula-Kubiszewska (2007) linked self-regulatory learning to learning independence through active participation, rather than teacher-reliance for external control, which would reinforce the need for teachers actively to involve pupils in their learning to enable them to become self-supporting learners. Stobart (2008) also claims that it is the learner's responsibility to become independent and it is the teachers' task to use appropriate methodology to enable learners to become autonomous: 'Part of being a self-regulated learner is to accept responsibility for learning, just as teachers must take responsibility for creating a context which helps learning' (p. 179). This view stresses the value of the quality of interactions between teachers and learners and the importance for teachers to create purposeful learning environments where students can be effectively supported in developing their independent learning skills. Such independence would be not just for a pupil's own benefit but for the benefit of their peers and for mutual learning in a classroom hallmarked by a culture of cooperation and collaboration. It is to this sort of classroom culture that I now turn and the learning activities conducive to self-regulatory behaviour.

LAYING THE FOUNDATIONS FOR FORMATIVE ASSESSMENT IN THE LANGUAGES CLASSROOM

In this section, I propose the necessary conditions for effective formative assessment to take hold in the languages classroom and provide examples. It is not just a question of tweaking techniques but of a more profound culture change.

Developing a culture of trust

The first thing to discuss is the need for a culture of trust in the classroom as a precondition. This takes time to establish as Webb and Jones (2009) assert. New demands are made of pupils and they have new responsibilities; learners will be expected to take considerable ownership of their own learning, show initiative, loosen the tight dependence on the teacher and collaborate with peers as a matter of course. Pupils may need some training in this, rules negotiated and agreed, new parameters established. Teachers also have to undergo role-change and assure pupils, for example, that their TL efforts will be welcomed, however imperfect, and that feedback will always be constructive. Horwitz (2000) writes about the anxiety that secondary learners feel with regard to the content and level of their TL and how it might not reflect their intellectual level; such anxiety needs to be assuaged. Language classrooms are likely to be quite noisy and the learning a bit messy in the sense of more trial-and-error than usual. The learners need to know that they will be safe in their language-learning environment and that the genuine efforts of all learners, whatever their learning differences and needs, will be welcomed (Beltran *et al.*, 2013).

Creating a collaborative learning community

Learners are more likely to collaborate with their peers when they are trustful of each other and understand the role of the teacher in supporting them. There is often an imbalance in TL use between teachers and pupils and a collaborative approach whereby pupils work for a good deal of the time in groups creates a better ratio of pupil-talking opportunity. Collaboration requires much more than grouping of pupils and assignment to task. Collaboration is difficult for pupils to do and in interview with pupils (Jones, 2010), there was much complaint found about fairness and arguing. Learners need to learn to cooperate before they can collaborate in their work. Time invested in developing good team working, assigning roles, for example, and the creation of the group identity, is time well spent. Coyle's (2007a) concept of the strategic classroom as one in which the establishment of a language-learning community, which nurtures the development of learner strategies, is useful. She describes the classroom as 'a physical and social place where learners not only learn a foreign language but "learn how to learn" in order that they can become effective future learners' (p. 66). She suggests that strategic behaviour can grow out of the learning context in which scaffolding, seeking opportunities, mediation and self-regulation are key ideas at the centre of pupil learning activity.

Opportunities for pupil talk

Teachers often do most of the talking in language lessons. A shift needs to be made to centre learning on pupil talk. Alexander (2008), drawing on his research, albeit in general subjects not specifically languages, identified three broad aspects of pedagogical interaction that he calls repertoires and which resonate with common interactions in the languages classroom:

- *Organising interaction* includes whole-class teaching, collective group working (where groups are teacher-directed in a structured way), collaborative group work, and one-to-one teaching/learning as in pair work, for example. These are typically present in a great many languages lessons, and frame a lesson plan.
- *Teaching talk* consists of, most frequently, rote in the form of drilling and repetition; recitation through questioning designed to test recall or to elicit

responses to questions that contain the answers and instruction/exposition, telling the pupils what to do, giving explanations. Again, many of these are standard practice in the classroom, and provide opportunities for repeated use of the TL.

- *Learning talk* concerns the pupil use of talk to explain, instruct, ask questions, analyse, discuss, speculate, evaluate responses, argue, negotiate. Some of this will take place in group work although where the TL is the exclusive medium, the talk may be limited (see next section).

Alexander proposes a more dialogic classroom that stresses the talk of pupils and where the teaching is more collective (addressing learning together); reciprocal (where teachers and pupils listen to each other, share ideas and propose additions/extensions; and supportive (learners expressing their ideas without fear of being embarrassed or of giving wrong answers, and helping each other). This sits well with the idea of the learning community where the learners take both individual and collective responsibility for their learning and with a languages-adapted task-based approach such as described by Klapper (2003) in which the learners have time to reflect on and explore the language to create extended TL dialogues or pieces of writing for group work. Pupils also need structured time to reflect on their learning and opportunities to discuss their learning. Flutter and Rudduck (2004: 7) write that: 'pupils of all ages can show a remarkable capacity to discuss their learning in a considered and insightful way, although they may not always be able to articulate their ideas in the formal language'. However, such a language can be taught and practised and integral to this is the development of well-honed assessment skills enabling pupils to be effective monitors and evaluators of their learning. This brings us to the issue of TL use.

More target language not less

Where other subjects can encourage extensive talk in English about the learning tasks involved, there is the danger of languages lessons being once again windswept in a gale of English as Hawkins (1999) so memorably put it. In fact, with careful coaching, practice and language prompts on the classroom walls and ceiling, and in pupils' learning diaries, then pupil use of pupil TL can be significantly increased. The giving of feedback is a potential opportunity for training the learners to make use of a stock of well-chosen comments in group work for example, and a real context for TL use, so phrases such as: 'Who has an idea? I agree. I disagree. I'm not sure. What about…? I suggest. I like that. I don't like it. That's good. Let's practise/write it up etc.' This kind of talk also provides an opportunity for a considerable amount of the use of question formats.

In a German comprehensive school, 14–15-year-old pupils were observed engaging in discussion using such phases in the TL in their English lessons. Countering the argument that their exposure to English would enable this, this also happened in their French lessons as such practice had been established as the norm. I have also observed ten-year-old pupils do the same in primary schools in England, where it was noticeable that the children undertook similar routines in groups in their English (as mother tongue), science and languages lessons. The critical issue is to start early and to persevere. Structured pupil TL use is especially useful at transition periods, primary to secondary, for example, when teachers can take the opportunity to find out what the pupils' repertoire of TL use is and extend it immediately with extended meta-language.

The practice of feedback needs to be extended from the customary teacher-to-pupil to include pupil-to-pupil and pupil-to-teacher. Ideally, lessons are a rich interplay of feedback based on, for example, comments, questions, traffic lighting and extensions. Such activity privileges sentence and text-level work. Giving feedback needs to be practised since not all feedback is helpful per se; time and adjustment are also necessary to be able to respond to feedback. Thinking about grade allocation can be a useful exercise if the pupils are trained to think critically about grade criteria. Differentiation comes into its own when pupils act as mediators for each other, the abler or more experienced language users supporting their peers. Feedback may be in the TL, in English or a mixture of codes according to personalised needs, given an appropriate meta-linguistic vocabulary. Christie's research (2011) has shown the potential of what he terms the 'target language lifestyle' where the TL is used as the main vehicle of communication, supported by 'target language management' by the teacher to ensure continuous use of the TL by pupils. Christie challenges the assertion by Jones and Wiliam (2008) that judicious use of English may be necessary and that 'learners being active and analytical in their use of the TL... suggests that this could equally well be transferred to the context of assessment for learning' (p. 306). Increasing pupil TL use empowers the learners, assists with the development of their linguistic self-regulatory skills and shifts responsibility more towards the learners in decreasing their dependence on the teacher.

FORMATIVE ASSESSMENT AS PEDAGOGICAL COMMON SENSE

The disquiet surrounding formative assessment as AfL, as practised in some language classrooms, that has led to some unhelpful routines such as formulaic learning objectives, rather superficial target-setting and feedback and over-use of English, has provided a useful opportunity to reflect on how languages teachers want to and can better incorporate formative assessment into language lessons. Furthermore, a period of critical reflection provides an opportunity for teachers to reposition themselves in terms of formative assessment and make it work for them rather than submitting to certain predefined techniques that can become trivialised. It is important to understand and embrace the fundamental principles of formative assessment – pupil talk; collaborative working; feedback and effective questioning; making these languages appropriate and enhancing of language teaching and learning, for there is no one template for formative assessment.

Much of what is inherent in a formative assessment approach is based on pedagogical common sense and the tenets of effective teaching. The above principles of learning outlined chime with Claxton's view (1995) of lifelong learning as based on five (not three!) Rs and which consist of readiness, resourcefulness, resilience, remembering and reflectiveness. Each of these needs to be built into the overall learning plan as well as into each lesson so that learners show readiness in the form of quick thinking and contingent action, resourcefulness in terms of taking responsibility for learning and being a strategic learner, resilience in terms of, for example, not being afraid to get it wrong but to find alternatives, remembering capacity in terms of good recall and recombination with new structures and reflectiveness at all times with teachers giving pupils time to think about their learning and an expectation that learners will think things out for themselves. Claxton asserts that self-assessment is to a large extent intuitive and that the development of learning acumen drawing on what Atkinson and Claxton (2000) call 'intuitive knowledge' is crucial rather than merely responding to pre-determined criteria. It would seem, then, that the five Rs could prove useful in formal assessments at examination time.

Examinations and grades

We cannot dissociate ourselves from an examination system where a grade culture is strong, where assessment for accountability is enshrined in the tropes of inspection and school improvement and in which summative assessment predominates. Although the relationship between formative assessment, resulting in modifying teaching and learning, and summative, aimed at monitoring progress, is not so clear-cut (Stobart, 2008; Harlen and James, 1997), there has been some criticism of the recent preoccupation with assessment for learning rather than with providing measurement, which prompted Broadfoot (1996: 46) to present the query: 'To measure or to learn: that is the question'. Since education is primarily concerned with learning, no opportunities should be missed to improve pupils' progress and understanding. As James (1998: 171) puts it rather vividly, one 'cannot fatten a pig by simply weighing it' and the real value in assessments is to give guidance for the advancement of learning and education, as measuring per se does not contribute to improvement. We can, however, turn an unhealthy obsession with grades into a healthy interest in and understanding of grades that are meaningful as way-stage markers in the learner's progress. Summative assessments and formative assessment practice can be difficult to reconcile at a practical level as Stobart claims:

> The image is still that formative assessment is a 'good thing', but, once preparation for examinations starts, we need to get on with the 'real thing'.

> This means frequent summative assessments and direct teaching-to-the-test, even though there is evidence that self-regulated learners will perform better.
>
> (2008: 159)

There is nothing to lose in turning this round and keeping the main focus on formative assessment in the languages classroom, mindful of evidence from Black and Wiliam (1998) that formative assessment can improve grade profiles. But the integrity of effective assessment to drive language learning forward and to develop rich self-assessment skills is best disassociated from the 'thin skills' of government branding (that tends to construe formative assessment as 'serial summative', that is to say summative style assessments in rapid and regular succession), and of assessment for accountability.

Being reflective

Formative assessment is reflective assessment in that it demands reflectivity on the part of both teachers and learners. It needs to be learnt and to be practised, but first it needs to be conceptualised and made sense of by teachers themselves who need time and space to think about how formative assessment works for them in their context by collecting and interpreting data. This can be done as action research or in teacher learning communities/groups (Wiliam, 2006; DuFour, 2004), for example, investigating assessment issues of real importance to languages teachers collaboratively, thus researching from the classroom 'inside-out' (Cochran-Smith and Lytle, 1993). Logan's research (2011) suggested that collaborative professional learning (CPL) with colleagues offers a powerful form of sustained CPD that can heighten critical reflection on practice, which in this case might involve rejecting the unsatisfactory aspects of AfL in terms of what does not work for languages, and embracing a more fully rounded, languages-sensitive, formative assessment approach. Investment in training/CPD can pay dividends across the whole curriculum when the school develops and exemplifies formative assessment across the whole school.

Conclusion

Much more research is needed into what it is that teachers and learners do in classrooms where formative assessment is visible, that promotes effective learning, learning habits and pupil assessment literacy. In particular, small-scale critically reflective studies carried out by practitioners on questions such as those below would be valuable in deriving evidence to construct a broad tapestry of transferable 'practice that works' to the advantage of the language learner. In this, listening to the genuine pupil voice is essential, paying attention to the 'students' expertise as insightful commentators on teaching and learning' found by Rudduck and McIntyre (2007: 12) in their research with pupils. In trying to ascertain what works, the conditions, the variables, the impact all need careful exploration.

Teachers need to take a lead, be a bit disruptive, stirring things up a little rather than accepting and being disappointed with the status quo and develop agency in reforming assessment, trialling materials, and doing action research as part of their professional learning and their activist subject leadership agenda. Rather than assessment having an unhelpful washback effect, teachers need to take the lead in assessment matters in the languages classroom, improving the alignment of summative–formative assessment so that assessment becomes more holistic, and privileging assessment through dialogue. Teachers would then be effectively positioned to strengthen the culture of assessment and be agents of change in the broader field of evaluation in languages teaching and learning, introducing more innovative, diverse and interactive assessment.

Reflective enquiry

1   What are the implications of the use of English in the languages classroom if we promote collaborative talk around learning tasks? In classrooms where an AfL approach is being practised, to what extent is more English used as opposed to in more traditional teaching styles? Identify and compare the use of English in differently assessment-cultured classrooms.

2   When and how do (1) teachers and (2) learners give feedback, what is the nature of the feedback and what seems to have the biggest impact on learning? Classify the types of feedback and consult learners for their views on feedback they find useful.

3   What triggers self-regulatory strategies and what kinds of activities might teachers plan to enable the development of self-regulatory skills?

4   In what ways can formative assessment be useful to pupils with learning differences and/or Additional Support Needs, for example? Identify tools and strategies to support such learners.

Further reading

Harlen, W. (2007) *Assessment of Learning*, London: Sage.

Leung, C. and Mohan, B. (2004) 'Teacher formative assessment and talk in classroom contexts: assessment as discourse and assessment of discourse', *Language Testing*, 21(3): 335–359.

Torrance, H. and Pryor, J. (2001) 'Developing formative assessment in the classroom: using action research to explore and modify theory', *British Educational Research Journal*, 27(5): 615–631.

Chapter 12

Making progress in languages
Issues around transition

Amanda Barton

Introduction

Much debate surrounds the issue of pupil transition across the designated Key Stages in the English educational system: Key Stage 2 to 3, as children progress from primary to secondary school; Key Stage 3 to 4, as many children move onto study that will culminate in an external examination; and Key Stage 4 to 5 as children opt into, or out of, further language study beyond the age of sixteen. This chapter focuses on the most keenly debated transition stage – Key Stage 2 to 3 when children are first confronted by a very different environment and curriculum from that they have experienced for the first seven years of their educational careers.

Recent years have seen a surge in the teaching of languages in primary schools in England. This is a consequence of the National Languages Strategy, published in 2002 (DfES), which recommended that from September 2010 all pupils in Key Stage 2 should have an entitlement to learn a language. This recommendation was subsequently reinforced by the Independent (Rose) Review of the Primary Curriculum (DCSF, 2009) which recommended the promotion of languages to mandatory status. Some 92 per cent of primary schools now appear to be providing some foreign language tuition within class time, a 22 per cent increase on the numbers reported two years earlier (Wade *et al.*, 2009). As we await the introduction of legislation in September 2014 that will promote languages from an 'entitlement' to a statutory subject in the Key Stage 2 curriculum it appears timely to assess the issues that have impeded successful transition to date, as well as some approaches which might facilitate it, and which will be highlighted imminently when this change in policy is implemented.

The issues surrounding the Key Stage 2 to 3 transition are not restricted exclusively to languages. Much has been written about the initial regression in children's learning when they transfer to secondary school (see, for instance, Galton *et al.*, 2003). Some of the issues experienced by teachers of languages are shared by teachers of other subjects, notably issues of differing pedagogy and curriculum content at Key Stage 2 and Key Stage 3. However, it can be argued that the complexity of the issues in languages is amplified by a number of factors which are explored in greater depth below.

MOTIVATION

It goes without saying that enjoyment of the language learning experience should be a principal objective of any languages teaching. There is an obvious correlation between enjoyment, positive attitudes to learning and high attainment. Behind the government's proposal to make languages statutory at Key Stage 2 is the thinking that an early languages learning experience will enthuse pupils and encourage them to continue studying at a higher level, thus boosting the economy by creating a much-needed increase in the numbers of employees who can speak more than one language. The proposal of the previous government's Language Review in 2007 (DfES), which similarly advocated making languages compulsory in primary schools from 2010, was predicated on the belief that enjoyment of languages in primary school 'has the potential to feed through into the secondary schools, improve performance, and encourage pupils as they reach Key Stage 4 to continue with languages' (DfES, 2007: 3).

Teachers often describe the unfettered enthusiasm of primary-aged learners when they first begin learning a foreign language. This, allied with the theory (often referred to under the auspices of the 'critical age theory') that the younger the child, the more easily they will assimilate a new language (see, for instance, Doye and Hurrell in Bolster, 2009: 234) is a strong rationale for teaching foreign languages to young children. Some research has also shown that younger children tend to be less anxious than their older counterparts when learning a language, and that they find it easier to master accurate pronunciation (Johnston, 2008, in Tinsley and Comfort, 2012). Sustaining this enthusiasm at Key Stage 3, however, especially if children are continuing with a language that they have already learned for four years at Key Stage 2, as the latest government policy suggests they will do, may present more of a challenge. Prior to the introduction of languages into primary school, secondary teachers had benefited from pupils responding positively to the novelty value of learning an entirely new subject. Bolster (2009: 235) now describes secondary teachers' criticism of the primary languages initiative, claiming that pupil disillusionment with foreign language learning is a direct result of the length of time pupils have been studying – some even since Key Stage 1.

Teachers of mathematics and English would not hesitate, of course, to dismiss such precious-seeming arguments when their own subjects are taught throughout the primary and secondary curriculum and can, therefore, enjoy no such novelty value when children transfer to secondary school. There is also an implicit tension here in secondary teachers arguing for less curriculum time to be spent on languages when most teachers would argue that far more time is needed. Arguing for a reduction in the time spent on teaching languages in primary schools, or a complete abolition of the same, in order to increase the appeal of the subject at secondary level could result in a further marginalisation of languages which, many argue, was a consequence of languages being made a non-statutory subject at GCSE level. The inclusion of languages in the English Baccalaureate (E-Bacc) has heralded something of a revival of the status of languages in school and to remove it from the primary curriculum at this stage would surely send out a confusing message about the importance of languages to stakeholders.

Nonetheless, there are important lessons to be learned from the last attempt to introduce languages into primary schools, especially in terms of its impact on pupil motivation. In the mid-1960s a government-funded initiative, 'French from 8', was launched to test the feasibility of teaching languages, in practice French, to children in the last four years of primary school (Burstall *et al.*, 1974). The project was longitudinal and spanned a period of eight years, from 1966–1974. Its findings make interesting food for thought for both policymakers and practitioners: while the research found that there were high levels of motivation in learning French throughout the primary phase, at secondary school pupils' motivation went into decline so that after three years 'a bare majority of ... pupils were still in favour of learning French' (p. 160). This was one of the reasons why the teaching of languages in primary school was not implemented nationally. The factors that contributed to the creation of these negative attitudes may still have some resonance in today's context and are explored in more detail below.

CONTINUITY AND ASSESSMENT

While prolonged exposure to a single language may result in demotivation at Key Stage 3, it can equally be argued that progression is impeded if there is no continuity between languages from Key Stage 2 to 3. It is not uncommon for in excess of twenty primary schools – and sometimes far more – to feed into a single secondary school, rendering the likelihood of all pupils in Year 6 learning the same language in preparation for their transfer to secondary in Year 7 highly improbable. Although the way in which mathematics is taught at primary and secondary level may differ substantially, mathematics as a subject area is fundamentally one prescribed area of the curriculum. The same cannot be said of languages, which contains French, German, Spanish, Italian, Japanese, Mandarin Chinese, Arabic and Russian inter alia – all with their own very different lexis, syntax and cultural contexts – and it is this aspect that distinguishes languages from other subjects in debates about transition and renders transition arrangements which facilitate progression more problematic.

A lack of continuity between primary and secondary school languages teaching has been widely reported around the world as a major obstacle in ensuring progression between the primary and secondary phases and it is clearly a long-standing problem (see, for instance, Grenfell, 1993; Freudenstein, 1998; Nikolov and Curtain, 2000). One research report found that discontinuity was the single most damaging factor in languages learning programmes (Martin, 2002).

A number of research reports have underlined how poor, or non-existent, liaison between primary and secondary languages teachers can contribute to unsatisfactory progression (Driscoll *et al.*, 2004; Hunt *et al.*, 2008; Wade *et al.*,

2009; Evans and Fisher, 2012). Bolster's research, for instance, described in the *Language Learning Journal* (2009), underlines how the 'lack of liaison, lack of information, lack of assessment and recording at primary, and lack of differentiation at secondary level, all led to a situation where pupils' prior learning was completely ignored' (p. 234). Although the National Languages Strategy (DfES, 2002) recommended that pupils should reach a recognised level of competence on a nationally recognised scheme, *The Languages Ladder: Steps to Success* (DCSF, 2007), by the end of Key Stage 2, it would nevertheless appear that this assessment data is rarely used in secondary school. There are a number of theories why this might be the case. While the status of languages in primary school has been merely that of an 'entitlement', it may be the case that few schools have been using the Languages Ladder, or any other sort of formal assessment instrument, at all. Anecdotal evidence of mine, acquired through contact with schools on primary research projects and through an online forum for primary teachers of languages, suggests that this is certainly the case in a large number of schools.

Some of the reasons behind this lack of engagement in formal assessment practices are clear: languages are being squeezed into what some perceive to be an already overcrowded curriculum, leaving staff with very little time to teach, let alone assess. A further reason relates to the rationale teachers have for teaching languages. While teaching in secondary, especially at Key Stage 4, is driven by the pressures of an external examination, teaching at primary level is not, as one teacher makes clear on a recent posting about assessment to the early language learning forum:

> We would have to spend so much time assessing to be able to give conclusive data, and with 30 to 60 mins. per week, if lucky, there just isn't time. Aren't we here to try to make learning languages fun and a positive experience?
> (primarylanguages@mailtalk.ac.uk, 6 July 2012)

As this extract suggests, there is a perception that introducing formal assessment elements into languages teaching would make it less enjoyable for pupils and teachers and introduce an unwelcome source of pressure – a perception that is well-founded when one considers the levels of stress to which teachers at Key Stage 4 are currently exposed, especially since they have been required to both administer and examine the GCSE speaking tests to their pupils.

Such resistance to assessment at primary level echoes that found amongst primary staff when they were questioned about this as part of a government-funded research project (Muijs *et al.*, 2005). This large-scale study, based on a sample of 500 schools, found that assessment practices were 'underdeveloped' and that 'recording of assessment evidence was limited' (p. 5). Formal assessment practices were not widespread, even when assessment tools were available, and there was apprehension that introducing assessment would change the character of the subject:

> Where assessment formed part of the local authority Scheme of Work and devised units, it was not always carried out ... there was some resistance to the notion of an imposed scheme and the worry that introducing assessment would change the whole nature of the experience.
>
> (Muijs *et al.*, 2005: 5–6)

Primary teachers' resistance to assessment may also be attributed to the difficulty of assessing a multi-skill subject. While mathematics may be assessed reasonably simply with a paper-based test, assessing pupils' skills and knowledge in languages needs to take into account four discrete skills: listening, speaking, reading and writing. It does not seem unreasonable to suggest that, if we require primary teachers to produce accurate and useful assessments of their pupils' achievements, they urgently require more professional development in this area.

We should be wary of laying the blame for the absence of assessment data at the beginning of Key Stage 3 squarely at the feet of primary colleagues; some primary teachers' accounts suggest that even when they do assess their pupils' attainment, the data which they pass on to their secondary colleagues is not used (Cable *et al.*, 2010). It is possible that secondary teachers choose to ignore such data in order to avoid the unnecessary evils of differentiation and, instead, opt to teach the pupils in their classes as if they were all *ab initio* learners. It is possible that there is a reluctance to move on from the legacy of an era when languages were not taught in primary school since that was considerably easier. We may also speculate that secondary teachers regard the 'Languages Ladder', with its 'can do' statements, as a fairly crude means of assessment of limited usefulness. Such broad statements of competence may be perceived as insufficiently precise and informative to enable secondary teachers to plan for personalised progression for individual pupils.

TEACHER CAPACITY

Given the irrefutable link between the quality of teaching and learning, one basic prerequisite for successful progression from Key Stage 2 to Key Stage 3 is the adequate subject knowledge of primary teachers. A recent longitudinal study into language learning at Key Stage 2 (Cable *et al.*, 2010) reported that there was a clear need for more training in developing primary teachers' languages skills, especially in cross-curricular learning, intercultural understanding and the learning and teaching of reading and writing as well as developing teachers' own languages skills (p. 5). In many primary schools foreign language teaching remains the responsibility of one member of staff, and staffing, especially staff turnover, is a source of concern for many head teachers. As a result, many schools continue to have to employ external language specialists to compensate for the lack of subject expertise on their staff (Wade *et al.*, 2009) or depend on input from visiting colleagues in secondary schools. Although this may plug the gap in the curriculum, some research suggests that is not the most effective model. It has been found that the best provision of languages at primary level is made by the children's class teacher, rather than by a visiting specialist (Driscoll *et al.*, 2004) and there are concerns that secondary teachers may not be sufficiently familiar with primary pedagogy and psychology, as outlined below. Although some government funding has been injected into initial teacher education in order to boost languages expertise, there is still some doubt that new entrants to the profession, many of whom will have opted out of languages study at the age of fourteen, will be able to redress the balance (McLachlan, 2009).

PEDAGOGY

Although not well documented in the research, there are significant differences between the pedagogies employed by teachers of languages in primary schools and those in secondary schools. This is bound to be the case, given the difference in age and cognitive maturity of the pupils in these different sectors, but the choice of pedagogy is also determined by the teacher's personal preferences, experience of teaching or learning languages, and attitudes to the place of literacy in languages teaching programmes. Many primary teachers place very little emphasis on literacy in languages lessons, focusing instead on developing pupils' listening and speaking skills (Cable *et al.*, 2010). The rationale behind this can be easily inferred: pupils, especially very young pupils, may lack the requisite literacy skills in English to support their learning of reading and writing in a foreign language. There may also be an argument that primary teachers resist teaching the 'harder' skills since there is no requirement for them to be assessed at the end of Key Stage 2. Their focus, instead, and understandably, is on making languages learning 'fun'.

Ongoing research (Roberts, 2012) has underlined how primary and secondary teachers afford greater or lesser importance to different aspects of the curriculum. Grammar, for instance, is attributed far greater value by secondary teachers than their primary colleagues (ibid.) and it has been found that there is little emphasis on verbs in primary classrooms (Cable *et al.*, 2010).

There are also considerable variations in the way languages are taught in different primary schools. In some schools, languages are 'embedded' in the curriculum, with little discrete language teaching time devoted to them. In this model, teachers teach chunks of language as they fit into the curriculum or the school day, such as during register time or while studying other areas of the curriculum such as geography or history. In other schools, languages provision may be made in a discrete half or full hour each week. The CILT 7–14 project set out to find examples of good practice in transition and to research successful approaches to teaching, especially at Key Stage 3, which support effective transfer. The study highlights some of the difficulties faced in Key Stage 2 to Key Stage 3 transition by today's secondary MFL departments:

Even if all pupils in a Year 7 class have studied the same language at primary school they may have been taught in very different ways or have covered very different areas of vocabulary and different grammatical structures. Some may have been used to a much more kinaesthetic approach to learning while others may have been exposed to much more listening and speaking as opposed to reading and writing. A number will have had experienced specialist or native speaker input, whilst others will have been taught by their class teacher. Some may only have received short taster sessions with a focus on learning a few set phrases or key words.

(CILT, 2007)

STRATEGIES TO FACILITATE TRANSITION

Although it is clear that numerous challenges surround the issue of Key Stage 2 to 3 transition in languages teaching it should not be assumed that strategies to facilitate this process are nowhere to be found. Some schools, secondary and primary, are developing their own ways of facilitating transition.

One such strategy used by some secondary schools is based on a more holistic model of teaching languages, rather than adhering to a model which sets out simply to equip pupils with functional knowledge of one language. An example of one school using this approach is King Edward VII School in Sheffield where one cohesive scheme of work begins in Year 3 in the feeder primary schools and continues into Year 7 and beyond, bridging the gap between Key Stage 2 and 3. The methodology for teaching at Key Stage 3 has undergone a complete paradigm shift with the emphasis shifting from the teacher as provider of knowledge to a facilitator of opportunities for pupils to learn from each other, sharing the knowledge and skills they acquired in primary school.

Rather than working on increasing their knowledge of one language, children in Years 7 and 8 foster their language learning skills, such as techniques for memorisation, and look at word families, identifying the links between different languages. There is also a cross-curricular element based on CLIL – Content and Language Integrated Learning – involving pupils being taught aspects of science, PSHE, geography, citizenship and RE through the medium of the foreign language. An increased focus on the culture of the target language country and the development of Personal, Learning, Thinking and Social skills (PLTS) provides additional focus on 'Meanings that Matter', rather than language being taught as an end in itself. In this way language can be developed in new and meaningful contexts, with students working cooperatively, irrespective of whether individual lexical items have been met at primary school or not.

Some of the features of this approach are shared by other programmes, designated language awareness or multilingual programmes, which set out to give primary pupils a taster of a range of different languages. The aims of such programmes include fostering generic language learning skills and linguistic sensitivity, and encouraging pupils to analyse different languages and draw comparisons with their mother tongue, thereby enhancing literacy. Such programmes also generally incorporate an element of cultural awareness, allowing pupils to contextualise the languages which they are learning about in the countries where they are spoken, and to learn about the cultures and ways of life in those countries. Part of the rationale behind such programmes is that they are much more accessible to non-specialist primary teachers who may lack the requisite subject and pedagogical knowledge to teach effectively at Key Stage 2. Teachers learn alongside their pupils with the help of interactive audiovisual resources which model language accurately.

One example of such an approach is the Discovering Language programme which is currently taught in around a hundred schools in Cambridgeshire and was piloted in seven schools in three different local authorities between 2004 and 2006. The programme involves teaching five to six languages, which may include French, German, Spanish, Japanese, Latin and Punjabi, to children in the last two years of primary school. An evaluation of the programme tracked the children from the start, in Year 5, through to Year 10 to establish how effective it had been in sustaining motivation as children opted into, or out of, languages study at Key Stage 4. When pupils were surveyed at the end of Year 7 it was found that those who had taken part in the Discovering Language programme were more confident than their peers who had had other language learning experiences in primary school, or who had not learned any languages at all (Barton and Bragg, 2007). Teachers also claimed to notice differences in pupils' motivation and confidence at the beginning of Year 7. By Year 10, it was found that these pupils were more likely to enjoy learning a language at Key Stage 4 and a slightly higher percentage opted for a language in Year 9 than from the other two cohorts (Barton and Bragg, 2010).

Conclusion: looking to the past and the future

It is widely acknowledged that the earlier children start learning other languages, the better. There are strong arguments for teaching languages at Key Stage 2, not least those relating to the importance of increasing foreign language capacity in order to boost the UK economy. Businesses commonly report on the adverse effects of not having enough capacity to sustain business within a global market (Tinsley and Comfort, 2012) and support the idea of an early start for learners.

What is less well known is that the learning gains pupils make during this time are largely dependent on the quality of the teaching they receive, as well as the length and frequency of their exposure (Tinsley and Comfort, 2012). Teachers, and head teachers, are keenly aware that introducing languages as a statutory part of the Key Stage 2 curriculum will not be without significant challenges, not the least of which is ensuring that pupils are enabled to build on the knowledge and skills they have acquired at primary school in the new secondary environment. A number of recent large-scale national languages studies have identified Key Stage

2/3 continuity and progression as a key area for further research (Driscoll *et al.*, 2004; Muijs *et al.*, 2005; NFER, 2007). The point has also been acknowledged by Government; a previous Government report recommends that more research is undertaken in order to support effective Key Stage 2/3 transfer in languages (Cable *et al.*, 2010).

Discussions about possible strategies for alleviating the dissonance that is currently experienced when pupils move from primary to secondary school often focus on primary schools as the location where practice needs to be adapted in order to fall into line with secondary practices. It is worth pointing out that facilitating transition to enable pupil progress needs to be a two-way process:

> Secondary language teachers' practice needs to be built on an openness to the diverse, unpredictable, and uncontrollable nature of the prior language learning experiences that Year 7 pupils now bring with them to the languages classroom. It will be increasingly counter-productive to ignore or repress this prior knowledge (or 'unlearn' as one of the case study heads of department said).
>
> (Evans and Fisher, 2012: 172)

Without wishing to take sides, it might not be completely unreasonable to suggest that secondary teachers, with their undoubtedly superior language qualifications, might be somewhat possessive of the curriculum and tempted to criticise the provision in primary school without being properly informed of its quality. As Evans and Fisher argue (2012), secondary teachers need to work with primary teachers, rather than denigrate what they do, and can no longer afford to regard languages as their sole domain. It is interesting that one of the findings of a recent longitudinal survey revealed some primary teachers' apprehension that information that they were passing onto their secondary colleagues about schemes of work and children's achievements in language learning was not being used effectively. These teachers were concerned that Year 7 work would fail to consolidate children's prior learning and that this would impact negatively on children's motivation and enthusiasm for language learning (Cable *et al.*, 2010). In the light of this, Cable and colleagues suggests the following ways of moving forwards:

- entering into learning partnerships with primary school colleagues to share and develop knowledge and expertise;
- reviewing the school's languages curriculum in the light of the objectives for children's learning in primary schools;
- deciding how children's prior achievements in languages can be built on in secondary schools to maintain children's enthusiasm for languages learning.

(Cable *et al.*, 2010: 151)

Such partnerships might begin to address the current deficit in knowledge that currently exists in a large number of primary schools. Effective provision of languages – in the primary and secondary classroom – is dependent, to a very large extent, on the knowledge of teachers – both in terms of subject knowledge and pedagogy. A recent Ofsted project, undertaken to identify primary schools which exemplified good practice, described one such school in the following terms: 'Teachers delivering modern language lessons have excellent subject knowledge and combine their skills as primary practitioners with a clear understanding of modern language methodology to excellent effect' (Ofsted, 2012).

If this is the standard to which primary schools need to aspire in order to ensure excellent provision then clearly there is a pressing need for ongoing training in order to enhance many schools' capacity as well as to sustain languages teaching in the long term. The Government's current pledge of no further funding for languages – as stated in the recent consultation document about the provision of primary languages – does not, unfortunately, suggest this will happen.

The answer might be to look beyond the provision of one language at Key Stage 2, as the government currently recommends, and to advocate a skills-based, rather than knowledge-based, course at Key Stage 2. This might eradicate the problems that are currently experienced at the transition stage when, often, a new language is introduced at Key Stage 3, interrupting continuity, or pupils who have learned a language at Key Stage 2 are forced to 'unlearn' in order to bring them into line with their classmates. Such a situation is reminiscent of the earlier 1960s 'Primary French' initiative which resulted in the abandonment of languages in primary schools. We must hope that the launch this time round will not meet the same fate for the same reasons.

Reflective enquiry

1   What differences have you observed between how languages are taught in the primary school classroom and in the secondary classroom?
2   If you were confronted by a Year 7 class consisting of some children who had learned languages in primary school and some who had not, how would you try to accommodate this in your lesson planning?
3   How would you set about incorporating the assessment data passed on from primary colleagues in your own teaching?
4   What steps would you take to ensure there was effective Key Stage 2 to 3 transition in languages in your own school?

Further reading

Barton, A., Bragg, J. and Serratrice, L. (2009) 'Discovering language in primary school: an evaluation of a language awareness programme', *Language Learning Journal*, Vol. 37, No. 2, pp. 145–164 (for an outline of an existing primary language awareness programme. What advantages/disadvantages does such a model seem to offer compared with a conventional single language programme?).

Kirsch, C. (2008) *Teaching Foreign Languages in the Primary School* (Continuum) (for an overview of how languages are taught in the primary school in other countries; theories of second language acquisition; case studies of primary schools which exemplify successful languages teaching; and approaches to teaching languages including assessment, transition and intercultural competence).

Chapter 13

The many faces of motivation

Suzanne Graham

Introduction

Most teachers would agree that motivation is vital for successful learning, and indeed research in second language learning suggests that it is one of the key factors influencing outcomes and may even be more important than aptitude (Gardner and Lambert, 1972). Yet despite several decades of research, we still do not have a definitive answer for what L2 motivation is or how it is best fostered. This is in part because motivation has many different sub-components and contributing factors, as signalled by this statement by Dörnyei (1998: 118) regarding key areas of importance in L2 motivation research: '*what* mental processes are involved in motivation, *how* these operate and affect learning and achievement, and *by what means* they can be enhanced and sustained at an optimal level' (emphasis in the original). In addition, he highlights the centrality of the '*temporal organisation of motivation*' (p. 131), i.e. the way it may fluctuate over time. These questions are of particular relevance for the UK context, not only because of continuing low levels of uptake and persistence beyond the age of 14 but also because English-L1 contexts such as in the UK pose particular questions regarding motivation to learn a second or foreign language. In such a context for pupils with English as L1, 'only non-world language learning can take place' (Dörnyei and Csizér, 2002: 455). Hence any 'utilitarian' reasons to learn a foreign language are likely to be much lower than in contexts where the L2 is the globally dominant English. Furthermore, changes in motivation over time are important in the UK context, given what we know about how it seems to wane at key milestones in our educational system, particularly at points of transition from one level of schooling to another.

A useful definition of motivation is provided by Weiner (1992: 17, original emphasis): 'Motivation is the study of the determinants of thought and action – it addresses *why* behavior is initiated, persists, and stops, as well as what choices are made'. These issues are very relevant to the context in England. Between 1992 and 2004, language study up to the age of 16 was compulsory there. During that time, the number of learners choosing to study a language beyond GCSE decreased sharply, especially in French, which saw a fall from 31,261 A-level entrants in 1992 to 15,173 entrants in 2004 (CILT, 2005). Since 2004, when it became optional to study a foreign language at Key Stage 4 (KS4), the number of pupils taking a GCSE in a language has decreased year on year. Numbers of pupils studying an MFL in KS4 have fallen particularly among pupils of lower socio-economic standing (Dearing and King, 2007; Vidal Rodeiro, 2009), with numbers remaining relatively stable in the independent and selective sector. The lack of popularity of MFL study, however, is not a new phenomenon. Indeed, a report by the DES in 1977 refers to low levels of uptake and enthusiasm for language learning among 15–16-year-old pupils, comments which echo the findings of more recent studies (see below). It would seem that numerous curriculum innovations since then (e.g. communicative language teaching, the GCSE) have had little positive impact on learners' motivation for language learning. Against this background, this chapter seeks to outline some of the main themes in motivational research and the different perspectives that have been adopted over the years, and to consider their relevance to the UK context on both a practical and a more theoretical level. From the above, it would seem that issues of persistence and 'motivational maintenance' (Dörnyei and Ottó, 1998: 46) are of particular relevance for the UK context.

L2 MOTIVATIONAL RESEARCH – TRENDS AND DEVELOPMENTS

A socio-educational approach

In the development of L2 motivational research, work in the 1970s and 1980s largely concentrated on the 'why' question, i.e. why do people choose to study a foreign language in the first place. This was the focus of the well-known work by Robert Gardner and colleagues in Canada, who argued that people choose to learn a language largely for two main reasons. First, they may adopt what he calls an *integrative orientation*. This refers to 'that class of reasons that suggest that the individual is learning a second language in order to learn about, interact with, or become closer to, the second language community' (Gardner, 1985: 54). Or their 'orientation' may be *instrumental*, where the reason for learning a second language is 'to gain social recognition or economic advantages through knowledge of a foreign language' (Gardner and Lambert, 1972: 14). In other words, learning a language in this case has a more utilitarian focus – the language is learnt for the use or benefit it will have for the learner's future life, perhaps employment prospects. Of course, the extent to which these two orientations will apply is bound to vary according to the learning context. In bilingual Canada, the setting of much of Gardner's work, interaction with the target language community is likely to be more important and possible than it is in a foreign language context such as England, where learners have little or no contact with speakers of French, German or Spanish, etc. on a regular basis. Similarly, while the importance of

English as a global language of communication means that for non-English speakers learning that language may have strong instrumental benefits, in terms of needing English to gain a job or entry into university, for English-speaking foreign language learners, instrumental reasons for foreign language study are likely to be of much less importance. Furthermore, school-aged learners have little choice until they get to a certain age as to whether they study a language or not, so that we might be better off considering instead the factors that influence levels of persistence and effort during language learning, rather than what influences initial choices – in other words, our attention might be less directed towards motivational influences that operate at the choice level, 'how intentions are formed', and more towards those that affect 'motivational maintenance' during task completion, perseverance and staying with the task or activity, once the choice has been made to undertake it (Dörnyei and Ottó, 1998: 46).

A CHANGE IN FOCUS: A COGNITIVE PERSPECTIVE

Gardner's work also maintains that motivation for L2 learning is fundamentally different from motivation for any other kind of learning, in that it is not just a subject of study: speaking a language also has implications for one's sense of identity in a way that, say, knowing about physics or chemistry does not. A language is also closely related to another culture, so that learners' attitudes to that culture may influence their learning in a way that applies much less, if at all, to other school subjects. On the other hand, it would be unwise to say that motivation for language study has nothing in common with motivation for other school subjects. This was the view expressed in the 1990s, most clearly in an article by Crookes and Schmidt (1991), which argued that research into L2 motivation could be enhanced if studies drew much more on perspectives from cognitive and educational psychology and also if they were much more clearly focused on classroom-based motivational forces. These perspectives can be clearly seen in more recent studies, where arguably L2 motivation is held to be much less about attitudes to the L2 community, i.e. relating to social factors, as in Gardner's model, and more about the individual's thoughts and beliefs, i.e. relating to cognitive factors, and about what happens in the classroom – i.e. about the influence of the teaching materials/approaches (as well as the teacher) and of the class dynamics.

   In more recent models of motivation, emphasis is placed particularly on the impact of learners' *thoughts and beliefs* on the choices they make and the degree of persistence they show. Ryan (2000, cited in Hufton *et al.*, 2002) asserts that cognitive studies of motivation are interested in two main questions that learners typically pose themselves: 'Can I do my homework?' and 'Do I want to do my schoolwork and why?' These questions reflect the concerns of 'expectancy-value' models of motivation (Eccles, 1983) which consider that an individual's level of motivation is influenced by: (1) their expectations of success in a given area; and

(2) the value they place on such success. They also suggest that the relationship between motivation and success is a complex one. The early work of Gardner and colleagues indicated that it was high levels of motivation that led to higher levels of achievement in language learning, i.e. that motivation caused success. By contrast, it also seems highly probable that the reverse is true – i.e. that the experience of success (or expectation of success) leads to higher levels of motivation. In what follows I will consider in particular studies that highlight the importance of expectations of success for heightened motivation for language learning.

In terms of expectations of success, an important perspective is offered by what is known as self-efficacy theory (Bandura, 1993, 1995). This suggests that individuals' choices, efforts and degree of persistence with tasks are influenced by their beliefs about their own abilities and competences to accomplish specific tasks (self-efficacy beliefs). Research in a variety of curriculum areas has consistently found that self-efficacy beliefs have a considerable impact on both levels of persistence and academic achievement (Mills *et al.*, 2007), yet relatively few studies of language learning motivation have included self-efficacy as a variable. Dörnyei and Ottó (1998: 44), who present language learning motivation as a 'dynamically evolving and changing entity, associated with an ongoing process in time', emphasise the centrality of persistence and engagement in the 'actional' phase of motivation, i.e. the phase where learning activities are being undertaken and need to be maintained for progress to be made. Bandura (1995) identifies two factors in the development of positive self-efficacy beliefs which are relevant to academic learning in general and arguably very important for MFL learning in the UK. First, what he calls mastery experiences, the achievement of success but not just 'easy success', which is less likely to promote perseverance and a problem-solving approach. Second, 'social persuasion', verbal persuasion from others, that one is capable of achieving well in a given area. Individuals need to receive positive appraisals of the likelihood of their success, but also need to be encouraged to 'measure their success in terms of self-improvement rather than triumphs over others' (Bandura, 1995: 4).

VALUE OR DIFFICULTY?

If we consider language learning motivation from an expectancy-value framework, then within the UK, several studies indicate that on the one hand, foreign languages are largely viewed by learners as subjects of little relevance or value to their current or future lives (Blenkinsop *et al.*, 2006). There is some evidence from Stables and Wikeley (1999) and Court (2002) to suggest that pupils see the 'value' and 'importance' of a subject mainly in utilitarian terms, that is, the extent to which they will enhance their job opportunities, or the likelihood of them going to the target language country to speak the language. Indeed, this utilitarian focus seems to be especially predominant where pupils express negative attitudes towards languages, while those who show more enthusiasm for them may see a value in language learning for its own sake, i.e. for intrinsic motivational reasons (Graham, 2002, and see also 'Motivation and autonomy', below).

Low motivation for MFLs does not, however, seem to be solely attributable to learners' failure to see the value of language learning in utilitarian terms. Indeed, some studies suggest that learners *are* aware of the potential usefulness of language learning for their future lives (Fisher, 2001; QCA, 2006). It might be argued that many subjects in the school curriculum that are popular with learners, such as drama or PE, are not perceived by learners to be directly *useful* in terms of getting a job. The perceived *difficulty* of foreign languages, especially when compared with other school subjects, seemed to be a more important reason for not choosing an MFL as a GCSE option among pupils in a study by the QCA (2006). This suggests that rather than *causing* achievement, motivation may *result* from achievement. The difficulty aspect may negatively affect motivation for MFLs for two reasons. First, it may persuade learners that MFLs have a 'boffer' or 'square' image (Bartram, 2006: 49; O'Reilly Cavani, 2000: 36), with peer pressure making some pupils reluctant to be seen choosing them, if being 'smart' is not considered positively within the school culture. Second, perceived lack of success or progress is unlikely to enhance pupils' desire to continue learning a subject, particularly within an expectancy-value theory of motivation as discussed earlier, i.e. where both expectations of success and the perceived value of a subject are held to influence motivation. Learners who are aware of the importance of good grades at GCSE and A-level for job prospects and university entrance may well be reluctant to risk taking a subject like MFL which they see as too much of a gamble in terms of likely success.

Studies that have looked at pupils' perceptions of their success or lack of it in MFL suggest that learners in England lack a sense of control over their language learning, and are unclear about how they might improve or make progress (Graham, 2002, 2004; Williams *et al.*, 2002). Even learners predicted top examination grades at GCSE seem to sense this lack of progress or real achievement (Graham, 2004), a feeling that may have a greater impact on pupils' decision to continue language study or not than the instrumental value they place in language learning. Indeed, a recent study (Erler and Macaro, 2011) suggests there is an important link between low self-efficacy (in a particular aspect of French, namely decoding, i.e. being able to 'sound out' a written word) and learners' reluctance to pursue study of the language after the age of 14. Furthermore, there is also evidence that this perception of lack of progress mirrors reality (an argument supported by successive reports by Ofsted, e.g. Ofsted, 2011). Erler and Macaro (2011) found that between Years 7 and 9, learners made almost no progress in their ability to decode French, even from a very low base.

ATTRIBUTIONS

Learners' sense of self-efficacy, and hence their levels of motivation, can also be influenced by what is called their 'attributions' (Weiner, 1979). Attribution theory argues that the reasons people subconsciously give to explain why they have been successful or unsuccessful can have either a positive or negative impact on how motivated they will feel to attempt a similar task in the future. Hence, if learners believe that they did badly on a vocabulary test because they used ineffective memorisation strategies (something that could be put right for subsequent tests), then it is more likely that they will feel motivated to try again on a later test, as this 'attribution' is internal to them and under their control. By contrast, learners who attribute lack of success to less controllable, and to external factors, such as poor teaching or simply being 'no good' at languages, may be less motivated to make another attempt. A small number of studies of language learners in the UK have looked at learners' attributions and how these relate to their motivation for language learning (for example, Erler and Macaro, 2011; Graham, 2004; Williams *et al.*, 2004), but have drawn important conclusions regarding the impact of attributions on learners' motivation to continue with language learning beyond the compulsory phase. Thus, in the Erler and Macaro (2011: 508) study referred to earlier, the authors found, through questionnaire data, that nearly 50 per cent of their large, representative sample (1,735 Key Stage 3 learners across 25 schools in England) made attributions for success/failure in French to external factors such as luck or chance, and to the 'weirdness' of the French language and its sounds. The authors go on to comment that 'the very nature of the language was seen to place control over learning it beyond the student's power. The student was then less likely to envisage continuing with French'. Likewise, in another large study, this time of Year 11–13 learners (involving a total of 594 learners, and using questionnaires and interviews) Graham (2004) found that Year 11 (sample size 286) learners who planned to continue with language study post-16 were more likely to make attributions linked to internal, controllable factors such as effort and effective use of learner strategies than non-continuers. Overall, however, few of the learners in the study made strategy-related attributions, with task difficulty and low ability in languages being common 'explanations' for lack of success, which may be interpreted as a sense of 'helplessness' and passivity regarding meeting the challenge of language learning.

MOTIVATION AND TRANSITION

A sense of a lack of progress, or even of regression referred to in the above studies, seems to occur particularly at points of transition, e.g. from primary to secondary school, from GCSE to A-level language study. Prior to the widespread implementation of Primary Languages, a number of studies found that demotivation for MFL sets in very early at secondary school. Davies (2004) claims that it begins as early as Year 7, while a large-scale study by Coleman *et al.* (2007) suggests that motivation for MFL dips in Year 8. It seems that periods of transition are crucial, because they bring with them new challenges. Learners' ability to cope with such challenges, to deal with problems when the 'going gets tough', seems to be vital for persistence in language learning. In turn, this ability to cope seems to be more likely to occur when learners attribute setbacks to controllable factors (Ushioda, 1996, in Erler and Macaro, 2011). Ushioda (2012) refers to the importance of motivational resilience at points of increased difficulty in one's language learning career, a point also made in Graham (2006b) in the depiction of how different Year 12 students cope with the challenge of moving to post-GCSE work. In that study, students termed 'minimalists' and 'stagnators' were those who up to GCSE had experienced few challenges in their language learning, and who felt that success was possible with little effort and largely attributable to some 'inborn' language talent. For them, the challenges of Year 12 were harder to deal with, as they had not developed any means earlier at school for solving language learning problems. By contrast, so-called 'mastery' students showed marked insights into the role of effort and suitable strategies in dealing with new challenges, and as a result, showed fewer signs of waning motivation post-GCSE. In such situations of increased difficulty, experiencing 'fun' or 'enjoyment' from language learning is simply not sufficient to bolster learners' motivation, and more fundamental forms of motivation are needed to sustain learners. These factors may be especially important at the primary/secondary transfer point. Bolster *et al.* (2004) report that where inadequate transfer mechanisms exist between primary and secondary school, and pupils' early language learning is not built upon or is even ignored, the impact on learners' motivation for MFLs is a negative one, as they perceive that their progress in language learning slows down once they reach secondary school. In a later study, Bolster (2009) comments that while both anecdotal and more systematically collected evidence seems to suggest that language learning in primary schools fosters high levels of motivation for languages within the primary setting, whether this motivation is maintained in the secondary school is at best unclear. From her own small-scale study, it is interesting to note that the most demotivated 'continuer' was the learner who seemed to have made the least progress at primary school and to find the subject difficult, suffering from low self-esteem and lack of a sense of achievement (Bolster, 2009).

IMPROVING MOTIVATION

The strong link between motivation and achievement is made especially clear by Macaro (2003: 115) who claims: 'Whatever the causal direction, it seems to me we have to start with the self-efficacy issue. Demotivated learners have to be given the tools with which to find the subject easier and make more rapid progress'. Some studies that have investigated how to improve language learning motivation have had considerable success by giving learners such 'tools'. For example, working with Year 7 and 8 learners of French, Macaro and Erler (2008) not only helped improve learners' ability to read in French by teaching them how to apply learner strategies to solve reading 'challenges' (through a structured programme of reading strategy instruction over 14 months), they also saw an improvement in the learners' level of motivation for reading and for French overall. Likewise, working with Year 12 learners of French, Graham and Macaro (2008) improved learners' self-efficacy for listening through a programme of listening strategy instruction which taught learners strategies to apply to listening 'problems'. In both studies, feedback, in the form of Bandura's (1995: 4) 'social persuasion' played an important role. This feedback was on the extent to which learners had used the strategies they had been taught and how this had led the learners to solve the particular language challenges they had faced. It also made suggestions for ways in which strategies might be applied on future tasks, helping learners, in the words of one learner, to 'get in the right frame of mind to do it ... If something's difficult, I don't sort of like panic about it' (Graham, 2007: 90). Hence feedback made learners more aware of the direct link between how they approached the task and how well they did on the task, giving them a greater sense of control over the learning outcome.

MOTIVATION AND SENSE OF SELF

Self-efficacy, and how confident one feels to carry out a learning task, is also likely to relate closely to one's sense of identity. Arguably, if learners feel they are unable to express themselves clearly and fully in the foreign language, their sense of 'self' in the foreign language classroom is likely to be a fairly negative one. Indeed, the notion of 'self' and 'identity' is an important one in recent L2 motivational research. Perhaps the most influential work in this area is by Dörnyei (e.g. 2005) with his 'ideal self' theory. This argues that an important element in strong L2 motivation involves the learner having an 'ideal self' image that includes the ability to speak a second language (Dörnyei, 2005). It has been argued that the 'ideal self' is less important for younger, adolescent learners, as their self-image is not yet fully formed (Kormos and Csizér, 2008; Lamb, 2011). Busse and Williams (2010), however, studying university-level learners of German in England did find a relationship between students' enjoyment of German and 'the ability to envision oneself as a successful speaker of that language' (p. 75). However, if, as I have argued earlier, language learning has negative image connotations for learners in England, then the ability to speak a language is unlikely to form part of their 'ideal self'. By contrast, in countries where the L2 is English, being a successful language learner is more closely associated with being able to access employment, travel and popular culture, and therefore more likely to form a positive 'ideal self' image. Dörnyei (2005) also refers to the 'ought to self', a self whereby being a successful language learner is something that is imposed externally by others (e.g. by parents or by teachers). This is likely to have a much less positive impact on motivation.

MOTIVATION AND AUTONOMY

Indeed, having an element of choice as to whether one learns a foreign language or not, and regarding how one learns a language, is also an important factor for motivation, and ties in with another influential, if less recent, theory of motivation that is frequently applied to learning in general. Deci and Ryan's (1985) self-determination theory places motivation on a continuum from intrinsic to extrinsic. The former is held to be based on innate human needs for competence and 'self-determination' – i.e. undertaking an activity for its own sake, for the sense of satisfaction and accomplishment it brings in meeting the challenge of a task. By contrast, extrinsic motivation is experienced for activities that are somehow imposed on us, or are carried out to avoid punishment or gain some kind of reward. Freely choosing to undertake an activity rather than because of some external imposition is more likely to foster a sense of autonomy in learners and thus the more deeply rooted form of intrinsic motivation. This has important implications for MFL study within the UK context, with policy measures that somehow impose language study on learners unlikely to lead to heightened and lasting intrinsic motivation. Earlier it was argued that negative attitudes towards language learning were more closely associated with learners viewing languages in terms of the extrinsic rewards they might bring, i.e. whether they would lead to improved employment prospects, while learners with positive attitudes to language learning are more likely to value them for their own sake, i.e. for intrinsic reasons. Evidence from other contexts (e.g. in the US) indicates that more intrinsically motivated students are likely to continue studying a foreign language while extrinsic (i.e. more instrumental) motivation characterises discontinuing students (Ramage, 1990). These studies suggest that while it might be necessary to foster both intrinsic and extrinsic motivation in language learning, an emphasis on intrinsic motivation may be a more fruitful approach for encouraging further language study.

Conclusion

The above gives some idea of the complexity of motivation as a construct, and the myriad of different theories that have been developed to try to explain it. There is still much to be done in terms of deepening our understanding. Important gaps in our knowledge concern the relative contribution to motivation of 'value' and 'expectations of success' in different educational contexts (especially in English L1 contexts like the UK); what impact so-called 'motivational teaching strategies' such as allowing learner choice, promoting a positive classroom environment and others (Guilloteaux and Dörnyei, 2008) might have on learners' motivation; and how teachers' own motivation influences that of learners. Given the positive impact on self-efficacy that has been found, however, from teaching approaches that give learners the 'tools' to deal with language learning challenges by teaching them how to apply learning strategies successfully and to see how this leads to successful learning outcomes, we need in particular more studies that explore this avenue of work across a wider range of learners.

Reflective enquiry

Reflective questions

1   Think back to your own subject choices at age 16 and 18. What factors determined your choices? Job prospects, being good at the subject, wanting to live abroad, or others? What insights do these reflections give you regarding what might influence learners' motivation for different school subjects?

2   Look at these two different forms of feedback. Which might have a more positive impact on the learner's motivation to do better on the task next time? Justify your comments.

   a   'You have used a range of different verbs in your writing. Well done! Now let's see if next time you can get all the endings right.'
   b   'I'm glad to see you are reading accompanying questions and blurb to get an overall sense of the passage before you start – that's important, so that you don't get bogged down by detail too soon. Try to think quite broadly at first about what you might hear, especially for the first listening – and remember that you might not hear the exact word you have predicted, but a synonym for it or a phrase.' (Graham, 2007: 86)

3   Think about the motivation of learners with English as an additional language to learn a European language such as French, German or Spanish. What might be positive or negative influences on their levels of motivation?

Suggestions for small-scale research studies

You might consider exploring e.g. what attributional tendencies do your learners show? Try exploring them using one or more of the following suggestions:

1   Give them a simple questionnaire like this one (from Graham, 2004):

---

1   Please complete the following statements:

   a   'When I do well in French, it's usually because_____'
   b   'When I don't do so well in French, it's usually because _____
   _____'

2   Think about areas in French in which you have done well (e.g. listening, speaking, reading, writing, grammar, etc.). Name the *one* area where you have had the *most* success: _____
   _____

---

3   Why have you been successful in this area, do you think? Circle the *one* number from 1 to 6 which best matches how you feel about each reason below.

I've been successful in this area because...	Agree strongly				Disagree strongly	
I'm just good at that kind of thing	1	2	3	4	5	6
It's just luck	1	2	3	4	5	6
I try hard	1	2	3	4	5	6
I use good techniques or strategies	1	2	3	4	5	6
We're given easy work	1	2	3	4	5	6
Are there other reasons? Write them here.						

4   Now think about areas in French in which you have not done so well (e.g. listening, speaking, reading, writing, grammar, etc.). Name the *one* area where you have had the *least* success: _____
_____

5   Why have you been less successful in this area, do you think? Circle the *one* number from 1 to 6 which best matches how you feel about each reason below.

I've been less successful in this area because...	Agree strongly				Disagree strongly	
I don't try very hard	1	2	3	4	5	6
I use poor techniques or strategies	1	2	3	4	5	6
I'm just no good at that kind of thing	1	2	3	4	5	6
We're given difficult work	1	2	3	4	5	6
It's just bad luck	1	2	3	4	5	6
Are there other reasons? Write them here.						

See also Williams *et al.* (2004).

If your learners mainly seem to attribute lack of success to low ability and getting difficult work, try changing the type of feedback you give, to help them focus on how using different strategies or ways of working may help them improve. Then give the questionnaire again to see if their attributional tendencies have changed.

2   Consider the various factors believed to influence motivation in this chapter (e.g. learner autonomy, seeing the link between success and strategies used, perception of 'value', etc.). Choose one that you might be able to manipulate in your teaching as an 'intervention' (e.g. giving learners more choice in how they complete tasks). Administer a questionnaire (see Coleman *et al.*, 2007 and Williams *et al.*, 2002, for examples, which you can adapt to suit your context) before doing this, to assess your class's level of motivation. Then administer it again after your intervention, to see if it has had any impact.

NB   For both of the above suggestions, you should seek further guidance regarding how to interpret any questionnaires you administer.

Further reading

Chambers, G. (1999) *Motivating Language Learners*, Clevedon: Multilingual Matters.
——(ed.) (2001) *Reflections on Motivation*, London: CILT.
Coleman, J.A. (2009) 'Why the British do not learn languages: myths and motivation in the United Kingdom', *Language Learning Journal*, 37(1): 111–127.
Dörnyei, Z. (2001) *Motivational Strategies in the Language Classroom*, Cambridge: Cambridge University Press.
Dörnyei, Z. and Ushioda, E. (2011) *Teaching and Researching Motivation*, Harlow: Longman.
Macaro, E. (2008) 'The decline in language learning in England: getting the facts right and getting real', *Language Learning Journal*, 36(1): 101–108.

Chapter 14

Learning strategies, autonomy and self-regulated learning

Michael Grenfell and Vee Harris

Introduction

This chapter seeks to bring together three large areas of research and debate in second language learning and teaching: learning strategies, autonomy and self-regulation. A key argument in the chapter to state at the outset is that the three are intimately connected, although curiously often treated separately in much of the research literature. The chapter begins with a historical perspective.

THE HISTORICAL VIEW

Why should we be interested in such notions as learning strategies, autonomy and self-regulation in language learning and teaching? Is it not true that our main focus in the classroom is the imparting of a good lexical knowledge in the target language, and a developed understanding of the necessary grammar? The historical view somewhat confirms this position. The dominant linguistic paradigm for language learning until well into the twentieth century was essentially structural: that linguistic competence *was* knowledge of syntax and vocabulary. Such a belief had a direct correlation on classroom practice. So, if the goal was vocabulary and grammar proficiency, the best way to teach them was direct transmission; for example, through dictation, translation, comprehension exercises and testing. This is essentially the 'intellectualist' view of learning and teaching, that languages are learnt through analysis and re-application of rules.

A counterposing 'behaviourist' view has language as a 'skill' that is learnt like any other skill – through practice and repetition. The prevailing perspective here is psychological and follows the general course of behavioural theory from the 1930s in its explication of mental processes (see the work of Watson and Skinner). This issue raises the interesting question of the relationship between learning theory and actual pedagogy, as well as the time delay from one impacting on the other. So, although behavioural views of learning were prevalent from the 1930s, their impact on actual teaching did not fully flower until the 1960s, in this case with the rise of the 'language laboratory' with their tapes and endless series of drilling exercises. Audio-visual and audio-lingual courses also assumed this relationship, if somewhat more semantico-globally between the drilling of stock phrases and the acquisition of a second language.

The Chomskyan revolution of the 1950s offered a radically different view. Here, language competence was seen much less as a knowledge base or skill than an inherent characteristic of the human brain. Indeed, a Language Acquisition Device (LAD) was posited, which was seen as being innate to all humans and giving rise to any number of languages depending on particular linguistic environments. In this world, whilst 'surface structures' followed individual languages, they all shared the same 'deep structures'. This natural view of language, language proficiency, and indeed competence leads to an obvious conclusion that second language (L2) learning could match and follow processes in the first (L1) (although it should be noted that this position was never argued by Chomsky himself). This conclusion was most famously articulated by Stephen Krashen who argued that L2 competence was gained through comprehensible input (note, much as in our L1), and that the formal learning of linguistic rules could never impact on real acquisition. His 'Natural Approach' to language teaching (1996) attempted to operationalise this theory in pedagogic practice. All of these models are, however, singularly psychological and language itself is treated entirely 'in itself': that both language learning and teaching operated still through its syntax and vocabulary. A single statement by Hymes (1972) shows up the doubtful nature of such a belief: 'There are rules of use without which the rules of grammar would be useless'. In other words, language is never 'in-itself' and is always 'for-itself', and this 'for' is social, personal and cultural.

The rise of Communicative Language Teaching (CLT) suggested that this need not be a problem and, in effect, one could have one's own theoretical cake and eat it. CLT is very much predicated on a social cultural view of language teaching; so, the communicative classroom is designed around the personalisation of language work, information gap activities, legitimate, authentic materials, and on linguistic fluency as opposed to accuracy as its focus. It is easy to see that, from this perspective, such a social, cultural approach to language pedagogy fits quite nicely with the sort of 'natural' method promoted by Krashen and his advocates.

A British perspective

Of course, one might ask what all this has got to do with teachers and pupils in the British context? Crucially, quite a lot. It is well known that classroom pedagogy is heavily influenced by assessment format and procedures which, until the early 1990s, were essentially designed around grammar-translation tests demanding accuracy over fluency and writing over speaking. Teaching therefore remained highly 'structural' – with a high preponderance of translation, dictation and comprehension tests – albeit supplemented with a wide range of audio-visual and audio-lingual techniques.

The introduction of the national curriculum in modern foreign languages in 1990 changed all that, with its reformulation of the aims and objectives of language learning in terms of the four skills, pupil-as-tourist interacting with the sympathetic native speaker. Suddenly, personal communication was prominent in teaching and testing materials, and so-called 'authentic' learning situations were designed to develop 'communicative competence'.

One effect of this change was an instant impact on motivation, as pupils who previously were being drilled into accurate submission, were able to play and experiment with the language more. A national inspection report from 1988 refers to the samey, predictable nature of language classrooms pre-national curriculum (Gathercole, 1990: 4). The latter, together with a national 'language for all' drive heightened the sense of expectation that at last, in CLT, we had a methodology that would deliver in terms of enhanced linguistic competence for a substantial majority of our pupils. Sadly, this vision turned out to be a mirage. As early as 1998, inspection findings reported on how pupils seem to be plateau-ing out in their language learning after initial years, producing little independent language away from drilling – again! – in stock (now communicative) phrases (see Dobson, 1998). The Nuffield inquiry (Nuffield Foundation, 2000) made for even more gloomy reading, and painted a picture of most pupils dropping languages as soon as they were able and of the lack of motivation and direction in many lessons. The language teaching profession responded robustly (see Grenfell, 2000). However, despite this, the years following the report saw the withdrawal by government of the 'languages for all' policy, which itself has exacerbated pupil drop-out in languages with the subsequent knock-on effect in terms of undergraduate recruitment, and the number of language teachers joining schools. But, what has this got to do with autonomy and learning strategies?

THE 'WHAT' OF AUTONOMY

One of the key features of both the traditional language classrooms as described is their highly prescriptive nature. Whether grammar-translation or CLT, the teacher is still in control: designs the lessons, decides the content, sets the pace, organises the assessment. The pupil can simply rely on the teacher to make all these decisions. 'Lack of independence' is also mentioned in both Nuffield and inspection reports as a feature of the classrooms they observed. So, we can surmise that independence is a desirable outcome of language learning; indeed, it is difficult to conceive of a successful language user who is not also an autonomous language user, choosing what to say and how to say it. But, what if autonomy is not simply a desired feature of successful language learning, but a means to that end; that autonomy *is* the key to linguistic achievement? How can that be?

In a classic definition of autonomy, Holec (1981) describes it as, 'the ability to take charge of one's own learning'. This would seem to be quite a broad definition and, as such, is not without problems. For example, what is ability, and is it the same as capacity, or even skills?; whilst 'to take charge' might imply 'control', 'intention', or 'responsibility'. Behind such questions lay an issue already alluded to in this chapter, a rather basic one, but no less problematic for that: the relationship between the learner and the learner environment. So, although Holec was writing very much in terms of an attribute of the learner, others have been much more concerned with the actual learning situation. Allwright (1988: 35), for example, refers to learner autonomy as 'associated with a radical restructuring of language pedagogy'. Indeed, many of the early enthusiasts came at autonomy in terms of classroom activities, for example the French and German coursebooks *Auto* and *Solo*, which built a pedagogy around a commitment to the autonomous language learner. Leni Dam (1990, 1995; Dam and Gabrielsen, 1988) was also a key individual in showing how to create the 'autonomous classroom'. Quoting from various documents, she lists learner autonomy as:

- choosing aims and purposes;
- choosing methods and tasks;
- exercising choice and purpose in organising and carrying out the chosen tasks;
- choosing criteria for evaluation and using them in evaluation.

(Dam, 1990: 16)

Whilst Little insists that it is essentially 'a matter of the learner's psychological relation to the process and content of learning' (1991: 4), more recent books again refer to autonomy very much in terms of classroom pedagogy (see for example Jiminez Raya *et al.*, 2007) and of the environment that teachers should create in their classroom. This has inspired some teachers to make radical changes in attempting to create more autonomous conditions for language learning.

AUTONOMY AND LEARNER STRATEGIES

However, no matter how inspirational the goal of autonomy is, and however creative teachers have proved to be in setting up classrooms to foster independent learning, something still appears to be missing. In 1993 Grenfell and Harris described how the initial enthusiasm of the students in their London inner-city classroom soon waned. They struggled to read the authentic materials they were presented with. They failed even to recognise cognates, seeming to perceive the new language as wholly unrelated to their existing knowledge. Furthermore, their search to express their own meanings was thwarted by their inability to use the dictionary. They did not even know that the dictionary was divided into two halves. From these challenges emerged for them the connection between autonomy and the research field of language learner strategies (LLS). It seemed that it was not enough to provide opportunities for students to learn independently, they needed the tools or strategies to be able to exploit those opportunities.

The development of research into language learner strategies

Rubin's seminal study 'What the "Good Language Learner" can teach us' (1975) sought to uncover what it is that they do that separates them from their less-proficient peers. Her list included: Monitoring, Memorisation and Inferencing. With some notable exceptions (Wong-Fillimore, 1979), most of the early studies into language learner strategies (LLS[1]) could be characterised as being more from this psycholinguistic perspective. Oxford (1990: 8) for example, defines learning strategies as: 'Specific actions taken by the learner to make learning easier, faster, more enjoyable, more self-directed, more effective, and more transferable to new situations'.

We will return to Oxford's definition towards the end of the chapter. Based in the USA, many of these earlier studies focused on adult learners, often learning English either as a second language or a foreign language.

Although the 'Good Language Learner' (GLL) was a key concept in establishing the study of learner strategies as a legitimate field of research, the approach was subsequently criticised for two main reasons; the first broadly psychological, the second sociocultural. From a psychological stance, in place of the perfect learner consistently using a large number of strategies, the focus has shifted to the qualitative and symbiotic deployment of clusters of strategies appropriate to the particular task in hand (Cohen and Macaro, 2007). Thus what characterises the successful learner is not *the number* of strategies used but *how* they are used and orchestrated in combination with other strategies. For example, simply looking for cognates can lead to 'wild card guessing' unless the student combines this strategy with monitoring and inferencing to double check that the cognates are not 'false friends'. These are words that appear to have a similar meaning to L1 words but in fact mean something else. Thus *car* in French means 'coach' or 'for' not 'a car'. Recognition of the complexity of strategy use has provided a richer picture of the language learning process.

The second limitation of the GLL research is the emphasis on the individual, rather than on the group, on the cognitive rather than sociocultural. In her work with immigrant adult learners in Canada, Norton (2000: 125) argues that: 'the relationship between the individual and the social in the context of second language learning should be reconceptualised', drawing on notions of power, identity, economy and capital. She stresses that even when individuals possess some of the characteristics of the 'Good Language Learner', if they are shy or unforthcoming, they can often be socially marginalised by busy, impatient native-speaker peers or colleagues. Their opportunities to engage in communication and thus to develop their language are severely restricted (Norton and Toohey, 2001). The importance of the context is also clear in Levine *et al.*'s study (1996). They found that the prior learning experiences of recently arrived ex-Soviet ESL learners in Israel, who had been educated within the highly structured and uniform system, meant that their strategies were more rigid and less creative than those used by people who had lived in Israel for at least five years. Moving from these wider learning contexts to the sociocultural aspects of the classroom itself, Donato and McKormick (1994) in the USA draw on Vygotsky's work to suggest the value of establishing a community of language learning practice in which learners share how they reflect on, plan and monitor their learning. Such a focus connects closely to the definition of autonomy discussed earlier which emphasises choice of aims, tasks and criteria for evaluation. In England, Coyle (2007a) describes how strategic classrooms can be created to foster the development of LLS even with young beginner learners of German.

Oxford and Schramm (2007) have sought to reconcile these two critiques of early LLS research, one from a psycholinguistic and one from a sociolinguistic stance, urging future studies to recognise the complex interaction between the individual and the world in which they operate.

Theoretical constructs underlying learner strategies

A further debate characterising current LLS research is the call for: 'theoretical research to develop precision in our conception of strategies' (McDonough, 1999: 14). Similarly, Grenfell and Macaro (2007) emphasise the need to clarify the learning theory underlying a LLS approach. For example, strategy taxonomies may include the rather mechanical skill of effective dictionary use alongside the more process-based behaviour involved in 'inferencing'. At issue is whether both can be understood from the same theoretical perspective. Dörnyei (2009b: 183), for example, argues that rather than being a separate research field, LLS are simply expressions of each individual's 'idiosyncratic self-regulated behaviour'. The range of categories and the overlap in LLS taxonomies compounds the problem and makes cross-study comparison particularly difficult. In their seminal study, O'Malley and Chamot (1990), for example, distinguished between the cognitive skills used to handle the language itself, the metacognitive skills of planning, monitoring and evaluating the learning and the social and affective skills of collaborating with others and managing one's own anxieties. Other authors concentrate on particular skill areas such as reading or writing (Macaro, 2001b). In an attempt to address the problem, Macaro (2006) defines strategies as conscious mental actions directed towards the achievement of a particular goal. In contrast to Oxford's definition discussed earlier (op. cit.), he stresses that: 'strategies do not make learning more efficient; they are the raw material without which L2 learning cannot take place' (Macaro, 2006: 332). Grenfell and Harris (1999) also see strategies as lying at the heart of the learning process since all language learning is problematic to a greater or lesser extent, and therefore inherently 'strategic' in character. However, Grenfell and Harris do not limit strategies to *conscious* behaviour. For us, strategies operate on a continuum between the conscious and the unconscious. The deployment of a particular cluster of strategies may well only rise to the conscious level when the learner encounters a particular problem; the rest of the time, they may be deployed automatically. We thus draw on Anderson's distinction between *declarative* and *procedural* thinking. The successful learner may well have proceduralised a whole set of strategic behaviour. Their automatic response to some aspects of the learning situation is an advantage since it means there is a minimal impact on short-term memory, leaving plenty of mental capacity for the more challenging aspects. For example, instinctively knowing to skip some words in order to grasp the overall meaning of a sentence frees up space to identify those words that are essential to understand and to use inferencing to try to make sense of them.

Whatever the issues in terms of definitions, LLS has proved a rich area of research as is evident even in the title of Cohen and Macaro's book (2007) *Language Learner Strategies: Thirty years of research and practice*. One of the areas of interest it has generated is in Strategy-Based Instruction (SBI). Given that it cannot be assumed that all students will develop the necessary learner strategies, it is claimed that: 'intervening in learners' strategic behaviour can improve learning processes and ultimate attainment' (Cohen and Macaro, 2007: 4). Teaching students how to develop their LLS is all the more important for students in an autonomous learning environment, since they must become less dependent on the teacher and more reliant on their own skills.

TEACHING LEARNERS HOW TO LEARN

It is unsurprising that LLS research became increasingly interested in SBI. Rubin (1990: 282) highlights its potential benefits for low attainers, linking it to motivation: 'Often poor learners don't have a clue as to how good learners arrive at their answers and feel they can never perform as good learners do. By revealing the process, this myth can be exposed'.

Initially there was some debate as to whether the SBI should just be embedded in the materials (O'Malley and Chamot, 1990). However, there was increasing consensus that it should be made explicit, given that the aim is to promote the development of autonomous self-management. Thus students need to be able to choose the appropriate strategies in the service of their own particular goals, and for the specific tasks they are faced with (Gu, 2003; Oxford *et al.*, 2004; Rubin, 2005). For the same reasons, it is more likely to be effective if integrated into regular language lessons rather than taught in a separate, generic 'study skills' course. Learners need to see exactly how and where to apply the strategies within their everyday language-learning activities.

A number of models for teaching LLS have been developed (National Capital Language Resource Center, 2003; Chamot *et al.*, 1999; Grenfell and Harris, 1999; O'Malley and Chamot, 1990). However, Rubin *et al.* (2007) point out that there is a sequence of four steps common to all of them, so that although the initial instruction is highly scaffolded, it is gradually lessened to the point that students can use the strategies independently. The sequence begins by raising awareness of the strategies the students are already using and moves on to the teacher modelling new ones. There is then an extensive practice stage, preferably in pairs or groups after which students evaluate the effectiveness of the strategies used and transfer strategies to new tasks. An illustration of each step can be found in Rubin *et al.* (2007).

The importance of a communicative focus to the SBI is underlined by Little (1996: 26) who argues that:

> Some pedagogical traditions have devoted so much time to the explanation, illustration and memorisation of grammatical rules that no time has been left to develop communicative ability. Much the same danger attends the current obsession in some quarters with 'strategy training'.

A particular concern is that often the awareness-raising step of the SBI is conducted in the L1, especially with beginners. This reduces the time students spend engaging with the L2. Others justify the use of L1 (Macaro, 2001b; Grenfell and Harris, 1999) on the grounds that time spent on this initial step will ultimately be worth it as students are then better equipped to grapple with the language independently.

A further challenge in relation to SBI is how to pitch it at the appropriate level. As Chamot *et al.* (1999: 99) warn:

> If the task is too easy, students will not need strategies to succeed; they may therefore see strategies as a waste of time. However, if the task is too difficult students may not be able to succeed even when they do use appropriate strategies.

Harris and Prescott (2005) illustrate this dilemma when they record the difficulties beginner students of French experienced when they were presented with unfamiliar authentic materials and at the same time invited to exploit a wide range of reading strategies. Students' initial enthusiasm rapidly disappeared as a result of the burden placed on their mental processing capabilities. The teachers responded by scaffolding the learning into smaller steps. So students first practised a small cluster of related strategies using familiar textbook material. It was only once they were comfortable with this type of activity that an extended group work presentation encouraged them to move on to using all the strategies independently to tackle authentic material.

The need to explore the match between the level of learner and the nature of the SBI activities is evident in one of the aims of the EPPI[2] review (Hassan *et al.*, 2005), namely to:

> Uncover differential effectiveness for different languages, different learners (school, university, adult), different stages of learning (beginner, intermediate,

advanced) and different language skills (reading, writing, listening, speaking, overall ability etc.). In doing so, we hoped to explore why different types of strategy training might or might not work.

Although initial findings as to the effectiveness of SBI were somewhat discouraging (McDonough, 1995), the EPPI review provides some promising evidence for the value of strategy training, especially in reading and writing. The evidence for listening and speaking is less conclusive and studies have not yet been conducted across all these skills as to whether any positive effects last over time. One reason why the listening and speaking SBI may be less successful is the demands of online processing, which leaves little time to reflect on the optimum strategy. For example, in engaging in conversation the student is both struggling to think of how to say what he wants as well as deciding which strategies are appropriate to tackling the gaps in their linguistic repertoire. Similarly one 12-year-old student who had experienced both listening and reading SBI explained why she found the reading SBI more useful: 'it is hard to use listening strategies because you can't go back to the words you don't understand' (Harris, 2007: 197). In contrast, reading and writing allows the student time to reflect on possible strategies to make sense of a particular word, or to express a particular opinion. Hence it is possible that SBI in listening and speaking is more suitable for advanced learners. However, as Rubin *et al.* (2007) point out, few studies indicate whether and how the choice of skill areas and strategies has been tailored to meet students' proficiency level. Furthermore they argue that in terms of reliable research evidence, there is often insufficient detail as to the nature of the SBI; for example, over what period of time it lasts, the type of activities used to model and practise the strategies and the extent to which it includes metacognitive strategies to ensure that students learn to reflect, plan and monitor their learning.

AUTONOMY, LANGUAGE LEARNER STRATEGIES, GOVERNMENT POLICY AND TEACHER EDUCATION

So far in this chapter we have looked at the rationale and theoretical underpinnings for autonomy and language learner strategies and autonomy. In sum, this perspective offers a new approach to second language teaching per se; one that is predicated much more on the organisation of the learning environment, and where learners take much more control of their own learning, than on the actual teaching of language in itself. Given the weight of evidence in favour of at least some aspects of autonomy and LLSs it might be thought that significant policy changes in the UK have emerged as a result. However, the picture is at best ambiguous.

If we take the last decade or so, we see that governmental policy planners have to some extent been sympathetic to the idea that teaching for all pupils should include a large component of learning skills; for example, McGuinness' lists of *thinking skills*: sequencing, sorting, grouping, comparing, hypothesising, recognising, predicting, testing, concluding, classifying, etc. (McGuinness, 2000). Many of these skills overlap, or indeed, would appear as being synonymous with the sorts of strategies listed in language learning strategy research itself. However, such 'strategy' work has often been adopted simply for its utilitarian potential – helping students with tips for learning – rather than as a principled base to language learning. The approach to 'language learning' for bilinguals seems to take a similar line. The Modern Foreign Languages KS3 Strategy (DfES, 2003a) itself was conceptualised in terms of skills and techniques, which may in some ways be understood as 'strategic'; for example, how to check written work, how to memorise, how to select, plan and monitor. These skills and techniques were spread out over 100 items listed for development over the first three years of secondary language learning. 'Strategies' are then conceptualised within an existing dominant curriculum model of language of the National Literacy Strategy (DfEE, 1998): 'word level', 'sentence level' and 'text level'.

More clearly needs to be known about the patterns of language learning strategy deployment of the learner. How do learners differentiate themselves in terms of individual differences (gender, bilingualism, motivation, aptitude, etc.)? And how do these impact on SBI, levels of independence and LLS deployment? To take the case of bilingual learners, for example, do they have a wider range of cognitive strategies than monolingual students across certain skill areas? What differences are there across skills? Do bilingual learners transfer some strategies like 'substitution' – acquired through extensive exposure to two languages – from listening to other skills? Do they perhaps have more advanced metacognitive strategies? If they are indeed more 'language aware', it might be expected that they have greater knowledge, but do they use it? What features of their environment contribute to the development of these strategies? Norton and Toohey (2001) suggest that the whole 'Good Language Learner' research agenda itself has given insufficient attention to the relationship between the individual and the social aspects of access into classroom discourses. The cultural background and psychotypology of individual learners obviously interacts with their ability to employ strategies. It might be that traditional approaches to 'strategy instruction' do not tap into what learners already know about language and how to use it; in other words, they are simply not processing language in *this* way, or indeed, operationalising strategies *like that*. Clearly, learners need to locate strategy instruction in their own sociocultural background to language learning, which might include a range of contexts, and make distinctions between new strategies for them and the ones they already use. Curriculum documents, which are based around a model of language which expresses it in terms of word, sentence and text levels may actually impair learners, as it offers a uniform approach to language learning as well as stressing writing and reading rather than the oral/aural skills. Indeed, a more social psychological focus might complement a broader 'strategic classroom' approach to MFL learning for learners.

Many of these points resemble some of the hunches that practising teachers have about language learners. It would be true to say that language policies of recent years have been much more proscriptive and prescriptive than was traditionally the case. Forcing autonomy and LLS on teachers as something else to teach is therefore very 'un-autonomous'. This is why it is only really possible to have autonomy with learners if teachers share in that autonomy (see Little, 1995).

AN AGENDA FOR FUTURE RESEARCH

As yet the causal link between strategy use and performance remains to be proved, rather than just remaining on the level of correlation (Cohen and Macaro, 2007). Is it the case, for example, that it is their deployment of strategies that renders learners successful? Or rather is it that proficiency levels determine particular kinds of strategy use? In other words, 'the research question "why do certain learners behave in certain ways?" has rarely been asked' (p. 23).

Some of the other issues to be included on the agenda for future research emerge from the earlier discussion. The paucity of studies into schoolchildren as opposed to adults or university students remains a source of concern. Similarly, whilst investigations have moved beyond English to examine the strategies used to learn French, German or Spanish, the cultural imperialism discussed by Wharton (2000) continues to be an issue. It is only in the last decade or so that research has been conducted into the strategies used to learn a language with a non-alphabetic script. For example, Shen (2005), Tseng (2000) and Ke (1998) have explored the LLS used to study Mandarin Chinese – a character-based language (see Jiang and Cohen [2012] for a review of LLS studies into Mandarin Chinese). In an increasingly global economy, there is likely to be ever more demand to learn languages such as Urdu, Arabic and Mandarin Chinese. Indeed by 2012, there has been a 40 per cent increase in the number of students taking the GCSE exam in Mandarin Chinese (NARIC, 2012). Whilst many strategies may be common to all languages (for example, inferring the meaning from the context), others are unique to a particular language. Using an example from Mandarin Chinese again, Shen (2005: 64) reports her students: 'try to recognise the radicals that I have already learned'.[3] Understanding the full repertoire of strategies needed to learn a particular language can be helpful for teachers wishing to undertake SBI with their students.

Within the SBI research field, more longitudinal studies are needed, along with more detailed descriptions of the SBI, and comparison with control classes. Little is known also regarding the most suitable skill areas for beginners as compared to advanced learners. Furthermore, over and above differences between school and university contexts suggested in the EPPI review, Chamot (2005) indicates the importance of comparing children in foreign language immersion to non-immersion programmes, and children in bilingual to second language programmes. Differences in the learning situation may well impact on the strategies already used and students' 'receptiveness' to new ones. Similarly Grenfell and Harris (forthcoming) argue that more studies are needed of the strategies used by bilingual students to learn a third language in school. They suggest that some bilingual students may find the beginners' classroom so far removed from the natural learning context of their home environment that they may fail to transfer valuable strategies.

Finally, returning to Little's point, there is still some discussion as to whether the progress made following SBI might equally well result from alternative pedagogical approaches. For example, in one of the few investigations of primary school students, apart from studies like those of Chamot and El-Dinary (1999), Macaro and Mutton's (2009) study compared a group of 10–11-year-old students who underwent SBI in inferring meaning with those who studied 'graded readers' and a control group. Whilst the SBI group outperformed the graded readers group in inferring the meaning of the new words in six sentences, there was no significant difference in the reading comprehension test. The subsequent discussion as to possible reasons for the latter findings highlights some of the difficulties in carrying out research with younger students, including difficulties in devising appropriate tests at this level. This may be a priority for future studies.

There are then a range of exciting avenues to explore, widening out the research to younger as well as adult learners, to non-European languages, and the wide variety of contexts in which languages are learned; from formal to autonomous classrooms. Discovering what remains the same and what changes and how may give us further insight into the language learning process. Hopefully it may allow us to identify just what is the most fruitful way to support confident and successful independent learners.

Conclusion

This chapter has explored a range of experience and knowledge within the area of autonomy and language learner strategies. We saw how both of these can be situated historically and need to be understood in terms of learning theory. They are both predicated on a generative–cognitive view of language learning; in particular, the latter with its 'learning to learn' rather than 'teaching the learner'. We have seen how autonomy and language learner strategies are inextricably linked; it is not possible to be a 'successful' language learner and not be an 'independent language learner', and this principle implies a range of 'good language learner learning behaviour'. However, we have also seen that such an approach is fraught with challenges and assumptions, and that underlying teaching/learning processes are a complex mix of the social and the psychological. Moreover, there is a chronic tension between language learning and teaching research, government policy and classroom pedagogy. We made the point that the type of autonomous learning classroom that may be envisaged assumes teacher independence; whilst recent history is one of intervention and prescription.

Finally, it is worth pausing to consider the ways in which what is discussed in this chapter is predicated on different types of knowledge. So, traditional techniques to be found in the language classroom – role-plays, listening tasks, reading comprehension, etc. – are simply ways of organising the input and manipulation of language; briefly, cognitive activity. Recent research suggests that such activity can be designed to develop particular dimensions of linguistic proficiency, for example, accuracy, fluency, sophistication, etc. As we have seen, learner strategies are of a different order of knowledge and mental activity. We have called these 'metacognitive' – 'beyond mental activity' – as a way of drawing attention to the skills, tricks, techniques, behaviours and attitudes that learners adopt in managing their own learning. That learning presupposes a degree of choice, and therefore independence, but autonomy takes us one step further from actual practice itself. Indeed, it is probably best understood as a 'condition' of language learning, rather than a technique of strategy. But, as a condition, a little goes a long way and may impact on several levels at once. Moreover, it may well act as a kind of catalyst to learning, an accelerator of learning and teaching. This is why, finally, it is such a critical aspect of the successful language classroom.

Reflective enquiry

Reflecting back on when you were a student in school learning a new language, what strategies did you use? Were you always conscious/aware of using them?

1   What opportunities are there for a busy classroom teacher to identify students' strategies? e.g. asking them how they worked out an answer to your question, observing how they tackle pair work?
2   What further opportunities could you create? e.g. brainstorming the strategies they use, setting up group work, focusing on one table at a time.
3   What strategies do most of your students use? What strategies are they lacking? Are they cognitive or metacognitive strategies? In which skill areas?
4   Read Harris and Snow (2004) – the details are in the further reading section, below.

   a   What way of conducting strategy instruction with your classes suits you best?
   b   How would you persuade your students that it was worthwhile spending time and effort to learn new strategies?

5   How could you tell if the strategy instruction had been successful? e.g. in improving students' performance or their motivation level?

Further reading

Cohen, A.D. and Macaro, E. (eds) *Language Learner Strategies: Thirty years of research and practice*, Oxford: Oxford University Press.

Coyle, D. (2007) 'Strategic classrooms: learning communities which nurture the development of learner strategies', *Language Learning Journal*, 35(1): 65–79.

Dam, L. (1995) *Learner Autonomy 3: From theory to classroom practice*, Dublin: Authentik.

Gathercole, I. (ed.) (1990) *Autonomy in Language Learning*, London: CILT.

Grenfell, M. and Harris, V. (1999) *Modern Languages and Learning Strategies: In theory and practice*, London: Routledge.

——(2013) 'Learning to learn languages: the differential response of learners to strategy instruction', *Curriculum Journal* (in press).

Harris, V. and Snow, D. (2004) *Classic Pathfinder: Doing it for Themselves – Focus on learning strategies and vocabulary building*, London: CILT.

Notes

1   There is a degree of discussion in the relevant literature as to whether the correct term should be language learner strategy or language learning strategies. In the past, these were used synonymously. Issues of taxonomy and definition remain. For the purpose of this chapter, we do not draw a sharp distinction between the two forms.

2   The EPPI-Centre (Evidence for Policy and Practice Information and Co-ordinating Centre) was established to develop a systematic approach to the organisation and review of evidence-based work. Its work and publications engage health and education policymakers and practitioners in discussions about how researchers can make their work more relevant and how to use research findings.

3   Radicals can sometimes provide useful clues to meaning since they can indicate the general semantic category of the character (such as water- or fire-related). For example, the radical for liquid occurs in both 汤 (tāng) meaning soup and 汗 (hàn) meaning sweat.

Part III

Educational debates

Chapter 15

Making the case for the future of languages

Rosamond Mitchell

Introduction

Against a background of the debate about the relative value of languages at different ages, this chapter considers the contribution it makes to learners' general education. A rationale for the subject will emerge which will delineate the unique place of languages in school life and the way forward as the curriculum is shaped to meet the needs of the next generation.

THE WIDER SOCIAL CONTEXT FOR LANGUAGES IN EDUCATION

The twenty-first century is self-evidently an era of globalisation. In this context, linguistic landscapes have outgrown traditional ideas grounded in nineteenth century nationalism, of one nation – one language (Blommaert and Rampton, 2012). Some sociolinguists have used the term 'superdiversity' to describe the state of affairs in today's post-industrial cities. The example of London is a striking one; thanks to many decades of economic and social migration, a recent survey showed that 40 per cent of London schoolchildren are multilingual users who report using at least one language other than English at home (Economic and Social Research Council, 2012). Over 230 different languages are involved (Baker and Eversley, 2000), and over 40 of these languages have more than 1,000 speakers. For such speakers, complex multilingual practices and language 'crossing' are routine parts of self-expression.

In the wider UK, linguistic diversity has also been increasing steadily, alongside new patterns of economic activity and related migration. For the first time, in 2012, over one million children in English schools have been reported to speak languages other than English; this includes one in six primary school age children, and 12.9 per cent of the secondary school population (NALDIC, 2012). Across England the most frequently reported languages are Punjabi, Urdu, Bengali and Polish; numbers for Polish have doubled between 2008 and 2012 (to *c.*54,000 school-aged speakers).

Multilingualism is thus becoming increasingly usual, even in societies traditionally strongly associated with a single national language. However, multilingualism is itself hierarchically structured. According to the Dutch sociologist, Abram de Swaan, the world's 5,000 or so languages are organised as a 'global language system' (Swaan, 2001). Almost all languages alive today are spoken locally for face-to-face communicative purposes (and in Swaan's system, these count as 'peripheral' languages). Around 100 'central' languages are vehicles of education and government (and are likely to be acknowledged as 'national' languages). However, a much smaller number of languages possess at least 100 million users, and perform the functions of a regional/international lingua franca: Swaan's list of these 'supercentral' languages includes Arabic, Chinese, English, French, German, Hindi, Japanese, Malay, Portuguese, Russian, Spanish and Swahili. Swaan's central thesis is that multilingualism is typically one-directional, and involves speakers of a peripheral or central language, learning a central or supercentral language; while speakers of languages higher up the hierarchy are much less likely to master lower-level languages.

In such a global language system, English occupies today a historically exceptional place, as 'the world's primary language for international communication' (Neil Kinnock, quoted in Graddol, 2006: 2). It is the pre-eminent language of international relations, business and science, of travel, media and much popular culture (Crystal, 2003), and remains – just – the pre-eminent language in the dynamic and fast evolving world of the internet (Internet World Stats, 2013). Against this background, knowledge of English is highly prized, and around two billion students are currently learning it, at ever younger ages, and increasingly through English-medium instructional models (Graddol, 2006). A recent survey of proficiency in languages conducted in 14 European countries on behalf of the European Commission found that 42 per cent of secondary school students tested could perform at levels B1/B2 of the Common European Framework of Reference for Languages in their first foreign language (almost always this was English: European Commission, 2012a). New communities of middle-class English users are emerging in different parts of the world (India, Africa, Singapore), and the dominance of 'native speaker' English is being challenged by local varieties and uses of English, and by the spread of 'lingua franca' usage among professional groups across Europe and beyond.

Despite the current standing of English as supercentral language, however, it is clear that any global language system is far from static. Chinese, Hindi and Spanish are identified by Graddol (2006) as potential contenders to displace English in key regions of world economic activity. Trends in media, telecommunications and the internet clearly show strongly increasing linguistic diversity, as rising economies become better connected (Internet World Stats, 2013). Rising standards in education are seen internationally as central to economic success, in a post-industrial 'knowledge economy' – hence the enormous interest in international educational 'league tables' such as PISA or TIMSS, and worldwide investment in sending ever increasing proportions of young people to higher education. Internationally there is a strong emphasis on language learning (often but not always with English learning as key driver) as an integral part of this educational effort, and in combination with the migration patterns mentioned earlier, this is systematically producing greater levels of multilingualism in many populations and particularly among mobile professionals.

Against this backdrop, many commentators view the monolingual bias of traditional anglophone societies as problematic (see e.g. Graddol, 2006). The 2002 National Languages Strategy argued that:

> In the knowledge society of the 21st century, language competence and intercultural understanding are not optional extras, they are an essential part of being a citizen ... Likewise in the global economy too few employees have the necessary language skills to be able to engage fully in international business.
>
> (DfES, 2002: 5)

A British Academy report (Tinsley, 2013) continues to stress the need for multilingual skills within the British economy. Tinsley concludes that language skills are needed not only by an internationally mobile elite, but also in very varied administrative, clerical and manual contexts (e.g. among health-care professionals). This report argues that while the languages most popularly taught in the UK (French, German, Spanish) are all useful from an employment perspective, a much wider range of languages is used in business and in public sector organisations, and there is considerable unmet need for multilingual staff. Specialist linguist roles (teacher, interpreter) account for only a small proportion; main needs are for language skills in combination with other workplace skills, and also for the intercultural awareness that accompanies foreign language learning. These needs can partly be met by harnessing the language skills of the existing multilingual population (e.g. for Polish or Chinese), but the main argument of Tinsley (2013) is for a more strategic approach to languages at all educational levels.

OVERALL RATIONALES FOR LANGUAGES IN EDUCATION

While employment-related needs are a significant part of the context for education, the inclusion of any given subject in the curriculum requires a broader rationale (Alexander, 2010). The leading thinker on the contribution of languages to the curriculum in the era of comprehensivisation, and proponent of 'languages for all', was arguably Eric Hawkins of the University of York. Hawkins (1981: Chapter 2) acknowledged the instrumental value of high levels of language achievement, for at least some school students. However, he also developed general arguments relating to intercultural learning ('emancipation from parochial prejudice'; 'escape from the monoglot's prison', etc.), and also above all relating to 'language awareness', favouring a systematic and comparative relationship between English mother tongue instruction, and foreign language learning. In a 2005 article, Hawkins revisited these ideas, arguing for 'educational' encounters with foreign languages centring on the development of language awareness in Key Stages 2 and 3, but including a 'serious attack' on an 'apprenticeship language' in Key Stage 3, and 'instrumental' language learning from age 14 onward (Hawkins, 2005).

The educational value of languages was elaborated further during the initial development of the National Curriculum from the late 1980s onward. The MFLs Working Group chaired by Martin Harris articulated eight 'educational purposes' of foreign language teaching in their Initial Advice to government (National Curriculum MFL Working Group, 1990: 4–5):

- to develop the ability to use the language effectively for purposes of practical communication;
- to form a sound base of the skills, language and attitudes required for further study, work and leisure;
- to offer insights into the culture and civilisation of the countries where the language is spoken;
- to develop an awareness of the nature of language and language learning;
- to provide enjoyment and intellectual stimulation;
- to encourage positive attitudes to foreign language learning and to speakers of foreign languages and a sympathetic approach to other cultures and civilisations;
- to promote learning of skills of more general application (e.g. analysis, memorising, drawing of inferences);
- to develop the pupils' understanding of themselves and their own culture.

The National Curriculum itself went through several versions in the 1990s, and statements of educational purpose evolved somewhat for languages. Thus the 1999 version stated:

> Through the study of a foreign language, pupils understand and appreciate different countries, cultures, people and communities – and as they do so, begin to think of themselves as citizens of the world as well as of the United Kingdom. Pupils also learn about the basic structures of language. They explore the similarities and differences between the foreign language they are learning and English or another language, and learn how language can be manipulated and applied in different ways. Their listening, reading and memory skills improve, and their speaking and writing become more accurate. The development of these skills, together with pupils' knowledge and understanding of the structure of language, lay the foundations for future study of other languages.
>
> (DfEE and QCA, 1999: 14)

This somewhat more streamlined statement is interesting on the one hand for its clearer commitment to broad intercultural learning ('citizenship of the world' replaces a narrower focus on a particular culture and civilisation); and on the other, for its more explicit commitment to learning about 'basic structures of language', and how these work in L1 and in the foreign language, in place of the earlier, more general statement about developing 'awareness of the nature of language'. Nonetheless, Hawkins' major educational themes are recognisable, along with the assumption that a practical experience of language learning will develop transferable skills for the future.

The National Curriculum rationale statements are cast in general terms, though in practice they were operationalised with reference to the 11–16 age group (and from 2004, when learning a language in Key Stage 4 ceased to be mandatory, the 11–14 age group). In the following sections, arguments supporting the teaching of languages in primary and secondary education are examined more closely.

EARLY LANGUAGE LEARNING: SAME OR DIFFERENT FOR TWO LANGUAGES?

First, however, it is necessary to examine briefly claims and beliefs about young children's natural language learning abilities, and the implications for promotion of second language learning at very young ages. Everyday observation tells us that young children are predisposed to learn language implicitly, through engagement in meaningful interaction, and the availability of rich input in their immediate environment. Theoretical explanations of these abilities still differ, but however they are conceptualised in detail, current research supports the view that these capacities can comfortably support the learning of more than one language, in the early years, where these languages are available and used in immediate family and community settings (Meisel, 2004). Simultaneous-bilingual children can master the distinctive features of each language (phonology, grammar, form-meaning connections), though in varying degrees depending on exposure and use; uses may gradually become differentiated, and one language may in due course become dominant, but these are functions of later use, not of any limitations to mental capacity.

There are thus no obvious reasons, from a child development perspective, to delay or restrict naturalistic exposure to more than one language in the pre-school stage. Indeed, some positive cognitive benefits have been demonstrated for early-onset and sustained bilingual development, including increased metalinguistic awareness and capacity to 'objectify' and analyse language (Bialystok, 2004). There are also no obvious developmental reasons to delay languages learning in the educational system, though teaching and learning approaches must be appropriate for children's maturational level (e.g. for early learners, mostly implicit and meaning-oriented), and the same cognitive benefits cannot be assumed for instruction offering just a few minutes' learning per day or per week.

Is there a 'critical age' for second/foreign language learning, which might influence educational decision-making re starting times for languages instruction? Or does language learning ability remain available throughout life? There have been longstanding debates on this issue, and there is still no full consensus among researchers (see e.g. review in Singleton and Ryan, 2004). It is clear that languages *can* be learned to an advanced level at any age, though learning processes and strategies will differ by age, and 'native speaker' capacity is not normally attained by later starters. An early start to languages instruction has many positive features, but it does not constitute any kind of 'magic carpet' or shortcut to advanced proficiency.

RATIONALES FOR LANGUAGES AT DIFFERENT EDUCATIONAL STAGES

If the provision of a positive language-learning experience is seen as an integral part of every child's education, for the educational and societal reasons outlined earlier, then, what are the particular advantages attaching to language study at particular ages and phases? Here, the discussion will focus on a number of overall objectives derived from the foregoing discussion, and consider them at each phase:

- providing a successful language learning experience;
- providing experience of intercultural learning, promoting intercultural understanding;
- boosting language learning motivation and confidence, and reducing anxiety about language learning;
- contributing to children's broader cognitive, academic and social development;
- promoting higher levels of ultimate language learning proficiency.

RATIONALE FOR PRIMARY LANGUAGES

A successful language learning experience

Over the years, many individual projects and initiatives have demonstrated that successful language-learning experience can be provided within the primary school curriculum. In accordance with their level of cognitive maturity, younger primary school children learn best through implicit approaches, receiving rich input, engaging in large amounts of varied practice, and using the new language for meaningful purposes (Muñoz, 2006b). This makes immersion and/or content and language integrated learning (CLIL) particularly appropriate for this age group, and internationally, primary school immersion or partial immersion programmes have frequently been shown to develop substantially children's second/foreign language competence (see for example, Thomas *et al.*, 1993). UK primary immersion/CLIL initiatives are unusual, but the evaluators of the Aberdeen partial French immersion programme, for example, reported levels of foreign language achievement equivalent to that achieved in the upper secondary school (Johnstone and McKinstry, 2008).

Where a language is taught as a subject, again, many individual projects in the 2000s in England have demonstrated successful language learning, including Pathfinder projects (Muijs *et al.*, 2005), and schools following the Key Stage 2 Framework for Languages (DCSF, 2005a) and/or the QCA Schemes of Work for Key Stage 2 Languages (QCA, 2007b, 2009). Cable *et al.* (2010) documented achievement in some schools approximating to *Breakthrough* level on the Languages Ladder/Common European Framework of Reference for Languages (CEFR) schemes (DCSF, 2005b; Council of Europe/Council for Cultural Cooperation, 2001). However, it was clear from much work in the 2000s that sustainable language learning success depends on adequate teacher training/ supply, as well as on strong curriculum planning and overall commitment on the part of head teachers and schools more generally (Wade and Marshall, 2009).

Development of intercultural understanding

There is a general international consensus around the key educational contribution of languages to the development of intercultural understanding – a change from more traditional ideas which saw language study as the means of accessing and understanding a particular 'external' culture (Byram, 1997; and see Hennebry, Chapter 10, this volume). From this perspective:

> The goal of learning is to decentre learners from their own culture-based assumptions and to develop an intercultural identity as a result of an engagement with an additional culture. Here the borders between self and other are explored, problematised and redrawn.
>
> (Scarino and Liddicoat, 2009)

As explained by Hennebry in Chapter 10, Byram (1997) has argued that learners need to develop a set of knowledge and skills to achieve intercultural competence: he labels these in French as *savoir, savoir être, savoir comprendre, savoir apprendre/ faire*, and *savoir s'engager*. Primary school age children already possess some knowledge (*savoir*) about their own social group's cultural practices, together with some less fixed ideas about linguistic and cultural difference (Liddicoat, 2004). Byram suggests that attitudes of openness and curiosity (*savoir être*) particularly characterise primary-aged students; the upper primary age group is also seen as capable of empathy with others.

Again, research studies of primary languages initiatives in the 2000s generally provide evidence of schools giving some attention to this domain. For example,

Muijs *et al.* (2005) observed engagement with native speakers, themed days, email-based exchanges, activities with children in other countries, and trips to countries where the language was spoken. Cable *et al.* (2010) reported similar practices, and documented impact on children's knowledge and attitudes in some cases. More generally they observed that where language learning was being complemented by other wider school initiatives (such as international partnerships), the combination offered great potential for the development of both empathy and *savoir être*. However, it is clear that considerable development of teacher skills, curriculum and resources is needed for intercultural competence to become a central goal for the mainstream.

Motivation, confidence and anxiety

There is a very longstanding tradition in language acquisition research which links high levels of motivation and positive attitudes to learning success (though the direction of influence has been much debated: Dörnyei and Ushioda [2011]; and see Graham, Chapter 13, this volume). Demotivation is known to affect teenage learners to greater or lesser degrees, especially boys in anglophone settings; a major reason to teach languages in the primary school is to try to forestall this problem, by building on young children's known curiosity and empathy, and promoting confidence and feelings of self-efficacy by providing an experience of learning success. (Dörnyei [2001] provides many suggestions for making the languages classroom a motivational environment, and others are reviewed in Graham, Chapter 13, this volume.)

Many empirical studies of primary languages report high levels of enjoyment of languages learning, together with positive attitudes (e.g. Muijs *et al.*, 2005; Johnstone and McKinstry, 2008; Cable *et al.*, 2010), with no striking gender differences. Nikolov (1999) reports some evolution in primary children's attitudes; from ages six to eight, positive attitudes derived largely from the immediate classroom context ('we have fun'/'the teacher is nice'). However, older children displayed more instrumental thinking ('it will be useful when I travel'); other researchers have argued that older primary students can acquire a positive image of themselves as a language learner, and may experience intrinsic motivation (enjoyment of the language learning process itself: Cable *et al.*, 2010: 43–44).

The obverse of learning confidence is foreign language anxiety, associated with lower participation and success in classroom learning. Again, numbers of teachers involved with the introduction of languages to the primary school have claimed that lower-attaining children acquire confidence and become less anxious in the languages lesson, because of a sense that everyone is on a level playing field for once (and perhaps also because oracy typically receives greater attention than literacy: Cable *et al.*, 2010: Chapter 4).

Cognitive and academic development

Earlier in this chapter, claims were mentioned briefly that early bilingualism leads to certain cognitive advantages, connected with metalinguistic awareness. There is persistent interest in the possibility that languages learning in the primary school may also confer wider benefits for other aspects of education.

In the international literature, there has been extensive research on immersion education models for the primary stage, which has generally shown that broader academic achievement of experimental groups at least keeps pace with control groups being taught exclusively through their first language. Some studies show academic advantages for immersion students; thus for example, Thomas *et al.* (1993) tracked over 700 'volunteer' students through an early partial immersion programme (Grades 1 and 2) in Virginia, USA. These children were receiving instruction in mathematics, science and health through one of French, Japanese and Spanish. They were carefully matched to a control group being taught in English, and statistical comparisons were made between their mathematics and English achievement and that of (1) the control group, (2) the general primary population in the area. This study showed that the immersion students performed as well as the control group in mathematics, and significantly better than the general primary population. In English language tests, they performed significantly better than both the control group, and the general primary population.

Some international research on foreign languages as a primary curriculum subject has also claimed wider academic benefits for participating children. For example, a recent Louisiana study (Taylor and Lafayette, 2010) tracked a cohort of 600+ children attending schools which taught French or Spanish for a minimum of 30 minutes a day (FLES schools), from Grade 3 to Grade 5. Their progress on regular state tests of (English) language, reading, mathematics, etc. was compared with that of comparable children attending non-FLES schools. The language learners regularly outperformed the control group on English language tests, and sometimes outperformed them in other subjects.

These studies are not directly comparable with UK learning contexts (most importantly, the amount of target language exposure was considerably greater than that in most UK primary school contexts). They also deal with slightly atypical populations (individual volunteers for immersion in the study of Thomas *et al.*, children attending volunteer FLES schools in the study of Taylor and Lafayette). Nonetheless the common finding of a benefit for first language development, is striking and encouraging for primary languages.

Over a number of years, Richard Sparks, Leonore Ganschow and their associates have followed a research agenda trying to document and explain the relationship between L1 attainment and FL learning (see e.g. Sparks *et al.*, 2006). In longitudinal studies extending over nine to ten years they have tracked the relationship between early achievement in L1 literacy, foreign language aptitude, and later success in instructed foreign language learning, providing evidence that early literacy achievement in L1 is predictive of later foreign language learning success. However, in their later work (e.g. Sparks *et al.*, 2009) they place increasing emphasis on the idea of common underlying metalinguistic skill, i.e. the ability to 'think about, reflect on and manipulate language' (p. 746). This metalinguistic skill is developed through early literacy development, and provides a strong foundation for later instructed FL learning (i.e. language aptitude).

There is little UK research to fully test these ideas, though an early study by Skehan and Ducroquet (1988) showed that children designated as early/fast developers in the Bristol study of first language acquisition had an advantage as foreign language learners many years later, in secondary school. The belief persists among primary educators that L1 and L2 attainment must be related and can mutually support each other (see e.g. comments of professionals reported in Cable *et al.*, 2010). However, given the limited amount of overall teaching time typical for languages, and the limited attention given to FL literacy in most UK primary languages projects, it is difficult to draw substantial conclusions about this relationship.

Boosting ultimate proficiency

Some past experience (the 1970s 'French from Eight' project) has suggested that under UK conditions, starting language learning in the primary school confers no particular advantage, at least in terms of the eventual proficiency level which is reached (Burstall *et al.*, 1974). International research provides conflicting evidence on this issue. Muñoz (2006a) reports a longitudinal study of primary and secondary school learners of English in Catalonia, which showed consistent relative advantages for the 'later starters' (i.e. secondary school starters), in terms of their rate of learning, over equivalent numbers of hours of instruction. The suggestion of Muñoz and her associates is that older post-primary learners are more efficient classroom learners, reflecting their greater cognitive maturity. Scarino *et al.* (2011) report 'no discernible advantage' for an early start in Asian languages in the Australian context. On the other hand, the recent EU comparative study of language learning draws the clear conclusion that 'For the majority of educational systems, languages and skills, ... an earlier onset of foreign language teaching means a higher score on the language tests [at age 14 or 15]' (European Commission, 2012a: 74).

It seems obvious that focus on particular target languages, curriculum coordination and effective management of transition from primary to secondary school will all be needed, if an early start is to influence the proficiency levels which are eventually obtained. Problems with transition were a likely cause of the disappointing Burstall findings (1974); this issue surfaced again in all of the studies of early language learning conducted in the UK in the 2000s (e.g. Driscoll *et al.*, 2004; Muijs *et al.*, 2005; Cable *et al.*, 2010), and in the Australian research of Scarino *et al.* (2011). Evidence provided in the last of these studies, and also from experience with the Asset Languages scheme (Jones, 2007), shows that under current primary school conditions, it is possible to bring children to approximately level A1 on the CEFR scheme by the end of Year 6, given a consistent weekly hour of instruction throughout Key Stage 2. However, it is only when all or most children are achieving to a similar level, and the secondary school curriculum takes clear account of this, that consistent measurable impact on ultimate attainment can be expected.

RATIONALE FOR LANGUAGES IN SECONDARY SCHOOL

This section focuses on rationales underpinning the study of languages for all, in Key Stage 3 (and perhaps in Key Stage 4). The lower secondary school is known to be a crucial stage for children's decision-making about eventual specialisations and career paths (Schoon and Parsons, 2002). A successful language-learning experience at this point is therefore highly relevant to achieving the broader societal aims for languages set out by Tinsley (2013).

A successful language-learning experience

Many research studies show that teenage learners acquire a foreign language initially at a faster rate than younger learners, even if early starters may outperform them in the long run. In the classic study of Snow and Hoefnagel-Höhle (1978), for example, learners of Dutch aged 12–15 were initially more successful at acquiring syntactic and morphological rules as well as vocabulary, and showed greater metalinguistic ability, than younger comparison groups. A recent study reported by Myles and Mitchell (2012) also showed that 11-year-old learners acquired French grammar more quickly than five- and seven-year-old learners, after the same amount of instructional time. At this age, increasing cognitive maturity allows for the conscious deployment of more learning strategies, including planning and evaluation of one's own learning. Target language literacy can build on literacy skills in the first language, and will support increasingly independent learning. But European research evidence strongly suggests that early teenage learners will succeed best where systematic language study is complemented by opportunities for meaningful target language use, face to face and virtual, in and out of the classroom (European Commission, 2012a).

Development of intercultural understanding

Michael Byram has consistently argued that the development of intercultural communication competence (ICC) is an essential justification for inclusion of language learning in the curriculum for all students (Byram, 1997, 2008). He sees lower secondary school pupils as diverse in their personal development:

some ready to handle abstract concepts, others not, some more readily able to decentre and take another's perspective, others largely ethnocentric. Their existing knowledge of their own national culture is probably substantial, as they are well into their process of secondary socialisation, but will have significant, but not easily predictable gaps ... insufficient knowledge and experience of [target language] countries, and the stereotypes and prejudices which arise, suggest that particular attention must be paid to these.

(Byram, 1997: 83)

Byram and associates have made numerous proposals for both classroom-based and structured 'external' experiences of 'otherness' for this age group, which can develop the various *savoirs* of his model. He has summed up the type of competence which can be developed as a 'threshold' ICC, including substantial knowledge about at least one target culture, the ability to analyse and interpret texts and events from that culture and learners' own, identifying values, and coping with different perspectives and conceptualisations of the world (1997: 84–85). Once again, these ideas have been trialled successfully in local projects and initiatives (Byram, 2001), but have never been fully operationalised e.g. in the UK curriculum, at least to GCSE level. (At the time of writing, in spring 2013, a fresh national consultation is taking place regarding National Curriculum content. The draft curriculum for modern languages omits any explicit reference to ICC and its development: DfE, 2013.)

Motivation, confidence and anxiety

As Graham has discussed in Chapter 13, the lower secondary school is a point in pupils' school careers where motivation for languages is likely to decline, perhaps after a positive beginning in Year 7. Language learning frequently comes to be seen as difficult, by younger English-speaking teenagers, as not relevant to daily life, and as unlikely to be useful in future careers.

When considering rationales for primary languages in an earlier section, it was argued that young children's positive attitudes and relative curiosity about other people were reasons favouring an early start to languages. On the other hand, a decline in motivation in the secondary school years is a challenge to be addressed. Some research has shown inconsistent progress in language learning in Key Stage 3; for example, Milton (2006) and David (2008) both report striking 'plateau' effects in French vocabulary development between Year 8 and Years 10/11. (The children in Milton's study learned on average only 50 new words during all of Year 8.) It seems highly likely that this 'plateau' is associated with lower motivation, and that the two issues need to be tackled together.

That is to say, sustaining motivation and engagement for this age group is key to ongoing progression and successful outcomes in languages. Graham argues that promotion of feelings of self-efficacy (confidence in one's own language learning abilities and likelihood of success) should be central to pedagogy. Other commentators on secondary school motivation also stress the role of curriculum content and activities:

> It is particularly in these years [Key Stage 4] that the context of the learning needs to be stimulating to pupils and to engage them in discussion, debates and writing about subjects that are of concern and interest to teenagers.
>
> (Dearing and King, 2007: 11)

Examples of motivational content offered by Dearing and King accord well with the suggestions of Byram regarding the teaching of intercultural competence (Byram, 2001), and with those of the European Commission (2012a) regarding exploitation of external resources. CLIL also provides means to link target language with meaningful content, and the research literature describes numerous successful examples of CLIL programmes with this age group (Hood, Chapter 17, this volume).

Cognitive and academic development

When considering rationales for primary languages, research evidence was mentioned showing strong positive relationships between general academic attainment and (substantial) programmes of school foreign-language learning. The research of Sparks, Ganschow and associates linking L1 literacy, L2 aptitude and L2 attainment, and their proposals regarding an underlying metalinguistic capability, remain highly relevant for the 11–16 age group. That is, students in this group have reached a level of cognitive maturity where they can draw much more consistently on metalinguistic knowledge, and undertake L1/L2 comparisons, to support developing practical control of the target language. In turn, this developing metalinguistic capability can be expected to support the learning of additional languages, either concurrently, or at a later stage of education.

Boosting ultimate proficiency

Following present trends, for many children in English schools, languages learning will cease at age 14, and for most it will cease post-GCSE, i.e. at age 16. (In 2010, just 44 per cent of the age cohort took a language at GCSE [CILT, 2011].) What have they achieved at this point, in their languages learning, and what platform has been established for further specialist learning, and/or for embarking on additional languages at a later stage?

At first glance, it seems that the GCSE system is generating a reasonable degree of language knowledge – in 2010, over 70 per cent of students taking French, Spanish and German GCSEs achieved an A–C grade. However, the recent European Commission study (2012a) showed that less than 10 per cent of the British children tested (Year 11 French GCSE students) were achieving at the B1 (independent user) level on the CEFR, the lowest proportion of any country. Perhaps this 'bar' is simply too high, in the English context, given the low time allowance for languages in school, and limited support for languages outside school. More worryingly however, around 30 per cent of the French learners tested were below A1 level (basic user). Thus it seems that there remains a relatively long tail of underachievement even within the GCSE cohort.

There is a consensus that curriculum reform is urgently needed, for the English GCSE examination (see e.g. the critique of Dearing and King, 2007). More generally, it would seem appropriate to set achievement targets which are actually attainable under local conditions (as advocated e.g. by Scarino *et al.*, 2011), and desirable to link these to an international comparison scheme (such as the CEFR). In setting language-learning targets, careful consideration needs to be given at the same time to the motivational and ICC dimensions of foreign language study, discussed earlier, given their known influence on student engagement and their interaction with linguistic achievement. Assessment schemes in turn also need reconsideration.

In sum, where a high proportion of students has a successful learning experience, terminating in a meaningful level of proficiency (even if only that of a 'basic user'), a platform has been laid for the emergence of future language specialists on the one hand, and for the meeting of unpredictable language learning needs later in life, of the kind described by the British Academy (Tinsley, 2013).

Conclusion

This chapter has surveyed recent rationales for languages learning in general education, paying particular attention to the anglophone/UK context. It has reviewed the potential contribution of languages learning to the development of metalinguistic understanding (and hence to academic achievement more generally); to the development of intercultural understanding and competence; to a broadening of the learner's actual communicative repertoire; and to their prospects for further developing this repertoire in the future, in line with future societal and employment needs in a globalised environment. As seen throughout the chapter, all of these basic goals are feasible, given appropriate resourcing and commitment. The broader challenge to educators is to convert them into a coherent curriculum for all students in general education and to complement them with appropriate learning targets, and pedagogic and assessment practices.

Reflective enquiry

1   How far do you find the arguments for 'languages for all' developed in this chapter to be convincing?

   a   What are the strengths and weaknesses of these arguments?

b   How would you go about convincing other educators about the value of 'languages for all' within general education, (i) in Key Stages 1 and 2, (ii) in Key Stages 3 and 4?

2   What is the right balance to be aimed for in general foreign-language education, between the development of proficiency in a particular language, and the development of language awareness and/or intercultural awareness?

3   In an English-speaking context, how should we decide what language(s) should be on offer in our schools? What is the right balance to be aimed for among European languages, world languages and community/heritage languages?

Further reading

Byram, M. (2008) *From Foreign Language Education to Education for International Citizenship: Essays and reflections*, Clevedon: Multilingual Matters. A recent work by Michael Byram developing the case for foreign language learning as a distinctive route to intercultural understanding.

Scarino, A. and Liddicoat, A.J. (2009) *Teaching and Learning Languages: A guide*, Australian Government: Department of Education, Employment and Workplace Relations. A rationale for foreign language education developed in another English-speaking context (Australia), together with related pedagogical proposals.

Taylor, C. and Lafayette, R. (2010) 'Academic achievement through FLES: a case for promoting greater access to foreign language study among young learners', *Modern Language Journal*, 94(1): 22–42. Recent empirical research study showing positive links between foreign languages in the primary school and overall academic development.

Tinsley, T. (2013) *Languages, The State of the Nation: Demand and supply of language skills in the UK, Summary Report*, London: British Academy. Review of societal needs for multilingual capabilities in the twenty-first century.

Chapter 16

Creative practice in the languages classroom

Marie Ryan

Introduction

This chapter brings together a range of evidence in its exploration of the transformative qualities of creative practice in the languages classroom. It will argue that creativity is both a necessity and a skill which can be actively and constructively nurtured with, and for, all learners within the context of languages pedagogy. This chapter will seek to identify ways in which creative practice can be encouraged in the languages classroom, both as a process and a product.

WHAT IS UNDERSTOOD BY THE TERM 'CREATIVITY'?

> Language and creativity are mental faculties which form part of the natural skills of human beings.
>
> (European Commission, 2009: 7)

Creativity is one of the few characteristics that distinguishes humans from other animal species. The apparent 're-discovery' of creativity by government, policymakers, advertisers and many teachers may be a 'belated realisation of the importance of maximising those abilities which make humans distinctive' (Barnes, 2007: 171).

In order to consider the place of creativity in the languages classroom, one must first explore the broad term of 'creativity'. Not all creative people are alike, which makes defining creativity a challenge and assessing it an even greater feat. Professor of Psychology, Mihaly Csikszentmihalyi's definition of creativity is a helpful starting point: 'Creativity is any act, idea, or product that changes an existing domain, or that transforms an existing domain into a new one' (Csikszentmihalyi, 1997: 28).

Csikszentmihalyi's research indicates that a creative contribution must be regarded by members of the field as significant and transformative within the domain. 'Domain' is a many-layered term; some view a domain as physical territory, others an emotional realm, some may regard it as social, and still others as a mental sphere. Furthermore, the boundaries of domain(s) are not necessarily fixed, since a creative process may transform one or more spheres, depending on a range of factors including participants' age, attitude, skills, knowledge, mindset, ability, subject(s), theme(s), skill(s), confidence, timing and sense of 'flow'. This critique of Csikszentmihalyi's research into the shifting effect of creativity on one or more domains may be best represented by a Venn diagram, representing different, overlapping spheres.

Creativity has been variously described as 'the ability to solve problems and fashion products and to raise new questions' (Gardner, 1993: 15); 'knowledge, control of material and command of ideas' (NACCCE, 1999); 'a state of mind in which all our intelligences are working together' (Lucas, 2001: 38); 'making, forming or bringing something into being' (Fisher, 2004: 8); and 'a faculty which we believe is present in all the pupils we teach, and which is possible to develop' (Fautley and Savage, 2007: 3). Whilst years of research have gone into trying to arrive at a definition, the elusive and contested nature of creativity means that we are still unable to explain fully the creative power of the brain (Sternberg, 1999). Creativity is clearly multifaceted and it appears to be easier to define the product than the mental process itself.

This chapter will take as its premise Gardner's avowal that creativity entails the ability both to find answers and to ask new questions, Csikszentmihalyi's statement that creativity engenders change and/or transformation, and the

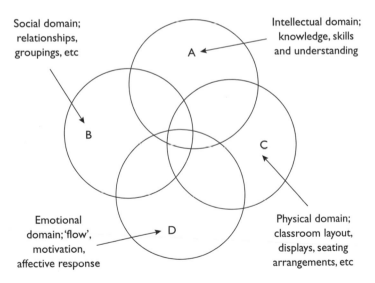

NB Different creative processes may influence and permeate different domains, e.g. 'A', 'AB', 'ABC', 'ABCD' etc.

Figure 16.1 Interpretations of Csikszentmihalyi's 'domain'.

inclusive assertion made by Fautley and Savage that creativity is present in all our students to varying degrees, and is something which we can develop. With this premise as our starting point, let us turn our attention to creative practice within modern languages education.

THE MODERN LANGUAGES CONTEXT

Modern languages pedagogy has undergone a dramatic transformation over the past forty years. Long gone are the days of the grammar-translation method, with its emphasis on reading and writing, its teaching of language through rules rather than through its use, and its dependency upon the use of closed questions to which the answer was either right or wrong. Gone also is the audio-lingual method, which proposed that students learn in a behaviourist manner, from repetition and habit-forming, offering few opportunities for 'authentic' communication. With its emphasis on interaction as both the means and the goal of language learning, communicative language teaching (CLT) situates the student at the heart of learning activities, and makes links between social and linguistic functions both within and beyond the classroom. One might be forgiven therefore for thinking that the current practice of CLT should be key in generating opportunities for, and in support of creativity in the languages classroom. Yet in our increasingly standardised, assessment-driven culture, recent studies (Nieto, 2006; Ofsted, 2010 *inter alia*) show that creativity in language learning appears to be lacking.

ANALYSIS OF THE KEY THEMES AND DEBATES

In its analysis of key themes and debates centred around creativity within the modern languages classroom, this chapter will take a holistic approach to the issues considered. Whilst the four skills are discussed, they will not be examined discretely. The examination of key themes and debates begins with an investigation into the parameters of creativity.

Is creativity the preserve of a talented few or in fact attainable by and for all?

> I used to think only posh people or very clever people wrote poetry. I never thought I could write it in French! But in our French lesson on Valentine's Day we wrote poems called '*Comme Moi sans Toi*' and mine was really good. Miss put my poem up on display.
>
> (Casey, Year 9 student)

Casey's observation was made during a small-scale research project conducted by Ryan into Year 9 students' perceptions of creative writing in MFL. The research was conducted in a non-selective, mixed, 11–16 school in an area of significant socio-economic deprivation. As Casey's comment implies, rather than elitist and exclusive, creative practice can be inclusive. Creativity should be the norm, not the exception in language lessons. Fasco (2006) and Craft (2002) both investigate the notion of a creativity continuum which extends between two extremities: *little-c* and *Big-C*. The little-c creativity includes everyday, routine problem-solving, implies basic functionality and can be found in nearly all people. Most creative output will be at what Fasco and Craft term the little-c end of the continuum. The poem to which Casey refers above and which is included here, is a good example of 'little-c creativity'. Big-C creativity encompasses high-impact creative activities that result in new social, cultural and scientific products and affect how others think, feel and live.

Figure 16.2 'Comme Moi sans Toi', poem written by Casey, Year 9.

The research cited above indicates that for students to produce creative work, they need two distinct things in a languages classroom:

1   Their *creative skills need to be nurtured* in a caring ethos where errors are tolerated and experimentation encouraged.
2   Students' *knowledge and understanding of both content and skills needs development* in an environment where language is viewed both as a process and a product; where communication is as valued as accuracy; and where students are equipped with vocabulary and structures needed in order to feel comfortable and confident using them within the context of a creative activity.

To return to Casey, the Year 9 student who surprised herself by writing poetry in French, had she not been equipped with a knowledge and understanding of the poem's structure, the language content and a grasp of dictionary skills, she would have been unable to approach the activity comfortably. Creativity and knowledge are not in competition with one another therefore, but are in fact interdependent, since creative thinking cannot take place if the thinker does not possess a significant body of knowledge (Boden, 2001: 95). Underlying any language are complex rules which enable speakers to understand and invent an infinite variety of sentences, most of which they will never have encountered before. Such creativity would be impossible if students were relying merely on learnt behaviour; it is only made possible because learners have internalised a knowledge and understanding of rules (Littlewood, 1984: 5).

Creativity is not the preserve of an elite minority therefore; instead, individuals move backwards and forwards to a greater or lesser degree along a continuum, which stretches from the lower ends of little-c to the upper echelons of Big-C creativity. Casey's success in, and enjoyment of, writing a poem in French engendered a striking Csikszentmihalyian transformation in her attitude, both to creative work and more importantly to her own abilities. Having previously dismissed poetry as the preserve of the elite, she began to question this assumption and to view creative output as enjoyable and within her reach. In keeping with Gardner's observation that creativity entails the ability both to find answers and ask new questions, Casey not only addressed her misconceptions, but also started to wonder whether her limitations were partly self-imposed. As Fautley and Savage assert, creativity is present in all to varying degrees, and is something which can be developed.

Creative activities in the MFL classroom – exciting or intimidating?

> Creative stuff scares me. I don't like putting myself out there. I'll look stupid.
> (Language teacher or language learner?)

Creativity can engender a sense of apprehension for both teacher and student, due to the apparent removal of familiar structures and a change to the 'normal' classroom culture. Anxiety in language-learning situations has been almost unanimously shown to be detrimental to successful learning (MacIntyre and Gardner, 1991; Horwitz, 2001). In contrast to unease is the genuine sense of satisfaction experienced during a state of consciousness which Csikszentmihalyi terms 'flow'. In this highly focused state of concentration, one is completely absorbed in and by an enjoyable activity, and especially an activity which involves one's creative abilities. Key characteristics are that one typically feels strong, alert, in effortless control, unselfconscious, and on top form (Csikszentmihalyi, 1990). Students' learning, motivation, achievement and enjoyment of languages are maximised, whilst a sense of discomfort and fear of failure are minimised.

So what are the optimal conditions that reduce anxiety and fear and encourage 'flow' in the context of language teaching and learning? Answers may vary but, as a minimum, an environment in which students feel accepted and secure; able to make mistakes without fear of ridicule; an environment in which all contributions are valued; in which the process is as important as the product; and where fluency is prized as much, if not more, than accuracy. The better the conditions, the further creative output may advance along the creativity continuum. As language teachers, we have to create an environment in which intellectual curiosity is nurtured in a bid to get the best out of our students.

Affording language students the freedom to take risks and to make mistakes is an essential component of any creative activity, since if they are to be creative, students must feel sufficiently self-assured to try things out, to experiment and, even more importantly, to fail (Robinson, 2001: 12). The process is as valuable as the end product. As Caleb Gattegno (1963: 31) observed, 'every mistake is a gift'. Whilst Gattegno's remark regarding mistakes may initially appear somewhat glib, it is an essential mindset if anxiety is to be dispelled and confidence developed. A mispronounced word may be a golden opportunity for the teacher to re-cast and to explain, for the student to learn, and for both teacher and learner to explore together shared knowledge and understanding of language. Mistakes can indicate that students are trying, and reveal that they are testing their ideas about, and knowledge of, language.

The languages teacher who conceives of, instigates and exploits activities which develop students' knowledge and understanding of language, and which at the same time offer a vehicle for creative expression and experimentation, encourages and induces this feeling of 'flow'. Incorporating creative practice into language lessons as a matter of course motivates students to *want* to learn and reduces worry. To paraphrase Craft (2005), the skilful language teacher develops students' desire to be creative, providing an environment in which they go beyond what is expected and are rewarded for doing so; helping them to find personal relevance in learning activities; giving them enough time to incubate their ideas; and encouraging the adoption of different perspectives.

Experience shows us that many language students at the little-c end of the creativity continuum have the capacity to express unusual thoughts and/or experience the world in new ways and/or effect significant changes within their own culture, yet are unwilling to do so. Many lack confidence in working independently, are reluctant to 'get it wrong' and need constant reassurance in order to experiment creatively with language! This can be addressed in part through the integration of project work into languages lessons, which can encourage students to work more autonomously, imaginatively and creatively, and can reduce fear of failure by developing an understanding that effort, cooperation and persistence can lead to success. Project work can enable students to make (guided) decisions regarding topic, theme, content, skills and presentation, and can encourage development of collaborative work and inter-personal skills, helping students to grow socially, emotionally and academically. Questioning is encouraged; learners are challenged to make connections, play with ideas and apply their learning in new ways and new contexts (Cox, 2011). Crucially, students are afforded that most precious commodity; time, in order to explore language, to learn, to reflect on progress, and to devise strategies for improvement and further development. It is factors such as these that serve to motivate students to persist, go some way to dispelling fears and insecurities and lead ultimately to success.

Similarly, the inclusion of ostensibly unstructured creative activities in languages lessons can open up less confident teachers to concerns about behaviour management; the class which usually listens attentively in the (familiar) language classroom may seem far more difficult to manage in the (excitingly unfamiliar) drama studio. Clear parameters and sound scaffolding are essential; amongst other things, the teacher needs to ensure that activities have clear objectives, a sound rationale, careful underpinning and specific learning outcomes. Likewise, students need to know what is expected of them. They need a clear timeframe, with regular reminders, and need to understand what rewards and sanctions will be applied and in what circumstances. Rigorous scaffolding and distinct parameters encourage a sense of security and help to reduce feelings of discomfort and anxiety for teachers and learners alike.

Creativity does not need to be feared therefore. This section has considered some of the challenges which arise in the MFL classroom and how one might use activities such as project work to engender a sense of 'flow', in order to address the anxieties which are so detrimental to language learning. If students and teachers alike are to experience a sense of transformation through the creative process, they need to be able to make, and accept, mistakes along the way. Gattegno demonstrates the power of a positive mindset towards error correction, and his view of mistakes as learning opportunities still rings true four decades later. This leads us to consider whether the correct answer should always come from the teacher.

'Miss, how do you say...?' Should the teacher be the fount of knowledge?

> The effective promotion of creative learning depended on the quality of leadership and management and on teachers' subject knowledge being secure and extensive enough to support pupils' enquiry, independent thinking and debate.
>
> (Ofsted, 2010: 6)

Ofsted's observation that effective promotion of creative learning is dependent upon teachers' subject knowledge being secure and extensive enough to support pupils' enquiry, independent thinking and debate is crucial. In order to inspire our students, we must be completely familiar with our own subject area, since this allows us to concentrate fully on the delivery of that knowledge within the classroom (Fautley and Savage, 2007).

Nevertheless, secure subject knowledge is not in itself enough; in tandem with this, the creative MFL teacher needs to enable students to become actively involved in learning. This entails meticulous planning and setting suitable learning objectives that both allow for, and facilitate opportunities for students to become creative learners (Fautley and Savage, 2007: 25). This can be achieved through meticulous scaffolding on the part of the MFL teacher, careful use of questioning, offering guided choices, developing dictionary skills, providing a selection of resources, allowing students to elect topic/theme/skill if and when appropriate, and judicious use of self- and peer-assessment alongside, and at times in place of, teacher-assessment.

Just as we scaffold learners' journeys through language from word to sentence to text level, so must we support students' creative experiences if we are to instil confidence, and they are to become accustomed to, and comfortable in creative activities. Having researched the assessment of creativity in academic domains, Grigorenko *et al.* (2008: 297) observe that 'the level of creativity is determined both by the demonstrated mastery of the skill of creativity (i.e. creativity proficiency level) as well as by the demonstrated mastery of the content of the domain (i.e. the knowledge)'.

For students and/or teachers who may feel uneasy using creative activities, suitable, early 'orientation' exercises may include:

1   *At word level*: closed activities such as the creative gap-fill 'As red as a ...', 'As blue as a ...' or a closed-structure song or poem such as '*Bonjour ..., Au revoir ....*' in which students think of one word opposites, e.g. 'Bonjour *collège*, Au revoir *vacances*'.

2   *At sentence level*: semi-structured activities such as 'freeze frame', whereby groups of students 'freeze' in a pose and come up with a target language phrase which sums up their pose (e.g. 'Tickets please'; 'Will you marry me?'), and which others have to guess; or a poem with a tight, repetitive structure as exemplified by '*Comme Moi sans Toi*' (see Figure 16.2).

3   *At text level*: more open-ended activities such as 'Complete the story', in which students read an incomplete account, and then devise an ending which they act out, record, write, perform, etc. It is essential that students be given the chance to hone their skills at word and sentence level before moving to text level activities.

In short, to support students' enquiry, independent thinking and creative output, the MFL teacher does not need to be the fount of knowledge, and in fact, operating as such does not help the MFL student in the long term. Instead, the MFL teacher needs to give students the means to experiment with vocabulary and structure, in order to shift the focus away from the teacher's knowledge and more towards students' creativity, their divergent thinking, their ability to make new connections and to produce original outcomes (NACCCE, 1999; Craft, 2005; Fautley and Savage, 2007). Where this is most successful, students take increasing responsibility for, and a growing degree of autonomy within, their own learning, regarding their teacher not as the fount of knowledge, but over time as the facilitator in a creative, transformative, inclusive learning environment.

Are assessment and creativity mutually exclusive?

Data, data everywhere,
Curricula did shrink;
Data, data everywhere,
No time to stop and think.
   (Ryan, with apologies to Samuel Taylor Coleridge)

The current education system is in the throes of a data-rich, assessment-ridden culture, dominated by league tables. Schemes of work are driven by the assessments they teach towards; content is narrow and unappealing. Many MFL teachers are reluctant to deviate from a straitened, prescriptive curriculum for fear of time 'wasted' on unexamined language. This clearly mitigates against creativity being afforded any genuine status in the classroom, reducing it to an occasional add-on and a filler if precious time is available.

Gardner's research shows that the brain learns best and retains most when actively involved in exploring physical sites and materials and asking questions to which it actually craves the answers (Gardner, 1999). Despite this, assisting students to pass endless assessments takes precedence over enabling them to relish learning a language. How often do we see Key Stage 3 language classes lurch half-heartedly from one uncreative, formulaic end of module test to the next as a direct consequence? Spontaneity is lost, creativity is squeezed out and boredom sets in for teacher and student alike. The straitjacket of conventional practice has not gone unnoticed by Ofsted, whose recent report into creative approaches in teaching and learning makes explicit reference to languages:

[w]as more effective when pupils were given scope to experiment with vocabulary and sentence structure. An incorrect response was not simply dismissed; when appropriate, differences between the intention of the initial response and its likely interpretation by a native speaker were explored.

(Ofsted, 2010: 24)

Ofsted's observation that learning is more effective when students are given the time to experiment with, and explore language (all too often omitted in our haste to meet the next assessment deadline), supports Csikszentmihalyi's (1996: 345) reflection that education must go beyond an accumulation of information, to provoke interest, awe and enjoyment. Whilst our current assessment-driven system may promote an accumulation of information, it affords scant space or time for awe, and doubts as to whether prevalent assessment-led practices even encourage interest and/or enjoyment are not unjustified.

In the MFL classroom, assessing the *outcome* of a piece of work would generally entail considering the language knowledge and skills applied, for example 'Has the concept of adjectival agreement been understood and applied correctly?' However, in considering the *creative process* itself, where the learning lies in doing, the assessment needs to be focused on the *process* rather than the outcome, for example 'Are students working collaboratively on developing their understanding of sound and syllable, in preparation for writing haiku?' Although summative assessment is not a useful tool for measuring creative learning, assessment for learning is invaluable in helping to measure creative learning (Barnes, 2007). Prior learning feeds into the creative process, which is refined through formative assessment practices such as dialogues (student(s) and teacher; student(s) and student(s)), formative feedback, subsequent target setting and further refinement.

The reduction of opportunities for genuine creativity within the MFL classroom is not solely the responsibility of teachers. This chapter has already touched on some of the not-inconsiderable pressures teachers find themselves under. In addition, Ofsted pays scant attention to creativity, implying that it is of little value. The Ofsted report *Modern Languages: Achievement and challenge 2007–2010* (2011) runs to sixty-four pages, yet creativity merits three brief mentions. Rarely mentioned and/or undervalued by Ofsted, and unexamined in an assessment-drive culture, there is little wonder that creativity is marginalised. The message to teachers and students alike is clear; concentrate on more important aspects of language learning. Yet GCSE data underlines the importance of creativity in language teaching and learning, as we will now see.

GCSE data – every picture tells a story...

Where my reason, imagination or interest were not engaged, I would not or I could not learn.

(Winston Churchill, *My Early Life*)

With creativity valued neither by Ofsted nor the examination system, it is not hard to find reasons for its marginalisation in language lessons. Time is short, the pressures are great. Yet the sidelining of creativity is having disastrous effects with regard to students' motivation, as data analysis shows. In 2001, 53 per cent of all pupils took French at GCSE with 321,207 entries. However, in 2012, fewer than 25 per cent of the cohort took GCSE French, with just 153,436 entries. The picture is equally bleak in German: 22 per cent of all pupils took German at GCSE in 2001 (130,627 entries), but by 2012 this figure had dropped below 10 per cent, to just 57,547 entries. This represents a 54 per cent decline in both subjects over the last decade. Spanish is the only language to have remained fairly constant with around 8 per cent of all pupils taking Spanish (72,606 entries in 2012). Whilst MFL is in decline, subjects often regarded by students as 'easier', 'more fun' and 'more creative' have seen a sharp rise in popularity; PE entries rose from 49,698 in 1999 to 101,580 in 2012, with media studies entries rising from 34,812 in 2003 to 61,680 in 2012. It seems that MFL students are voting with their feet.

Research into students' reasons for dropping languages post-14 yield depressingly familiar responses: 'I don't understand it', 'It's boring', 'It's too hard'. Yet students' answers seem to drill down into the same concern. In attempting to simplify language, presenting it in bite-sized chunks with little grammatical underpinning, we have over-complicated it. The current approach relies on memory skills, with an expectation that students learn apparently disconnected phrases, in pedestrian settings and in mechanistic ways. Yet, manipulation of a language relies on an understanding and an accommodation of patterns, structures and rules. By attempting to simplify language, in order to make it more appealing, we have all but removed grammar, rendering patterns virtually undetectable. Students have been dis-abled rather than enabled as language learners. It is little wonder that learners complain they do not understand.

A recent small-scale research study with Year 8 language learners (Ryan, conducted in 2012) revealed some interesting findings regarding motivation and perceived degree of difficulty. Students from six non-selective schools were invited to participate in 'E-Bacc MFL Day' at Canterbury Christ Church University. E-Bacc Day focused on the use of creative, active learning strategies, and sought to examine the effect on MFL students' attitudes and motivation. Selected by their schools as capable of (but not necessarily considering) taking a language at GCSE, Year 8 students took part in a 'total immersion' French day. Pre- and post-event questionnaires were administered and findings analysed.

Prior to the event, 67 per cent of participants agreed with the statement 'Languages are more difficult than other subjects'. When questioned about their future intentions, 82 per cent of participants intended to carry on with a language. After the event, students were asked the same questions. Just as before, 67 per cent of participants agreed with the statement 'Languages are more difficult than other subjects'. Although their perception of the degree of difficulty involved had not changed, students' attitudes towards language learning shifted over the course of the day. One may infer from this that it is not the degree of difficulty which dissuades learners, since those figures had not changed. After a day in which language was used for purpose in creative contexts, 91 per cent of students intended to continue with a language, a 9 per cent increase over the course of the day. This small-scale research study implies that creative approaches to content and methodology are more significant than the degree of difficulty.

Creativity entails a lot of work. Is it a risk worth taking?

> I am always doing that which I cannot do, in order that I may learn how to do it.
>
> (Pablo Picasso, quoted in Krieger, 2002: 132)

The teachers we best remember are those who made the greatest impact upon us, whether for good or bad. The ideal MFL teacher ignites a passion for language(s) and makes learning exciting. This ideal languages teacher teaches creatively and enables creative learning, and is a teacher whose mindset is that of a risk-taker, engendering imaginative, creative risk-taking on the part of students. Likewise, ideal learners are resourceful, innovative, independent and motivated students, who have been afforded the opportunity to develop their creative skills to match their level of language competency. In taking risks, teachers and students may make errors, but these are discussed, explored and exploited as learning opportunities. A languages classroom in which imagination and innovation are encouraged, errors are tolerated, and the emphasis is on students' participation, experimentation and process rather than simply on product is one which enables and, in the best cases, ensures a confident approach to risk-taking and to creative activities.

Incorporating creativity into language lessons as a matter of course motivates students to *want* to learn and teachers to *want* to teach. GCSE data analysed earlier indicates that the 'safe' approach of 'teaching to the test' is demotivating and that, when given the choice, more students drop a language than continue with it. Ryan's small-scale research (carried out in 2012) shows that students enjoy creative approaches, and are not dissuaded by their perception that MFL is difficult. It is imperative therefore that language teachers embed creativity into lessons as a matter of course, rather than allow it to be regarded as an optional extra. Teaching creatively encourages creative learning.

Conclusion

> Creativity now is as important in education as literacy, and we should treat it with the same status ... We don't grow into creativity, we grow out of it. Or rather, we get educated out of it.
>
> (Sir Ken Robinson, 2006)

If the MFL teaching profession is to develop a generation of enthused, creative linguists, we need to heed the advice offered by Sir Ken Robinson, and afford creativity its rightful standing by embedding it into language lessons systematically, rather than sidelining it in favour of more 'academic' pursuits.

So, why is creativity now as important as literacy for MFL? Because MFL students who have learnt to use language creatively and have developed a good range of skills draw upon these successfully when meeting new, unfamiliar content (vocabulary). They are creative and literate 'decoders', inferring, using context and experimenting both to understand and to make themselves understood. However, MFL students who have a high level of content (vocabulary) but a low skills base are ill-equipped once confronted with new, unfamiliar content. In today's ever-changing world, content is constantly evolving with technological developments moving so fast that learners require the skills and creativity to be able to adapt constantly. They need to be capable of thinking creatively and adept at seeking and finding new solutions, as well as raising new questions. Students' creative experiences truly will be transformative – we have no idea what the world will even look like by the time the current secondary cohort retires.

This chapter began by taking as its premise Gardner's (1993) avowal that creativity entails the ability both to find answers and to ask new questions, Csikszentmihalyi's (1997) statement that creativity engenders change and/or transformation, and the inclusive assertion made by Fautley and Savage (2007) that creativity is present in all our students to varying degrees, and is something which we can develop. Sir Ken Robinson (2006) raises the legitimate concern that rather than harnessing students' creative abilities, the current education system inhibits and ultimately destroys them. Research considered within the course of this chapter appears to show that there is merit in all these perspectives, alongside a raft of others. Whilst all individuals have creative abilities, these need to be nurtured alongside the simultaneous development of MFL learners' knowledge, skills and understanding.

As this chapter seeks to show, current MFL practice needs urgent adaptation if the latter part of Sir Ken Robinson's assertion is to be disproved, which it must. Students must be educated *in* creativity, not out of it. It is imperative that we teach languages creatively if we are to facilitate creative language learning. Instead of placing emphasis wholly on the final outcome, we must attach greater importance to the creative learning process *per se* if creativity is to be an integral component, and not the unfortunate victim, of MFL teaching practice.

Reflective enquiry

1   Product or process? Which is more important to you? And to your students? Why? Revisit this question on a number of occasions, and in discussion with your students. How, when and why do responses differ?

2 Critique MFL assessment practice in your current context. Is it a tool or a straitjacket for creative learning? How might assessment be used more creatively?

3 Undertake a small-scale research project into teaching creatively and creative learning with a selected class over a module of work. Analyse and evaluate your findings. What does the research show?

4 Consider a current scheme of work in use in the MFL department. Apply Csikszentmihalyi's theories of flow to this. How and where might creative elements best be incorporated?

5 Audit and reflect upon a series of lessons with regard to teaching creatively and creative learning. Categorise the teaching and learning activities accordingly. What does the audit reveal? How might you address issues arising?

Further reading

Barnes, J. (2007) *Cross-Curricular Learning 3–14*, London: Paul Chapman.

Csikszentmihalyi, M. (1997) *Creativity: Flow and the psychology of discovery and invention*, New York: Harper Perennial.

Fisher, R. (2002) 'Teaching thinking and creativity', keynote address at the 'Teaching Qualities Initiative' international conference held in Hong Kong, online, available at: www.teachingthinking.net/thinking/web%20resources/robert_fisher_creative-minds.htm

Kaufman, J.C. and Sternberg, R.J. (2010) *The Cambridge Handbook of Creativity*, Cambridge: Cambridge: University Press.

Ofsted (2010) *Learning: Creative approaches that raise standards*, Manchester: Ofsted.

Savage, J. and Fautley, M. (2010) 'Creativity as a way of teaching and learning' in J. Savage and M. Fautley, *Secondary Education Reflective Reader*, Exeter: Learning Matters.

Chapter 17

Content and language integrated learning

Has its time come?

Philip Hood

Introduction

The use of an additional language as a medium of instruction for other curriculum subjects is now a well-established part of language learning provision in mainland Europe and increasing attention is being given to its potential in the UK. But do teachers know what it is? This chapter addresses some frequently asked questions about the CLIL (Content and Language Integrated Learning) approach. What is the rationale for this integrated approach and what are the learning theories that underpin it? Through an exploration of these issues this chapter suggests viable frameworks for practice with exemplifications. The chapter also reviews some findings about CLIL and considers the implications for learner motivation and achievement in schools that adopt a CLIL approach.

A SHORT HISTORICAL INTRODUCTION TO THE CONTEXT

While Content and Language Integrated Learning (CLIL) is a relatively new term, dating from the 1990s, the approach has been an intermittent part of language learning throughout history. As long ago as 3000 BC Sumerian was the language for learning of a range of curriculum subjects for aspirant scribes who spoke other languages (Germain, 1995). We should remember also that across Europe Latin was the language of general learning in the medieval era. Comenius, who lived across the sixteenth and seventeenth centuries in central and northern Europe and was a major educational innovator, believed that language should be learned through nature's way, learning about things not grammar. He lives on, having given his name to EU funding programmes and the former UK foreign language support centres. All of this demonstrates that when we speak of CLIL we are not referring to a very new trend and as we shall see it is certainly not untried, untested and without an evidential basis.

During the 1960s and 1970s, when a major primary school French experiment took place in England (Burstall *et al.*, 1974; Hood, 1994) and when the comprehensivisation of secondary schools was a major educational force, language learning began to be opened up to all. At that time a predominant approach was the audio-lingual/audio-visual method, which was founded on behavioural learning theory (Skinner, 1948, 1971). The prescription around this pedagogy changed during the 1980s and 1990s to what might be seen as a different kind of straitjacket, that of communicative language teaching (CLT) (Littlewood, 1981). In many ways this was seen as (and could be) liberating but where the focus was firmly on survival language (van Ek and Alexander, 1975) and topic-based transactional language, it tended to set boundaries to what could be learned as the audio-lingual approach had done. Furthermore, CLT was adopted in a fundamentally reduced version which, despite being apparently different from the audio-visual approach, was in fact closely linked to it through the rather teacher-centred so called 3Ps lesson structure (presentation, often characterised by the use of flashcards; practice, characterised by the use of pair 'drills'; and production, characterised rather too often by the learners reading self-created dialogue from a script rather than speaking spontaneously with understanding). The result of the predominance of these two movements in language teaching was that access to a broader vocabulary, more geared to the learner's interest was restricted and the receptive skills of listening and reading came to be used mainly to consolidate and check on material already presented, rather than as a vehicle for meeting and learning new language. It is true that the 'problem-solving' element associated with the communicative movement, where essential meaning was extracted by strategic reading and listening was a more positive aspect, but in essence the message was to ignore the text that was not part of the 'main message', not to explore it and learn with it. Grammar was first of all reduced to drilling during the audio-lingual phase and then to an area of knowledge which was expected to grow organically from experience and use under CLT. Although the apocryphal claim from the 1980s of grammar being 'thrown out of the window' was never really realised in classroom practice, teachers at the time sometimes spoke of erasing grammar lesson notes from their whiteboards before any colleagues could see them.

An alternative to the 3Ps, adopted in the 1990s on the Nottingham PGCE (teacher training) programme, was outlined in Hood and Tobutt (2009) and this approach (the 3Ms approach) centred on learners *meeting* language in a variety of ways, then *manipulating* it and finally *making it their own*. This may not seem to represent a major difference in direction but does emphasise some important aspects of language learning which aim to decentralise the teacher and focus more on the learner. It allows a range of ways learners can meet new language and some of these can be under their own control in terms of source, timing and amount. It emphasises both a 'practice' and a 'production' phase which are more shaped by spontaneity and less by narrow form- or content-specification by a teacher holding a pure language learning rather than communication objective. As early as the 1970s, Naiman *et al.* (1978: 30–37) when characterising the good language learner had identified five major strategies for language learning and had indicated that: good language learners actively involve themselves in the language learning task; they develop or exploit an awareness of language as a system; they realise that language is a means of communication and interaction, i.e. the vehicle rather than the focus; they realise initially or with time that they must cope with the affective demands made upon them by language learning (and succeed in doing so); and they also know how to monitor their performance in the target language.

These are still very important considerations for anyone who is doing any kind of language learning, because they draw together the affective, motivational aspects (Dörnyei, 2010; Dörnyei and Ushioda, 2011) and the language structure understanding aspects (Long and Robinson, 1998). It could be argued that neither the behaviourist nor the communicative teaching approaches encouraged a deep understanding of language learning but rather relied on either habit forming or pattern recognising and that neither was guaranteed to be motivational, although clearly communicative approaches do stress authenticity of material and purpose and so could be said to engender both intrinsic and extrinsic motivation (Gardner and Lambert, 1972) on the part of those who already really see language learning as desirable.

As indicated above, the role of text in the last forty years has been interesting because – unlike for example in Germany, where it is a major contributor to the forming of vocabulary, grammatical awareness and motivation (depending on subject content) – it has been used in England more as a means of testing knowledge and the ability to utilise reading skills and strategies. Stories, for example, have a power which teachers of young children take for granted as a major stimulus for enriching vocabulary for listening and speaking, engendering discussion and stimulating creativity in the form of writing, painting, music making. Yet they are used little in early stages of language learning, or indeed at all before GCSE. Non-fiction text has similar powers when a learner has a particular interest but material such as short magazine articles tends to be left as extension for the more able when there is time.

If we go back to the essentials of communicative language learning and teaching and couple this with the ideas contained within the task-based learning approach (Willis, 1996; Ellis, 2003; Samuda and Bygate, 2008) we begin to see a rationale for CLIL, which can locate it as a part of a continuum of approaches rather than as a completely separate direction. This tends to reassure language teachers that they have a legitimate right to participate in CLIL programmes.

What is CLIL and how does it fit into this pattern of teaching approaches?

The current definition of CLIL is as follows:

> CLIL is a dual-focused teaching and learning approach in which the L1 and an additional language or two are used for promoting both content mastery and language acquisition to pre-defined levels.
>
> (CLIL Essentials,[1] n.d.)

In other words CLIL involves having on a teaching plan primarily objectives about content as well as objectives about language, but the language learning is more likely to be enabled through the tasks geared to content mastery than through any overt language teaching. Interestingly, in this most recent definition the emphasis on CLIL classrooms as bilingual learning settings shows a move towards seeing learning as potentially occurring through any vehicular language. This does not mean, however, that when the content gets difficult, we switch back to L1; it might though involve learners working in groups on tasks using a mix of the two languages to make combined and collaborative sense of material before reformulating their understanding through the CLIL language. As we shall see, good CLIL practice also emphasises problem-solving, thinking skills and collaboration in an active learning focus.

What worries teachers about CLIL?

The frequently asked questions from *content* teachers who begin to consider a CLIL approach are:

- Doesn't it just 'dumb down' the content?
- What would I or the students gain from this?
- Can I still demand *thinking*?
- Is there a CLIL methodology? What do people mean when they say we should plan for content but with 'sensitivity to language'?

The equivalent questions from *language* teachers tend to be:

- But I'm not a scientist/historian/geographer – how will I implement these lessons?
- What levels of language do the learners have?
- Are English for Academic Purposes (EAP) and English for Specific Purposes (ESP) CLIL?
- Do I need to pre-teach or practise vocabulary?
- Is there a CLIL methodology? Do I still use language teaching techniques?

The response to some of these worries is contained in the visual portrayal of CLIL practice generated by Coyle (2002, 2006, 2007b) and Coyle *et al.* (2010). This is referred to as the 4Cs and is largely accepted by many CLIL teachers and researchers as a planning tool as well as a means of explaining how the approach is intended to operate.

> The 4Cs Framework integrates four contextualized building blocks: *content* (subject matter), *communication* (language learning and using), *cognition* (learning and thinking processes) and *culture* (developing intercultural understanding and global citizenship). In so doing, it takes account of

integrating content learning and language learning within specific *contexts* and acknowledges the symbiotic relationship that exists between these elements.

(Coyle *et al.*, 2010: 41)

If we see this as a triangle with the three points content, cognition and communication then we start to address what happens in any learning and teaching scenario. The triangle can also be seen to be sitting in a circle which is culture, but it is worth focusing initially on the three points.

Teachers planning any lesson will always consider a theme or topic and ways in which they will engage learners and make them apply thinking to the 'content' (even if this involves physical or creative activity rather than more conventional 'academic' tasks). By doing this they hope to enable learning and the more the cognitive challenge, the greater the concentration is required and, if the motivation is there, the deeper the learning (as long as the material and the tasks are accessible to the learners). Ellis and Robinson (2008: 3) in a cognitive linguistics view of how we can learn both content and language at the same time, assert that: 'What is attended is learned and so attention controls the acquisition of language itself'. CLIL, just as much as any other challenging learning programmes, focuses on higher order thinking skills as exemplified by Bloom *et al.* (1956) later modified by Anderson and Krathwohl (2001), and by Mohan's Knowledge Framework (1986).

Higher order thinking by students involves the transformation of information and ideas. This occurs when learners combine facts and ideas and synthesise, generalise, explain, hypothesise, or arrive at some conclusion or interpretation. Manipulating information and ideas through these processes allows students to solve problems and gain understanding and discover new meaning.

(Department of Education, Queensland, 2002: 1)

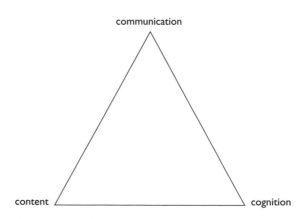

Figure 17.1 3Cs, following The 4Cs Framework (source: Coyle *et al.*, 2010: 41).

Anecdotal evidence from evaluation interviews (H learners will speak of a CLIL programme as hard, but good thing – it makes you concentrate more and when y remember it better. Of course the motivation to w accessibility of both input and tasks are not to be taken

But all teachers (whether of L1 or L2 or in CLIL mo how language either enables or acts as a barrier to this c is also a need, of course, in L1 teaching to provide acces language impairment or poorly developed skills. So teachers, when considering how their CLIL subject content is being expressed, must ask themselves what language the learners have to comprehend the content and to express their thinking about it, how this can be scaffolded and whether the learners need to learn more language in order to function effectively. This does not imply that the teachers need to move into language-teacher mode, but that they should seek ways in which the language needed can be integrated into the discourse of the classroom with much *natural* repetition and in purposeful tasks and activities. In natural repetition a teacher asks open questions around the class to gather facts or opinions, with a genuine intention to hear different responses, i.e. not as a repetition exercise. The teacher can ensure that the relevant content vocabulary and concepts and the necessary language forms are heard several times and can demand more from more able learners so that further natural repetition occurs in their answers. Reading can be a source of simultaneous concept and language encounter and learning if a problem-solving task is used (see the appendix to Ting [2010] for an example of this).

If we consider also the side of the triangle linking communication and cognition we must ask ourselves how we can set tasks at the right cognitive level to allow thinking processes and the desire to communicate a meaningful thought to 'push' language use (Swain, 1985) and enable both language and thinking to develop. Studies appear to show that if people are learning something else in L2 then the desire to think and talk about the concepts involved is strong. This means that for many learners, along with more concentration and, therefore, potentially deeper learning, more motivation is generated. The actual task set may be a motivator too, and we will look at collaborative learning shortly after a brief summary of the effectiveness of evaluations of CLIL.

How do we know that it is effective?

Teachers using immersion approaches in Canada (Swain and Lapkin, 1986; Genesee, 1987; Lapkin *et al.*, 1991) discovered that if the curriculum is taught through another language via sound pedagogical practice then children will learn both the content (the subject matter) and the language. They also discovered that to ensure grammatical accuracy in this language, children do need more formal language lessons to accompany the immersion approach.

pare this with the situation we have here in the UK with English as an ...tional Language (EAL), where incoming new arrivals benefit hugely from ...ing immersed in the classroom and also having some more specific language work directed just at them. The combination works well as long as the teaching is good and appropriate scaffolding approaches are used.

In practice this means that, provided we use natural language in manageable amounts and for real purposes, and we structure tasks carefully, children can learn both the content and the language effectively. So in an ideal CLIL lesson the written objectives will focus on the content and the thinking involved in learning it, and will consider how best to use language to enable those objectives to be met. Evaluations of CLIL programmes in Europe (Admiraal *et al.*, 2006; Alonso *et al.*, 2008; Campo *et al.*, 2007; Ruiz de Zarobe, 2008; Lasgabaster, 2008; Ruiz de Zarobe and Celaya, 2011) have shown that children do make substantial language gains and where they have compared CLIL and non-CLIL groups, the CLIL groups have made more progress. There has not been so much research focusing on the content learning of CLIL, but there have been no indications so far that this is problematic.

To return to Naiman *et al.*'s (1978) criteria again, we can say that in order to learn language effectively, we need:

- meaning and purpose
- motivation and very positive affect
- awareness of how language works.

Rather than just putting those things into a language learning scenario, CLIL proponents suggest that with a focus on using language to learn something else, it is easier to achieve these aims.

CLIL models such as the one proposed by Coyle *et al.* (2010) and in the CLIL Essentials statements[2] work best with highly active learning contexts and collaborative inquiry approaches. O'Donnell (2006: 781) suggests that:

> Cognitive elaboration approaches to peer learning are based on information processing theory. Peer interaction is used to amplify individual performance of basic information processing activities such as encoding, schema activation, rehearsal, metacognition and retrieval. Information processing theory suggests that performing these activities in the presence of peers will result in deeper processing and more active engagement with the tasks at hand.

Similarly, Ting (2010: 3) suggests: 'CLIL automatically changes classroom dynamics: rather than downloading information onto passive learners, teachers guide learners towards deep-level understanding of concepts through interactive knowledge-construction processes. Such active learning processes are coherent with how the brain learns'.

Recent neural research suggests that rather than having particular areas of the brain exclusively for particular functions, the brain is wired so that different parts of it are being used constantly and if you are trying to learn a concept or a piece of content and you are working with the language that goes with that it is actually wiring up different sections of the brain quite substantially and that should result in deeper learning because more of the brain is being used more of the time. If we are thinking and learning and if we are using language to do this, then we will learn more deeply. We are also more likely to be doing those things when we are learning content than when we are simply learning language because it is actually activating a whole range of different thoughts, concepts and ways of combining the material that is actually inside our heads and then expressing that.

How might we start to include CLIL in our curriculum?

As we plan a unit of CLIL work, the question to ask ourselves as teachers is: 'How much is this intended content the same as it would be in English in that subject at this age?' If the response is that it resembles more the work they did in English three or four years earlier, then we can be sure that the content will function really just as a vehicle for language practice. It is a starting point and may help to bring a little more thinking into the learning, but it could not really be considered as CLIL. Simple two digit addition with Year 7 (age eleven) learners is an example of this; it is not age appropriate cognitively challenging mathematics.

It is common to begin to include some cross-curricular material in foreign language work through the inclusion of culture and surface links to other topics. A good starting point is the oral/mental starter section of the mathematics lesson, where careful choice of calculations supported by numbers written on the whiteboard, for example division sums which result in lower number answers or multiplication sums where one of the multipliers is gapped, can give both skills practice and a chance to hear higher numbers spoken by the teacher in a meaningful context.

So, $90 \div 15 = ?$ lets children hear the higher number ninety but only need to produce the easier number six. Similarly $15 \times ? = 255$ elicits the known number seventeen while including an example of a number in the hundreds. This begins to look more like age-appropriate work for the children.

Two other common starting points are science (for example, through healthy eating or the structure of plants or types of ecosystems) and geography (through elements relating to target-language-speaking countries such as tourism, physical features such as rivers or mountains, or comparisons between different countries such as population-related statistics).

When we start to build new material onto what is already known or to teach a completely new topic in the foreign language, then we have to consider the content as a very real focus in designing how we teach. For example, the former Primary Strategy (DfES, 2006) Year 3 objectives in 'Understanding shape' in the mathematics framework included (p. 77): 'Read and record the vocabulary of position, direction and movement, using the four compass directions to describe movement about a grid'. If we look across to Year 4 we find (p. 79): 'Recognise horizontal and vertical lines; use the eight compass points to describe direction; describe and identify the position of a square on a grid of squares'.

A Year 4 CLIL lesson in mathematics might well start by taking the Year 3 objective and carrying out simple work around the four compass points on a grid, perhaps superimposed on a map of the country; the teacher would be using the fact that the children remember the previous year's work encountered through English to establish the foreign language terminology, so using content familiarity to build new language knowledge. A couple of lessons later, when the children are understanding and beginning to use that language with confidence, new content can be introduced, in this case the extra compass points and the more complex directions involved in describing relationships between places.

One very easy entry (again aimed more at primary learners perhaps) into the more complex thinking required for a content subject (when compared with the more repetition-based language learning approaches) is to structure simple decision tasks. Here children must choose between options such as yes/no to questions relating to whether certain artefacts existed at historical points – did the Vikings have chocolate/jewellery/televisions? – or options such as where an object is likely to be – in a factory/garden/town centre/office. Similarly the Matisse PowerPoint included in *A La Française* (Tobutt and Roche, 2008) and also available in German, uses common animals in multi-choice questions designed to elicit the names of two Matisse collages, the wolf and the snail. Children may already know the words for cat and dog which appear as distractors here, but it actually does not matter if they do not. These techniques, with visual scaffolding, actually teach the vocabulary set involved through usage and thinking and without the need for repetition techniques. A further example might be the use of a visual of the food pyramid (see Figure 17.2) with a labelling task, first for the food vocabulary and then of the suggested frequency of consumption.

The focus here is on the decisions around the content area – healthy eating – and the language items are learned through using the language in this way. This is a task that can easily be used in the first term of Key Stage 3. So this piece of very simple source material, easily constructed from internet sites, exemplifies a range of aspects of a CLIL approach. First of all it is immediately accessible with small amounts of text which interact with a clear visual image. Despite the simplicity of presentation, it offers an opportunity for potentially complex thinking and discussion and it taps into prior knowledge. It combines a role as a content and language teaching tool with one as a stimulus for interaction, decision-making and report. If learners do not already have the food vocabulary and are unsure about the detail of healthy eating, it gives a meaningful context for this to be introduced. For these learners a 'presentational' stage involving repetition and memory games is not necessary as open questions around '*magst du...?*' (do you like...?) or '*isst du oft...?*' (do you often eat...?) allow a great deal of natural repetition to occur and for the forms to be fixed in memory without

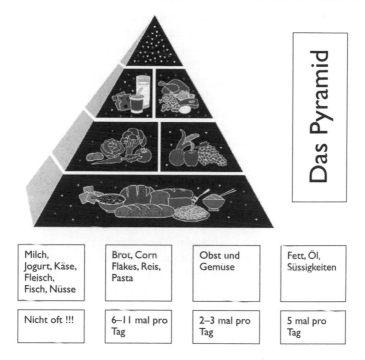

Milch, Jogurt, Käse, Fleisch, Fisch, Nüsse	Brot, Corn Flakes, Reis, Pasta	Obst und Gemüse	Fett, Öl, Süssigkeiten
Nicht oft !!!	6–11 mal pro Tag	2–3 mal pro Tag	5 mal pro Tag

Figure 17.2 A possible worksheet for oracy and literacy work on the food pyramid (adapted from an image by the US Department of Agriculture).

parroting. In all cases the language will be used for a legitimate purpose while it is being fixed and not just 'practised' to learn the vocabulary or structures before a final production task. A teacher can also offer personal views and extend these a little by gradually introducing the health agenda. The food labels can be added to the pyramid as a group consolidation task after a period of oral interaction and then the groups can go onto deciding about the recommended intakes. Again this is a content task which uses the L2 as a vehicle for that decision-making. Similarly, if they have not come across the phrase *pro Tag* this will be taught and learned through this process without any specific language teaching. In a CLIL approach this will then be taken further at a level appropriate to the age of the learners (i.e. according to what they should learn in the science or PSHE context at their stage). This extension will certainly involve giving reasons for the intake proportions of different types of food and may start by being teacher-led through, for example, a PowerPoint presentation about the effects caused by different types of intake or a video (there are several short clips available in German on YouTube for example, including a song). Although this sort of material is likely to push the language level further than the learners can easily manage, the teacher can set appropriate tasks to accompany the resource and can also stop and interpret with the class and not just expect the resource to do all the work.

If most or all of the vocabulary is already known, then immediately the labelling tasks can be undertaken as a quick group brainstorm and the source can be supplemented by a series of 'daily intake' sheets of varying quality as regards healthy eating and the groups can also prioritise these and prepare to report reasons for their desirability. A successful and very simple format for report is a matrix which acts as a stimulus for different aspects. In one Year 4 primary class, for example, the four headers on the matrix were (in German): I like it and it's healthy; I like it but it's not healthy; I don't like it even though it's healthy; I don't like it and it's not healthy!

Often the questions asked in a CLIL context may have a range of answers (such as happens normally in content subjects across the curriculum). This enables a teacher to ask the same question of several different pupils because there may be different answers, and this type of repetition sets up a more natural language-rich classroom, where children hear the target language more frequently without this being done simply for the sake of fixing the language forms.

It forms the kind of comprehensible input which Krashen wrote about in his work during the 1980s and 1990s (e.g. Krashen, 1982) and which underpins real communicative language teaching as well as CLIL. In addition it also takes the 'parroting' pressure away from children where they are required to repeat without a real reason for doing so. In fact children are more likely to want to speak in the target language if there is a message to deliver than if they are simply asked to do so in order to practise the language.

Some teachers may feel that this is very demanding on their own language competence, but it is important to remember that children will learn best if the language is rich but controlled to include more cognates and to avoid excess complexity. Questioning and the tasks set must always be broken into manageable stages and be clear and well supported with visuals and mime and with references to prior learning. So, by scripting the input carefully and building from a simpler base, teachers help pupils to build both confidence and competence effectively.

CLIL brings other dimensions of interest into language classes, offers hands-on work, for example through science and maths investigations and brings language work into the whole curriculum, joining it up rather than making it something separate.

Conclusion: why CLIL?

This chapter has attempted both to show the positive attributes a CLIL approach can bring to learners of an additional language and give a brief insight into how this process might begin without too much of a move into the unknown. It is, however, formulated on quite a radical step for language teachers in changing the *mindset* they hold on the classroom threshold. It needs a teacher to walk into lessons with an intention to teach first and foremost something other than a set of language items or even language skills. The notion of 'I'm doing some science today' (and not just as a distraction but as an integral part of the science curriculum) can feel very different from 'Today I'm presenting some key vocabulary for a topic which will enable the learners to survive when buying food and drink in the target language country'. It has pointed out that in research projects to date language learning has occurred while the focus has been on content. In addition, the chapter has also tried to address the key role that text and reading have in this – and has suggested that reading becomes much more a means of learning rather than consolidating. It has stressed the importance of collaboration and active learning and the importance of finding the motivation which can arise from tapping into learners' other academic interests. CLIL, like any other approach, needs to be used thoughtfully, imaginatively and perhaps also rather bravely in order to succeed, but it can offer exciting results when it does.

Reflective enquiry

1   Have a look again at the section on teacher worries earlier in this chapter. Did you have any of these worries and have they become less acute after reading the chapter?

2   How convincing do you find the arguments for CLIL in this chapter? Do you have any further evidence to add for it or against it?

3   If you are involved in secondary age learning, what are the advantages and disadvantages of the current national curriculum and examining system? Consider learner motivation as well as learner attainment.

4   If you are involved in primary age learning, what are the aspects of language learning that younger learners seem to find most enjoyable and interesting?

5   How helpful do you find the 4Cs framework (a) as a way on envisaging how a CLIL programme should be constructed and (b) as a concrete planning aid?

6   If you work with language teaching, consider content areas where you do feel more confident about integration?

7   If you are a content subject teacher, which aspects of language do you feel most confident about?

8   If you were to write an action plan towards using CLIL, what would be the first three items you would focus on?

Further reading

Coyle, D., Hood, P. and Marsh, D. (2010) *CLIL: Content and Language Integrated Learning*, Cambridge: Cambridge University Press.

Dale, L. and Tanner, R. (2012) *CLIL Activities with CD-ROM*, Cambridge: Cambridge University Press.

Dalton-Puffer, C., Nikula, T. and Smit, U. (2010) *Language Use and Language Learning in CLIL Classrooms*, Amsterdam: John Benjamins Publishing.

Llinares, A., Morton, T. and Whittaker, R. (2012) *The Roles of Language in CLIL*, Cambridge: Cambridge University Press.

Notes

1   www.ccn-clil.eu/index.php?name=File&nodeIDX=5060
2   See note 1.

Chapter 18

Managing learners' needs

Policy, research and practice

Jill Llewellyn-Williams

Introduction

The concept of inclusion is grounded in the right of all individuals to have a full and appropriate education. The infinite and disparate variety of humankind makes this a challenge and in recent decades educationalists have found that a differentiated approach can provide a means of meeting the needs of a wide spectrum of learners. The concepts of inclusion and differentiation have experienced substantial shifts in the United Kingdom in order to adapt to a changing educational landscape. Following the introduction of comprehensive schools in the 1960s and 1970s, when new systems were settling into place after a process of radical reform, educationalists began to see the necessity of finding new ways of meeting learners' individual needs. In the previous school system, where learners had been grouped more homogeneously, there had been less need to consider the full range of abilities. In the case of modern foreign languages, some learners did not have access to this subject prior to comprehensive education, so new thinking was required to give access to languages for all. However, large-scale changes were needed throughout the system in order to provide a more equitable learning experience. The Warnock Report (Warnock Committee, 1978) had begun to develop thinking on learners' needs and the Education Act of 1981 had affirmed the idea of an inclusive approach for learners with Special Educational Needs (SEN).

Throughout the 1990s, there was an intensive period of educational legislation which transformed thinking on inclusion and promoted ideas of catering for the wide spectrum of learners' needs. During this period, there was much debate about inclusion, though many saw it in terms of the integration of SEN pupils, paying little regard to how their learning could be managed or to ways of allowing them to become included in the wider education community. These reforms have continued, over the years, with the publication of *Every Child Matters* (DfES, 2003b) and the White Paper *Higher Standards, Better Schools for All* (DfES, 2005b). The notion of differentiation, while still at the heart of curriculum delivery, has developed into the wider concept of personalised learning. Changes in government have not diminished legislation and recent government advice defines the right of all learners to have an education that is appropriate to their ability, learning aptitudes and disposition. An inclusive and differentiated approach to learning, though not always expressed in those precise terms, continues to be at the top of the educational agenda.

KEY ISSUES, THEMES AND RESEARCH

Learning is a highly individual process; we are all different in terms of our ability, interests, needs and motivation. We learn differently and have varying strengths and areas of difficulty. We learn at differing paces and use different strategies. The learning process is highly complex and research is far from understanding its intricacies. Planning and delivering a curriculum that caters for such complex and diverse learning capacities and proclivities seems an impossible task and the more we learn about the processes involved, the more daunting it seems.

DIFFERENTIATION

For many modern foreign languages teachers, some guidance has come from the notion of differentiation. Convery and Coyle (1999) categorise differentiation by text, task, outcome, support, ability, interest, variety and range. In recent years, three of these categories have become more prevalent and appear more regularly in guidance on differentiation.

These can be summarised as differentiation by:

- Task (setting different tasks for learners of different abilities)
- Support (varying the level of support to match the learners' needs)
- Outcome (where learners are set the same open-ended task but respond differently according to their individual level).

However, each of these approaches to differentiation can be challenging. Differentiation by task can be translated into limiting students' learning by the teacher's expectations of what they can do and, in any case, it can be extremely difficult to plan differentiation by task for large numbers of learners with diverse needs. However, task-based language learning (Pachler *et al.*, 2007) provides opportunities for learners to discover language through tasks, rather than using tasks to practise language forms that they have already learned. Differentiation by support, in practice, often relies on the help of teaching assistants assigned to students with specific learning needs, yet recent research on the Achievement for All pilot (Maddern, 2011) highlights the importance of teachers taking responsibility for all pupils in the classroom rather than leaving pupils with SEN to teaching assistants. Finally, differentiation by outcome can fail to challenge pupils unless they have a clear idea of what is expected of them, leading to only moderate learning gains.

Differentiation in the forms described above tends to begin in the planning stage of teaching and learning, in activities such as the preparation of differentiated work sheets, planning questions and setting homework. However, O'Brien and Guiney (2001) point out that when a teacher teaches, a learner does not necessarily learn. Knowledge of the learner and of learning processes increases the chances of successful learning and feedback on learning can help to identify needs. Careful planning is therefore essential to the process of differentiation. However, they point out that teaching and learning is a dynamic and unpredictable process. Teachers therefore need to develop the skills of thinking on their feet and to practise 'differentiation on the hoof' (O'Brien and Guiney, 2001: 91). Many teachers develop these skills intuitively as a way of responding effectively and routinely to learners' needs.

Reasons for differentiation are often practical and pragmatic, rather than theoretical and philosophical. Learning is likely to be more effective if learners undertake tasks that match their particular learning needs. Differentiation can mean that they are more engaged in their learning and less liable to be disruptive, consequently increasing their levels of motivation and self-confidence. However, it is the concept of ability and how to match the diverse spectrum of learners to tasks that match their needs that requires the most careful consideration.

Learners' ability

Differentiation is sometimes a difficult concept to grasp and this confusion is shared by many trainee teachers as well as some of the more experienced practitioners. Most of the guidance offered to teachers on differentiation is based on the premise that learners can be sorted, managed and taught according to their ability. In teacher training programmes, the concept of differentiation is often included in lesson plans in the form of a section where trainees define what all, most and some learners should be able to do. The starting point for differentiation seems therefore clearly rooted in the concept of ability. This notion of ability does not have to be limited to the subject specialism but can be based on more generic abilities and skills (Hramiak and Hudson, 2011). It is also possible that this idea of ability per se can be affected by learners' general communication skills, particularly for those for whom English is not their first language.

Teachers keep detailed records of learners' profiles right across the range of perceived learning abilities, from SEN learners to those considered to be gifted and talented. A clear understanding of learners' abilities will evidently make the complex business of differentiation more manageable. However, differentiation, as an approach, applies to all learners, not just those at the extreme ends of the ability spectrum, although attention currently seems to be concentrated on SEN and gifted and talented learners. Differentiation is therefore an inclusive concept. Learners should be seen as having common needs as well as distinct and individual ones. This allows learning disability to be seen as 'an element of diversity rather than as a deficit within the community. This is an inclusive view of a learning community' (O'Brien and Guiney, 2001: 15). Differentiation should not therefore be reactive (seeing a learner in difficulty) but should be a normal part of the relationship between teacher and learner.

There are, however, some inherent difficulties in the idea of ability as a basis for differentiation. Harris (1995) points out that much ability-based differentiation is often founded on teachers' instincts rather than on any sound or rigorous theoretical basis. Much thinking on differentiation conveniently glosses over the difficulties of accurately assessing either learners' abilities or task difficulty and whether (or how) they can be properly matched. There seems to be a lack of clear and cogent thinking on this point. Booth points out that:

> The division of children according to their attainment is generally bolstered by the ascription of ability labels to children from a very early age, a practice which constrains thinking about what they will achieve in the future and affects their self-expectations.
>
> (Booth, 2011: 304)

Another assumption is that learners' ability is fixed, static and unchanging. This has been challenged by much recent research (Greenfield and Sharples, 2008; Dweck, 2006; Hart et al., 2004). Recognising and planning for changes in proficiency need to be at the heart of a differentiated approach.

Currently the teaching of modern foreign languages is organised into a wide range of ability groupings. Many learners are taught in sets based on ability while others find themselves in mixed-ability classes. The benefits and drawbacks of such groupings are hotly debated by teachers, though in most cases, they have little choice but to accept the systems imposed upon them by their senior school managers, owing to the complexity of the timetabling arrangements. Boaler and Wiliam (2000), in their comparison of setted and mixed-ability contexts, found that learners in a setted school were significantly disadvantaged. More able learners suffered from inappropriate expectations and pressure to succeed while other learners became disaffected by perceived limitations placed on their attainment. The study suggested that mixed-ability groupings make differentiation a necessity whereas sets encourage a 'one size fits all' approach. Boaler and Wiliam's 2000 study was in the context of mathematics teaching. A later study in a language learning setting came to very different conclusions. Joyce and McMillan (2010) concluded that there are advantages to streaming for both lower and higher ability groups. They assert that in both setted and mixed-ability contexts, learners establish their own ability-based hierarchy within the groupings. Such differentials are bound to be greater in a mixed-ability group and this is likely to be demotivating for less proficient learners whereas the more able might be inclined to conceal their skills in order to enable them to manage social interaction with their classmates.

In the differentiated classroom, when learners are allocated different tasks, it will not take them long to work out their position on the ability scale if they compare their work with that of their peers. Moreover, for group work, the teacher has the choice of either placing learners in similar or mixed-ability groupings. If they are organised into homogeneous ability groups, this risks causing tension in the class as a whole, unless it is managed carefully and diplomatically. On the other hand, if each individual group contains learners of differing abilities, it could be argued that the benefits for all learners differ and some would contend that the high attainers might not be adequately challenged. Joyce and McMillan (2010) observe that in a mixed-ability language class, opportunities for peer tutoring can disadvantage the more proficient learners as the ability to cooperate and contribute meaningfully to tasks is closely aligned to language proficiency.

INCLUSION

It is the balancing of the needs of all learners in an effective and equitable way that is the real challenge to inclusive education. The rigorous attention to data in the current educational climate has serious implications for the inclusion of less able learners in the wider education community. Tomlinson (2005) comments that 'as long as teachers are pressed to deliver higher standards in the form of more children passing examinations and reaching targets, they will understandably be reluctant to take on the education of all children'. She points out that for learners who are unlikely to succeed, 'inclusive schooling is a sham'.

While there has been much debate about managing the needs of SEN and gifted and talented learners, it is worth noting that there has been less attention paid to those who fall in the middle ground. Lee et al.'s study of Year 9 language learners in *The Invisible Child* (1998) observes that learners of average ability are frequently overlooked or neglected, mainly because they are compliant and undemanding. However, in some instances, schools pay very careful attention to these learners who fall in the middle ability range as extra tuition of this group can push them over grade boundaries that have a crucial impact on published examination results. The harsh climate of performance-based education means that schools feel constrained to divert resources in an inequitable way in order to compete with other schools in the local area.

This difficulty of managing a wide range of learners' needs is particularly acute when applied to the study of modern foreign languages, owing to the hierarchical patterns of language acquisition which make teaching mixed-ability groupings a more challenging task than for most subjects. This challenge of inclusive language learning provision is not unique to the United Kingdom; language learning is compulsory in most European countries (European Commission, 2012b), so this problem is faced in classrooms across Europe. However, the situation is perhaps more challenging in the United Kingdom owing to significant shifts in the role of modern foreign language learning in the school curriculum in recent years. The profile of the subject has changed substantially and ways of making language learning meaningful and appropriate for all types of learners with differing abilities has been a constant concern of language teachers.

Booth (2011) contends that the inclusion debate has become increasingly narrowed in recent years and that it is seen mainly in the context of Special Educational Needs, with the latter being the dominant partner. In fact, the debate needs to move beyond impairment, which to an extent diminishes the learners and defines them in an inappropriate way. Concepts of inclusion need to be broadened and increased to managing the curriculum for the full spectrum of learners, regardless of their ability, impairments, socio-economic background, gender, ethnicity or language. A learner with family problems or difficulties in social integration needs consideration along with other disadvantaged learners (ibid.). This will require system-wide changes:

> Increasing participation for all implies not only that everyone is entitled to participate in their local educational settings, but that education systems and settings are developed to be responsive to diversity in ways that *value equally* all children, young people and their families and the adults who work with them.
>
> (Booth, 2011: 304)

Catering for learner diversity and the need for a differentiated approach does not therefore only apply to ability (and the inherent difficulties of defining it) but also to age, prior learning, experience, gender, disposition and learning styles.

LEARNING STYLES AND THEORIES

Educational theory, cognitive research and neuroscience have increasingly been more present in the classroom in the form of thinking about learning. From Piaget's cognitive and developmental theories in the early twentieth century to the latest advances in brain scanning, there is a thirst for a greater understanding of the process of learning as a means of helping learners to develop their cognitive skills. Howard Gardner's Multiple Intelligences, Visual Audio and Kinaesthetic Learner Styles and other approaches to learning have had a significant impact in the classroom. Evidently, in managing the learning of diverse groups of individuals, identifying strategies that will support their learning is likely to benefit them. For such approaches, there is less emphasis on what causes difficulty for the learner but more on focusing on what they can do and creating circumstances for them to make optimal progress.

Professor Frank Coffield stands out, perhaps, as one of the main critics of using learning theories as a basis for managing differentiation in the classroom. With three colleagues from the London Institute of Education, he carried out a review of 13 different learning style instruments but found that only one met the minimal criteria for effectiveness (Coffield *et al.*, 2004b). He is highly critical of inspectors and senior school managers who continue to encourage teachers to use low-grade research to differentiate lessons by means of learning styles. While learning styles are a good starting point to a discussion about how students learn (or fail to do so), discussions need to go beyond such categorising (Coffield, 2008). Gardner's concept of multiple intelligences has also been subjected to harsh criticism from Professor John White who questioned whether ministers of education 'should be in the business of sponsoring iffy theories and recommending them to teachers'. (White, 2004).

The fundamental problem with using learning-styles thinking to inform differentiation and promote inclusion is that learning preferences are likely to vary according to developmental stage, external factors and even mood. It could even be argued that it would be more worthwhile to examine the learning preferences of the teachers themselves and to research the impact this has on their selection of methods to deliver the curriculum. However, specific intelligences and learning styles have particular relevance to the learning of modern foreign languages so teachers would be well advised to at least be abreast of these emergent ideas even though they might conclude that some are (to a certain degree) questionable.

Greenfield and Sharples (2008), observe that a wider vision of the learner's place in the rapidly changing world is helpful when deciding how to manage the curriculum and meet all learners' needs: 'As we move into an information-rich world where knowledge is available from a broad range of sources, educationalists and policymakers increasingly recognise the importance of being able to process, question and assess that information rather than just retain it'.

This is not about learner preferences, styles or intelligence, it is a question of helping learners develop an inquisitive and questioning mind that is open to the diverse and disparate learning experiences that they will encounter throughout their lives.

MOTIVATION AND CHALLENGE

Providing learners with appropriate learning opportunities is a complex challenge when all the factors that affect successful learning are taken into account. For past generations, if schooling was enjoyable, it was a pleasant and unexpected bonus, there was little expectation of having to consider pupils' interests. Times have changed. If today's teachers fail to engage and motivate their learners, they are expected to review their planning and delivery. If they fail to do so, they risk poor behaviour and declining attainment levels. Differentiation can therefore become a classroom management tool, a means of avoiding demotivation and unacceptable behaviour. Differentiation, according to Anstee (2011), can result in higher levels of motivation, better behaviour and greater progress. Although he accepts that differentiation by learner interest can be 'a can of worms' (Anstee, 2011: 39), he claims that learner motivation will be boosted and it will therefore be easier for teachers to engage learners in their tasks. While the notion of preparing all lessons to include bespoke activities for every single pupil is obviously impractical, it would also be unwise to omit activities that reflect the interests of some of the learners some of the time. If learners appreciate that the teacher has made an effort to recognise them as individuals beyond the classroom, they are likely to respond positively.

Taking into account learner interest can also extend to allowing a choice of activities. Once again, common sense dictates that the range of choices needs to be limited, otherwise lesson preparation becomes at the best daunting and at the worst impossible. Tobin and McInnes (2008) observe that increased choice improves learners' focus and concentration. A differentiated approach benefits a wide range of learners but they will differ in the levels of support they need and the areas in which they need it. It is the level of challenge and how learners perceive it that is problematic for most teachers, who fear that learners will deliberately select undemanding activities. Most will agree that learners are likely to be motivated when they feel successful and interested in what they are learning. In order to push learners to their upper capacity for learning, into Vygotsky's *zone of proximal development*, teachers require an acute understanding of the learner's psychology. For every learner who is motivated by a teacher's demands for improved performance, other learners might interpret this as a dismissal of their potential. Managing motivation and challenge is extremely complex and learner attitudes are highly individual. Claxton (2005) suggests that personalising learning can be viewed as helping learners to become better learners: 'This means creating a school climate that cultivates generic, portable "learning dispositions and learner identities". To be "disposed" to persist, for instance, means to show persistence in a broad range of occasions and in the face of obstacles'.

Some teachers might argue that this persistence in the face of difficulty is not fostered by allowing learners to select only tasks that interest them and to limit their choice to activities that provide merely a moderate challenge. O'Brien and Guiney (2001) outline the principles for effective differentiated learning, summarised as follows:

- all children have the right to a high quality education
- every child can learn
- every teacher can learn
- learning is a process that involves mutual relationships
- progress for all will be expected, recognised and rewarded
- people and learning systems can change for the better.

By recognising the intricate and complex relationship between the teacher and the learner, positive interaction can be fostered. We need to recognise that the learner is at the centre of the learning process, rather than the teacher, the school or the education system.

PERSONALISED LEARNING

Although differentiation as a means of promoting an inclusive learning experience has become a daily reality for most teachers, talk of differentiation seems to have been largely displaced by the debate on personalised learning. Ideas of shaping teaching around the way different youngsters learn and taking the care to nurture the unique talents of every pupil were floated by David Miliband, then Minister for School Standards, in the North of England Conference in January 2004. These echoed the debate on personalisation in the public sector (Leadbeater, 2003), in which service becomes more attuned to customers' needs, giving them a greater say in how services operate. In a school setting, this would mean a basic curriculum with many interpretations. Hargreaves (2006) advocates nine gateways to personalised learning, accessed via what he terms as deep learning, deep experience, deep support and deep leadership:

Deep learning:
• student voice
• assessment for learning
• learning to learn.

Deep experience:
• new technologies
• curriculum.

Deep support:
• advice and guidance
• mentoring and coaching.

Deep leadership:
• workforce development
• school design and organisation.

By organising personalised learning into this structure, a culture of co-construction between learners, teachers and the wider community can be established. He draws parallels with the business world, where moves from mass production to mass customisation requires significant shift in practices.

So what is the difference between personalised learning and differentiation? On the surface, it seems that personalised learning tends to be mostly concept-based whereas differentiation is more of an operational approach, particularly when one considers differentiation by task, support and outcome. Practical guides exist for differentiation (Anstee, 2011; Convery and Coyle, 1999) yet discussion on personalised learning tends to relate to ideas and aspirations. Campbell *et al.* (2010) judge that although personalised learning is an attractive concept, it rests on 'substantial ambiguities' (Campbell *et al.*, 2010: 138), such as the lack of equal distribution among the population of the ability to take advantage of the opportunities that it offers. It is therefore likely that more articulate, professional class parents will gain an advantage from personalised learning and that it will consequently increase inequality in society. Beach and Dovemark (2009) contend that personalised learning can lead to 'a private appropriation of teacher time for personal gain at the expense of others' and see it as 'a form of privatisation' (p. 698). Leadbeater (2003) anticipated this problem and proposed the idea of skewing provision to compensate disadvantage. Campbell *et al.*, however, point out that trying to redress inequality in education has 'a long and dismal record of ineffectiveness' (2010: 139). Hopkins, in contrast, believes that personalised learning 'will not only generate excellence, it will also make a strong contribution to equity and social justice' (2007: 54).

Miliband (2004: 9) outlined five key processes necessary for personalised learning:

- assessment for learning (planning, strategies and target setting)
- a wide range of teaching techniques supported by ICT
- curriculum choice and the development of subject specialism
- school organisation (structure of the school day and lessons, teaching and learning reforms)
- links beyond school (parents, families, local education authority and the community).

Personalised learning can be defined as an education that is 'tailored to the learner, within systems that are responsive to learner needs, rather than expecting the learner to adapt to existing systems within the school' (Muijs and Reynolds, 2011: 236). Personalised learning does not mean that learners work alone, as in individualised instruction, but that they have a varied approach to learning, a balance of group work and individual tasks (Hopkins, 2007). In personalised learning, there is still a general aim to the lesson but this is broken down into personalised tasks and collaborative learning (Hramiak and Hudson, 2011). Learners are supported by learning mentors or coaches who help them to focus on how they are learning and what they need to do in order to progress. Learners are set targets and have individual plans; reviewing targets and frequent feedback are essential to the process. The use of data is a key component in the learning process and parents are encouraged to see themselves in partnership with schools. There has been much criticism of what is perceived to be a lack of clear thinking in the implementation of personalised learning. White (2006) observes that:

> People differ about what learners' needs are. Everyone can subscribe to the idea that education should be tailored to needs. If that is what personalised learning is about, it's hard not to be a supporter of it. But this gets us nowhere. Talk of a needs-based education glosses over huge ideological differences.

It is the absence of a clear theoretical framework for personalised learning that seems to be its greatest stumbling block. Campbell *et al.* provide a thorough review and analysis of the progress on thinking on personalised learning, including the Nuffield Review of 14–19 provision (Hayward *et al.*, 2005), the Economic and Social Research Council Teaching and Learning Programme (Pollard and James, 2004), the National College for School Leadership special supplement (2004), the Government White Paper (DfES, 2005b) and a review by HM Chief Inspector of Schools (Gilbert, 2007). Of the White Paper (2005b), they conclude that 'there is descriptive rhetoric but no conceptualisation' (Campbell *et al.*, 2010: 143). What has remained constant, however, is the intention of successive governments to promote the concept of inclusive education. Personalised learning is central to the aims of inclusivity and the Department for Education (DfE, 2011c) sets out three principles for inclusive education:

- setting suitable challenges
- responding to learners' diverse needs
- overcoming potential barriers to learning and assessment for individuals and groups of learners.

These principles are a clear reflection of the thinking associated with the notions of differentiation and personalised learning. However, many educationalists would hesitate to connect these principles to what is actually the state of the national education system:

> On the face of it, in Britain, state education is provided free for all children. All children are taught the skills, knowledge and understanding required by statutory curriculum documentation and therefore this would seem to suggest that education provides an equal opportunity for all children and that each child, therefore, has an equal chance of achieving equally well as another child. That not all groups are achieving equally suggests that there are still barriers to learning occurring for some children.
>
> (Knowles and Lander, 2011: 5)

Education has experienced radical developments in recent decades and is likely to change exponentially in the years to come. Technological innovation and an increase in evidence-based research will, it is hoped, provide opportunities for improved equity, inclusion and a truly personalised learning experience.

FUTURE TRENDS

Recent initiatives have attempted to translate notions of personalised learning into practical recommendations for the classroom. A revised structure of the school day, peer-to-peer instruction and creating a less hierarchical partnership between teachers and learners have been some instances of practical interpretations of the personalised learning agenda (Stewart, 2008). By restructuring the school day, learners are given a choice about when they attend school in order to fit learning into their lifestyles. The creation of pupil-tutors is a further innovation, and one that can give learners responsibility, inspire respect for teachers and extend resources available in schools. Such co-constructive collaboration between learners, it is argued, would change the relationships that they have with teachers and allow them to become partners in learning.

Changes in the patterns of learning are also likely to take place. Sir Ken Robinson (2010) is highly critical of the 'production line mentality' that persists in seeing learners in age group batches and limits learning experiences to narrow subject specialisms. He champions divergent thinking and points out that 'collaboration is the stuff of growth'. Vertical tutoring, where age groups are mixed in order to improve relationships between learners in form groups, is developing into vertical learning groups, where age groups are mixed within lessons throughout the day, echoing Robinson's demand to end age group learning and find more appropriate ways of developing homogeneous learning groups. Increasingly educationalists are considering a 'stage not age' approach to learning. There is a widespread rethinking of the traditional structures of school organisation as a means of meeting learners' needs in more imaginative ways. Much of the difficulty in motivating learners is often due to a lack of challenge. Macaro (2008) points out that some language learners could gain a GCSE Grade A after only two years of study, given the right conditions; vertical learning systems could provide a framework for such gains.

These new patterns of learning can support a more inclusive education for a wide and diverse range of learners, facilitating a more individual and personal approach to learning and allowing teachers to differentiate more effectively. Major advances in technology, such as the digitisation of the curriculum, will support this personalised approach to learning. While South Korea plans to digitise its entire curriculum by 2015 (Eason, 2011), Secretary of State for Education, Michael Gove, in his criticism of the resistance of British schools to embrace technology noted that 'it's clear that technology is going to bring profound changes to how and what we teach. But it's equally clear that we have not yet managed to make the most of it' (Gove, 2012).

In his view, the benefits of using advances in technology in learning can be summarised as the dissemination of learning, a review of the way we teach and new methods of assessment. These advances will create unprecedented opportunities to differentiate and personalise learning and to create an inclusive environment for the complete spectrum of learners. In such a rapidly changing world, it is impossible to predict future opportunities but it is to be hoped that we shall seize the chance to create new ways of meeting the needs of all learners and that we prioritise their needs over those of system-led schools and governments.

Personalised learning is not a new idea; tailoring the curriculum and teaching methods to individual needs have been part of the educational system for many years. Constructivist learning is a key feature of Vygotsky's social theory of pedagogy, an approach that enables learners to construct their own knowledge and personalise it to their individual needs. What has changed, however, is a widespread shift in educational thinking that allows for such approaches to develop in a less constrained manner, in a system that is open to change and has technological and professional knowledge to support it.

Conclusion

Managing all learners' needs in a fast-paced languages classroom and in dynamic and demanding school settings is a daunting challenge for teachers with all levels of experience. Whether learners are taught in mixed-ability or setted groupings, all learners are highly individual and have very different needs from their peers. This complexity operates at many different levels, not only relating to ability, which is variable at different educational stages but also to many other factors, such as predominant learning styles, differing backgrounds and dispositions.

Ensuring equality of opportunity for all language learners is problematic in the current political climate. The numbers of learners opting to study languages beyond the age of compulsory language learning is declining. The study of languages is perceived as difficult and in an employment market that is increasingly competitive, learners are reluctant to invest time and effort without discernible returns. Making language learning relevant to the whole spectrum of learners is therefore the greatest challenge facing educationalists in their attempts to promote language learning that is truly inclusive.

For the teaching profession, it is sobering to recognise the substantial changes that have taken place over the past decades. In the 1990s, as the UK was preparing itself to become a full member of the European Community, language teachers were full of optimism about the future of language learning and saw the new century as the end of a radical shift from the language learning elitism of the grammar schools to the provision of language learning opportunities for all. The sad reality of falling numbers has brought the realisation that language learning, in its current state, needs reform. There is a disconnect between language learning provision and the perceptions of learners, who, in their failure to engage with language learning, seem to feel that their needs are not being met. A substantial rethink is required to ensure that learners begin to understand that languages are relevant to them and that it responds to their needs and aspirations in the modern world.

Reflective enquiry

1   What are the main strengths and weaknesses of differentiation?
2   How feasible is differentiation in a mixed-ability classroom?
3   What are the principal barriers to inclusion?

4   In what ways are differentiation and inclusion particularly challenging in a modern foreign languages context?
5   How can the needs of learners be balanced with the requirements of schools to demonstrate improved performance?

Further reading

Knowles, G. and Lander, V. (2011) *Diversity, Equality and Achievement in Education*, London: Sage.
O'Brien, T. and Guiney, D. (2001) *Differentiation in Teaching and Learning: Principles and practice*, London: Continuum.

Chapter 19

A new era for primary languages

Patricia Driscoll

Introduction

The long awaited and welcome policy decision to make languages compulsory for all children at Key Stage 2 (KS2) from 2014 (DfE, 2013) marks a new and exciting era for a subject that has been hovering on the margins of acceptability for many years. Rather than a blank canvas, this new statutory subject will build upon a complex web of established practices and beliefs about how to teach foreign languages to young learners and the factors that lead to successful and sustainable provision (Driscoll *et al.*, 2004; Muijs *et al.*, 2005; Wade *et al.*, 2009; Cable *et al.*, 2010; Ofsted, 2011).

In this chapter I aim to explore how practice has developed over the last fifteen years or so. I draw upon research evidence to indicate how some aspects of primary languages have changed and conversely how some aspects of learning and teaching have remained constant. I present some previously unpublished findings from my doctoral thesis conducted in eight schools between 1996 and 1999 (Driscoll, 2000), and compare this practice with evidence from our findings from a three year longitudinal study (2006–2009) in forty case-study schools across England (Cable *et al.*, 2010). By considering changes that have taken place as well as aspects of practice that have been sustained, I hope to shed some light on the distinct nature of the subject for those unfamiliar with the field, and suggest possible areas of development as we move into the new statutory era. I shall also draw upon other studies and in particular two national studies which plotted the rapid growth of primary language learning in England: the baseline study (Driscoll *et al.*, 2004); and a later NFER study (Wade *et al.*, 2009) which draws upon the same methodological instruments as the baseline study, in order to map the rapid expansion of languages over time.

Throughout this period of growth, specialist language teachers and advisers played a key role in shaping the subject, through training courses and by creating curriculum guidance materials, for example, the Key Stage 2 Framework (DfES, 2005a). Specialist teachers have also played an important part in teaching the subject in primary schools. In some cases, specialist teachers have worked together with non-specialist teachers in primary classrooms, which has supported primary teachers' confidence to teach the subject (Cable *et al.*, 2010) but, in most cases, class teachers leave the classroom as soon as the specialist teacher arrives which diminishes the potential for modelling and coaching (Cable *et al.*, 2010; Wade *et al.*, 2009). I argue in this chapter that developing an ongoing and personalised collaborative approach within a community of primary and secondary colleagues who learn from each other's expertise will be important as we move into the next phase of development.

A GLIMPSE BACKWARDS

One of the main reasons languages were excluded from the primary National Curriculum over twenty years ago was because there were too 'few teachers in primary school … equipped to teach it' (DES/Welsh Office, 1990: 5). Despite this policy viewpoint, about 20 per cent of schools experimented with teaching the subject. Programme aims varied considerably and teachers, both internal and external to the school, with language skills ranging from basic to fluent, added to this rich variety of provision (Driscoll, 1999). After about a decade of experimentation in individual schools and local authorities, the government published National Curriculum guidelines which, although non-statutory, promoted a coherent set of aims for the subject (QCA, 1999).

Alongside this move towards consistency, the government also funded nineteen Pathfinder authorities to work with schools to further develop their distinct and varied practice. Muijs *et al.*'s (2005) evaluation of the Pathfinder Projects distinguished three broad aims and approaches to teaching languages: language competence programmes (which develop knowledge and skills in one or two languages, similar to secondary school practice); sensitisation programmes (where children encounter different languages as an introduction to the world of foreign languages) and language awareness/multi-lingual programmes (which emphasise meta-linguistic and cultural awareness). Each approach requires a different type of knowledge base and teaching methods. At that time, language programmes were chosen for ideological reasons and to meet the needs of the pupil population or for practical reasons such as staffing or time availability. Barton *et al.* (2009), for example, report that headteachers and teachers in their study endorsed language awareness/multi-lingual programmes as they considered them to be less demanding on specialist knowledge of language.

In 2000, the Nuffield Foundation reported the need for greater language skills in the workforce to ensure economic prosperity, recommending a coherent lifelong language-learning programme starting in primary school (Nuffield Foundation, 2000). The value-added of learning in primary schools in terms of increased competence at a later stage was the central drive, therefore. Two years later, the National Languages Strategy, *Languages for All, Languages for Life* (DfES, 2002) recommended that all children be offered an 'entitlement' to learn languages with the intention that languages be made statutory in 2010/2011. The Strategy suggested creating a 'cadre' of specialist teachers from secondary schools and the community, in order to maximise language capability and capacity in schools. Significant funding also followed to develop primary teachers' skills (King, 2011). Rafts of in-service language methodology and language proficiency short courses were implemented and funded. A greater number of language graduates were attracted to specially designed and funded primary postgraduate teaching courses (Driscoll and Rowe, 2011). Funding was also allocated to Specialist Language Colleges (SLC) and many supported primary schools as part of their outreach work.

At the same time as primary teachers and, in some cases, teaching assistants and headteachers were developing their knowledge and skill, a steady flow of secondary MFL teachers and peripatetic specialist teachers delivered languages to one or more primary classes. From 2005, all schools received curriculum guidance for languages in the form of the Key Stage 2 Framework (DfES, 2005a). The Framework offered a theoretical structure for teaching primary languages which combined aspects of communicative language teaching with text analysis and translation. Progression in listening, speaking, reading and writing were mapped against learning objectives, with separate strands for intercultural understanding, knowledge about language and language-learning skills. For the first time, one coherent approach was offered as a common frame of reference for primary languages pedagogy. Over time, both specialist and non-specialist teachers reported using the Framework as a basis for planning (Cable et al., 2010).

Within this culture of intense government support, provision spread rapidly. Wade et al. (2009) reported that by 2009, 92 per cent of primary schools offered languages with almost 70 per cent of schools teaching across all year groups in KS2. As provision increased, the number of primary teachers incorporating language teaching as part of their professional portfolio also increased. The latest figures show that only about a quarter of teaching is undertaken by secondary MFL teachers and other linguists external to primary schools (Wade et al., 2009). At present, the number of teachers teaching languages per school varies from one to five, but with 30 per cent of schools not teaching languages across KS2 (Wade et al., 2009), it is likely that more teachers will be needed by September 2014 when the subject becomes statutory. The implications in terms of training and support for new teachers to the subject are considerable.

The expectations and assumptions regarding the level of subject knowledge and fluency needed to teach primary languages has shifted significantly. Tinsley and Comfort (2012) argue from their international review of evidence that primary teachers with relatively low levels of language competence do in fact teach languages effectively, if well trained. Non-specialist teachers have developed their confidence to use the target language within the confines of the content taught in primary lessons. Ofsted (2011) reported that only *a minority* of the primary teachers observed were unable to sustain the target language when teaching and then only occasionally (my italics). Despite the apparent shift in attitudes about the levels of proficiency needed to teach languages and the growing number of language graduates teaching in primary schools (Driscoll *et al.*, 2004; Wade *et al.*, 2009), finding and retaining language teachers remains a major challenge for schools, not only in England, but also across Europe, the United States and Hong Kong (Blondin *et al.*, 1998; Wade *et al.*, 2009; Enever, 2011; Extra and Yagmur, 2012; Rhodes and Pufhal, 2009).

The new National Curriculum will be implemented at a time when most of the central funding for promoting languages has been withdrawn and redirected to the general school budget (King, 2011). The Ofsted report (2011), which draws on evidence gathered between 2007 and 2010, indicates that practice is good or outstanding in just over two-thirds of the primary language lessons observed. For this tradition to continue and for practice to improve further, in the absence of government-funded training and resources, primary schools will need to find more specialist teachers to teach languages or local sources of professional development for non-specialist teachers and most likely, a combination of both.

COMMUNITIES OF PRACTICE: SHARING PROFESSIONAL KNOWLEDGE AND EXPERIENCE

The concept of 'communities of practice' (Lave and Wenger, 1991; Wenger, 1998), which promotes learning-through-participation and through engagement with an activity or enterprise is useful when applied to the professional community of teachers who teach primary languages. Lave and Wenger (1991: 98) suggest that a community of practice can be seen as, 'an activity system in which participants share understandings'. They also present the idea of 'legitimate peripheral participation' which is a way of understanding the relationship of a newcomer to the activity as they move towards full participation with established members of the community. Within a languages community, linguists external to primary schools could learn about how to apply 'good pedagogical practice for the teaching of young children' which Tinsley and Comfort (2012: 69) argue is essential for primary languages, and primary teachers new to the subject could tap into a localised source of support to help build their confidence and skill in handling the subject matter.

Non-specialist primary teachers are the mainstay of primary languages and are key to establishing the subject into the life of the school. Wade and colleagues' study found that by 2009, approximately three-quarters of the teachers, headteachers and teaching assistants teaching languages had an A-level, GCSE-level or no qualification. Many of these teachers had undertaken 'funded' training courses (Wade and Marshall *et al.*, 2009). If teachers, who are new to the subject, can connect and collaborate with a group or community of experienced practitioners some of whom are linguists, we have more of a chance to maintain and improve the good practice that has been established.

The primary context

According to the Cambridge Primary Review (CPR), which 'makes fair claim to being the most comprehensive review of primary education for 40 years' (Alexander, 2010: 2), primary teachers work within a distinct professional culture. Within this culture there is an intense loyalty to the class-teacher system and many class teachers are happy to define the essence of their work as 'the whole child' and 'the whole curriculum' (p. 407). The class-teacher model, Alexander argues, is still at the heart of the primary ethos and suggestions for specialist teaching are considered by many as 'tantamount to sacrilege' (p. 408). Alexander has promoted the benefits of specialist teaching for primary-age learners since 1992 (Alexander *et al.*, 1992), but the deployment of specialist teachers in primary schools is still limited and generally confined to specific subjects such as music and foreign languages. Alexander (2010) suggests that once schools realise the benefits of specialist teachers, particularly for upper-primary-age children, they may be more open to deploying specialists in other subjects or domains. To date, in primary foreign languages, part of these benefits have been realised through professional support and coaching as well as through specialist teachers, external to the primary school, undertaking the teaching.

Specialist MFL teachers

The benefits of specialist teachers in terms of increased gains in pupil attainment (Cable *et al.*, 2010), is a powerful argument for specialist teachers for languages in the upper-primary stage. Pupils' attainment was assessed in eight out of the forty case-study schools (Cable *et al.*, 2010). Children in two schools in particular attained high ratings when assessed in listening and speaking. These schools consistently promoted progression and it was also noticeable that Year 6 performed among the highest in writing. The teachers in these schools, both internal and external to the schools, possessed high levels of proficiency. Conversely, children in the lowest performing school were taught by teachers with limited proficiency who had recently taken on the role of teaching languages. The study concluded that different types of teaching staff can deliver successful progression, but teachers' subject knowledge and linguistic skills are factors in learners' attainment.

Specialist teachers can offer much in the way of methodological support. Their deeper subject knowledge provides a rich source of learning which cannot be replaced by a commercially produced resource. Specialists are more able to draw from a wealth of possible explanations and examples when teaching which impacts on children's attainment. They can provide children with high levels of differentiated language and cultural input and they themselves provide the model for pronunciation. They understand the language-learning process well and can plan for medium- and long-term learning. They can model the foreign language and facilitate learning efficiently across all four skills as well as identify and monitor error (Driscoll, 2000; Driscoll *et al.*, 2004; Muijs *et al.*, 2005; Ofsted, 2005; Cable *et al.*, 2010; Driscoll *et al.*, 2013).

A number of studies in the past, however, have found that some specialist teachers, full of good intentions, deliver language lessons that are out of alignment with primary practice which can create unfavourable learner engagement (Blondin *et al.*, 1998; Driscoll, 2000; Chesterton *et al.*, 2004; Ofsted, 2005). The expertise to teach languages in primary schools is not simply a matter of teacher proficiency and fluency. If the subject is taught by primary teachers, there is a greater potential for making connections between foreign languages and other curriculum subjects. Where specialists, external to primary schools, have worked alongside primary teachers they are better placed to fit within the primary school culture and understand how to teach primary learners (Cable *et al.*, 2010).

The ideal primary language teacher understands primary pedagogy and has high levels of linguistic proficiency. There are, however, too few of these ideal teachers at present, but by working collaboratively within a community, teachers with different types of professional knowledge and experience can mutually support, develop and help improve each other's practice.

THE NATIONAL CURRICULUM

The newly published National Curriculum indicates that pupils should make substantial progress in one modern or ancient foreign language, and teaching should provide both spoken and written language activities (DfE, 2013). At present, French is the most common language taught in schools (89 per cent), followed by Spanish (25 per cent) and then German (10 per cent). Some schools teach two languages but only a few teach any other language with 3 per cent or less teaching, 'Italian, Chinese, Japanese and Urdu' (Wade *et al.*, 2009: 3). Elsewhere in Europe, the picture is quite similar. The percentage of students learning languages other than English, French, Spanish, German or Russian is below 5 per cent and in many countries below 1 per cent (Eurydice, 2012).

Some schools may decide to teach an ancient language but widespread adoption of the classics as the main language is unlikely, due to the lack of resources to support the pedagogy. The emphasis on practical communication remains. Combining the purpose of study and aims for language learning across KS2 and KS3 highlights progression in the curriculum from seven to fourteen.

KEY THEMES AND DEBATES – CHANGES OVER TIME

In this section, I draw upon evidence from my unpublished doctoral study. I conducted over 150 language lesson observations of specialist and non-specialist language teachers, but the evidence presented below is drawn from observations of eight non-specialist primary teachers' lessons and ongoing open-ended and semi-structured interviews and semi-structured interviews with them. I also conducted interviews with headteachers and Year 6 children in the eight schools. I present data from my doctoral study which used an ethnographic approach to the methodology (Hammersley and Atkinson, 1983), and compare these findings with those gathered from the case studies in the longitudinal study (Cable *et al.*, 2010). These two studies, different in size and methodology and conducted ten years apart, reveal some interesting insights into the constancy of some areas of practice as well as an indication of how primary practice has changed. For the Cable *et al.* study (2010), we interviewed specialist and non-specialist teachers and headteachers in forty schools and observed language lessons using semi-structured observation schedules every year for three years. We also interviewed focus groups of children in each year using semi-structured interviews, and assessed children's attainment in each year in eight of the case-study schools (see Mitchell's chapter in this volume for an overview of assessment findings). Rather than an ethnographic approach and grounded theory (Glaser and Strauss, 1967), we conducted a thematic analysis of the observations and interviews across the case-study sites. Despite these differences in research design, methodology and time frame, the comparison of findings highlight interesting insights into the developing nature of languages as a curriculum subject.

Teachers' qualifications

All the eight teachers who participated in the ethnographic study (Driscoll, 2000), were experienced primary teachers who had taught French for several years. Their qualifications ranged from none, to GCSE-level or equivalent, or to A-level in languages. One teacher had a degree in languages but it was not possible to include this teacher as a central part of the study. Primary teachers undertake a variety of roles. Six class teachers in this study were subject coordinators for up to four curriculum subjects and two teachers were deputy headteachers. They had all undertaken language methodology training and one teacher attended a French evening class to improve her language skills. All these teachers, who were experienced language teachers, indicated a general confidence in teaching the facts and concepts of the programme and in promoting listening and speaking skills. They also expressed confidence in using simple classroom commands. The majority indicated they were extremely reluctant to attempt the complex structures and range of vocabulary needed for classroom communication and even the teachers who had French A-level were reluctant to use too many verbs when teaching. Similarly, all teachers were hesitant about writing more than a few words on the board. They expressed concern about inadvertently making mistakes with accents or spelling.

Despite the increase in teachers with a degree in languages, the majority of practitioners teaching languages have 'school-level' language competence (Driscoll *et al.*, 2004; Wade *et al.*, 2009). Commercial resources and technology have both improved since the 1990s but there are still only a few resources available which specifically support non-specialist teachers.

Teachers' aims in teaching languages

The class teachers in the ethnographic study knew their children well (Driscoll, 2000). They personalised the curriculum through their knowledge and understanding of the children's abilities, strengths, interests and their home life. The teachers frequently expressed the importance of an inclusive language programme so *all* pupils felt confident to participate in the lessons and engage in simple conversations. The following quotation is typical of teachers' comments over the three years of the study:

> One of the nice things ... is that children ... that are generally academically weaker are at the same point as the stronger ones. They can speak this new language just as easily ... So you see all the children, well nearly all of them anyway, tackle this confidently and with enthusiasm.
>
> (Marian, W4)

Teachers placed the highest priority on children's enjoyment, the importance of maintaining children's self-esteem and developing activities that were fun. In relation to cognitive aims, teachers indicated that they were introducing children to the 'basics' in preparation for later learning. One teacher expressed this in the following way:

> I hope it gives them ... a familiarity ... a grounding for something they can then work on later ... just the whole concept of working in a different language because they don't meet it here otherwise.
>
> (Glenda, W6)

On rare occasions, teachers made brief connections between the target language and English by highlighting or comparing the roots of words, language structure or punctuation. Although perfectly placed to make connections with the English curriculum and other cross-curricular links, teachers tended to stick to the formula of phrases and vocabulary outlined in the resources. There was evidence that their lack of subject knowledge in the foreign language impeded the impetus to make connections between the two languages and there were and still are few resources to support this. The general lack of language awareness and curriculum connections is also noted by Low (1999) in her discussion of primary teachers teaching languages in Scottish primary schools at the time. Cable *et al.*'s (2010) study suggests that where foreign languages are integrated into the life of the school, literacy coordinators indicated an impact on children's wider literacy, but specific literacy gains were difficult to determine. Many of the teachers in the Cable *et al.* (2010) study, described fun and enjoyment as key motivational factors and the majority of children reported that they enjoyed the subject and were keen to learn more.

A comparison of teachers' beliefs about why they teach languages indicates that teaching aims are more extensive and generally encompass a greater conceptual framework of the subject. Rather than an introduction to speaking and listening, teachers speak more about the importance of including cultural understanding, reading, aspects of knowledge about language and grammatical structures. Half of the teachers in the Cable *et al.* study (2010) reported that teaching cultural awareness and intercultural understanding were core aims which formed an integral part of the school's broader curriculum (cultural references were rarely observed in language lessons but there was evidence of increased whole-school cultural activities). Teachers remain committed to promoting an enthusiasm for languages, developing positive attitudes and encouraging listening and speaking skills (Driscoll, 2000; Driscoll *et al.*, 2004; Wade *et al.*, 2009; Cable *et al.*, 2010). The comparison of evidence also reveals that whole-class teaching continues to dominate practice, with limited opportunities for pair work and very little individual work offered to learners (Driscoll, 2000; Cable *et al.*, 2010). It is not surprising therefore, that writing, which is generally an individual task, is underdeveloped. Differentiated tasks, assessment and connecting language learning across the curriculum also remain underdeveloped.

Pedagogy

The observations data from the 1996–1999 study indicate that teachers focused on children's engagement through songs, games and activities which involved actions or physical activity. Broadly speaking, much of the pedagogy remains the same. Teachers continue to provide young learners with concrete, interactive and creative activities that involve movement, songs and stories (Driscoll *et al.*, 2004; Cable *et al.*, 2010). The major part of most lessons observed during the ethnographic study (Driscoll, 2000), were taught to the whole class as teachers used the video resource as the main source of language input. Once the vocabulary or phrases had been introduced, the teacher organised different types of activities and tasks to give children the opportunity to practise the language in different ways. Children repeated chorally as a whole class, then practised the vocabulary or phrases in pairs or groups using word games, running vocabulary games, role-play activities and songs. Game-like competitive team activities provided an authentic context for language learning as children were focused on winning. These activities gave an impression of pace, although the content introduced was limited and confined to speaking and listening.

In lessons, children were encouraged to respond with physical cues when listening to songs or stories to encourage participation and memorisation of lists of nouns or phrases. Following listening activities, children were prompted to substitute single words within a phrase or refrain for another. Teachers focused on a set of vocabulary within a small number of topics – personal information, family, pets, colours, numbers, days of the week, months of the year, school vocabulary, shopping. Very few verbs or adjectives (apart from colours and size) were introduced. Generally, teachers used the audio resources and video for reading stories or singing songs to ensure that children heard the correct pronunciation and intonation. On occasion children were given single words or very short sentences on cards or worksheets to read but in general reading and writing were considered a barrier to children's enjoyment. Lessons were mainly timetabled for thirty minutes a week but on numerous occasions teachers moved the lesson to another time, shortened the lesson or decided not to teach languages as they had more pressing demands on their time.

By 2009, the majority of lessons observed over three years were timetabled for thirty to forty minutes a week. In many schools language lessons continue to be low priority: they were frequently moved to another time or cancelled completely. Wade and colleagues (2009) found that lessons had a more solid position on the timetable if they were taught by specialist teachers. Cable *et al.* (2010) found whole-class teacher-led activities which focused on speaking and listening skills. The subject content of the majority of lessons observed were topic-based. Reading and writing activities did not form a substantial part of most lessons although there is evidence of an increased attention to reading. On occasions, children read aloud as a whole class or followed a text as the teacher read the story supported by a resource. Teaching aspects of knowledge about language (KAL), however, were regularly noted in many lessons. The majority of teachers drew attention to specific sounds and phonemes; singular and plural forms of verbs and nouns and rules of agreement with regard to gender. Teachers also highlighted pronunciation and intonation, the similarity of some words across languages and the use of accents on letters. Target language writing remains the most underdeveloped skill in primary languages and most children assessed were unable to generate verb forms in writing (Cable *et al.*, 2010).

Planning with resources

There was a distinct difference in the 1996–1999 study between the teachers who had no qualifications or a GCSE-level and those with A-levels. Teachers with an A-level in languages had much more confidence in planning in the medium and long term and sometimes from lesson to lesson. The following quote is from a Year 6 teacher who had the equivalent to a GCSE-level, and who expresses his lack of confidence in the following way:

> I still worry a lot about giving the children the wrong idea and some of them come up with some quite perceptive questions … We often reach the limit of my knowledge … not to teach it, but to support it, so that you are absolutely certain that your choice of the bit that you are teaching is relevant to what comes after it.
>
> (Joe, W7)

All teachers had developed a bank of games and activities for each topic covered such as laminated boards depicting images of animals for games of lotto. However, their limited experience of the language-learning journey meant they had to rely on resources for planning as well as providing the language model when teaching. One teacher expressed her use of the resources in the following way:

> I follow (*named materials*) quite closely ... without your own skills it would seem foolish not to. I mean if you were better at French yourself then maybe you could go off at tangents ... I haven't got the basic underlying skills to do the French probably any differently than I do it.
>
> (Maude, W3)

Limited subject expertise was not isolated to languages in these primary schools. One headteacher expressed this in the following way:

> Well, it's the same with any subject, you can only do the strengths you've got within your school ... take science – we haven't got a science expert ... why should I have expertise for French ... Each teacher has got different strengths ... I think we're very lucky ... it's a lovely, friendly, secure atmosphere here and children like being with the same teacher – it gives them security.
>
> (Headteacher, WG)

Using suitable resources to supplement subject knowledge is part of the primary context, however, if the design of resources determines the mapping, planning and sequencing of pedagogy, provision could be restricted to the resources available in the school. The paucity of primary resources for the subject is well documented (Driscoll *et al.*, 2004; Wade *et al.*, 2009) and without support from language teaching experts, curriculum innovation in primary foreign languages may over-rely on existing materials in the school which is not the best foundation for curriculum change.

Differentiation

Teachers in the ethnographic study indicated they differentiated learning by asking more able pupils to develop longer and more detailed dialogues and by directing their questions to the stronger or more able pupils first. The following extract illustrates this practice.

> I get the brighter children to say, and hopefully the others can hear ... I might ask them to do maybe four sentences – introducing themselves, brothers and sisters, their pets names, you know go through the whole caboodle where some of the others you might only ask them, 'how old are you?'
>
> (Marian, W 4)

Over the three years, a small number of children in each class indicated their frustration about this practice, comments such as, 'She always points to Liam or Grace first, even when I know the answer' were made reasonably frequently. A few children also expressed their exasperation about the constant repetition of words, phrases and questions and the lack of more challenging work. The following comment illustrates this point:

> We go over the same things all the time ... We did it in Year 5 and now we're doing it again ... We never learn any of the joining words so it's difficult to speak when we go to France.
>
> (Year 6 pupil)

Ten years later, a minority of children in each class during the longitudinal study also indicated that they were frustrated by the constant repetition of lists of words and practising pronunciation over and over again (Cable *et al.*, 2010). Similar findings were reported by other studies in 2004, 2005 and 2009 (Driscoll *et al.*, 2004; Muijs *et al.*, 2005; Wade *et al.*, 2009). This represents fairly robust evidence that some children are frustrated by the lack of challenge and differentiation in language classes. Even though the majority of children report being enthusiastic about learning (Cable *et al.*, 2010), we need to take notice of the important few. Rather than simply researching and reporting disaffection or boredom of a few learners before they begin secondary schooling we need to address this shortfall in good practice. Pooling expertise across key stages could be one way of finding new and creative approaches which benefits all learners.

Conclusion and reflections

This chapter has explored some of the key components of primary languages and outlined the changing nature of the subject over the last fifteen years or so. I argue that a major challenge for non-specialist teachers is communicating in the target language and long term planning. Teachers reported they tended to, 'follow the course materials', but primary languages resources remain limited in most schools. As languages becomes statutory the need for high quality resources to enhance planning and differentiated learning will increase. Limitations and constraints of time, resources, funding and expertise are the major factors influencing the sustainability of primary languages (Driscoll, 2000; Driscoll *et al.*, 2004; Wade *et al.*, 2009; Cable *et al.*, 2010).

The great majority of primary children participate actively in their language lessons for most, if not all of the time, and the majority of primary learners report that they enjoy languages (Driscoll, 2000; Driscoll *et al.*, 2004; Cable *et al.*, 2010). Primary teachers' relationship with their learners, their creative use of school space, and their knowledge of teaching all subjects can be brought to bear on their teaching of languages. Specialist MFL teachers, particularly those in the early stages of their careers, could learn considerably from this fluid and complex construct of professional knowledge.

Provision has rapidly increased over recent years and practice is at least 'good' in many schools (Ofsted, 2011), but central funding for training and resources has ceased. The National Curriculum spans Key Stages 2 and 3 and it makes sense therefore to drive forward these communities of primary and secondary language teachers where expertise is pooled to enrich all members of the community but particularly those new to teaching languages.

One of the legacies of the National Languages Strategy is a greater number of linguists were trained in universities as primary teachers to teach foreign languages as well as across all subjects in the primary curriculum. If this trend can be encouraged to continue, eventually there will be a critical mass of specialist language teachers within a locality, but as discussed at the beginning of this chapter, this scenario has yet to be achieved in many countries in the world. To date, in England, the combination of specialist and generalist teachers has enabled the subject to become more widespread so now the majority of schools offer timetabled lessons (Wade et al., 2009), but there is much more work to be done. Lessons remain vocabulary based with few adjectives and very few verbs. There are indications that some non-specialist teachers need further support in teaching grammatical structures. Writing also remains an undeveloped skill despite the balance of reading and writing set out in the KS2 Framework in 2005 (DfES, 2005a). The lack of writing may stem from the lack of time to organise creative writing tasks but some teachers continue to lack confidence in teaching writing skills. Assessment strategies also remain underdeveloped (Driscoll, 2000; Driscoll et al., 2004; Muijs et al., 2005; Ofsted, 2011), and it is likely that statutory status will prompt a greater need for schools to monitor, assess and report children's progress to parents.

There is a significant body of work which considers how early language learning influences second language acquisition, as well as how it impacts on ultimate attainment in classroom or naturalistic settings (see reviews of Birdsong, 2006, or Munoz and Singleton, 2011). Rosamond Mitchell in this volume also highlights interesting studies about the relationship between age, additional learning time from starting early and success in foreign language learning.

The avid interest in what can be achieved by starting early is understandable, but before we focus too obsessively on the 'value-added' of early learning, we should ensure that our full attention has been given to the process of learning and teaching. Subject knowledge is merely one ingredient in successful pedagogy. Instrumental questions about how much more students will know or how much more they will be able to do, are more prominent in languages than many other primary subjects. Subjects such as primary art, music, science, physical education or geography highlight the intrinsic educational, social, physical, emotional, psychological and neurological values of learning for young children as they develop as individuals, rather than what learners will be able to achieve at some point in the distant yonder.

The focus on eventual gains in languages led to the demise of the ten-year initiative of teaching French to children from the age of eight in 1964 (Burstall *et al.*, 1974). This initiative was primarily conceived as an attempt to provide more linguists for the workforce (Hoy, 1977), and as the early start did not deliver the expected increase in outcomes at the age of sixteen, the pilot was abandoned and languages rapidly disappeared in most primary schools. Today, languages are arguably more established, but provision is still fragile and we need to address issues in the process before we weigh the product. Many of the challenges during the French-from-eight project (Buckby, 1976; Hoy, 1977; Hawkins, 1981) prevail today: for example, finding fixed and adequate curriculum time; the need for well-designed assessment procedures that are tailored to young learners, and the need for primary/secondary school liaison (see Amanda Barton's chapter in this volume).

The heyday of primary languages may have dwindled in terms of government-funded professional development and resources but if communities of specialist and non-specialist language teachers can find creative spaces to collaborate and share their professional knowledge and skills, we will improve practice not just in primary languages but potentially across the early stages of secondary school.

Reflective enquiry

1   Think about three things you feel strongly about in relation to teaching and learning in MFL. What does this tell you about your own beliefs, values and ideology? How do these aspects of your practice shine through when teaching? How could you help a new non-specialist primary language teacher develop aspects of their practice?

2   Observe a range of activities in MFL lessons in Year 7 and Year 10. When do you think students are learning best? Why? How do you know? Repeat in Year 3 and Year 6 in a primary school. What does this tell you about age, attainment and learning? What does this tell you about pace, practice, use of space and relationships with learners?

3   Explore the key professional benefits and workplace barriers of collaborating with teachers who teach in another Key Stage in a different school. How could these barriers be overcome?

Further reading

Hood, P. and Tobutt, K. (2009) *Modern Languages in the Primary School*, London: Sage Publications Ltd.

Kirsch, C. (2008) *Teaching Foreign Languages in the Primary School*, London: Continuum.

Driscoll, P., Earl, J. and Thomae, M. (2013) 'The role and nature of the cultural dimension in primary modern languages', *Language Culture and Curriculum*, 26(2): 146–160.

References

Admiraal, W., Westhoff, G. and de Bot, K. (2006) 'Evaluation of bilingual secondary education in the Netherlands: students' language proficiency in English', *Educational Research and Evaluation*, 12(1): 75–93.

Aitchison, J. (1987) *Words in the Mind: An introduction to the mental lexicon*, Malden, MA: Blackwell Publishing.

Alderson, J.C. (2005) *Diagnosing Language Proficiency: The interface between learning and assessment*, London: Continuum.

——(2007) 'Judging the frequency of English words', *Applied Linguistics*, 28(3): 383–409.

Alexander, R. (2008) 'Culture, dialogue and learning: notes on an emerging pedagogy', in N. Mercer and S. Hodgkinson (eds) *Exploring Talk in School*, London: Sage.

——(ed.) (2010) *Children, Their World, Their Education: Final report and recommendations of the Cambridge Primary Review*, Abingdon: Routledge.

Alexander, R., Rose, J. and Woodhead, C. (1992) *Curriculum Organisation and Classroom Practice in Primary Schools*, London: Department for Education.

Allwright, R.L. (1988) 'Autonomy and individualisation in whole-class instruction', in A. Brookes and P. Grundy (eds) *Individualisation and Autonomy in Language Learning*, London: Modern English Publications and the British Council, pp. 35–44.

Alonso, E., Grisaleña, J. and Campo, A. (2008) 'Plurilingual education in secondary schools: analysis of results', *International CLIL Research Journal*, 1(1): art. 3, online, available at: www.icrj.eu/11-742.

Anderson, J.R. (1983) *The Architecture of Cognition*, Cambridge, MA: Harvard University Press.

Anderson, L.W. and Krathwohl, D. (eds) (2001) *A Taxonomy for Learning, Teaching, and Assessing: A revision of Bloom's taxonomy of educational objectives*, New York: Longman.

Andon, N. and Wingate, U. (2012) 'The contribution of textbooks to sustaining motivation for second language learning', paper presented at Beyond the Beginner: Sustaining Second Language Learning, 8th Annual Conference of the British Association for Applied Linguists Language Learning and Teaching SIG, Oxford University Department of Education, 4–5 July 2012.

Anstee, P. (2011) *Differentiation Pocketbook*, Alresford: Teachers' Pocketbooks.

ARG (Assessment Reform Group) (2002) *Assessment for Learning: 10 Principles*, online, available at: www.aaia.org.uk/afl/assessment-reform-group/ (accessed 26 July 2013).

Atkinson, T. and Claxton, G. (2000) *The Intuitive Practitioner: On the value of not always knowing what one is doing*, Maidenhead: Open University Press.

Baddeley, A.D., Gathercole, S.E. and Papagno, C. (1998) 'The phonological loop as a language learning device', *Psychological Review*, 105(1): 158–173.

Baker, C. (2011) *Foundations of Bilingual Education and Bilingualism*, fifth edition, Bristol: Multilingual Matters.

Baker, P. and Eversley, J. (2000) *Multilingual Capital: The languages of London's schoolchildren and their relevance to economic, social and economic policies*, London: Battlebridge.

Bandura, A. (1993) 'Perceived self-efficacy in cognitive development and functioning', *Educational Psychologist*, 28(2): 117–148.

——(ed.) (1995) *Self-Efficacy in Changing Societies*, Cambridge: Cambridge University Press.

Bardovi-Harlig, K. (2002) 'A new starting point? Investigating formulaic use and input and future expression', *Studies in Second Language Acquisition*, 24(2): 189–198.

Barnes, J. (2007) *Cross-Curricular Learning 3–14*, London: Paul Chapman.

Barton, A. and Bragg, J. (2007) *Discovering Language Project: Evaluation (Phase 2)*, online, available at: www.ascl.org.uk/resources/library/discovering_language/ The-Discovering-Language-project-Phase-2-report.

——(2010) *Discovering Language Project: Evaluation (Phase 3)*, online, available at: www.ascl.org.uk/resources/library/discovering_language/ The-Discovering-Language-project-Phase-3-report.

Barton, A., Bragg, J. and Serratrice, L. (2009) ' "Discovering Language" in primary school: an evaluation of a language awareness programme', *Language Learning Journal*, 37(2): 145–164.

Bartram, B. (2006) 'Attitudes to language learning: a comparative study of peer group influences', *Language Learning Journal*, 33(1): 47–52.

Bauer, L. and Nation, P. (1993) 'Word families', *International Journal of Lexicography*, 6(4): 253–279.

Baumert, J. (1993) 'Lernstrategien, motivationale Orientierungen und Selbstwiksamkeitsuberzeugungen, im Kontext schulischen Lernens', *Unterrichtswissenschaft*, 21: 327–354.

Beach, D. and Dovemark, M. (2009) 'Making "right" choices? An ethnographic account of creativity, performativity and personalised learning policy, concepts and practices', *Oxford Review of Education*, 35(6): 689–704.

Belcher, D. (2012) 'Considering what we know and need to know about second language writing', *Applied Linguistics Review*, 3(1): 131–150.

Beltran, E., Abbott, C. and Jones, J. (forthcoming 2013) *Inclusive Education, Languages and Digital Technology*, Clevedon: Multilingual Matters.

Bereiter, C. and Scardamalia, M. (1987) *The Psychology of Written Composition*, Hillsdale, NJ: Erlbaum.

Bertram, R., Baayen, H.R. and Schreuder, R. (2000) 'Effects of family size for complex words', *Journal of Memory and Language*, 42(3): 390–405.

Bialystok, E. (1979) 'Explicit and implicit judgments of L2 grammaticality', *Language Learning*, 29(1): 81–103.

——(2004) 'The impact of bilingualism on language and literacy development', in T.K. Bhatia and W.C. Ritchie (eds) *The Handbook of Bilingualism*, Oxford: Blackwell, pp. 577–602.

Biggs, J. (2003) *Teaching for Quality Learning at University: What the student does*, second edition, Maidenhead: Open University Press.

Bird, S.A. and Williams, J.N. (2002) 'The effect of bimodal input on implicit and explicit memory: an investigation into the benefits of within-language subtitling', *Applied Psycholinguistics*, 23(4): 509–533.

Birdsong, D. (2006) 'Age and second language acquisition and processing: a selective overview', *Language Learning*, 56(1): 9–49.

Birjandi, P. and Rahimi, A.H. (2012) 'The effect of metacognitive strategy instruction on the listening performance of EFL students', *International Journal of Linguistics*, 4(2): 495–517.

Bitchener, J. (2012) 'A reflection on "the language learning potential" of written CF', *Journal of Second Language Writing*, 21(4): 348–363 (Special Issue: Exploring L2 Writing–SLA Interfaces).

Bitchener, J. and Ferris, D.R. (2012) *Written Corrective Feedback in Second Language Acquisition and Writing*, New York: Routledge.

Black, P. and Wiliam, D. (1998) 'Assessment and classroom learning', *Assessment in Education: Principles, Policy and Practice*, 5(1): 5–74.

——(2009) 'Developing the theory of formative assessment', *Educational Assessment and Evaluation*, 21: 5–31.

Black, P., Harrison, C., Lee, C., Marshall, B. and Wiliam, D. (2002) *Working Inside the Black Box: Assessment for learning in the classroom*, London: GL Assessment.

——(2003) *Assessment for Learning: Putting it into practice*, Buckingham: Open University Press.

Blenkinsop, S., McCrone, T., Wade, P. and Morris, M. (2006) *How Do Young People Make Choices at Age 14 and Age 16?*, DfES Research Report 773, London: DfES, online, available at: https://www.education.gov.uk/publications/eOrdering-Download/RR773.pdf.

Blommaert, J. and Rampton, B. (2012) *Language and Superdiversity*, MMG Working Papers, 12, online, available at: www.academia.edu/1496858/Language_and_Superdiversity_Blommaert_and_Rampton_2012_.

Blondin, C., Candelier, M., Edelenbos, P., Johnstone, R., Kubanek-German, A. and Taeschner, T. (1998) 'Foreign languages in primary and pre-school education: context and outcomes', *A Review of Recent Research within the European Union*, London: Centre for Information on Language Teaching and Research.

Bloom, B.S., Englehart, M.D., Furst, E.J., Hill, W.H. and Krathwohl, D.R. (1956) *Taxonomy of Educational Objectives: Cognitive domain*, New York: McKay.

Boaler, J. and Wiliam, D. (2000) 'Students' experiences of ability grouping: disaffection, polarisation and the construction of failure', *British Educational Research Journal*, 26(5): 631–648.

Boden, M.A. (2001) 'Creativity and knowledge', in A. Craft, B. Jeffrey and M. Liebling (eds) *Creativity in Education*, London: Continuum, pp. 95–102.

Boekaerts, M. (1995) *Motivation in Education*, Leicester: British Psychological Society.

——(2002) 'Motivation to learn', in H. Walberg (ed.) *Educational Practices Series*, International Academy of Education/International Bureau of Education (UNESCO).

Bolster, A. (2009) 'Continuity or a fresh start? A case study of motivation in MFL at transition, KS2–3', *Language Learning Journal*, 37(2): 233–254.

Bolster, A., Ballandier-Brown, C. and Rea-Dickens, P. (2004) 'Young learners of modern foreign languages and their transition to the secondary phase: a lost opportunity?', *Language Learning Journal*, 30(1): 35–41.

Booth, T. (2011) 'The name of the rose: inclusive values into action in teacher education', *Prospects*, 41(3): 303–318.

Borg, S. (2010) 'Language teacher research engagement', *Language Teaching*, 43(4): 391–429.

Boyle, B., Lamprianou, I. and Boyle, T. (2005) 'A longitudinal study of teacher change: what makes professional development effective? Report of the second year of the study, school effectiveness and school improvement', *International Journal of Research, Policy and Practice*, 16(1): 1–27.

Bozorgian, H. (2012) 'Metacognitive instruction does improve listening comprehension', *ISRN Education*, Article ID 734085, online, available at: www.hindawi. com/isrn/education/2012/734085/ (accessed 9 August 2013).

Breidbach, S. (2002) 'European communicative integration: the function of foreign language teaching for the development of a European public sphere', *Language, Culture and Curriculum*, 15(3): 273–283.

Brighouse, T. and Moon, B. (2012) 'Taking teacher development seriously: a proposal to establish a national teaching institute for teacher professional development in England', The New Visions For Education Group, online, available at: www. newvisionsforeducation.org.uk (accessed 25 March 2013).

British Academy (2013) *Languages: The State of the Nation – Demand and Supply of Languages Skills in the UK, Summary Report*, London: British Academy.

Broadbent, D. (1958) *Perception and Communication*, London: Pergamon Press.

Broadfoot, P. (1996) 'Liberating the learner through assessment', in G. Claxton, T. Atkinson, M. Osborn and M. Wallace (eds) *Liberating the Learner*, London: Routledge.

Brown, G. (1990) *Listening to Spoken English*, second edition, Harlow: Longman.

Buckby, M. (1976) 'Is primary French in the balance?', *Modern Language Journal*, 60(7): 340–346.

Burstall, C., Jamieson, M., Cohen, S. and Hargreaves, M. (1974) *Primary French in the Balance*, Windsor: NFER Publishers.

Busse, V. and Williams, M. (2010) 'Why German? Motivation of students studying German at English universities', *Language Learning Journal*, 38(1): 67–85.

Bygate, M. (1996) 'Effects of task repetition: appraising the developing language of learners', in J. Willis and D. Willis (eds) *Challenge and Change in Language Teaching*, Oxford: Macmillan, pp. 136–146.

——(2001) 'Effects of task repetition on the structure and control of oral language', in M. Bygate, P. Skehan and M. Swain (eds) *Researching Pedagogic Tasks, Second Language Learning, Teaching and Testing*, London: Longman, pp. 23–48.

Byram, M. (1992) 'Foreign language learning for European citizenship', *Language Learning Journal*, 6(1): 10–12.

——(1997) *Teaching and Assessing Intercultural Communicative Competence*, Clevedon: Multilingual Matters.

——(ed.) (2001) *Developing Intercultural Competence in Practice*, Clevedon: Multilingual Matters.

——(2008) *From Foreign Language Education to Education for International Citizenship: Essays and reflections*, Clevedon: Multilingual Matters.

Byram, M. and Risager, K. (1999) *Language Teachers, Politics and Cultures*, Multilingual Matters: Clevedon.

Byram, M., Gribkova, B. and Starkey, H. (2002) *Developing the Intercultural Dimension in Language Teaching: a practical introduction for teachers*, Language Policy Division, Strasbourg: Directorate of School, Out-of-School and Higher Education, Council of Europe.

Byram, M., Morgan, C. and colleagues (1994) *Teaching-and-Learning Language-and-Culture*, Clevedon: Multilingual Matters.

Cable, C., Driscoll, P., Mitchell, R., Sing, S., Cremin, T., Earl, J., Eyres, I., Holmes, B., Martin, C. with Heins, B. (2010) *Languages Learning at Key Stage 2: A longitudinal study research report no. 198*, London: DCSF, online, available at: https://www.education.gov.uk/publications/standard/publicationDetail/Page1/DCSF-RR198 (accessed 17 February 2013).

Campbell, R., Robinson, W., Neelands, J., Hewston, R. and Mazzoli, L. (2010) 'Personalised learning: ambiguities in theory and practice', *British Journal of Educational Studies*, 55(2): 135–151.

Campo, A., Grisaleña, J. and Alonso, E. (2007) *Trilingual Students in Secondary School: A New Reality*, Bilbao: Basque Institute of Educational Evaluation and Research.

Canale, M. and Swain, M. (1980) 'Theoretical bases of communicative approaches to second language teaching and testing', *Applied Linguistics*, 1(1): 1–47.

Carrell, P.L. (1991) 'Second language reading: reading ability or language proficiency?', *Applied Linguistics*, 12(2): 159–179.

Carver, R.P. (1977) 'Toward a theory of reading comprehension and "rauding"', *Reading Research Quarterly*, 13(1): 8–63.

Chamot, A.U. (2005) 'Language learning strategy instruction: current issues and research', *Annual Review of Applied Linguistics* 25: 112–130.

Chamot, A.U. and El-Dinary, P.B. (1999) 'Children's learning strategies in language immersion classrooms', *Modern Language Journal*, 83(3): 319–338.

Chamot, A.U., Barnhardt, S., El-Dinary, P.B. and Robbins, J. (1999) *The Learning Strategies Handbook*, White Plains, NY: Longman.

Chesterton, P., Steigler-Peters, S., Moran, W. and Piccioli, M.T. (2004) 'Developing sustainable language learning pathways: an Australian initiative', *Language, Culture and Curriculum*, 17(1): 48–57.

Chien, C. and Wei, L. (1998) 'The strategy use in listening comprehension for EFL learners in Taiwan', *RELC Journal*, 29(1): 66–91.

Christie, C. (2011) 'Speaking spontaneously: an examination of the University of Cumbria approach to the teaching of modern foreign languages', unpublished PhD thesis, Institute of Education, University of London.

CILT (2005) *Languages Yearbook*, London: CILT.

——(2007) *The CILT 7–14 Project*, online, available at: www.primarylanguages.org. uk/policy__research/research_and_statistics/languages_research/cilt_projects.aspx.

——(2011) *Language Trends 2010 Secondary: Full Statistical Report*, London: CILT, online, available at: www.cilt.org.uk/home/research_and_statistics/language_ trends_surveys/secondary/2010.aspx.

Claxton, G. (1995) 'What kind of learning does self-assessment drive? Developing a "nose" for quality: comments on Klenowski', *Assessment in Education: Principles, Policy and Practice*, 2(3): 339–343.

——(2004) 'Learning is learnable (and we ought to teach it)', in J. Cassell (ed.) *National Commission for Education report Ten Years On*, Bristol: National Commission for Education.

——(2005) 'This time it's personal', *Times Educational Supplement*, 28 January, online, available at: www.tes.co.uk/article.aspx?storycode=2069111 (accessed 4 November 2012).

Coady, J. (1997) 'L2 vocabulary acquisition through extensive reading', in J. Coady and T. Huckin (eds) *Second Language Vocabulary Acquisition*, Cambridge: Cambridge University Press, pp. 225–237.

Cobb, T. (2007) 'Computing the vocabulary demands of L2 reading', *Language Learning and Technology*, 11(3): 38–63.

Cochran-Smith, M. and Lytle, S.L. (1993) *Inside Outside: Teacher Research and Knowledge*, New York: Teachers College Press.

Coffield, F. (2008) *Just Suppose Teaching and Learning Became the First Priority*, London: Learning and Skills Network.

Coffield, F., Ecclestone, K., Hall, E. and Moseley, D. (2004a) *Learning Styles and Pedagogy in Post-16 Learning*, London: Learning and Skills Development Agency.

Coffield, F., Moseley, D., Hall, E. and Ecclestone, K. (2004b) *Should We be Using Learning styles? What research has to say to practice*, London: Learning and Skills Research Centre, Learning and Skills Development Agency.

Cohen, A.D. and Macaro, E. (eds) (2007) *Language Learner Strategies: Thirty years of research and practice*, Oxford: Oxford University Press.

Coleman, J.A., Galaczi, A. and Astruc, L. (2007) 'Motivation of UK school pupils towards foreign languages: a large-scale survey at Key Stage 3', *Language Learning Journal*, 35(2): 245–281.

Commission of the European Communities (2008) *Commission outlines strategic plans for European co-operation on education and training*, 16 December, online, available at: http://europa.eu/rapid/pressReleasesAction.do?reference=IP/08/1 986&format=HTML&aged=0&language=EN&guiLanguage=en (accessed 30 June 2012).

Convery, A. and Coyle, D. (1999) *Differentiation and Individual Learners*, London: CILT.

Cook, V. (2001) *The Neglected Role of Written Language in Language Teaching*, online, available at: http://homepage.ntlworld.com/vivian.c/Writings/Papers/ RoleOfWriting.htm (accessed 31 July 2013).

Cordingley, P. (2004) 'Teachers using evidence: using what we know about teaching and learning to reconceptualise evidence-based practice', in G. Thomas and R.

Pring (eds) *Evidence-Based Practice in Education*, Maidenhead: Open University Press, pp. 77–91.

Council of Europe/Council for Cultural Cooperation (2001) *Common European Framework of Reference for Languages: Learning, teaching, assessment*, Cambridge: Cambridge University Press.

Court, K. (2002) *Why Are Boys Opting Out? A study of situated masculinities and foreign language learning*, CRILE Working Paper No. 57, online, available at: www.ling.lancs.ac.uk/groups/crile/workingpapers.htm.

Cox, R. (2011) 'The classroom', in J. MacLusky and R. Cox (eds) *Teaching Creative Writing in the Primary School*, Maidenhead: Open University Press, pp. 13–24.

Coyle, D. (2002) 'Against all odds: lessons from content and language integrated learning in English secondary schools', in W.C. Daniel and G.M. Jones (eds) *Education and Society in Plurilingual Contexts*, Brussels: VUB Brussels University Press.

——(2006) *Developing CLIL: Towards a Theory of Practice*, in APAC Monograph 6, Barcelona, pp. 5–29.

——(2007a) 'Strategic classrooms: learning communities which nurture the development of learner strategies', *Language Learning Journal*, 35(1): 65–79.

——(2007b) 'Content and language integrated learning', *Encyclopaedia for Language Learning Vol. 4*, Berlin: Springer.

Coyle, D., Hood, P. and Marsh, D. (2010) *Content and Language Integrated Learning*, Cambridge: Cambridge University Press.

Craft, A. (2001) 'Little 'c' creativity', in A. Craft, B. Jeffrey and M. Leibling (eds) *Creativity in Education*, London: Continuum, pp. 45–61.

——(2002) *Creativity and Early Years Education*, London: Continuum.

——(2005) *Creativity in Schools: Tensions and dilemma*, Abingdon: Routledge.

Creese, A. and Blackledge, A. (2010) 'Translanguaging in the bilingual classroom: a pedagogy for learning and teaching?', *The Modern Language Journal*, 94(1): 103–115.

Crookes, G. and Schmidt, R.W. (1991) 'Motivation: reopening the research agenda', *Language Learning*, 41(4): 469–512.

Cross, J. (2010) 'Raising L2 listeners' metacognitive awareness: a socio-cultural theory perspective', *Language Awareness*, 19(4): 281–297.

Crystal, D. (1997) *English as a Global Language*, Cambridge: Cambridge University Press.

——(2003) *English as a Global Language*, second edition, Cambridge: Cambridge University Press.

Csikszentmihalyi, M. (1996) *Creativity: Flow and the psychology of discovery and invention*, New York: HarperCollins.

——(1997) *Creativity: Flow and the psychology of discovery and invention*, New York: HarperPerennial.

——(2002) *Flow: The psychology of happiness* (reprint), London: Rider.

Cunningham, A.E. and Stanovich, K.E. (1998) 'What reading does for the mind', *Journal of Direct Instruction*, 1(2): 137–149, reprinted from *The American Educator*, 22(1/2): 8–15.

Cutler, A. (1994) 'Segmentation problems, rhythmic solutions', *Lingua*, 92: 81–104.

Cutler, A. and Carter, D.M. (1987) 'The predominance of strong initial syllables in the English vocabulary', *Computer Speech and Language*, 2(3): 133–142.

Cutler, A., Mehler, J., Norris, D. and Segui, J. (1986) 'The syllable's differing role in the segmentation of French and English', *Journal of Memory and Language*, 25(4): 385–400.

——(1992) 'The monolingual nature of speech segmentation by bilinguals', *Cognitive Psychology*, 24(3): 381–410.

Dadds, M. (1997) 'Continuing professional development: nurturing the expert within', *Journal of In-Service Education*, 23(1): 31–38.

Daller, H., Milton, J. and Treffers-Daller, J. (2007) *Modelling and Assessing Vocabulary Knowledge*, Cambridge: Cambridge University Press.

Dalton, C. and Seidlhofer, B. (1994) *Pronunciation*, Oxford: Oxford University Press.

Dam, L. (1990) 'Learner autonomy in practice', in I. Gathercole (ed.) *Autonomy in Language Learning*, London: CILT.

——(1995) *Learner Autonomy 3: From theory to classroom practice*, Dublin: Authentik.

Dam, L. and Gabrielsen, G. (1988) 'Developing learner autonomy in a school context', in H. Holec (ed.) *Autonomie et Appretissage Autodirige: Applications dans le context Europeene*, Strasbourg: Council of Europe.

David, A. (2008) 'Vocabulary breadth in French L2 learners', *Language Learning Journal*, 36(2): 167–180.

Davies, B. (2004) 'The gender gap in modern languages: a comparison of attitude and performance in Year 7 and Year 10', *Language Learning Journal*, 29(1): 53–58.

Davies, M. and Gardner, D. (2010) *A Frequency Dictionary of Contemporary American English*, New York: Routledge.

Day, R.R. and Bamford, J. (1998) *Extensive Reading in the Second Language Classroom*, Cambridge: Cambridge University Press.

DCSF (Department for Children, Schools and Families) (2005a) *Key Stage 2 Framework for Languages*, Nottingham: DCSF Publications.

——(2005b) *The Languages Ladder*, Nottingham: DCSF Publications.

——(2007) *The Languages Ladder. Steps to Success*, London: DCSF.

——(2008) *The Assessment for Learning Strategy*, London: DCSF.

——(2009) *Independent Review of the Primary Curriculum: Final Report*, London: DCSF.

Dearing, R. and King, L. (2007) *Languages Review*, London: DfES.

Deci, E.L. and Ryan, R.M. (1985) *Intrinsic Motivation and Self-Determination in Human Behavior*, New York: Plenum.

DeKeyser, R. (2007a) 'Skill acquisition theory', in B. VanPatten and J. Williams (eds) *Theories in Second Language Acquisition*, Mahwah, NJ: Lawrence Erlbaum, pp. 97–113.

——(ed.) (2007b) *Practice in a Second Language: Perspectives from applied linguistics and cognitive psychology*, New York: Cambridge University Press.

Department of Education, Queensland (2002) *A Guide to Productive Pedagogies: Classroom reflection manual*, Queensland: Department of Education.

Derwing, T. and Munro, M.J. (1997) 'Accent, intelligibility and comprehensibility: evidence from Four L1s', *Studies in Second Language Acquisition*, 19(1): 1–16.

DES (Department of Education and Science) (1977) *Modern Languages in Comprehensive Schools: A discussion paper by some members of H.M. Inspectorate of Schools based on a survey of 83 schools in 1975–76*, London: HMSO.

DES (Department of Education and Science)/Welsh Office (1990) *Modern Foreign Languages for Ages 11 to 16: Proposals of the Secretary of State for Education and Science and the Secretary of State for Wales, Harris Committee*, London: HMSO.

DfE (Department for Education) (2010) *The Case for Change*, London: Stationery Office, online, available at: www.education.gov.uk/publications/cOrdering-Download/DFE-00564-2010.pdf.

——(2011a) *Modern Foreign Language Programmes of Study*, online, available at: www.education.gov.uk/schools/teachingandlearning/curriculum/secondary/b00199616/mfl/programme (accessed 20 August 2012).

——(2011b) *Training our Next Generation of Outstanding Teachers*, London: Stationery Office, online, available at: https://www.education.gov.uk/publications/standard/publicationDetail/Page1/DFE-00083-2011 (accessed 20 March 2013).

——(2011d) *Including all Learners*, online, available at: www.education.gov.uk/schools/teachingandlearning/curriculum/b00199686/inclusion (accessed 4 November 2012).

——(2013a) *The National Curriculum in England: Framework document for consultation*, London: Department for Education.

——(2013b) *The National Curriculum Programmes of Study (A Consultation)*, London, DfE, online, available at: www.education.gov.uk/schools/teaching andlearning/curriculum/nationalcurriculum2014.

DfEE (Department for Education and Employment) (1998) *National Literacy Strategy: A Framework for Teaching*, London: HMSO.

DfEE and QCA (Department for Education and Employment and Qualifications and Curriculum Authority) (1999) *The National Curriculum: Modern foreign languages*, London: The Stationery Office.

DfES (Department for Education and Skills) (2002) *Languages for All: Languages for life, a strategy for England*, London: DfES Publications.

——(2003a) *Key Stage 3 National Strategy: Framework for Teaching Modern Foreign Languages, Years 7, 8, and 9*, London: HMSO.

——(2003b) *Every Child Matters*, Norwich: The Stationery Office.

——(2005a) *Key Stage 2 Framework for Languages*, Nottingham: DfES Publications.

——(2005b) *White Paper: Higher Standards, Better Schools for All*, London: Department for Education and Skills.

——(2006) *Primary Framework for Literacy and Mathematics*, London: DfES, online, available at: www.educationengland.org.uk/documents/pdfs/2006-primary-national-strategy.pdf (accessed 17 August 2013).

——(2007) *Languages Review*, London: DfES.

Dobson, A. (1998) *Modern Foreign Languages Inspected*, London: CILT.

Dombey, H. (2010) *Teaching Reading: What the evidence says*, Leicester: UKLA.

Donato, R. and McCormick, D. (1994) 'A sociocultural perspective on language learning strategies: the role of mediation', *Modern Language Journal*, 78(4): 453–464.

Dornyei, Z. (1998) 'Motivation in second and foreign language learning', *Language Teaching*, 31(3): 118.

——(2001) *Teaching and Researching: Motivation*, Harlow: Longman.

——(2005) *The Psychology of the Language Learner: Individual differences in second language acquisition*, Mahwah, NJ: Lawrence Erlbaum.

——(ed.) (2008) *Motivational Strategies in the Language Classroom*, Cambridge: Cambridge University Press.

——(2009b) 'The L2 Motivational Self System', in Z. Dornyei and E. Ushioda (eds) *Motivation, Language Identity and the L2 Self*, Bristol: Multilingual Matters.

——(2010) 'The relationship between language aptitude and language learning motivation: individual differences from a dynamic systems perspective', in E. Macaro (ed.) *Continuum Companion to Second Language Acquisition*, London: Continuum, pp. 247–267.

Dörnyei, Z. and Csizér, K. (2002) 'Some dynamics of language attitudes and motivation: results of a longitudinal nationwide survey', *Applied Linguistics*, 23(4): 421–462.

Dörnyei, Z. and Ottó, I. (1998) 'Motivation in action: a process model of L2 motivation', *Working Papers in Applied Linguistics*, Thames Valley University, London, 4: 43–69.

Dörnyei, Z. and Ushioda, E. (2011) *Teaching and Researching: Motivation*, second edition, Harlow: Pearson Education.

Driscoll, P. (1999) 'Teacher expertise in the primary modern foreign languages classroom', in P. Driscoll and D. Frost (eds) *The Teaching of Modern Foreign Languages in the Primary School*, London: Routledge, pp. 27–49.

——(2000) 'Modern foreign languages in English primary schools: an investigation of two contrasting approaches', unpublished PhD thesis, University of Kent.

Driscoll, P. and Rowe, J. (2012) 'Broadening the lens: an investigation of student teachers' changing perceptions of pedagogy following a teaching placement in a primary school in mainland Europe', *Education*, 40(4): 3–13.

Driscoll, P., Earl, J. and Thomae, M. (2013) 'The role and nature of the cultural dimension in primary modern languages', *Language Culture and Curriculum*, 26(2): 146–160.

Driscoll, P., Jones, J. and Macrory, G. (2004) *The Provision of Foreign Language Learning for Pupils at Key Stage 2*, DfES Research Report RR572, London: DfES.

DuFour, R. (2004) 'What is a Professional Learning Community?' *Schools as learning communities*, 61(8): 6–11.

Dupoux, E. (1993) 'The time course of prelexical processing: the syllabic hypothesis revisited', in G. Altmann and R. Shillcock (eds) *Cognitive Models of Speech Processing*, Hove: Erlbaum.

Dweck, C. (2000) *Essays in Social Psychology. Self-theories: Their role in motivation, personality, and development*, Hove: Brunner/Mazel.

——(2006) *Mindset: How you can fulfil your potential*, New York: Ballantine Books.

Eason, G. (2011) 'Digital textbooks open a new chapter', *BBC News*, 19 October, online, available at: www.bbc.co.uk/news/business-15175962 (accessed 4 November 2012).

Eccles, J. (1983) 'Expectancies, values, and academic behaviors', in J.T. Spence (ed.) *Achievement and Achievement Motives*, San Francisco, CA: W.H. Freeman and Company, pp. 75–146.

Economic and Social Research Council (2012) *Language Diversity Will Make London a True Global Player*, Economic and Social Research Council, online, available at:

www.esrc.ac.uk/news-and-events/press-releases/20633/language-diversity-will-make-london-a-true-global-player.aspx (accessed 30 March 2013).

Egege, S. and Kutieleh, S. (2003) 'Critical thinking: teaching foreign notions to foreign students', *International Education Journal*, 4(4): 75–85.

Elley, W.B. (1989) 'Vocabulary acquisition from listening to stories', *Reading Research Quarterly*, 24(2): 174–187.

Elliott, J. (1990) 'Teachers as researchers: implications for supervision and for teacher education', *Teaching and Teacher Education*, 6(1): 1–26.

Ellis, N. (2005) 'At the interface: dynamic interaction of explicit and implicit language knowledge', *Studies in Second Language Acquisition*, 27(2): 305–352.

Ellis, N.C. and Robinson, P. (2008) 'An introduction to cognitive linguistics, second language acquisition and language instruction', in P. Robinson and N.C. Ellis, *Handbook of Cognitive Linguistics and Second Language Acquisition*, Abingdon: Routledge, pp. 3–24.

Ellis, R. (2003) *Task-based Language Learning and Teaching*, Oxford: Oxford University Press.

——(2004) 'The definition and measurement of L2 explicit knowledge', *Language Learning*, 54(2): 227–275.

——(2010) 'Epilogue: a framework for investigating oral and corrective feedback', *Studies in Second Language Acquisition*, 32(2): 335–349.

Enever, J. (ed.) (2011) *ELLiE: Early Language Learning in Europe*, London: British Council.

Erlam, R. (2003) 'The effects of deductive and inductive instruction on the acquisition of Direct Object Pronouns in French as a second language', *The Modern Language Journal*, 87(2): 242–260.

Erler, L. (2003) 'Reading in a foreign language – near-beginner adolescents' experiences of French in English secondary schools', unpublished DPhil thesis, University of Oxford.

Erler, L. and Macaro, E. (2011) 'Decoding ability in French as a foreign language and language learning motivation', *The Modern Language Journal*, 95(4): 496–518.

European Commission (1995) COM(95)590 *White Paper on Education and Training: Teaching and Learning; towards the learning society*, Brussels, online, available at: http://europa.eu/documentation/official-docs/white-papers/index_en.htm (accessed 24 May 2012).

——(2009) *Study on the Contribution of Multilingualism to Creativity – Compendium Part One Multilingualism and Creativity: Towards an Evidence-Base*, Brussels: European Commission.

——(2012a) *First European Survey on Language Competences: Final report*, Brussels: European Commission.

——(2012b) *Key Data on Teaching Languages at School in Europe 2012*, Brussels: Education, Audiovisual and Culture Executive Agency.

Eurydice (2012) *Key Data on Teaching Languages at School in Europe*. 2012 edition, Eurydice European Unit/European Commission, online, available at: http://eacea.ec.europa.eu/education/eurydice.

Evans, M. and Fisher, L. (2012) 'Emergent communities of practice: secondary schools interaction with primary school foreign language teaching and learning', *Language Learning Journal*, 40(2): 157–173.

Extra, G. and Yagmur, K. (eds) (2012) *Language Rich Europe, Trends in Policies and Practices for Multilingualism in Europe*, UK British Council.

Fasko, D. (2005) 'Creative thinking and reasoning: can you have one without the other?' in J.C. Kaufman and J. Baer (eds) *Creativity and Reason in Cognitive Development*, Cambridge: Cambridge University Press, pp. 159–176.

Fautley, M. and Savage, J. (2007) *Creativity in Secondary Education*, Exeter: Learning Matters.

Field, J. (2004) 'An insight into listeners' problems: too much bottom-up or too much top-down?' *System*, 32(3): 363–377.

——(2005) 'Intelligibility and the listener: the role of lexical stress', *TESOL Quarterly*, 39(3): 399–423.

——(2008a) *Listening in the Language Classroom*, Cambridge: Cambridge University Press.

——(2008b) 'Revising segmentation hypotheses in first and second language listening', *System*, 3(1): 35–51.

——(ed.) (2008c) Special issue: psycholinguistics for TESOL, *TESOL Quarterly*, 42(3): 361–374.

——(2008d) 'Bricks or mortar: which parts of the input does a second language listener rely on?', *TESOL Quarterly*, 4(3): 411–432.

——(2013) 'Cognitive validity', in A. Geranpayeh and L. Taylor (eds) *Examining Listening*, Studies in Language Testing 35, Cambridge: Cambridge University Press.

Finnish National Board of Education (2004) *National Core Curriculum for Basic Education*, online, available at: www.oph.fi/download/47672_core_curricula_basic_education_3.pdf (accessed 20 August 2012).

Fisher, L. (2001) 'Modern foreign language recruitment post-16: the pupils' perspective', *Language Learning Journal*, 23(1): 33–40.

Fisher, R. (2004) 'What is creativity?' in R. Fisher and M. Williams (eds) *Unlocking Creativity: A teacher's guide to creativity across the curriculum*, Abingdon: David Fulton.

Flutter, J. and Rudduck, J. (2004) *Consulting Pupils: What's in it for schools?*, London: RoutledgeFalmer.

Foster, P. (1999) ' "Never mind the quality, feel the impact": A methodological assessment of teacher research sponsored by the Teacher Training Agency', *British Journal of Educational Studies*, 47(4): 380–398.

Frantzen, D. (1995) 'The effects of grammar supplementation on written accuracy in an intermediate Spanish content course', *The Modern Language Journal*, 79(3): 329–344.

Freudenstein, R. (1998) 'Was Hänschen nicht lernt … *Grundschulunterricht*' 451, Beiheft.

Fullan, M. (1993) *Change Forces: Probing the depths of educational reform*, London: Falmer Press.

Furlong, J., Salisbury, J. and Combes, L. (2003) *Best Practice Research Scholarships: An evaluation*, Nottingham: DfES Publications.

Galanouli, G. (2010) *School-Based Professional Development: A report for the General Teaching Council for Northern Ireland*, online, available at: http://arrts.gtcni.org.uk/gtcni/bitstream/2428/96693/1/School_Based_Report_April2010.pdf (accessed 21 January 2013).

Galton, M., Gray, J. and Rudduck, J. (2003) *Transfer and Transition in the Middle Years of Schooling (7–14): Continuities and discontinuities*, Learning Research Report RR443, Nottingham: Department of Education and Science.

Gardner, D. and Davies, M. (2007) 'Pointing out frequent phrasal verbs: a corpus-based analysis', *TESOL Quarterly*, 41(2): 339–359.

Gardner, H. (1993) *Multiple Intelligences: The theory in practice*, New York: Basic Books.

——(1999) *The Disciplined Mind*, New York: Simon and Schuster.

Gardner, R.C. (1985) *Social Psychology and Second Language Learning: The role of attitudes and motivation*, Baltimore, MD: Edward Arnold.

Gardner, R.C. and Lambert, W.E. (1972) *Attitudes and Motivation: Second language learning*, Rowley, MA: Newbury House.

Gass, S. (1997) *Input, Interaction and the Second Language Learner*, Mahwah, NJ: Lawrence Erlbaum Associates.

Gathercole, I. (ed.) (1990) *Autonomy in Language Learning*, London: CILT.

Gathercole, S.E. and Baddeley, A.D. (1993) *Working Memory and Language*, Hove: Erlbaum.

Gattegno, C. (1963) *Teaching for Languages in Schools: The silent way*, Reading: Educational Explorers.

——(1976) *The Common Sense of Teaching Foreign Languages*, n.p.: Educational Solutions.

Genesee, F. (1987) *Learning Through Two Languages: Studies of immersion and bilingual education*, Rowley, MA: Newbury House.

Germain, C. (1995) *Évolution de l'enseignement des langues: 5000 ans d'histoire*, Paris: CLE International.

Gilbert, C. (2007) *2020 Vision: A report on behalf of the Teaching and Learning 2020 Review Group*, London: Ofsted.

Goh, C. and Taib, Y. (2006) 'Metacognitive instruction in listening for young learners', *ELT Journal*, 60(3): 222–232.

Goodman, J. (2011) 'Assessment practices in an independent school: the spirit and the letter', unpublished PhD thesis, King's College London.

Goodman, K. (1967) 'Reading: a psycholinguistic guessing game', *Journal of the Reading Specialist*, 6(4): 126–135.

Gough, P.B. and Wren, S. (1999) 'Constructing meaning: the role of decoding', in J. Oakhill and R. Beard (eds) *Reading Development and the Teaching of Reading*, Oxford: Blackwell.

Gove, M. (2012) 'Digital literacy campaign – Michael Gove's speech in full', *The Guardian*, 11 January, online, available at: www.guardian.co.uk/education/2012/jan/11/digital-literacy-michael-gove-speech (accessed 4 November 2012).

Grabe, W. (2004) '3. Research on teaching reading', *Annual Review of Applied Linguistics*, 24: 44–69.

——(2010) 'Fluency in reading: thirty-five years later', *Reading in a Foreign Language*, 22(1): 71–83.

Grabe, W. and Stoller, F.L. (2011) *Teaching and Researching Reading*, second edition, Harlow: Longman.

Graddol, D. (2006) *English Next*, Manchester: The British Council, online, available at: www.britishcouncil.org/learning-research-englishnext.htm.

Graham, S. (2002) 'Experiences of learning French: a snapshot at Years 11, 12 and 13', *Language Learning Journal*, 25(1): 15–20.

——(2003) 'Learner strategies and advanced level listening comprehension', *Language Learning Journal*, 28(1): 64–69.

——(2004) 'Giving up on modern foreign languages? Students' perceptions of learning French', *The Modern Language Journal*, 88(2): 171–191.

——(2006a) 'Listening comprehension: the learners' perspective', *System*, 34(2): 165–182.

——(2006b) 'A study of students' metacognitive beliefs about foreign language study and their impact on learning', *Foreign Language Annals*, 39(2): 296–309.

——(2007) 'Learner strategies and self-efficacy: making the connection', *Language Learning Journal*, 35(1): 81–93.

Graham, S. and Macaro, E. (2008) 'Strategy instruction in listening for lower-intermediate learners of French', *Language Learning*, 58(4): 747–783.

Graham, S., Santos, D. and Vanderplank, R. (2008) 'Listening comprehension and strategy use: a longitudinal exploration', *System*, 36(1): 52–68.

——(2010) 'Strategy clusters and sources of knowledge in French L2 listening comprehension', *International Journal of Innovation in Language Learning and Teaching*, 4(1): 1–20.

——(2011) 'Exploring the relationship between listening development and strategy use', *Language Teaching Research*, 15(4): 435–456.

Graham, S.J. (2004) 'Giving up on modern foreign languages? Students Perceptions of learning French', *The Modern Language Journal*, 88(2): 171–191.

Gray, C. (2013) 'Bridging the teacher/researcher divide: master's-level work in initial teacher education', *European Journal of Teacher Education*, 36(1): 24–38.

Green, P. and Hecht, K. (1992) 'Implicit and explicit grammar: an empirical study', *Applied Linguistics*, 13(2): 168–184.

Greenfield, S. and Sharples, J. (2008) 'Brain and behaviour: thinking differently', *Times Educational Supplement*, 23 May, online, available at: www.tes.co.uk/article.aspx?storycode=6001521 (accessed 4 November 2012).

Gregg, K. (1984) 'Krashen's Monitor and Occam's Razor', *Applied Linguistics*, 5(2): 79–100.

Grenfell, M. (1993) *The Caen Primary School Foreign Language Project*, Occasional Paper 16, University of Southampton, Centre for Language in Education.

——(2000) 'Modern languages: beyond Nuffield, and into the 21st century', *Language Learning Journal*, 22(1): 23–29.

——(2002) *Modern Languages Across the Curriculum*, London: Routledge.

Grenfell, M. and Harris, V. (1993) 'How do pupils learn?' (part 2) *Language Learning Journal*, 9(1): 7–11.

——(1999) *Modern Languages and Learning Strategies: In theory and practice*, London: Routledge.

——(forthcoming) 'The strategy use of learners of a third language', *Modern Language Journal*.

——(in press) 'Learning to learn languages: the differential response of learners to strategy instruction', *Curriculum Journal*.

Grenfell, M. and Macaro, E. (2007) 'Language learner strategies: claims and critiques', in A.D. Cohen and E. Macaro (eds) *Language Learner Strategies: Thirty years of research and practice*, Oxford: Oxford University Press.

Griffiths, C. (2008) *Lessons from Good Language Learners*, Cambridge: Cambridge University Press.

Grigorenko, E., Jarvin, L., Mei, T. and Sternberg, R. (2008) 'Something new in the garden: assessing creativity in academic domains', *Psychology Science Quarterly*, 50(2): 295–307.

Grosjean, F. (1985) 'The recognition of words after their acoustic offsets: evidence and implications', *Perception and Psychophysics*, 38(4): 299–310.

Gu, P.Y. (2003) 'Vocabulary learning in a second language: person, task, context and strategies', *TESL-EJ 7/2*, online, available at: www.tesl-ej.org/wordpress (accessed 12 September 2012).

Guilloteaux, M.J. and Dörnyei, Z. (2008) 'Motivating language learners: a classroom-oriented investigation of the effects of motivational strategies on student motivation', *TESOL Quarterly*, 42(1): 55–77.

Gula-Kubiszewska, H. (2007) *Efekty Dydaktyczne Samoregulowanego Uczenia sie Motorycznego*, Wroclaw: AWF.

Häcker, M. (2008) 'Eleven pets and 20 ways to express one's opinion: the vocabulary learners of German acquire at English secondary schools', *Language Learning Journal*, 36(2): 215–226.

Hamada, M. and Koda, K. (2010) 'The role of phonological decoding in second language word-meaning inference', *Applied Linguistics*, 31(4): 513–531.

Hargreaves, D. (2006) *A New Shape for Schooling?*, London: Specialist Schools and Academies Trust.

Harklau, L. (2002) 'The role of writing in classroom second language acquisition', *Journal of Second Language Writing*, 11(4): 329–350.

Harlen, W. and James, M.J. (1997) 'Assessment and learning: differences and relationships between formative and summative assessment', *Assessment in Education*, 4(3): 365–380.

Harmer, J. (1991) *The Practice of English Language Teaching*, first edition, London: Longman.

——(2007) *The Practice of English Language Teaching*, fourth edition, London: Longman.

Harris, A. (1998) 'Effective teaching: a review of the literature', *School Leadership and Management*, 18(2): 169–183.

Harris, V. (1995) 'Differentiation: not as easy as it seems', *Language Learning Journal*, 12(1): 13–15.

——(2007) 'Exploring progression: reading and listening strategy instruction with near-beginner learners of French', *Language Learning Journal*, 35(2): 189–204.

Harris, V. and Prescott, J. (2005) 'Learning strategy instruction: in theory and in practice', *Scottish Languages Review*, 11, online, available at: www.strath.ac.uk/scilt/slr (accessed 24 August 2012).

Hart, S., Dixon, A., Drummond, M. and McIntyre, D. (2004) *Learning without Limits*, Maidenhead: Open University Press.

Hassan, X., Macaro, E., Mason, D., Nye, G., Smith, P. and Vanderplank, R. (2005) 'Strategy training in language learning – a systematic review of available research', *Research Evidence in Education Library*, London: EPPI-Centre, Social Science Research Unit, Institute of Education, University of London.

Hattie, J. and Timperley, H. (2007) 'The power of feedback', *Review of Educational Research*, 77(1): 81–112.

Hawkins, E. (1981) *Modern Languages in the Curriculum*, Cambridge: Cambridge University Press.

——(1999) 'Foreign language study and language awareness', *Language Awareness* 8(3/4): 124–142.

——(2005) 'Out of this nettle, drop-out, we pluck this flower, opportunity: re-thinking the school foreign language apprenticeship', *Language Learning Journal*, 32(1): 4–17.

Hawkins, P.R. (1971) 'The syntactic location of hesitation pauses', *Language and Speech*, 14(3): 277–288.

Hay, J. (2001) 'Lexical frequency in morphology: is everything relative?', *Linguistics*, 39(6): 1041–1070.

Hayes, J.R. and Flower, L.S. (1980) 'Identifying the organization of writing processes', in L.W. Gregg and E.R. Steinberg (eds) *Cognitive Processes in Writing*, Hillsdale, NJ: Erlbaum.

Hayward, G., Hodgson, A., Johnson, J., Oancea, A., Pring, R., Spours, K., Wilde, S. and Wright, S. (2005) *Annual Report of the Nuffield Review of 14–19 Education and Training*, Oxford: University of Oxford Department of Educational Studies.

Heafford, M. (1990) 'What learners learn is not what teachers teach', *Language Learning Journal*, 1(1): 88–90.

Heibeck, T.H. and Markman, E.M. (1987) 'Word learning in children: an examination of fast mapping', *Child Development*, 58(4): 1021–1034.

Hennebry, M. (2011a) 'Modern foreign language learning and European citizenship in the Irish context', *Irish Educational Studies*, 30(1): 83–112.

——(2011b) 'Interactions between European citizenship and language learning among adolescent Europeans', *European Educational Research Journal*, 1(4): 623–641.

——(2012) 'Pedgagogy, citizenship and the EU', in J. Sayer and L. Erler (eds) *Schools for the Future Europe*, Continuum: London.

Hill, M. and Laufer, B. (2003) 'Type of task, time-on-task and electronic dictionaries in incidental vocabulary acquisition', *International Review of Applied Linguistics in Language Teaching*, 41(2): 87–106.

Hirsh, D. and Nation, P. (1992) 'What vocabulary size is needed to read unsimplified texts for pleasure?', *Reading in a Foreign Language*, 8(2): 689–696.

Hirvela, A. (2011) 'Writing-to-learn in content areas: research insights', in R.M. Manchon (ed.) *Learning-to-Write and Writing-to-Learn in an Additional Language*, Amsterdam: John Benjamins, pp. 37–60.

HM Inspectorate for Education and Training in Wales (2009) *Improving modern foreign languages in Wales: Advice and guidance for schools and local authorities*, Cardiff: Estyn.

HMI (HM Inspectors of Schools and Colleges) (1977) *Matters for Discussion: Modern Languages in Comprehensive Schools – HMI Report*, London: HMSO.

——(1985) *Inquiry into Practice in 22 Comprehensives Where Foreign Language Forms Part of the Curriculum for All or Almost All Pupils up to the Age of 16+*, London: HMSO.

HMI (HM Inspectors of Schools) (1989) *A Survey of the Teaching and Learning of Modern Languages in a Sample of Inner City and Urban Schools*, London: HMSO.

Hobbs, V., Matsuo, A. and Payne, M. (2010) 'Code-switching in Japanese language classrooms: an exploratory investigation of native vs. non-native speaker teacher practice', *Linguistics and Education*, 21(1): 44–59.

Hodgen, J. and Marshall, B. (2005) 'Assessment for Learning in English and mathematics: a comparison', *The Curriculum Journal*, 16(2): 153–176.

Hoey, M. (2005) *Lexical Priming: A new theory of words and language*, London: Routledge.

Holec, H. (1981) *Autonomy in Foreign Language Learning*, Strasbourg: Council of Europe.

Hood, P. (1994) 'Primary foreign languages: the integration model: some parameters for research', *Curriculum Journal*, 5(2): 235–247.

——(2006) Unpublished data from CLIL research interviews with students at Tile Hill Wood Language College, Coventry.

Hood, P. and Tobutt, K. (2009) *Modern Languages in the Primary School*, London: Sage.

Hopkins, D. (2007) *Every School a Great School*, Maidenhead: Open University Press.

Horwitz, E.K. (2000) 'It ain't over 'til it's over: on foreign language anxiety, first language deficits, and the confounding of variables', *Modern Language Journal*, 84(2): 256–259.

——(2001) 'Language anxiety and achievement', *Annual Review of Applied Linguistics*, 21: 112–126.

House of Lords European Union Select Committee (2005) *17th Report of the session 2004–2005 Proposed EU Integrated Action Programme for Life-Long Learning*, London: Stationery Office Books.

Hoy, P.H. (1977) *The Early Teaching of Modern Languages: A report on the place of language teaching in primary schools by a Nuffield Foundation Committee*, London: Nuffield Foundation.

Hramiak, A. and Hudson, T. (eds) (2011) *Understanding Learning and Teaching in Secondary Schools*, Harlow: Pearson.

Hu, H.M. and Nation, P. (2000) 'Unknown vocabulary density and reading comprehension', *Reading in a Foreign Language*, 13(1): 403–429.

Hudson, R.A. (2007) *Language Networks: The new word grammar*, Oxford: Oxford University Press.

Hufton, N.R., Elliott, J.G. and Illushin, L. (2002) 'Educational motivation and engagement: qualitative accounts from three countries', *British Educational Research Journal*, 28(2): 265–289.

Hulse, B. and Hulme, R. (2012) 'Engaging with research through practitioner enquiry: the perceptions of beginning teachers on a postgraduate initial teacher education programme', *Educational Action Research*, 20(2): 313–329.

Hunt, M., Barnes, A., Martin, C. and Powell, B. (2008) 'Moving on: the challenges for foreign language learning on transition from primary to secondary school', *Teaching and Teacher Education*, 24(4): 915–926.

Hyland, K. (2011) 'Learning to write: issues in theory, research and pedagogy', in R.M. Manchón (ed.) *Learning-to-Write and Writing-to-Learn in an Additional Language*, Amsterdam: John Benjamins, pp. 17–35.

Hymes, D. (1972) 'On communicative competence', in J.B. Pride and J. Holmes (eds) *Sociolinguistics: Selected Readings*, Harmondsworth: Penguin.

Internet World Stats (2013) *Internet World Users by Language: Top ten languages*, online, available at: www.internetworldstats.com/stats7.htm (accessed 30 March 2013).

Irish National Council for Curriculum and Assessment French Junior Cycle Curriculum (2012) *French*, online, available at: www.curriculumonline.ie/en/Post-Primary_Curriculum/Junior_Cycle_Curriculum/Junior_Certificate_Subjects/French/ (accessed 15 August 2012).

Jackson, D. and Street, H. (2005) 'What does collaborative enquiry look like?' in H. Street and J. Temperley (eds) *Improving Schools Through Collaborative Enquiry*, London: Continuum.

James, M. (1998) *Using Assessment for School Improvement*, Oxford: Heinemann.

——(2006) 'Assessment, teaching and theories of learning', in J. Gardner (ed.) *Assessment and Learning*, London: Sage.

James, M., Black, P., McCormick, R., Peddler, D. and Wiliam, D. (2006) 'Learning how to learn in classrooms, schools and networks: aims, design and analysis', *Research Papers in Education*, 21(2): 101–118.

Järvinen, H.-J. (2008) *Research in CLIL*, Bulletin 8J, Brussels: European Commission, Euro-clic.

Jiang, X. and Cohen, A.D. (2012) 'A critical review of research on strategies in learning Chinese as both a second and foreign language', *Studies in Second Language Learning and Teaching*, 2(1): 9–43.

Jiminez Raya, M., Lamb, T. and Vieira, F. (2007) *Pedagogy for Autonomy in Language Education in Europe*, Dublin: Authentik.

Johnson, K. (1996) *Language Teaching and Skill Learning*, Oxford: Blackwell.

Johnstone, R. and McKinstry, R. (2008) *Evaluation of EPPI: Early Primary Partial Immersion in French at Walker Road Primary School, Aberdeen, Final Report*, Stirling: University of Stirling, Scottish CILT, online, available at: www.strath.ac.uk/media/faculties/hass/scilt/research/eppi_book.pdf.

Jones, J. (2010) 'The role of Assessment for Learning in the management of primary to secondary transition: implications for teachers', *Language Learning Journal*, 38(2): 175–191.

——(2013) 'Modern foreign languages as an inclusive learning opportunity: changing policies, practices and identities in the languages classroom', in E.V. Beltrán, C. Abbott and J. Jones (eds) *Inclusive Language Education and Digital Technology*, Clevedon: Multilingual Matters.

Jones, J. and Wiliam, D. (2008) *Modern Foreign Languages Inside the Black Box*, London: GLA Assessment.

Jones, N. (2007) 'Assessment and the National Languages Strategy', *Cambridge Journal of Education*, 37(1): 17–33.

Joyce, P. and McMillan, B. (2010) 'Student perspectives of their learning experience in streamed and mixed-ability classes', *Language Education in Asia*, 1(1): 215–227.

Just, M.A. and Carpenter, P.A. (1987) *The Psychology of Reading and Language Comprehension*, Newton, MA: Allyn and Bacon.

Ke, C. (1998) 'Effects of strategies on the learning of Chinese characters among foreign language students', *Journal of Chinese Language Teachers Association*, 33(2): 93–112.

Kellerman, E. (1991) 'Compensatory strategies in second language research: a critique, a revision, and some (non-) implications for the classroom', in R. Phillipson, E. Kellerman, L. Selinker, M. Sharwood Smith and M. Swain (eds) *Foreign/Second Language Pedagogy Research*, Clevedon: Multilingual Matters.

Kellogg, R.T. (1994) *The Psychology of Writing*, New York: Oxford University Press.

King, L. (2011) *Overview of the National Languages Strategy (2003–2011)*, London: The Languages Company, online, available at: www.languagescompany.com/images/stories/docs/news/national_language_strategy.pdf (accessed 3 February 2013).

Kingston, A.J. (1961) 'A conceptual model of reading comprehension', in E.P. Bliesmer and A.J. Kingston, Jr (eds) *Phases of College and Other Adult Reading Programs: the Tenth Yearbook of the National Reading Conference*, Milwaukee, WI: National Reading Conference.

Kirkpatrick, A. (2007) *World Englishes: Implications for international communication and English language teaching*, Cambridge: Cambridge University Press.

Klapper, J. (2003) 'Taking communication to task? A critical review of recent trends in language teaching', *Language Learning Journal*, 27(1): 33–42.

Knowles, G. and Lander, V. (2011) *Diversity, Equality and Achievement in Education*, London: Sage.

Koda, K. (2007) 'Reading and language learning: crosslinguistic constraints on second language reading development', *Language Learning*, 57(1): 1–44.

Kohler, D.B. (2002) 'The effects of metacognitive language learning strategy training on lower-achieving second language learners', unpublished doctoral dissertation, Brigham Young University, Provo, Utah.

Kormos, J. and Csizér, K. (2008) 'Age-related differences in the motivation of learning English as a foreign language: attitudes, selves and motivated learning behaviour', *Language Learning*, 58(2): 327–355.

Kramsch, C. (1995) 'The cultural component of language teaching', *Language, Culture and Curriculum*, 8(2): 83–92.

Krashen, S. (1989) 'We acquire vocabulary and spelling by reading: additional evidence for the input hypothesis', *Modern Language Journal*, 73(4): 440–464.

Krashen, S.D. (1982) *Principles and Practice in Second Language Acquisition*, Oxford: Pergamon.

——(1985) *The Input Hypothesis: Issues and implications*, London: Longman.

——(1996) *The Natural Approach: Language acquisition in the classroom*, revised edition, Newcastle upon Tyne: Bloodaxe.

Krashen, S.D. and Terrell, T. (1988) *The Natural Approach: Language acquisition in the classroom*, London: Prentice Hall.

Krieger, R.A. (2002) *Civilization's Quotations: Life's Ideal*, New York: Algora Publishing.

LaBerge, D. and Samuels, S.J. (1974) 'Toward a theory of automatic information processing in reading', *Cognitive Psychology*, 6(2): 293–323.

Lamb, M. (2011) 'Young adolescents' home background and the L2 motivational self-system', paper presented at the 16th World Congress of Applied Linguistics, August 2011, Beijing Foreign Studies University, Beijing, China.

Lamb, T. and Simpson, M. (2003) 'Escaping from the treadmill: practitioner research and professional autonomy', *Language Learning Journal*, 28(1): 55–63.

Lapkin, S., Hart, D. and Swain, M. (1991) 'Early and middle French immersion programs: French language outcomes', *Canadian Modern Language Review*, 48(1): 11–40.

Larsen-Freeman, D. (2009) 'Adjusting expectations: the study of complexity, accuracy and fluency in second language acquisition', *Applied Linguistics*, 30(4): 579–589.

Lasagabaster, D. (2008) 'Foreign language competence in content and language integrated courses', *The Open Applied Linguistics Journal*, 1: 31–42.

Laufer, B. (1989a) 'What percentage of text lexis is essential for comprehension?' in C. Lauren and M. Nordman (eds) *Special Language: From humans thinking to thinking machines*, Clevedon: Multilingual Matters.

——(1989b) 'A factor of difficulty in vocabulary learning: deceptive transparency', *AILA Review*, 6: 10–20.

——(1991) 'How much lexis is necessary for reading comprehension?' in P.J.L. Arnaud and H. Béjoint (eds) *Vocabulary and Applied Linguistics*, Oxford: Macmillan, pp. 126–132.

——(1998) 'The development of passive and active vocabulary in a second language: same or different?', *Applied Linguistics*, 19(2): 255–271.

Laufer, B. and Ravenhorst-Kalovski, G.C. (2010) 'Lexical threshold revisited: lexical text coverage, learners' vocabulary size and reading comprehension', *Reading in a Foreign Language*, 22(1): 15–30.

Lave, J. and Wenger, E. (1991) *Situated Learning: Legitimate peripheral participation*, Cambridge: Cambridge University Press.

Lawes, S. (2003) 'What, when, how and why? Theory and foreign language teaching', *Language Learning Journal*, 28(1): 22–28.

——(2010) 'The principled practitioner: a model of knowledge acquisition', in R. Heilbronn and J. Yandell (eds) *Critical Practice in Teacher Education: A Study of Professional Learning*, London: Institute of Education, University of London, pp. 154–183.

Leadbeater, C. (2003) *Personalisation Through Participation*, London: Demos.

Lee, I. (2009) 'Feedback revolution: what gets in the way', *ELT Journal*, 65(1): 1–12.

——(forthcoming) 'EFL writing in schools', in R.M. Manchón and P. Matsuda (eds) *The Handbook of Second and Foreign Language Writing*, New York: De Gruyter Mouton.

Lee, J. and Schallert, D.L. (1997) 'The relative contribution of L2 language proficiency and L1 reading ability to L2 reading performance: a test of the Threshold Hypothesis in an EFL context', *TESOL Quarterly*, 31(4): 713–739.

Lee, J., Buckland, D. and Shaw, G. (1998) *The Invisible Child: The responses and attitudes to the learning of modern foreign languages shown by Year 9 pupils of average ability*, London: CILT.

Leech, G., Rayson, P. and Wilson, A. (2001) *Word Frequencies in Written and Spoken English Based on the British National Corpus*, Harlow: Longman.

Leki, I. (2001) 'Material, educational and ideological challenges of teaching EFL writing at the turn of the century', *International Journal of English Studies*, 1(2): 197–209.

Lennon, P. (1990) 'Investigating fluency in EFL: a quantitative approach', *Language Learning*, 40(3): 387–417.

Lessard-Clouston, M. (2006) 'Breadth and depth of specialized vocabulary learning in theology among native and non-native English speakers', *The Canadian Modern Language Review*, 63(2): 175–198.

Levelt, W.J.M. (1989) *Speaking*, Cambridge, MA: MIT Press.

——(1999) 'Language production: a blueprint of the speaker', in C. Brown and P. Hagoort (eds) *Neurocognition of Language*, Oxford: Oxford University Press.

Levin, B.B. and Rock, T.C. (2003) 'The effects of collaborative action research on preservice and experienced teacher partners in professional development schools', *Journal of Teacher Education*, 54(2): 135–149.

Levine, A., Reves, T. and Leaver, B.L. (1996) 'Relationship between language learning strategies and Israeli versus Russian cultural-educational factors' in R.L. Oxford (ed.) *Language Learning Strategies Around the World: Cross-Cultural Perspectives*, Manoa, HI: University of Hawai'i Press.

Li Wei (2011) 'Multilinguality, multimodality and multicompetence: code- and mode-switching by minority ethnic children in complementary schools', *Modern Language Journal*, 95(3): 370–384.

Liddicoat, A.J. (2004) 'The conceptualisation of the cultural component of language teaching in Australian language-in-education policy', *Journal of Multilingual and Multicultural Development*, 25(4): 297–321.

Little, D. (1991) *Learner Autonomy 1: Definitions, Issues and Problems*, Dublin: Authentik.

——(1995) 'Learning as dialogue: the dependence of learner autonomy on teacher autonomy', *System*, 23(2): 175–181.

——(1996) 'Strategic competence considered in relation to strategic control of the language learning process', in H. Holec, D. Little and R. Richterich (eds) *Strategies in Language Learning and Use*, Strasbourg: Council of Europe.

Littlewood, W. (1984) *Foreign and Second Language Learning*, Cambridge: Cambridge University Press.

Littlewood, W.T. (1981) *Communicative Language Teaching*, Cambridge: Cambridge University Press.

Liu, N. and Nation, I.S.P. (1985) 'Factors affecting guessing vocabulary in context', *RELC Journal*, 16(1): 33–42.

Logan, P. (2011) 'Teacher-led enquiry as a pathway to empowerment and professional transformation', unpublished PhD thesis, King's College London.

Long, M. and Robinson, P. (1998) 'Focus on form: theory, research and practice', in C. Doughty and J. Williams (eds) *Focus on Form in Classroom Second Language Acquisition*, Cambridge: Cambridge University Press, pp. 15–41.

Lortie, D. (1975) *Schoolteacher: A sociological study*, Chicago, IL: University of Chicago Press.

Low, L. (1999) 'Policy issues for Primary Modern Languages', in P. Driscoll and D. Frost (eds) *The Teaching of Modern Foreign Languages in the Primary School*, London: Routledge.

Lucas, B. (2001) 'Creative teaching, teaching creativity and creative learning', in A. Craft, B. Jeffrey and M. Liebling (eds) *Creativity in Education*, London: Continuum.

Macaro, E. (2000) 'Learner strategies in foreign language learning: cross-national factors', *Tuttitalia*, 22: 9–18.

——(2001a) 'Analysing student teachers' codeswitching in foreign language classrooms: theories and decision making', *The Modern Language Journal*, 85(4): 531–548.

——(2001b) *Learning Strategies in Foreign and Second Language Classrooms*, London: Continuum.

——(2003) *Teaching and Learning a Second Language: A review of recent research*, London: Continuum.

——(2006) 'Strategies for language learning and for language use: revising the theoretical framework', *Modern Language Journal*, 90(3): 320–337.

——(2008) 'The decline in language learning in England: getting the facts right and real', *Language Learning Journal*, 36(1): 101–108.

Macaro, E. and Erler, L. (2008) 'Raising the achievement of young-beginner readers of French through strategy instruction', *Applied Linguistics*, 29(1): 90–119.

——(2011) 'Decoding ability in French as a foreign language and language learning motivation', *The Modern Language Journal*, 95(4): 496–518.

Macaro, E. and Graham, S. (2008) 'The development of the passé composé in lower intermediate learners of French', *Language Learning Journal*, 36(1): 5–19.

Macaro, E. and Mutton, T. (2002) 'Developing language teachers through a co-researcher model', *Language Learning Journal*, 25(1): 27–39.

——(2003) 'Second language teachers as second language classroom researchers', *Language Learning Journal*, 27(1): 4–12.

——(2009) 'Developing reading achievement in primary learners of French: inferencing strategies versus exposure to "graded readers"', *Language Learning Journal*, 37(2): 165–182.

Macaro, E., Graham, S. and Vanderplank, R. (2007) 'A review of listening strategies: focus on sources of knowledge and on success', in A.D. Cohen and E. Macaro (eds) *Language Learner Strategies: Thirty Years of Research and Practice*, Oxford: Oxford University Press.

MacIntyre, P.D. and Gardner, R.C. (1991) 'Methods and results in the study of anxiety and language learning: a review of the literature', *Language Learning*, 41(1): 85–117.

Maddern, K. (2011) 'The importance of being included', *Times Educational Supplement*, 16 December, pp. 14–15.

Manchón, R.M. (2009) 'Broadening the perspective of L2 writing scholarship: the contribution of research on foreign language writing', in R.M. Manchón (ed.) *Writing in Foreign Language Contexts: Learning, Teaching, and Research*, Bristol: Multilingual Matters, pp. 1–19.

——(2011a) 'The language learning potential of writing in foreign language contexts: lessons from research', in T. Chimasko and M. Reichelt (eds) *Foreign Language Writing Instruction: Principles and practices*, West Lafayette, IN: Parlor Press, pp. 44–63.

——(2011b) 'Writing to learn the language: issues in theory and research', in R.M. Manchón (ed.) *Learning-to-Write and Writing-to-Learn in an Additional Language*, Amsterdam: John Benjamins, pp. 61–82.

——(2013) 'Teaching writing', in C. Chapelle (ed.) *Encyclopedia of Applied Linguistics*, Oxford: Blackwell.

Manchón, R.M. and Roca de Larios, J. (2007) 'Writing-to-learn in instructed language learning contexts', in E. Alcón and M.P. Safont-Jordá (eds) *Intercultural Language Use and Language Learning*, Dordrecht: Springer, pp. 101–121.

——(2011) 'Writing to learn in FL contexts: exploring learners' perceptions of the learning potential of L2 writing', in R. Manchón (ed.) *Learning-to-Write and Writing-to-Learn in an Additional Language*, Amsterdam: John Benjamins, pp. 181–206.

Markham, P. (1989) 'The effects of captioned television videotapes on the listening comprehension of beginning, intermediate, and advanced ESL students', *Educational Technology*, 29(10): 38–41.

——(1999) 'Captioned videotapes and second-language listening word recognition', *Foreign Language Annals*, 32(3): 321–328.

——(2001) 'The influence of culture-specific background knowledge and captions on second language comprehension', *Journal of Educational Technology Systems*, 29(4): 331–343.

Marslen-Wilson, W. (1973) 'Linguistic structure and speech shadowing at very short latencies', *Nature*, 244: 522–523.

Martin, C. (2002) 'An analysis of national and international research on the provision of foreign languages at primary schools', report prepared for the Qualifications and Curriculum Authority.

Martinez, R. and Murphy, V. (2011) 'Effect of frequency and idiomaticity on second language reading comprehension', *TESOL Quarterly*, 45(2): 267–290.

Martinez, R. and Schmitt, N. (2012) 'A phrasal expressions list', *Applied Linguistics*, 33(3): 299–320.

Maughan, S., Teeman, D. and Wilson, R. (2012) *What Leads to Positive Change in Teaching Practice*, NFER Research Programme: Developing the Education Workforce, Slough: NFER.

McDonough, S.H. (1995) *Strategy and Skill in Learning a Foreign Language*, London: Edward Arnold.

——(1999) 'Learner strategies: state of the art article', *Language Teaching*, 32(1): 1–18.

McGowan, P. and Turner, M. (1994) 'Raising reading attainment in modern languages', in A. Swarbrick (ed.) *Teaching Modern Foreign Languages in Secondary Schools: A reader*, London: Routledge.

McGuiness, C. (2000) 'ACTS: a methodology for enhancing thinking skills across the curriculum', a paper given at the conference ESRC Teaching and Learning Research Programme, University of Leicester, November 2000.

McLachlan, A. (2009) 'Modern languages in the primary curriculum: are we creating the conditions for success?', *Language Learning Journal*, 37(2): 183–203.

McPake, J., Johnstone, R., Low, L. and Lyall, L. (1999) *Foreign Languages in the Upper Secondary School: A study of the causes of decline*, final report to SOEID,

University of Glasgow: The SCRE Centre, online, available at: http://dspace.gla.ac.uk:8080/bitstream/1905/232/1/091.pdf.

McPake, J., Tinsley, T. and James, C. (2007) 'Making provision for community languages: issues for teacher education in the UK', *Language Learning Journal*, 35(1): 99–112.

McQueen, J. (2007) 'Eight questions about spoken word recognition', in G. Altmann (ed.) *Oxford Handbook of Psycholinguistics*, Oxford: Oxford University Press.

Meara, P. (2002) 'The rediscovery of vocabulary', *Second Language Research*, 18(4): 393–407.

——(2009) *Connected Words: Word associations and second language vocabulary acquisition*, Amsterdam: John Benjamins.

Mecartty, F.H. (2000) 'Lexical and grammatical knowledge in reading and listening comprehension by foreign language learners of Spanish', *Applied Language Learning*, 11(2): 323–348.

Meisel, J. (2004) 'The bilingual child', in T.K. Bhatia and W.C. Ritchie (eds) *The Handbook of Bilingualism*, Oxford: Blackwell, pp. 91–113.

Mendelsohn, D. (1994) *Learning to Listen: A strategy-based approach for the second-language learner*, San Diego, CA: Dominie Press.

Miliband, D. (2004) 'Personalised learning: building a new relationship with schools', North of England Education Conference, Belfast, 8 January, online, available at: https://www.education.gov.uk/publications/eOrderingDownload/personalised-learning.pdf (accessed 4 November 2012).

Mills, N., Pajares, F. and Herron, C. (2007) 'Self-efficacy of college intermediate French students: relation to achievement and motivation', *Language Learning*, 57(3): 417–442.

Milton, J. (2006) 'Language lite? Learning French vocabulary in school', *Journal of French Language Studies*, 16(2): 187–205.

Ministère Education Nationale (2012) *Les Programmes du Collège*, online, available at: www.education.gouv.fr/cid81/les-programmes.html#Langues vivantes (accessed 23 August 2012).

Ministerio de Educación y Ciencia (2007) *Real Decreto* 1629/2006, online, available at: www.boe.es/boe/dias/2007/01/04/pdfs/A00465-00473.pdf (accessed 20 August 2012).

Mitchell, R. (2003) 'Rethinking the concept of progression in the National Curriculum for Modern Foreign Languages: a research perspective', *Language Learning Journal*, 27(1): 15–23.

Mitchell, R., Parkinson, B. and Johnstone, R. (1981) *The Foreign Language Classroom: An observational study*, University of Stirling: Stirling Educational Monographs No 9.

Mitterer, H. and McQueen, J.M. (2009) 'Foreign subtitles help but native-language subtitles harm foreign speech perception', *PLOS ONE*, online, available at: www.plosone.org/article/info:doi/10.1371/journal.pone.0007785.

Mohan, B. (1986) *Language and Content Reading*, Boston, MA: Addison-Wesley.

Moon, R. (1987) 'The analysis of meaning', in J.M. Sinclair (ed.) *Looking Up: An account of the COBUILD Project in lexical computing*, London: HarperCollins, pp. 86–103.

Muijs, D. and Reynolds, D. (2011) *Effective Teaching: Evidence and Practice*, London: Sage.

Muijs, D., Barnes, A., Hunt, M., Powell, B., Arweck, E., Lindsay, G. and Martin, C. (2005) *Evaluation of the Key Stage 2 Language Learning Pathfinders*, London, DfES, online, available at: http://webarchive.nationalarchives.gov. uk/20130401151715/https://www.education.gov.uk/publications/standard/ publicationDetail/Page1/RR692.

Muñoz, C. (ed.) (2006a) *Age and the Rate of Foreign Language Learning*, Clevedon: Multilingual Matters.

——(2006b) 'The effects of age on foreign language learning: the BAF project', in C. Muñoz (ed.) *Age and the Rate of Foreign Language Learning*, Clevedon: Multilingual Matters, pp. 1–40.

——(2008) 'Symmetries and asymmetries of age effects in naturalistic and instructed L2 learning', *Applied Linguistics*, 29(4): 578–596.

Muñoz, C. and Singleton, D. (2011) 'A critical review of age-related research on LS ultimate attainment', *Language Teaching*, 44(1): 1–35.

Munro, M.J. and Derwing, T.M. (1995) 'Foreign accent, comprehensibility, and intelligibility in the speech of second language learners', *Language Learning*, 45(1): 73–97.

Myles, F. and Mitchell, R. (2012) *Learning French From Ages 5, 7, and 11: An investigation into starting ages, rates and routes of learning amongst early foreign language learners – ESRC End of Award Report*, RES-062-23-1545, Swindon: Economic and Social Research Council.

Myles, F., Mitchell, R. and Hooper, J. (1999) 'Interrogative chunks in French L2: a basis for creative construction?', *Studies in Second Language Acquisition*, 21(1): 49–80.

NACCCE (1999) *All our Futures: Creativity, Culture and Education*, Sudbury: DfES.

Nagy, W.E., Anderson, R.C., Schommer, M., Scott, J.A. and Stallman, J. (1989) 'Morphological families in the internal lexicon', *Reading Research Quarterly*, 24(3): 262–282.

Nagy, W.E., Herman, P.A. and Anderson, R.C. (1985) 'Learning words from context', *Reading Research Quarterly*, 20(2): 233–253.

Naiman, N., Fröhlich, M., Stern, H.H. and Todesco, A. (1978) *The Good Language Learner*, Clevedon: Multilingual Matters.

NALDIC (2011a) *EAL and Ethnicity in Schools Nationally and by LA*, January 2011, online, available at: www.naldic.org.uk/docs/resources/KeyDocs.cfm (accessed 4 September 2011).

——(2011b) *EAL Pupils in Primary and Secondary Schools 1997–2011*, online, available at: www.naldic.org.uk/docs/resources/KeyDocs.cfm (accessed 4 September 2011).

——(2012) *EAL Statistics*, National Association for Language Development in the Curriculum, online, available at: www.naldic.org.uk/research-and-information/ eal-statistics (accessed 30 March 2013).

NARIC (2012) *In the News: Chinese Language*, UKNARIC blog, online, available at: www.uknaric.org (accessed 18 August 2012).

Nassaji, H. (2003) 'L2 vocabulary learning from context: strategies, knowledge sources, and their relationship with success in L2 lexical inferencing', *TESOL Quarterly*, 37(4): 646–670.

Nation, I.S.P. (2001) *Learning Vocabulary in Another Language*, Cambridge: Cambridge University Press.

——(2004) 'A study of the most frequent word families in the British National Corpus', in B. Laufer and P. Bogaards (eds) *Vocabulary in a Second Language: Selection, acquisition, and testing*, Amsterdam: John Benjamins, pp. 3–13.

——(2006) 'How large a vocabulary is needed for reading and listening?', *The Canadian Modern Language Review*, 63(1): 59–82.

——(2008) *Teaching ESL/EFL Reading and Writing*, Abingdon: Routledge.

Nation, I.S.P. and Waring, R. (1997) 'Vocabulary size, text coverage and word lists', in N. Schmitt and M. McCarthy (eds) *Vocabulary: Description, acquisition and pedagogy*, Cambridge: Cambridge University Press, pp. 6–19.

National Capital Language Resource Center (2003) *The Elementary Immersion Learning Strategies Resource Guide*, Washington, DC: National Capital Language Resource Center.

National College for School Leadership (2004) *Personalised Learning, Special Supplement*, Nottingham: National College for School Leadership.

National Curriculum MFL Working Group (1990) *Initial Advice*, London: Department of Education and Science and the Welsh Office.

NFER (National Foundation for Educational Research) (2007) *Language Learning Provision at Key Stage 2: Findings from the 2007 survey*, London: DCSF.

Nieto, S. (2006) 'Language, literacy, and culture: Intersections and implication', in H. Luria, D.M. Seymour and T. Smoke (eds) *Language and Linguistics in Context: Readings and applications for teachers*, Mahwah, NJ: Lawrence Erlbaum Associates, pp. 315–331.

Nikolov, M. (1999) ' "Why do you learn English?" "Because the teacher is short": a study of Hungarian children's foreign language learning motivation', *Language Teaching Research*, 3(1): 33–56.

Nikolov, M. and Curtain, H. (eds) (2000) *An Early Start: Young learners and modern languages in Europe and beyond*, Graz: European Centre for Modern Languages.

Norris, J.M. and Ortega, L. (2000) 'Effectiveness of L2 instruction: a research synthesis and quantitative meta-analysis', *Language Learning*, 50(3): 417–528.

Norton, B. (2000) *Identity and Language Learning: Gender, ethnicity and educational change*, London: Longman/Pearson Education.

Norton, B. and Toohey, K. (2001) 'Changing perspectives on good language learners', *TESOL Quarterly*, 35(2): 307–322.

Nostrand, H. (1989) 'Authentic texts and cultural authenticity: an editorial', *Modern Language Journal*, 73(1): 49–52.

Nuffield Foundation (2000) *Languages the Next Generation: The final report and recommendations of the Nuffield Languages Inquiry*, Milton Keynes: The English Company.

Nygaard, L.C. and Pisoni, D.B. (1995) 'Speech perception: new directions in research and theory', in J.L. Miller and P.D. Eimas (eds) *Speech, Language and Communication*, San Diego, CA: Academic Press.

O'Brien, T. (2004) 'Writing in a foreign language: teaching and learning', *Language Teaching*, 37(1): 1–28.

O'Brien, T. and Guiney, D. (2001) *Differentiation in Teaching and Learning: Principles and practice*, London: Continuum.

O'Donnell, A.M. (2006) 'The role of peers and group learning', in P.H.E.A. Winne and A. Patricia (eds) *Handbook of Educational Psychology*, Mahwah, NJ: Lawrence Erlbaum Associates Publishers, pp. 781–802.

O'Hanlon, F., McLeod, W. and Paterson, L. (2010) *Gaelic-Medium Education in Scotland: Choice and attainment at the primary and early secondary stages*, Inverness: Bòrd na Gàidhlig.

O'Keeffe, A., McCarthy, M. and Carter, R. (2007) *From Corpus to Classroom: Language use and language teaching*, Cambridge: Cambridge University Press.

O'Malley, J.M. and Chamot, A. (1990) *Learning Strategies in Second Language Acquisition*, Cambridge: Cambridge University Press.

O'Reilly Cavani, J. (2000) 'Motivation in language learning: a Glasgow snapshot', in G. Chambers (ed.) *Reflections on Motivation*, London: CILT, pp. 31–41.

OECD (2005) *Formative Assessment: Improving learning in secondary classrooms*, Paris: OECD.

Ofsted (2005) *Implementing Languages Entitlement in Primary Schools: An evaluation of progress in 10 Pathfinder LEAs*, HMI 2476, London: Ofsted.

——(2010) *Learning: Creative approaches that raise standards*, Manchester: Ofsted.

——(2011) *Modern Languages: Achievement and challenge 2007–2010*, Manchester: Ofsted, online, available at: www.ofsted.gov.uk/resources/modern-languages-achievement-and-challenge-2007-2010 (accessed 3 January 2013).

——(2012) 'Everyone a linguist: Cherry Orchard Primary School', *Good Practice Example*, online, available at: www.ofsted.gov.uk/resources/good-practice-resource-everyone-linguist-cherry-orchard-primary-school.

Olson, M.W. (1990) 'The teacher as researcher: a historical perspective', in M.W. Olson (ed.) *Opening the Door to Classroom Research*, Newark, DE: International Reading Association, pp. 1–20.

Ortega, L. (2009) 'Studying writing across EFL contexts: looking back and moving forward', in R.M. Manchón (ed.) *Writing in Foreign Language Contexts: Learning, Teaching, and Research*, Bristol: Multilingual Matters, pp. 232–255.

——(2011) 'Reflections on the learning-to-write and writing-to-learn dimensions of second language writing', in R. Manchón (ed.) *Learning-to-Write and Writing-to-Learn in an Additional Language*, Amsterdam: John Benjamins, pp. 237–250.

——(2012) 'Epilogue: exploring L2 writing–SLA interfaces', *Journal of Second Language Writing*, 21(4): 404–415 (Special Issue: Exploring L2 Writing–SLA Interfaces).

Osler, A. and Starkey, H. (2005) *Citizenship and Language Learning: International Perspectives*, Stoke-on-Trent: Trentham Books.

Oxford, R. (1990) *Language Learning Strategies: What every teacher should know*, Boston, MA: Heinle and Heinle.

Oxford, R.L. and Schramm, K. (2007) 'Bridging the gap between psychological and sociocultural perspectives on L2 learner strategies', in A.D. Cohen and E. Macaro (eds) *Language Learner Strategies: Thirty years of research and practice*, Oxford: Oxford University Press.

Oxford, R.L., Cho, Y., Leung, S. and Kim, H.-J. (2004) 'Effect of the presence and difficulty of task on strategy use: an exploratory study', *International Review of Applied Linguistics*, 42(1): 1–47.

Pachler, N. (2002) 'Foreign language learning in England in the 21st century', *Language Learning Journal*, 25(1): 4–7.

Pachler, N., Evans, M. and Lawes, S. (2007) *Modern Foreign Language: Teaching school subjects*, Abingdon: Routledge, pp. 11–19.

Page, B. (2004) 'Graded objectives', in M. Byram (ed.) *The Routledge Encyclopedia of Language Teaching and Learning*, London: Routledge, pp. 245–248.

Palmer, H. (1921) *Principles of Language Teaching*, Oxford: Oxford University Press [reprinted 1972].

Paribakht, T.S. and Wesche, M. (1997) 'Vocabulary enhancement activities and reading for meaning in second language vocabulary acquisition', in J. Coady and T. Huckin (eds) *Second Language Vocabulary Acquisition: A rationale for pedagogy*, New York: Cambridge University Press, pp. 174–199.

Paris, S.G., Wasik, B.A. and Turner, J.C. (1991) 'The development of strategic readers', in R. Barr, M.L. Kamil, P.B. Mosenthal and P.D. Pearson (eds) *Handbook of Reading Research*, Volume II, New York: Longman.

Pawley, A. and Syder, F.H. (1983) 'Two puzzles for linguistic theory: native-like selection and native-like fluency', in J.C. Richards and R.W. Schmidt (eds) *Language and Communication*, London: Longman.

Pellicer-Sanchez, A. and Schmitt, N. (2010) 'Incidental vocabulary acquisition from an authentic novel: do things fall apart?', *Reading in a Foreign Language*, 22(1): 31–55.

Pennycook, A. (2001) *Critical Applied Linguistics: A critical introduction*, Mahwah, NJ: Lawrence Erlbaum Associates.

Perfetti, C.A. (1985) *Reading Ability*, New York: Oxford University Press.

Perrenoud, P. (1993) 'Touche pas à mon évaluation! Pour une approche systématique du changement pédagogique', *Mesure et évaluation en education*, 16(1/2): 107–132.

——(1998) 'From formative evaluation to a controlled regulation of learning processes: towards a wider conceptual field', *Assessment in Education: Principles, Policy and Practice*, 5(1): 85–102.

Peters, M. (1999) 'Les stratégies de compréhension auditive chez des élèves du Bain Linguistique en français langue seconde', unpublished doctoral dissertation, University of Ottawa.

Phillips, M. (2010) 'The perceived value of video-conferencing with primary pupils learning to speak a modern language', *Language Learning Journal*, 38(2): 221–238.

Phillipson, R. (1992) *Linguistic Imperialism*, Oxford: Oxford University Press.

Pichette, F. (2005) 'Time spent on reading and reading comprehension in second language learning', *The Canadian Modern Language Review*, 62(2): 243–262.

Pintrich, P.R. (2000) 'Multiple goals multiple pathways: the role of goal orientation in learning and achievement', *Journal of Educational Psychology*, 92(3): 544–555.

Poet, H., Rudd, P. and Kelly, J. (2010) *Survey of Teachers 2010: Support to improve teaching practice*, London: General Teaching Council for England.

Polio, C. (2012a) 'Second language writing', in S. Gass and A. Mackey (eds) *Handbook of Second Language Acquisition*, New York: Routledge, pp. 319–334.

——(2012b) 'The relevance of second language acquisition theory to the written error correction debate', *Journal of Second Language Writing*, 21(4): 375–389 (Special Issue: Exploring L2 Writing–SLA Interfaces).

Polio, C. and Williams, J. (2009) 'Teaching and testing writing', in M.H. Long and C.J. Doughty (eds) *The Handbook of Language Teaching*, Oxford: Blackwell, pp. 486–517.

Pollack, I. and Pickett, J.M. (1964) 'The intelligibility of excerpts from conversation', *Language and Speech*, 6(3): 165–171.

Pollard, A. and James, M. (2004) *Personalised Learning: A commentary by the Teaching and Learning Research Programme*, London: Economic and Social Research Council.

Postholm, M.B. (2009) 'Research and development work: developing teachers as researchers or just teachers?', *Educational Action Research*, 17(4): 551–565.

Poulisse, N. (1990) *The Use of Compensatory Strategies by Dutch Learners of English*, Berlin: Mouton de Gruijter.

Professional Development Consortium in Modern Foreign Languages (2013) *Oral Interaction*, online, available at: http://pdcinmfl.wordpress.com (accessed 24 March 2013).

Pulido, D. and Hambrick, D.Z. (2008) 'The virtuous circle: modeling individual differences in L2 reading and vocabulary development', *Reading in a Foreign Language*, 20(2): 164–190.

QCA (Qualifications and Curriculum Authority) (1999) *The Review of the National Curriculum in England: The Secretary of State's proposals*, London: QCA.

——(2006) *Pupils' Views on Language Learning*, online, available at: www.school-portal.co.uk/GroupDownloadFile.asp?GroupId=338117&ResourceID=2339971.

——(2007a) *The National Curriculum for England and Wales*, online, available at: www.education.gov.uk/schools/teachingandlearning/curriculum/secondary/b00199616/mfl/attainment (accessed 3 January 2013).

——(2007b) *Languages: A Scheme of Work for Key Stage 2, Units 1–12*, London: QCA, online, available at: http://webarchive.nationalarchives.gov.uk/20100612050234/http://www.standards.dfes.gov.uk/schemes3/subjects/primary_mff/?view=get.

——(2009) *Languages: A Scheme of Work for Key Stage 2, Units 13–24*, London: QCA, online, available at: http://webarchive.nationalarchives.gov.uk/20100612050234/http://www.standards.dfes.gov.uk/schemes3/subjects/primary_mff/?view=get.

Ramage, K. (1990) 'Motivational factors and persistence in foreign language study', *Language Learning*, 40(2): 189–219.

Ramaprasad, A. (1983) 'On the definition of feedback', *Behavioural Science*, 28(1): 4–13.

Rastle, K. (2007) 'Visual word recognition', in M.G. Gaskell (ed.) *The Oxford Handbook of Psycholinguistics*, Oxford: Oxford University Press.

Raupach, M. (1980) 'Temporal variables in first and second language speech production', in H.W. Dechert and M. Raupach (eds) *Temporal Variables in Speech*, The Hague: Mouton.

Rayner, K. and Pollatsek, A. (1989) *The Psychology of Reading*, Englewood Cliffs, NJ: Prentice Hall.

Read, J. (2004) 'Research in teaching vocabulary', *Annual Review of Applied Linguistics*, 24: 146–161.

Reda, G. (2003) 'English coursebooks: prototype texts and basic vocabulary norms', *ELT Journal*, 57(3): 260–268.

Reichelt, M., Lekkowitz, N., Rinnert, C. and Schultz, J.M. (2012) 'Key issues in foreign language writing', *Foreign Language Annals*, 45(1): 22–41.

Rhodes, N.C. and Pufhal, I. (2009) *Foreign Language Teaching in U.S. Schools*, online, available at: www.cal.org/resources/pubs/fl_teaching.html (accessed December 2012).

Roberts, K. (2012) 'Understanding teachers' conceptualisations of language teaching: an aid to effective pedagogical continuity and progression at Key Stage 2/3 transfer?', EdD dissertation, University of Manchester, work in progress.

Robinson, K. (2001) *Out of Our Minds: Learning to be creative*, Oxford: Capstone.

——(2006) *Do Schools Kill Creativity?*, online, available at: www.artiseducation.com/why-creative-learning-matters.

——(2010) 'Changing education paradigms', *Technology, Entertainment, Design, TED*, online, available at: www.ted.com/talks/ken_robinson_changing_education_paradigms.html (accessed 4 November 2012).

Rogers, C. (1991) *On Becoming a Person*, Boston, MA: Houghton Mifflin.

Romanini, A.C. (2008) 'The influence of production accuracy on suprasegmental listening comprehension', unpublished MA dissertation, Brigham Young University, Provo, Utah.

Rott, S. (1999) 'The effect of exposure frequency on intermediate language learner's incidental vocabulary acquisition and retention through reading', *Studies in Second Language Acquisition*, 21(4): 589–619.

Rubin, J. (1975) 'What the "good language learner" can teach us', *TESOL Quarterly*, 9: 41–51.

——(1990) 'Improving foreign language listening comprehension', in J.E. Alatis (ed.) *Georgetown University Round Table on Languages and Linguistics*, Washington, DC: Georgetown University Press.

——(2005) 'The expert language learner: a review of good language learner studies and learner strategies', in K. Johnson (ed.) *Expertise in Second Language Learning and Teaching*, Basingstoke: Palgrave Macmillan.

Rubin, J., Chamot, A.U., Harris, V. and Anderson, N. (2007) 'Intervening in the use of strategies', in A.D. Cohen and E. Macaro (eds) *Language Learner Strategies: Thirty years of research and practice*, Oxford: Oxford University Press.

Rudduck, J. and McIntyre, D. (2007) *Improving Learning Through Consulting Pupils*, Abingdon: Routledge.

Ruiz de Zarobe, Y. (2008) 'CLIL and foreign language learning: a longitudinal study in the Basque Country', *International CLIL Research Journal*, 1(1): art. 5, online, available at: www.icrj.eu/11-744.

Ruiz de Zarobe, Y. and Celaya, M. (2011) 'CLIL across languages research outcomes in two bilingual communities', *Número especial sobre: Sociedad de la Información, lenguas minoritarias y educación en bilingüismo*, 12(3): 200–214.

Rundell, M. and Fox, G. (2007) *Macmillan English Dictionary for Advanced Learners*, Oxford: Macmillan.

Sadoski, M. and Paivio, A. (2007) 'Toward a unified theory of reading', *Scientific Studies of Reading*, 11(4): 337–356.

Samuda, V. and Bygate, M. (2008) *Tasks in Second Language Learning*, Basingstoke: Palgrave.

Santos, D., Graham, S. and Vanderplank, R. (2008) 'Second language listening strategy research: methodological challenges and perspectives', *Evaluation and Research in Education*, 21(2): 111–133.

Savage, J. and Fautley, M. (2010) 'Creativity as a way of teaching and learning', in J. Savage and M. Fautley, *Secondary Education Reflective Reader*, Exeter: Learning Matters.

Saville-Troike, M. (2003) *The Ethnography of Communication: An introduction*, third edition, Oxford: Wiley Blackwell.

Scarino, A. and Liddicoat, A.J. (2009) *Teaching and Learning Languages: A guide*, Australian Government: Department of Education, Employment and Workplace Relations.

Scarino, A., Elder, C., Iwashita, N., Kim, S.H.O., Kohler, M. and Scrimgeour, A. (2011) *Student Achievement in Asian Languages Education. Part 1: Project Report*, Canberra: Australian Government Department of Education, Employment and Workplace Relations.

Schmitt, N. (2008) 'Instructed second language vocabulary learning', *Language Teaching Research*, 12(3): 329–363.

——(2010) *Researching Vocabulary: A vocabulary research manual*, Basingstoke: Palgrave Macmillan.

Schmitt, N. and Meara, P. (1997) 'Researching vocabulary through a word knowledge framework: word associations and verbal suffixes', *Studies in Second Language Acquisition*, 20(1): 17–36.

Schmitt, N. and Schmitt, D. (2012) 'A reassessment of frequency and vocabulary size in L2 vocabulary teaching', *Language Teaching*, doi: 10.1017/S0261444812000018.

Schmitt, N., Jiang, X. and Grabe, W. (2011) 'The percentage of words known in a text and reading comprehension', *The Modern Language Journal*, 95(1): 26–43.

Schneider, W. and Shiffrin, R.M. (1977) 'Controlled and automatic human information processing: I. Detection, search, and attention', *Psychological Review*, 84(1): 1–66.

Schoon, I. and Parsons, S. (2002) 'Teenage aspirations for future careers and occupational outcomes', *Journal of Vocational Behavior*, 60(2): 262–288.

Segalowitz, N. (2003) 'Automaticity in second languages', in C.J. Doughty and M.H. Long (eds) *The Handbook of Second Language Acquisition*, Malden, MA: Blackwell Publishing, pp. 382–408.

Seidelhofer, B. (2005) 'English as a lingua franca', *ELT Journal*, 59(4): 139–141.

Sercu, L. (2006) 'The foreign language and intercultural competence teacher: the acquisition of a new professional identity', *Intercultural Education*, 17(1): 55–72.

Sercu, L., Bandura, E., Castro, P., Davcheva, L., Laskaridou, C., Lundgruden, U., del Carmen, M., García, M. and Ryan, P. (2005) *Foreign Language Teachers and Intercultural Competence: An international investigation*, Clevedon: Multilingual Matters.

Share, D.L. (1995) 'Phonological recoding and self-teaching: sine qua non of reading acquisition', *Cognition*, 55(2): 151–208.

Sheen, Y. and Lyster, R. (eds) (2010) 'The role of oral and written corrective feedback in second language acquisition', special issue of *Studies in Second Language Acquisition*, 35(2).

Shen, H. (2005) 'An investigation of Chinese-character learning strategies among non-native speakers of Chinese', *System*, 33(1): 49–68.

Silva, T. (1993) 'Toward an understanding of the distinct nature of L2 writing', *TESOL Quarterly*, 27(4): 657–677.

Sinclair, J. (1987) *Looking Up: An account of the COBUILD Project in lexical computing*, London: Harper Collins.

——(1991) *Corpus, Concordance, Collocation*, Oxford: Oxford University Press.

Singleton, D. and Ryan, L. (2004) *Language Acquisition: The age factor*, second edition, Clevedon: Multilingual Matters.

Skehan, P. (1998) *A Cognitive Approach to Language Learning*, Oxford: Oxford University Press.

Skehan, P. and Ducroquet, L. (1988) *A Comparison of First and Foreign Language Ability*, ESOL Department Working Document No. 8, London: Institute of Education.

Skinner, B.F. (1948) *Walden Two*, New York: Macmillan.

——(1971) *Beyond Freedom and Dignity*, New York: Knopf.

Smith, P.D. and Berger, E. (1968) *An Assessment of Three Foreign Language Teaching Strategies Utilizing Three Language Laboratory systems, Final Report*, Washington, DC: U.S. Department of Health, Education and Welfare, Office of Education.

Snow, C.E. and Hoefnagel-Höhle, M. (1978) 'The critical period for language acquisition: evidence from second language learning', *Child Development*, 49(4): 1114–1128.

Snowling, M.J. and Hulme, C. (eds) (2005) *The Science of Reading: A handbook*, Oxford: Blackwell.

Sockett, G. and Toffoli, D. (2012) 'Beyond learner autonomy: a dynamic systems view of the informal learning of English in virtual online communities', *ReCALL*, 24(2): 138–151.

Sonbul, S. and Schmitt, N. (2010) 'Direct teaching of vocabulary after reading: is it worth the effort?', *Applied Linguistics*, 64(3): 253–260.

Spada, N. and Tomita, Y. (2010) 'Interactions between type of instruction and type of language feature: a meta-analysis', *Language Learning*, 60(2): 1–46.

Sparks, R.L., Patton, J., Ganschow, L. and Humbach, N. (2009) 'Long-term relationships among early first language skills, second language aptitude, second language affect, and later second language proficiency', *Applied Psycholinguistics*, 30(4): 725–755.

Sparks, R.L., Patton, J., Ganschow, L., Humbach, N. and Javorsky, J. (2006) 'Native language predictors of foreign language proficiency and foreign language aptitude', *Annals of Dyslexia*, 56(1): 129–159.

Stables, A. and Wikeley, F. (1999) 'From bad to worse? Pupils' attitudes to MFL at ages 14 and 15', *Language Learning Journal*, 20(1): 27–31.

Stæhr, L.S. (2008) 'Vocabulary size and the skills of listening, reading and writing', *Language Learning Journal*, 36(2): 139–152.

Stanovich, K.E. (1980) 'Toward an interactive-compensatory model of individual differences in the development of reading fluency', *Reading Research Quarterly*, 16(1): 32–71.

——(1986) 'Matthew effects in reading: some consequences of individual differences in the acquisition of literacy', *Reading Research Quarterly*, 21(4): 360–407.

Starkey, H. (2007) 'Language education, identities and citizenship: developing cosmopolitan perspectives', *Language and Intercultural Communication*, 7(1): 56–71.

Stenhouse, L. (1975) *An Introduction to Curriculum Research and Development*, London: Heinemann.

Sternberg, R. (1999) *Handbook of Creativity*, Cambridge: Cambridge University Press.

Stewart, W. (2008) 'Let them teach themselves', *Times Educational Supplement*, 11 July, online, available at: www.tes.co.uk/teaching-resource/Let-them-teach-themselves-2647097/ (accessed 4 November 2012).

Stobart, G. (2008) *Testing Times: The uses and abuses of assessment*, Abingdon: Routledge.

Stoll, L., Bolam, R., McMahon, A. and Thomas, S. (2006) 'Professional learning communities: a review of the literature', *Journal of Educational Change*, 7(4): 221–258.

Swaan, A. de (2001) *Words of the World: The global language system*, Cambridge: Cambridge Polity Press.

Swain, M. (1985) 'Communicative competence: some roles of comprehensible input and comprehensible output in its development', in S. Gass and C. Madden (eds) *Input in Second Language Acquisition*, New York: Newbury House, pp. 235–256.

——(1995) 'Three functions of output in second language learning', in G. Cook and B. Seidlhofer (eds) *Applied Linguistics: Studies in Honour of H.G. Widdowson*, Oxford: Oxford University Press, pp. 125–144.

Swain, M. and Lapkin, S. (1986) 'Immersion French in secondary schools: "The Goods" and "The Bads"', *Contact*, 5(3): 2–9.

Swan, M. (2008) 'Talking sense about learning strategies', *RELC Journal*, 39(2): 262–273.

Taylor, C. and Lafayette, R. (2010) 'Academic achievement through FLES: a case for promoting greater access to foreign language study among young learners', *The Modern Language Journal*, 94(1): 22–42.

The Guardian (2007) 'Useless research: an expensive waste of time', online, available at: www.guardian.co.uk/science/blog/2007/jul/13/uselessresearchanexpensive (accessed 27 March 2013).

Thomas, W.P., Collier, V.P. and Abbott, M. (1993) 'Academic achievement through Japanese, Spanish, or French: the first two years of partial immersion', *The Modern Language Journal*, 77(2): 170–179.

Thompson, I. and Rubin, J. (1996) 'Can strategy instruction improve listening comprehension?', *Foreign Language Annals*, 29(3): 331–342.

Timperley, H. (2008) *Teacher Professional Learning and Development*, Educational Practices Series 18, Geneva: International Bureau of Education, online, available at: www.ibe.unesco.org/fileadmin/user upload/Publications/Educational_Practices/EdPractices_18.pdf (accessed 22 February 2013).

Ting, Y.-L.T. (2010) 'CLIL appeals to how the brain likes its information: examples from CLIL-(neuro)science', *International CLIL Research Journal*, 1(3), art. 1, online, available at: www.icrj.eu/13/article1.html (accessed 18 January 2013).

Tinsley, T. (2013) *Languages, The State of the Nation: Demand and supply of language skills in the UK*, Summary Report, London: British Academy.

Tinsley, T. and Comfort, T. (2012) *Lessons from Abroad: International review of primary languages*, Reading: CfBT.

Tinsley, T. and Han, Y. (2011) *Language Learning in Secondary Schools in England: Findings from the 2011 Language Trends Survey*, Reading: CfBT.

Tobin, R. and McInnes, A. (2008) 'Differentiating learning in the literacy classroom', *Literacy*, 42(1): 3–9.

Tobutt, K. and Roche, C. (2008) *A La Française*, Dublin: Authentik.

Tomlinson, S. (2005) 'Inclusion', *The Guardian*, 19 April, online, available at: www.guardian.co.uk/politics/2005/apr/19/education.schools (accessed 4 November 2012).

Towell, R., Hawkins, R. and Bazergui, N. (1996) 'The development of fluency in advanced learners of French', *Applied Linguistics*, 17(1): 84–119.

Tseng, J.J. (2000) 'Character learning strategies among German students', *Language Research*, June.

Tsui, A.B.M. and Fullilove, J. (1998) 'Bottom-up or top-down processing as a discriminator of L2 listening performance', *Applied Linguistics*, 19(4): 432–451.

Ushioda, E. (2012) 'Sustaining L2 learning: the interplay of motivation, autonomy and metacognition', paper presented at the 8th BAAL Language and Learning Teaching Special Interest Group Conference, University of Oxford, July.

Valette, R.M. (1969) 'The Pennsylvania Project, its conclusions and its implications', *The Modern Language Journal*, 53(6): 396–404.

Van Ek, J.A. and Alexander, L.G. (1975) *Threshold Level English*, Oxford: Pergamon Press on behalf of the Council of Europe.

Van Lier, L. (1996) *Interaction in the Language Curriculum: Awareness, autonomy and authenticity*, Harlow: Pearson Education.

Vandergrift, L. (1997) 'The strategies of second language (French) listeners', *Foreign Language Annals*, 30(3): 387–409.

——(1998) 'Successful and less successful listeners in French: what are the strategy differences?', *French Review*, 71(3): 370–395.

——(2003) 'From prediction to reflection: guiding students through the process of L2 listening', *Canadian Modern Language Review*, 59(3): 425–440.

——(2005) 'Relationships among motivation orientations, metacognitive awareness and proficiency in L2 listening', *Applied Linguistics*, 26(1): 70–89.

Vandergrift, L. and Tafaghodtari, M.H. (2010) 'Teaching L2 learners how to listen does make a difference: an empirical study', *Language Learning*, 60(2): 470–497.

Vanderplank, R. (1988a) 'Implications of differences in native and non-native speaker approaches to listening', *British Journal of Language Teaching*, 26(1): 32–41.

——(1988b) 'The value of Teletext subtitles in language learning', *ELT Journal*, 42(4): 272–281.

——(1990) 'Paying attention to the words: practical and theoretical problems in watching television programmes with uni-lingual (CEEFAX) sub-titles', *System*, 18(2): 221–234.

——(1999) 'Global medium – global resource? Perspectives and paradoxes in using authentic broadcast material for teaching and learning English', in C. Gnutzmann (ed.) *Teaching and Learning English as a Global Language: Native and non-native perspectives*, Tübingen: Stauffenberg.

——(2010) 'Déjà vu? A decade of research on language laboratories, television and video in language learning', *Language Teaching*, 43(1): 1–37.

Vidal Rodeiro, C.L. (2009) 'Some issues on the uptake of modern foreign languages at GCSE', *Statistics Report Series No. 10*, Cambridge: Cambridge Assessment, online, available at: www.cambridgeassessment.org.uk/ca/digitalAssets/178744_Uptake_of_Modern_Foreign_Languages_-_Stats_Report_No_10.pdf (accessed 22 February 2011).

Wade, P. and Marshall, H. with O'Donnell, S. (2009) *Primary Modern Foreign Languages Longitudinal Survey of Implementation of National Entitlement to Language Learning at Key Stage 2*, Research Report No. RR127, London: DCSF.

Walczyk, J.J. (2000) 'The interplay between automatic and control processes in reading', *Reading Research Quarterly*, 35(4): 554–566.

Walter, C. (2007) 'First-to-second-language reading comprehension: not transfer, but access', *International Journal of Applied Linguistics*, 17(1): 14–37.

——(2008) 'Phonology in second language reading: not an optional extra', *TESOL Quarterly*, 42(3): 455–474.

Waring, R. and Takaki, M. (2003) 'At what rate do learners learn and retain new vocabulary from reading a graded reader?', *Reading in a Foreign Language*, 51(2): 130–163.

Warnock Committee (1978) *Special Educational Needs: The Warnock Report*, London: HMSO.

Webb, M. and Jones, J. (2009) 'Exploring tensions in developing assessment for learning', *Assessment in Education: Principles, Practice and Policy*, 16(2): 165–184.

Webb, S. (2007) 'The effects of repetition on vocabulary knowledge', *Applied Linguistics*, 28(1): 46–65.

Weiner, B. (1979) 'A theory of motivation for some classroom experiences', *Journal of Educational Psychology*, 71(1): 3–25.

——(1992) *Human Motivation: Metaphors, theories, and research*, Thousand Oaks, CA: Sage.

Wells, G. (1999) 'Using L1 to master L2: a response to Anton and DiCamilla's "Socio-Cognitive Functions of L1 Collaborative Interaction in the L2 Classroom"', *The Modern Language Journal*, 83(2): 248–254.

Wenger, E. (1998) *Communities of Practice: Learning, meaning and identity*, Cambridge: Cambridge University Press.

Wharton, G. (2000) 'Language learning strategy use of bilingual foreign language learners in Singapore', *Language Learning*, 50(2): 203–243.

White, J. (2004) 'Unpick woolly thinking', *Times Educational Supplement*, 12 November, online, available at: www.tes.co.uk/article.aspx?storycode=2047846 (accessed 4 November 2012).

——(2006) 'Individual learning? Let's cut the confusion', *Times Educational Supplement*, 7 July, online, available at: www.tes.co.uk/teaching-resource/Individual-learning-Let-s-cut-the-confusion-2259424/ (accessed 4 November 2012).

White, R. and Arndt, V. (1998) *Process Writing*, Harlow: Longman.

Wiliam, D. (2006) 'Assessment: learning communities can use it to engineer a bridge connecting teaching and learning', *National Staff Development Council*, 27(1): 16–20.

Williams, J. (2012) 'The potential role(s) of writing in second language development', *Journal of Second Language Writing*, 21(4): 321–331 (Special Issue: Exploring L2 Writing–SLA Interfaces).

Williams, J. and Polio, C. (forthcoming) 'Second language writing and second language development', in R.M. Manchón and P. Matsuda (eds) *The Handbook of Second and Foreign Language Writing*, New York: De Gruyter Mouton.

Williams, M. and Burden, R. (1997) *Psychology for Language Teachers*, Cambridge: Cambridge University Press.

Williams, M., Burden, R. and Lanvers, U. (2002) ' "French is the language of love and stuff": student perceptions of issues related to motivation in learning a foreign language', *British Educational Research Journal*, 28(4): 503–528.

Williams, M., Burden, R., Poulet, G. and Maun, I. (2004) 'Learners' perceptions of their successes and failures in foreign language learning', *Language Learning Journal*, 30(1): 19–29.

Willingham, D. (2007) 'Critical thinking: why is it so hard to teach?', *American Educator*, 31(2): 8–19.

Willis, J. (1996) *A Framework for Tasked-Based Learning*, London: Longman.

——(2011) 'Affiliation, autonomy and assessment for learning', *Assessment in Education: Principles, Policy and Practice*, 18(4): 399–415.

Winke, P., Gass, S.M. and Sydorenko, T. (2010) 'The effects of captioning videos used for foreign language listening activities', *Language Learning and Technology*, 14(1): 66–87.

Wolff, D. (2000) 'Second language writing: a few remarks on psycholinguistic and instructional issues', *Learning and Instruction*, 10(1): 107–112.

Wong-Fillmore, L. (1979) 'Individual differences in second language acquisition', in C.J. Fillmore, W.S.Y. Wang and D. Kempler (eds) *Individual Differences in Language Ability and Behaviour*, New York: Academic Press.

Woore, R. (2007) ' "Weisse Maus in Meinem Haus": using poems and learner strategies to help learners decode the sounds of the L2', *Language Learning Journal*, 35(2): 175–188.

——(2009) 'Beginners' progress in decoding L2 French: some longitudinal evidence from English modern foreign languages classrooms', *Language Learning Journal*, 37(1): 3–18.

——(2010) 'Thinking aloud about L2 decoding: an exploration into the strategies used by beginner learners when pronouncing unfamiliar French words', *Language Learning Journal*, 38(1): 3–17.

——(2011) 'Investigating and developing beginner learners' decoding proficiency in second language French: an evaluation of two programmes of instruction', unpublished DPhil thesis, University of Oxford.

Wray, A. (2003) *Formulaic Language and the Lexicon*, Cambridge: Cambridge University Press.

Yamashita, J. (2002) 'Mutual compensation between L1 reading ability and L2 language proficiency in L2 reading comprehension', *Journal of Research in Reading*, 25(1): 81–95.

Young, M.Y.C. (1996) 'Listening comprehension strategies used by university level Chinese students using English as a second language', unpublished doctoral dissertation, University of Essex.

——(1997) 'A serial ordering of listening comprehension strategies used by advanced ESL learners in Hong Kong', *Asian Journal of English Language Teaching*, 7(May): 35–53.

Zahar, R., Cobb, T. and Spada, N. (2001) 'Acquiring vocabulary through reading: effects of frequency and contextual richness', *Canadian Modern Language Review*, 57(4): 541–572.

Zechmeister, E.B., Chronis, A.M., Cull, W.L., D'Anna, C.A. and Healy, N.A. (1995) 'Growth of a functionally important lexicon', *Journal of Reading Behavior*, 27(2): 201–212.

Index

101–102; writing-to-learn approaches
96–107

X-medium education 17–18

Year 11 students 13
younger learners 15, 73–74, 164,
    207–208, *see also* primary school
    language teaching
Young, M.Y.C. 59

Zechmeister, E.B. 122, 123